Food Policies

WILEY SERIES ON
STUDIES IN ENVIRONMENTAL MANAGEMENT
AND RESOURCE DEVELOPMENT

Series Editor
Timothy O'Riordan
School of Environmental Sciences
University of East Anglia

Food Policies

John R. Tarrant
School of Environmental Sciences
University of East Anglia

Further Titles in Preparation

Food Policies

John R. Tarrant
School of Environmental Sciences
University of East Anglia

JOHN WILEY & SONS

Chichester · New York · Brisbane · Toronto

Copyright©1980, by John Wiley & Sons, Ltd.

British Library Cataloguing in Publication Data:

Tarrant, John Rex
  Food policies.—(Wiley series on studies in
  environmental management and resource
  development).
  1. Food supply—Political aspects
  I. Title
  338.1'9   HD9000.6   79-40740

  ISBN 0 471 27656 1

Typeset by Preface Ltd., Salisbury, Wiltshire and printed by Page Bros. (Norwich) Ltd., Norwich.

Acknowledgements

Table 6 and Figure 43 are based on material reproduced by permission of the Agricultural Economics Society and the authors. Table 7 is based on material copyright 1974 by the American Association for the Advancement of Science and is reproduced with the Association's permission. Table 11 and Figure 9 are based on material copyright 1975 by the American Association for the Advancement of Science and reproduced by permission of the Association and the author. Tables 5, 8 and 50 and Figure 16 are based on material reproduced by permission of IPC Business Press Limited. Tables 10, 57 and 69 are reproduced by permission of OECD. Tables 20, 21 and 48 are based on material which is copyright United Nations (1975) and is reproduced by permission. Tables 23 and 37 are reproduced by permission of Her Majesty's Stationery Office. Tables 27, 29, 31 and 32 are reproduced by permission of Centro Internacional de Mejoramiento de Maiz y Trigo (CIMMYT). Table 34 and Figure 40 are reproduced by permission of the American Association and Agricultural Economics. Table 39 contains material published by permission of W. B. Saunders Company. Tables 51 and 53 and Figure 44 are reproduced by permission of the Johns Hopkins University Press. Figure 56 is reproduced by kind permission of the Worldwatch Institute, Washington DC.

Contents

Abbreviations

ACP – Africa, Caribbean and Pacific (countries)

AFBF – American Farm Bureau Federation

AFL – American Federation of Labor

BADC – Bangladesh Agricultural Development Corporation

CAP – Economic Community Common Agricultural Policy

CCC – Commodity Credit Corporation

CIO – Congress of Industrial Organization

CPE – centrally planned economies

DC – developed countries

DSM – dried skimmed milk

EAGGF – European Agricultural Guidance and Guarantee Fund

FAO – Food and Agricultural Organization (of the United Nations)

GATT – General Agreement on Tariffs and Trade

IFPRI – International Food Policy Research Institute

ISMOG – Instituut voor Sociaal economische studie van Minders Ontwikkelde Gebieden

LDC – less developed countries

MAFF – Ministry of Agriculture, Fisheries and Food

MCA – monetary compensation amounts

NAS – National Academy of Sciences

NFO – National Farmers' Organization

NFU – National Farmers' Union

NRC – National Research Council

ODI – Overseas Development Institute

OECD – Organization for Economic Co-operation and Development

PRC – Peoples's Republic of China

UA – units of account

UNCTAD – United Nations Committee on Trade And Development

USAID – United States Agency for International Development

USDA – United States Department of Agriculture

WFC – World Food Council

WFP – World Food Programme

WHO – World Health Organization

Units

All units are metric unless indicated otherwise.

Ton	= metric ton (1000 kg)
Bushel (of wheat)	= 28.58 kg
Quintal	= 100 kg
Maund	= 37 kg
25 taka	= £1

Preface

I approached the writing of this book with some trepidation. An understanding of food policy incorporates a knowledge of a wide range of subjects from agricultural economics, through political science and nutrition to international relations. No one discipline has a monopoly of understanding in food policy, and indeed the synergism between nutrition, demography, agricultural policy, and economic development is such that there are considerable dangers if analysis and planning are left to one discipline alone. I have tried to approach the problems of national and international food policy in a multi-disciplinary way, but one result is certainly a less than satisfactory treatment of individual disciplines. This results partly from my ignorance and partly from the conflict between breadth and depth which exists in any attempt to combine results from several disciplines. The aim was a book providing enough of a synthesis of a very broad field to aid understanding of complex issues of national and international food policy.

The emphasis on understanding is important. The field of food policy is littered with writings which have an ideological or emotional appeal, but in which evidence to back up the arguments is highly selective or totally absent. Often the arguments made do not stand up to close scrutiny. Convincing and conclusive evidence on many issues of world food policy is often not available. Expert opinions differ and protagonists in any argument can bring forth evidence to support their positions. For example, there are different viewpoints on appropriate methods for increasing agricultural production in the developing world, or even if this increased production should be encouraged at all. There are similarly contrasting views on the impact of food aid on recipient countries. I have tried to present as much evidence as possible in this book, sufficient to allow readers to make their own judgements.

Unfortunately the evidence presented is not as well balanced as I would like. Although one of the major objectives has been to stress the connections and similarities between different parts of the world in terms of food policy, the choice of countries is necessarily limited. Whatever one's political ideology the United States must predominate in any such study. It has a substantial part of the world's food production and the lion's share of world food exports. Also, a great deal has been written about agricultural policies in the United States, so the emphasis in a review of this type is understandable. Other developed economies, particularly the European Economic Community, have certainly not been ignored, and for detailed country-by-country studies of agricultural policy the reader is referred to the OECD agricultural policy studies (OECD, 1973, 1974, 1975). In the Third World the concentration is on the countries of South and South-East Asia. Again writings on these countries dominate the literature. Also the countries of this region have very large and rapidly growing populations and so, in terms of population numbers, they must dominate world food issues. Many examples are taken from Bangladesh, a country of which I have practical experience, and which provides an extreme example of food and population problems. There remains, however, great danger in assuming that the conclusions reached about Asia are applicable to Latin America or to Africa. Conditions are very different, particularly a lower population density and greater arable land potential in the latter two continents.

The centrally managed economies of the world present a third important grouping. It contains about one-third of the population of the world, and the economic isolation from the rest of the world which was characteristic of these economies is decreasing with the recent impact on world markets of food imports, especially to the USSR. Detailed and accurate information remains scarce, especially for the People's Republic of China. This is particularly unfortunate as there are indications that the PRC is increasingly important in world cereal markets. Because the country covers such a vast geographical area, wheat and rice are produced and consumed in vast quantities. It is possible to switch a small part of this consumption from one crop to another, thereby releasing, say rice, to the world market when prices are high and purchasing wheat when prices for that crop are low. To this extent China may be the final arbiter of at least rice prices in South-East Asia.

The emphasis throughout the book is on government policies and their effects. This is not meant to imply that governments are the only significant influence in world food issues, although they are both universal in their effects and certainly important. Many agricultural commodities are dominated in their production, processing, packaging, and marketing by transnational corporations. These corporations also have a substantial stake in the provision of the necessary inputs to modern commercial agriculture, particularly fertilizers, pesticides, and machinery. In this respect the use of these inputs may have at least as much to do with the policies of the corporations as it does with the policies of governments. By their nature these corporations may be beyond effective control by individual governments and their influence certainly overlaps national boundaries. I have chosen not to dwell on such issues, not because I do not consider them important, but because their influence can be exaggerated, especially in the area of staple food production with which this book is mostly concerned. Extreme views have been put forward which suggests, for example, that the green revolution was propagated in the interests of big business because the basic research was organized under the auspices of the Rockefeller and the Ford Foundations, themselves the product of capitalist profits which avoided taxation. The claim continues that the same industrial interests which endowed the Foundations and supported the green revolution research benefit through increased sales of chemical fertilizer and machinery. The resulting economic development would also increase the size of the world market for all types of manufactured goods. I reject this view of the work of the Foundations, but to examine the significance of the transnational corporations in world food production and policy would require a complete book. This book will be restricted primarily to government influences.

In this respect readers looking for a single coherent section on each of such topics as United States' food policy, the green revolution, and nutrition policy will be somewhat disappointed. The interconnections between these and all other aspects of food policy are such that reference will be made to many of them throughout the book. The organization is built upon government actions in the spheres of production, consumption, trade and aid and deliberately intermixed discussion of the developed countries with the developing world to draw out the worldwide parallels and interconnections.

The book could not have been written without patient advice, teaching and help from a variety of sources. In particular, I would mention the staff of the International Food Policy Research Institute in Washington, DC, and the Food Research Institute, Stanford University, and various development specialists in Bangladesh, especially the field staff of the Ford Foundation. Special mention must also be made of Marion Pick who patiently interpreted my manuscript and typed it, editing as she went along; David Mew who drew the figures, and Seamus Doherty who helped with the bibliographic work. The book and its faults remain, of course, entirely my responsibility. Lastly my thanks to the Rockefeller Foundation from whom a grant-in-aid financed a period of study used for the preparation of the book. The Foundation was in no way responsible for the work, and the conclusions and the opinions expressed are entirely my responsibility.

July 1979 JOHN TARRANT

List of Tables

List of Figures

CHAPTER 1

Introduction

Two closely related spectres haunt the future world: a shortage of food and a shortage of energy. In both cases the trend in world consumption appears to be outstripping our capability to produce. In both cases exhaustion of resources have been delayed by technical fixes. Oil and gas reserves are discovered and exploited in more and more remote and technically difficult sites and nuclear power continues to provide some possibilities of an energy panacea for the future. With food resources the green revolution and associated plant breeding technology and fertilizer application have allowed large increases in food production in the developing and the developed countries, and possibilities for unconventional foods such as cultured single-cell proteins are put forward as providing some promise for future food provision. The importance of energy in an increasingly energy-short world and food in a food-short world allows for the strategic and political use of these resources by those countries lucky enough to have a surplus at any time. The national and international importance of these resources leads to national and international food and energy policies. There are further similarities. Energy sources are renewable or non-renewable, and technological development has allowed the exploitation of the non-renewable resources, coal, oil and gas, which, at least in the case of the latter two, are close to exhaustion. Technological development is now increasingly concentrated on renewable energy sources. Thus, man's use of energy is closing the circle from the exclusive use of renewable energy, the burning of firewood, the use of draft animal power and the wind, through a series of technological devices to use non-renewable energy and is now entering a phase of technological development which hopefully will enable a return to fuller use of renewable resources. Food production, although it relies on the renewable resources of solar energy and water, has shown a similar increasing reliance on technology to exploit non-renewable resources, especially those based on energy. With increasingly expensive energy, food production technology is turning to more self-contained, energy-efficient forms of production. As

1

with energy the world is a very long way from producing food based entirely on renewable resources.

With little assistance from man the better-quality land on the earth can produce about 6 kg/ha per year of protein suitable for human consumption. It is possible that such unintensive agriculture could support a population of about 200 million people. With a world population of 4000 million there is no choice but to adopt agricultural methods which use more or less fossil fuel to increase the productivity of the land (Slesser, 1975). The energy used in the manufacture of fertilizers, in providing motive power, in pumping for irrigation, in transport, packaging, and marketing of agricultural goods has meant that Western agriculture generally has become energy expensive and in the process has been able to become land and labour efficient. Energy use has in large measure substituted for land and labour (Leach, 1975). Although in the face of increasing energy costs there have been moves towards a less energy-intensive agriculture (Merrill, 1976), this can only be achieved on any scale at the expense of increased use of land and/or labour for the same agricultural production.

Many studies of energy use in agriculture have concentrated on the energy ratio, or the ratio between energy inputs to an agricultural system and the energy output (Pimentel et al., 1973; Leach, 1975; Slesser, 1975; Ward et al., 1977). In hunter/gatherer and subsistence farming systems the energy content of food output exceeds the muscular energy input of the cultivators and collectors by a factor of between 10 and 30. In modern systems the majority of energy input is derived from fossil fuels and not from human or animal power. As expected, the energy ratio is much lower and in some cases is less than unity (Gifford, 1976). While it is useful to measure energy costs alongside labour and capital costs of different agricultural systems it is confusing to appear to cost agriculture solely on this basis. There is nothing fundamentally wrong with expending more energy to produce food than the energy content of that food if for no other reason than the fact that we cannot eat coal and oil. The energy ratio for Australian agriculture is much larger than that for the United States or the United Kingdom, but this is achieved at the expense of using land much less intensively (Gifford, 1976). Similarly, rice production in the Philippines uses land much more intensively, but has a high energy ratio as a result of a very high labour input per unit of production. There are many circumstances where a shortage of land and labour is at least as serious as a shortage of energy (Chapter 2). An important confusion arises through the measurement of the output of agriculture in energy terms. Although a substantial proportion of our diets are used as energy, few would recognize a one-to-one relationship between food value and energy value. Thus, crops like sugar-cane come out of an energy budget analysis with a high energy ratio, while milk produced in the United Kingdom has a ratio of well below unity. We would hardly feed sugar to a child suffering from malnutrition, but in most cases milk would be very beneficial. Although the proteins in our diet can be converted to energy if necessary (Chapter 6) the conversion may not be very efficient and the reverse conversion is not possible. Therefore, foods we eat because of their protein content will tend to have low energy ratios. Although we could use less energy to produce such protein foods, and many of them can be considered as nutritional luxuries, it is unsound to compare quite different agricultural crops in this way. Estimating the energy costs of the production of 1 kg of protein by different methods (Leach, 1975) could be a legitimate exercise, but this is not a full energy budget.

The consideration of energy alone in a comparison of agricultural systems can lead to erroneous impressions about the 'efficiency' or desirability of agriculture of different types. For example, Slesser (1975) produces evidence which shows that there are three distinct agricultural systems in terms of their energy use. The first group, with very high energy ratios is typically vegetable production in New Guinea and rice production in the Philippines. The second group, with energy ratios of between 2 and 6, include many types of agriculture in the United States, including corn production in Iowa in 1915 and in 1969. Although energy *inputs* have nearly doubled over this time for this group, so also have energy yields. The energy ratio of American corn production actually improved in 1970 over 1954 and was only marginally worse than in 1959 and 1964 (Pimentel *et el*., 1973). The third group, with energy ratios of close to or less than unity, include irrigated rice production in Louisiana, sugar-beet production in California, and peanuts in North Carolina. All this last group are subject to large government subsidies, and the value of these payments have allowed a greater use of energy. It is grossly misleading to imply that all these systems of agricultural production represent points on a deteriorating continuum with regard to energy use.

Just as there are other significant factors besides energy in agricultural production so there are reasons why food production is perhaps even more significant, and certainly more complex, an issue than energy production and use. Firstly food is a basic element of life. Man can, and many societies encompassing many millions of people effectively do, exist without fossil fuels, relying on the energy of the sun, acting through photosynthesis to provide the plants to feed themselves and their animals. Furthermore, agriculture provides not only the direct means of life but also employment, and therefore livelihood, for many millions. The effect of technological changes in agriculture on employment means that the links between food production and economic development are as close or closer than the links between economic development and energy use. The majority of the world's population are engaged directly in agricultural production; most of which is food production; much is on the basis of at least partial self-sufficiency, and the majority with very low levels of fossil fuel use.

The interconnections between agriculture, employment, income distribution and food consumption and, in particular, a recognition that malnutrition is almost universally a consequence of people's inability to afford food which is available, has meant that the role of agriculture is now considered central to the development process. The cycle of poverty and malnutrition can only be broken by policies concentrating on agriculture, usually small-scale agriculture, in the developing countries.[1] The change towards an agricultural emphasis is slow but detectable in many countries and in most of the work of the major donor agencies.

The importance of agriculture, nationally and internationally, leads to the intervention of governments at all levels. Policies to protect producers, to subsidize consumers and to encourage trade are widespread. It is significant that although the United States government struggled through 1977 and 1978 to enact an energy policy, an agricultural policy had been in existence since the early 1930s. Very much more legislative time is devoted to agriculture in the United States and in the EEC than is devoted to energy matters. The political importance of agriculture has long been recognized.

An extra dimension, and one which food production shares with energy, is the international one. The world is characterized by a limited number of surplus food producers with the potential to export food, and a very much larger number of food deficit countries. The latter include developed and the developing world countries as well as, more recently, the centrally planned economies of Eastern Europe and the Far East. In periods of shortage and high international food prices, as between 1972 and 1975, food-importing countries concentrate on increasing domestic self-sufficiency (HMSO, 1975) while in times of world surplus production the exporting countries, especially the United States as the world's largest surplus food producer, concentrate on exports to relieve accumulating stocks at home and to improve their balance of payments. For example, in 1978 with substantial grain surpluses, the United States Agricultural Trade Act made resources available to upgrade the diplomatic rank of some of the agricultural attachés in US embassies in key grain-importing countries, to allow the People's Republic of China to purchase grain on credit terms, and to establish between six and twenty-five agricultural trade offices in major importing countries (Deaton, 1978).

The role of food exports is political as well as economic. The United States has long been the world's major source of food aid. The distribution of this aid, predominantly itself a result of a domestic need to dispose of surplus production in ways which do not significantly depress the world market price, has often been blatantly political. In 1974, when most of the

---

[1] Throughout this book the terms 'developing countries', 'less developed countries' and the 'developing world' are used interchangeably. All such terms have come in for criticism. Their use here continues a pattern of common usage and there is no implication that developing countries are necessarily set on a path of economic development which, if carried to its conclusion, will lead to an economy similar to that of the Western capitalist countries.

developing world was in need of food aid and when total food aid flows were halved, the United States sent the lion's share of aid to Cambodia and to South Vietnam. The sales of wheat to Russia in 1972, which were so closely associated with the subsequent food crisis, were as much a result of a political need for *détente* between the USSR and the USA as they were the result of commercial considerations. The sales were not encouraged for immediate political or commercial rewards. A swap deal was considered whereby the Russians would have supplied oil for wheat, but this was rejected in favour of commercial sales on generous credit terms which it was hoped would encourage the Russians to be more flexible in world affairs (Maddock, 1978). It was significant that even at the height of the Russian purchases from the United States, amounting to 23 million tons of grain in 1972–73, it was still possible for the USSR to re-export over 2 million tons of grain to her East European satellites. These shipments certainly encouraged political stability within the Soviet bloc and perhaps helped to provide a domestic climate which encouraged a more favourable attitude to issues of major concern to the West, especially in the Middle East and in Africa. Food aid to Egypt, one of the world's largest recipients, has helped to counterbalance American pro-Israel attitudes and other aid shipments. This food aid, coming not only from the United States but also from Canada, the EEC and elsewhere, has encouraged domestic stability and perhaps helped peace initiatives in the Middle East.

There is nothing new about economic weapons of this type. The Arab oil embargo is often seen as providing a striking precedent to the use of food as a political weapon, although the United States, through its food aid programmes, predated this action by more than two decades. The United States has an increasing domination of world food exports so that, although other countries of the world have tried operating commodity cartels, it is really only the United States which has the potential to use *food* to wield political influence. There are, however, important limitations to the effectiveness of using food as a political weapon. Firstly, unlike the case of oil with which comparison is frequently made, most countries are 90 to 95 per cent self-sufficient in food. Although the residual percentage may represent a very large amount of food, no country is totally dependent on an external source of supply under the control of a foreign government. Also, as supply is in most cases dominated by domestic production and imports are important only at the margin, import demand varies greatly from year to year. The fluctuations in the food import demand of the USSR, for example, have no relationship to the political situation in the Middle East or anywhere else. This situation is in contrast with the position over oil, the demand for which, although it can be altered by price, remains high and predictable in the developed countries. Although there is domestic production of other types of energy, this cannot be substituted for oil, at least in the short term.

In the United States, export earnings from farm produce are closely related to the national balance of payments and to the strength of the dollar on international exchanges. Certainly the United States as a whole, and farmers in particular, cannot forgo export earnings from food in the same way as the Arab rulers can afford to forgo export earnings from oil, at least for a short time. On the other hand, food exports have been linked to domestic inflation in the United States. Certainly, one of the effects of the wheat sales to Russia in 1972 was higher prices on the domestic market. Thus labour organizations (AFL–CIO) have been aligned with conservative elements in government in opposition to large food exports, at least in times of world food shortage. The domestic policy on food exports is therefore complicated by lobbies for and against those policies which could have international political significance.

To a limited extent the oil boycott was later turned against the major oil suppliers as demand for oil fell with a world economic recession. The boycott certainly contributed to falling world demand. In the case of food the weapon could be reversed even more effectively. The United States needs the food exports to avoid the costs of stockpiles and to reduce the costs of government support programmes to agriculture. In the event of a concerted action by a number of the major customers of the United States, the loss of exports would soon produce an unmanageable surplus at home.

Although, superficially, comparisons between oil and food as sources of world political strength are seductive, they do not really stand up to closer inspection. Perhaps most importantly it is difficult to see what political return to the United States could possibly be great enough to justify the threat or even the actuality of mass starvation (Hopkins, 1977). The withholding of food aid has been used, some would say squandered (Hopkins, 1977), on some matters of little importance to the United States' economy as a whole and of little world-wide impact. For example, there was the encouragement of the government of Bangladesh to eliminate its jute trade with Cuba, a matter of vastly more significance to Bangladesh than to the United States' foreign policy. The approval of large food sales to the USSR implied that it was not available for others for sale or as aid. This negative side to the sales probably did not form an overt part of the political decision-making and was dispersed in its effects. To the recipients of the food aid it was none the less of considerable importance and may have had adverse effects on relations with the United States.

Nothing so concentrates the mind as a crisis, real or imagined. Thus, the oil crisis provided the impetus to energy conservation programmes, smaller motor cars in the United States and many forms of alternative energy research. Similarly, the latest food crisis, starting in August 1972 when within a few months the price of the world's major grains tripled or even quadrupled, produced the World Food Conference and a rash of schemes for food security, increased food production and food aid. Good, often record, harvests in 1976, 1977 and 1978 defused much of the world food crisis debate, while qualified research and informed opinion continues to regard the long-term food/population balance as critical and most projections of the future food supply situation are pessimistic (Enzer *et al.*, 1978). The decade of the 1970s has seen food production go through a full circle from glut to shortage and return to glut. But the present glut of food is only partly the result of the improved harvests—it is also partly the result of a downturn in demand related to the world economic situation. From the 1960s to 1972 there was a 3.3 per cent annual growth in food consumption, between 1972 and 1976–77 this fell to a 1.6 per cent annual growth rate. A substantial part of this slow-down in consumption stems from the feeding of less grain to American livestock. If consumption had continued to grow at the rate of the 1960s and early 1970s the present increments in food consumptions would be higher than the increments in food production (Crosson and Frederick, 1977). With the world's population growing fast each harvest needs to be a record just to maintain food supply per capita, and there is no realistic prospect of significantly reducing the growth rate in world population over the next twenty-five years.

There are two reactions to the cycles of glut and shortage. One is to see in the 1970s a significant shift in the food/population equation to provide an increasingly ciritical world shortage of food. These neo-Malthusians do not envisage technological developments allowing yield increases sufficient to keep pace with population growth. This view is reinforced as the technological developments of the green revolution become less effective as they are applied in increasingly less suitable circumstances. The contrary view is that the physical potential exists for vastly increased food production and that the events of 1972–75 were the result of a particular combination of circumstances which is unlikely to recur. As usual in such debates the truth probably lies somewhere between the two positions. Although the technology does exist to greatly increase food production, it will produce expensive food, especially in the face of rising energy costs. Perhaps 40 per cent of the world's population are malnourished today, even when the world food situation seems to be one of oversupply. The world's poor, especially the rural poor in the developing countries, cannot purchase sufficient food at today's prices, let alone the more technologically intensive food of the future. The solution to the problem of future food supply does not lie with alternative food production, like the single-cell proteins, nor in vastly increased food production in the developed world, but rather in increased production in the developing countries, most of which have both the physical potential and also vast and rapidly growing populations (Wortman and Cummings, 1978). The links between economic growth and food supply are obvious, but there remains great concern over the distributional effects of growth. Economic growth in the recent past has shown no tendency to relieve poverty for the mass of the people, it has therefore done little to reduce world hunger (Hay, 1978).

The political will is needed, nationally and internationally, to shift the emphasis of development to the agricultural sector, using such technological developments as are available and appropriate to the scale of the small farmer. Although there are grounds for hope for the future (Wortman and Cummings, 1978) it seems most likely that the world will muddle on with shortages alternating with food gluts, the frequency of shortages increasing as the world population grows, but stopping short of the catastrophic effects foreseen by Malthus. Certainly the prospects for the world entering a period of unconcern over food issues are remote in the extreme. Target proposals for the elimination of world hunger, although technically feasible, are as unrealistic now as they were thirty years ago.

Food is an issue of great national and international significance, arguably of even greater importance than energy. The first consideration in this book is food production. Special attention is paid to the prospects of increasing world production by multiple cropping, irrigation, fertilizer use, and increasing the area of arable production. This second chapter concludes with a consideration of the effects of climate, and especially climatic change, on future agricultural production. Against this background the book proceeds in Chapter 3 with an examination of the reasons for government intervention in the agricultural sector. Such intervention, although taking different forms, is universal in the developed market economies, the centrally planned economies and in developing countries. Governments intervene directly in ways which affect agricultural production, food consumption, and food trade. The effects of policies in each of these areas are not independent. Production intervention, by fixing domestic produce prices above world price levels, may give rise to overproduction and the necessity to both protect the domestic producers from international competition through tariff barriers at the same time as government subsidies or other encouragements are needed to export the surplus production.

The reasons for government intervention (Chapter 4) may be similar throughout the world, but the methods chosen to protect or to subsidize producers and consumers are different. Particular contrasts exist between producers policies adopted in the United States and in the European Economic Community and between the policies of the United Kingdom and the EEC before the UK joined the Community. Different forms of consumer subsidy exist for different purposes in the developing countries and in the United States and the United Kingdom. The effects of government policies (Chapter 5) in food production, consumption and trade are not always what they are expected or supposed to be. While policies in Europe and the United States, for example, which may be supposed to help the small farmers unable to make satisfactory livings from their farms with low prices, in fact aid the large and the efficient farmers. Price-support policies obviously mean larger payments to those farmers with larger production. In the developing world the green revolution can be seen in the context of government encouragement to increased production. Again, the income distribution effects of such policies have been considerable. Policies to protect consumers are often in conflict with policies for producers as the first means low prices and the latter high prices. These conflicts are outlined at the end of Chapter 5.

The present and future world food position does not depend only on food production. Consumption, particularly changing food consumption patterns over time, is of great significance. Chapter 6 considers first the physiological requirements for different foods and the malnutrition of those whose diets do not meet these requirements. Although the world produces more than enough food to provide the entire population with a nutritionally adequate diet, gross maldistribution in food consumption means that perhaps two-thirds of the population of the developing countries suffer from malnutrition, while many in the developed countries and many of the remainder of the population of the developing countries overeat. Because these excesses cannot be set against the inadequate diets of the malnourished, actual food deficits in most developing countries are very large. Future world food demand will depend not only on the future world population but, perhaps more importantly, on the extent to which the physiological demands of the malnourished can be made into economically effective demand. Future changes in income distribution and general levels of economic development will significantly affect food demand.

The balance between production and consumption in any country must be made up either by trade or, in the case of the poorest of countries, by food aid. Chapter 7 is devoted to this important issue. In the context of a study of government policy, food aid is particularly important. It is useful for countries with surplus production which has to be disposed of in ways which will minimize price effects on either the domestic or the international markets. Such surpluses themselves are often the result of government domestic pricing policies, especially in the United States and in the European Economic Community. Food aid is a distinctly mixed blessing for recipients. Food availability is increased, but its distribution often means that the people most in nutritional need do not get the extra food and the resulting depressed domestic price may adversely affect the incomes and the incentives of producers. The pros and cons of food aid, bilateral and multilateral, are developed at the end of Chapter 7.

Much of the current concern with world food supplies dates from recent food crises in the mid 1960s and the early 1970s (Chapter 8). Both of these crises reflected a short-term inelasticity of supply. Rising demand increased world prices, in the case of the 1970s very dramatically. Contemporary analysis of the events of the early 1970s tended to blame adverse weather conditions for the price rises while later studies have shown that these rises were amplified by government actions, especially in the United States, the Soviet Union and the EEC. The food market instability led to a renewed uncertainty about future food supplies. Again, many contemporary reports saw these events as ushering in a new era of acute food shortage. In the short term at least, these prophecies have proved false, but there is very strong evidence for future major food gaps between supply and demand for much of the developing world. This book concludes with a discussion of these projections and various proposals for long-term world food security.

CHAPTER 2

Production

Introduction

Ever since the writings of Malthus consideration of the prospects for world food and agricultural production in the future have varied between extreme pessimism and relative optimism. The Food and Agriculture Organization (FAO) of the United Nations, in a review of the state of world food and agriculture in 1976, noted the distinct improvement which continued into 1977 with increased production and overflowing stocks in most developed and developing countries. The exception to this appears to be the USSR and some countries in Western Europe (IFPRI, 1977b). None the less, as we shall see in Chapter 8, this improvement has only served to reduce the expected deficit in food production in the developing world by 1985 from up to 100 million tons to perhaps 60 million tons, a very much larger deficit than occurs at present and there remains considerable doubt about the world's capability to fill it with trade and aid.

As production has fluctuated so also have commentators' attitudes to the world's available food stocks. What in one set of circumstances are 'troublesome surpluses' become 'highly desirable stocks' when conditions change. The overproduction of food, primarily in the United States, during the 1960s became by 1975 '...[a] comfortable reserve of surplus stocks and excess production capacity that the world has enjoyed over the past generation' (Brown, 1975). Ten years ago, the excess production was hardly considered comfortable. In fact, apart from a few years in the early 1970s, overproduction in the United States and how to control it has exercised successive secretaries of agriculture, Democrat and Republican alike, for at least forty years. President Eisenhower summed up the position in 1958/59 in a message to Congress as 'compelling higher prices to consumers, vanished foreign markets and staggering surpluses in the hands of the Federal Government which has to pay $1,000 million a year in carrying charges' (reported in the *New York Times*, 30 January 1959). Wilson reports 'that by the end of the 1950s officials at the United States

Department of Agriculture felt that a good harvest would finish them. Grain filled the proper stores and rotted in old liberty ships as the government spent a million dollars a day on storage fees' (Wilson, 1977). By the end of 1977 US stock levels for wheat were at 34.7 million tons, the highest level for sixteen years, following closely on a period when it was felt that the days of abundant supplies and high stock levels had gone for ever.

There are two related reasons for the variability of impressions about the seriousness of the world food position now and in the future. Firstly, as with all forecasts, any assessment of future production and consumption is beset with problems since there is little that can be done other than to project, with various degrees of sophistication, past trends. In the period following the dramatic rises in food prices and the lowering of stocks which made up the food crisis of 1972–75 it was quite legitimate, if on the basis of the track record of past prophecies, somewhat rash, for Lester Brown to conclude that 'a world of cheap abundant food with surplus stocks and a large reserve of idled crop land may now be history. The present augurs a somewhat grimmer future, one of more or less chronic scarcity enlivened by sporadic surpluses of a local and short-lived nature' (Brown, 1975).

Two years later crop land was again being withdrawn from production in the United States. Wheat land was cut by 20 per cent for the 1978 season. This represents more than $5\frac{1}{4}$ million ha which produce about 10 million tons or about two-thirds of the total United Kingdom cereal harvest for 1977. By December 1977, with increases in production and falling prices, farmers in parts of the United States went on strike threatening to reduce crop planting and demanding higher prices. While it is possible to argue that a basic concern over long-term food supplies is still very much with us and the position of 1977–78 is just a shortlived and sporadic surplus period, instability in food circumstances and therefore instability of predictions concerning the future are remarkable. Also, crop idling programmes, whether in the 1950s or the 1970s, indicate clearly that the problems of the hungry of the world have little or nothing to do with food production. Malnutrition and starvation continue more or less unchanged through periods of world food glut and food shortage. We shall return frequently to this point in identifying the real causes of hunger.

The second reason that impressions about the nature of the future world food position are so variable is that, as particularly during the 1970s, the world food position can change very rapidly indeed and the news media are concerned with the present position, whether it be shortage and escalating prices or overflowing food stocks and falling prices. In part this variability is the result of climatic variability. This is especially true in local or national circumstances, where, for example, a failure of the monsoon in India can reduce harvests by as much as a half. On a world scale weather fluctuations may tend to cancel one another out so that a bad year in one major production zone is countered by a good harvest in another. In cases where the weather is poor for a number of seasons in succession or where many of the world's major cereal-producing areas have bad seasons at the same time, total world production can be reduced significantly and, if this is not buffered by stocks in the producing or importing countries, large price rises will be experienced. But, even in 1972 world cereal production was perhaps only 2 per cent below trend—hardly enough one would have thought for the substantial price rises and shortages which occurred. One reason that small production shortfalls are magnified into major world shortages is that only a very small proportion of the world's food production is traded. Out of a world total cereal production of 1286.1 million tons in 1975 only 137.5 million were exported, or about 11 per cent.

Thus, as production shortfall in the world's major food producers is passed on more or less in its entirety to the export market, the effects on those countries which require to import a substantial proportion of their food is magnified several times. These effects are especially significant for those developing countries which have a shortage of foreign exchange and which are therefore not in a good position to pay the increased import prices required by the world market. In the following section outlining food and agricultural production it is important to bear in mind this difference between production and trade which will be developed more fully in Chapter 6.

Food and Agricultural Production

The most important part of agricultural production is food production. Although in certain countries the production of non-food agricultural crops, for example rubber and fibres, may be of considerable importance for exports and the balance of payments, on a worldwide basis food production is the most significant part of agriculture in terms of area of production and value of the resulting product. Most agricultural production is used for food, although not in all cases directly. The more advanced the economy of the country the less its agricultural production is used directly for food. The food is increasingly processed and packaged so that the value added by the processing and packaging may exceed the value of the original agricultural product. In addition, developed economies tend to use more advanced forms of agricultural products which may have gone through more than one production stage. The direct consumption of cereals by people varies very considerably between different countries. For example, in the United States although total cereal consumption per head may be very high at about 748 kg per person per year, most of this is consumed through animals that have been fattened on the grain so only just a little over 90 kg is used directly as food. The significance of such consumption differences will be developed more fully in Chapter 5.

Total world agricultural production is a somewhat meaningless concept

Table 1. World agricultural production, 1977

	Production	
	Million tons	%
Total cereals	1459	42.45
Total root crops	570	16.58
Total pulses	48	1.40
Vegetables and melons	319	9.28
Fruit and nuts	261	7.59
Oil crops (oil equiv.)	45	1.31
Sugar	92	2.68
Cocoa, coffee and tea	7	0.20
Vegetable fibres	21	0.61
Tobacco	6	0.17
Rubber	4	0.12
Meat	126	3.67
Milk	451	13.12
Eggs	25	0.73
Wool (greasy)	3	0.09
Total	3437	100.00

Source: FAO, *Production Yearbook* (1977).

as it involves adding together units of weight or value of unlike products as, for example, maize and coffee beans. Table 1 indicates the composition of world agricultural production in 1976 and illustrates the dominance of cereal crops and food crops generally, at least in so far as this table is based on weight. The FAO excludes industrial oilseeds, tobacco, fibres (vegetable and animal), rubber, coffee, and tea from food production in its current data, although coffee and tea have been considered as food in the tabulations of previous years.

Over the period 1952 to 1962, world agricultural production grew at a fairly steady rate of around 2.7 per cent per annum, though this growth rate increased to slightly over 3 per cent per annum between 1965 and 1976. The recent largest deviations from this trend occurred between 1971 and 1972 when indexed production, to a base of the average of the period 1961 to 1965, fell by one percentage point. There was also a virtual standstill in production between 1968 and 1969. In contrast the largest increase in agricultural production occurred immediately following the fall in 1971–72 when production increased a full seven percentage points over the 1961–65 base. As far as total agricultural production is concerned, 1972 was clearly an exceptionally poor year, well below the trend line, but there is no indication that it was the start of any more general downturn in the trend of production increases (Figure 1).

Of this total agricultural production, cereals have shown a faster rate of

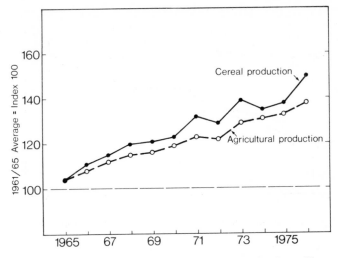

Figure 1. World agricultural and cereal production. The values plotted are for net agricultural production less amounts calculated for seeds and wastage. Because of the difficulties of comparing unlike commodities by weight, the values here are indexed on the basis of wheat price equivalents. The national producer price of all agricultural products are expressed as percentages of the national producer price of an equivalent quantity of wheat. Source: FAO, *Production Yearbooks*

growth, slightly over 4 per cent per annum over the last twelve years, reflecting the considerable technological improvements which have gone into cereal production through the breeding of new cereal varieties. More significantly perhaps, the rate of increase in production has been considerably more erratic with troughs in 1972 and again in 1974 and 1975. This is partly, but by no means entirely, a statistical phenomenon resulting from a smaller overall production and a more rapid rate of increase.

Total food production has increased considerably in all economic regions of the world (Figure 2). At first it is surprising to realize that the rate of increase in production has been considerably greater in the less developed countries (LDCs) than in the developed countries (DCs). However, when considering the potential for improvement in both the area of cultivated land and the yield of food crops on that land which existed in the LDCs in the early 1960s, the difference becomes explicable. With diminishing returns to fertilizers and other inputs becoming apparent in the developed world it appears likely that these different rates of growth between the developed and the developing worlds will continue and probably increase. Taking cereals as the major constituent of food production, the centrally

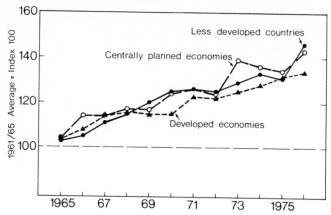

Figure 2. World food production. Source: FAO, *Production Yearbook* (1976)

planned economies of Asia and Europe (CPEs) have achieved their rate of growth in output by a better-than-average yield improvement, while the LDCs, where yield improvements still lag, seem to have achieved their rate of growth by increasing the area under cultivation (Table 2). To some extent this increase in cereal acreage has taken place at the expense of other food crops vital to a balanced diet, notably legumes and pulses, and we will return to this important topic in Chapter 5.

Although much of the blame for the instability in world food availability in 1972–74 has been placed on the United States, with her policies for reducing stocks and idling land, it is significant to note that in the developed countries as a whole food production has shown a remarkably constant increase, in contrast particularly to the centrally planned economies. The destabilizing effects of such great swings in production in some of the world's most important cereal-producing areas are obvious. As an example, in 1975 the Russian cereal harvest was 140 million tons while a year later it was 220 million tons.

Table 2. Harvested area, yield and production increases for cereals, 1961–65 to 1976

	% Change in yield	% Change in harvested area	% Change in production
World	33.2	12.2	49.6
DCs	27.8	10.8	41.7
LDCs	26.8	18.0	49.6
CPEs	46.7	7.2	57.2

Source: FAO. *Production Yearbook* (1976).

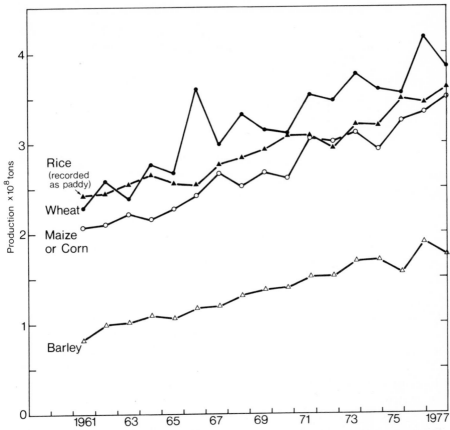

Figure 3. World major cereal production. Source: FAO, *Production Yearbooks* (1976, 1977)

All major cereals have shown a considerable increase in output (Figure 3) with wheat production showing the most erratic performance. Rice is generally a more significant crop as it is a direct food of such large sections of the world's poor populations, while wheat is used a great deal for the processed foods. The years 1971 and 1972 showed overall reductions in the production of rice. In such circumstances wheat, as the cereal which is traded more than any other (21 per cent of total production in 1975) normally becomes the relief food for food-short rice-growing areas. The significance of 1971 to 1972 as compared for example with 1966 and 1974 to 1975 was that production of both wheat and rice fell as did production of barley and maize, although to a lesser extent. Figure 4 illustrates the particular nature of the period 1971 to 1972 for cereal production. This drop in all cereal production at the same time is one of the conjunctional accidents which helped to precipitate the dramatic cereal price rises which followed, and made up the food crisis of, 1973–75.

18

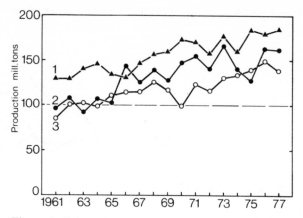

Figure 4. Selected cereal production. 1 = rice production — developing countries; 2 = wheat production — centrally planned economies; 3 = wheat production — developed economies. Source: FAO, *Production Yearbooks* (1976, 1977)

There is now considerable evidence, at least from the developing world, that the rates of increase of food production are slowing (IFPRI, 1977b; World Bank, 1976; OECD, 1976a). For all the LDCs the rate of growth of cereal production was 2.7 per cent per annum for the period 1960 to 1975. This had fallen to 2.3 per cent per annum for 1967 to 1975. The difference here is not as simple as it may seem as the rate of increase for the period 1960 to 1966 was only 2.1 per cent per annum and so the overall rate of growth for the whole period was faster than for both the individual parts of the period. This pattern is repeated for other cereals

Table 3. Rates of increase in cereal production, all developing countries, 1960–76

	All cereals	Wheat	Rice	Coarse grains
1960–66	2.1	2.4	0.9	2.9
1960–75	2.7	4.1	2.5	2.3
1967–76	2.3	4.0	2.4	1.4

Source: IFPRI (1977a).

	Cereals	Wheat	Rice	Coarse grains
1960–74	2.67	4.17	2.36	2.44
1960–65	2.90	4.29	1.56	3.26
1966–74	2.75	5.23	2.87	1.25
1969–74[a]	1.18	2.46	1.25	0.34

[a]Period rather short and adversely affected by bad weather, but the downturn was common to four of the six World Bank's production regions.
Source: World Bank (1976).

(Table 3). These rates of growth should therefore be treated with some caution as what has happened over the period in question is that the increased production in the mid 1960s has been in the form of a step function with a relatively slow rate of increase before the step and similarly after the step. If we fit a trend line to the whole period the rate of increase appears higher than for either of the two parts.

The 1967 to 1975 period would appear to be a better base from which to predict the future. On the other hand, recent substantial increases in investment in rural development in the developing countries can be expected to show returns over the next ten years or so; we might therefore expect a higher rate of increase in the future. The World Bank (1976) has produced a comparable set of data showing declining rates of increase in food production. The good crop years of 1975 and 1976 have done much to reverse this downward trend and have led to revised figures for future food deficits in the developing countries. Short-term fluctuations like these, however, illustrate the difficulties of prediction.

Considering aggregate data for all developing countries together hides intercrop and intercountry differences. Rates of increase in the production of wheat in Asian developing countries (6.6 per cent per annum over the period 1960–75) have been substantially faster than those for rice (2.4 per cent per annum over the same period). As a result wheat-growing countries like Pakistan have shown about twice the rates of increase of food production than have the predominantly rice-growing areas of Asia such as Bangladesh.

The location of production of different food crops is of major importance (Table 4). The most significant feature is the importance of cereal crops for food production in the developed countries. In fact the dominance is even more marked than the figures suggest because few of the root crops are grown for human consumption. Although over half the world's production of rice is found in the developing economies this crop accounts for only just over 22 per cent of food production in those countries. Even in the developing countries of the Far East milled rice accounts for less than half of total food production by weight. Roots, pulses, and other cereal crops remain significant. Root crops achieve most importance in Africa, making up 63 per cent of total food production by weight. This has great importance when considering food consumption by country and the nutritional status of populations because of the very low protein values of most root crops and the special malnutritional problems which arise in many African countries.

Food Production Per Capita

In contrast to total production, food production per capita presents a far less encouraging picture. World population increased by just over 2 per cent per year over the period 1965 to 1976, while food production

Table 4. World food crops

	Cereals	Milled rice[a]	Wheat	Coarse grains	Root crops	Pulses	Ground-nuts	Total
World	100	100	100	100	100	100	100	100
	63.93	14.25	22.55	26.13	33.26	2.80	1.02	100
Developed countries	35.54	6.38	36.26	50.83	14.14	6.48	11.74	27.37
	81.71	3.32	29.87	45.52	17.19	0.66	0.44	100
Centrally planned	36.63	41.34	41.79	19.98	54.00	42.58	16.61	39.86
	51.52	14.78	23.64	13.09	45.06	2.99	0.42	100
Developing countries	31.82	52.28	21.95	29.19	31.86	50.94	71.65	32.77
	61.10	22.73	15.10	23.28	32.32	4.35	2.33	100
Africa	3.41	1.52	1.07	6.47	13.42	9.15	19.07	7.06
	30.42	3.06	3.40	23.95	63.20	3.63	2.75	100
Latin America	7.05	4.03	3.00	12.21	8.29	9.80	6.47	7.54
	58.91	7.62	8.95	42.34	36.57	3.64	0.87	100
Near East	3.99	1.32	7.78	2.06	1.02	3.92	5.61	2.99
	83.05	6.31	58.74	18.00	11.36	3.67	1.91	100
Far East	17.41	45.40	10.11	8.45	8.87	28.02	40.49	15.10
	72.55	42.84	15.09	14.63	19.53	5.19	2.73	100

Note: In each column the upper figure, offset to the left, shows the proportion of the world production of that crop grown in each region. The figures in rows 5 to 8 may not sum to 100 per cent as other developing countries outside the four designated regions have not been included. Each row of the table shows the proportion of that region's total food production which is accounted for by each crop type. These data should be interpreted with caution as they have involved adding together production by weight of crops with very different food values. Not all the production indicated may be used directly or indirectly for food. The proportion not so used will be higher in the developed countries than elsewhere.
[a]Milled rice based on a paddy to rice ratio of 3 : 2.
Source: FAO, *Production Yearbook* (1977).

increased by more than 3½ per cent. At first sight the world's population should now be substantially better fed and Johnson (1975a) presents some convincing evidence that, despite the current awareness of famine and malnutrition on a worldwide basis, the position is an improvement over the past. There has been an undoubted reduction in the levels of world famine. Johnson estimates that in the last quarter of the nineteenth century 20 to 25 million people died from starvation. With the rate of population increase since that time the equivalent would be about 75 million today. For the whole of the twentieth century so far not more than 12 to 15 million people have died from famines. A much larger number of people in both periods died from weakness and susceptibility to infection resulting from malnutrition. With the rapid growth in population the absolute number of malnourished people has increased greatly, although the proportion has decreased. Estimates vary from around 450 million people to about 1000 million are malnourished at present (National Research Council, 1977).

The world has also seen a considerable increase in life expectancy. In 1950 the life expenctancy in the developing countries was between 35 and 50 years and the average for 1970–75 was 52 years. Probably the single most significant factor leading to a reduction in world famine has been improved transport and communications of all sorts. The world generally hears about acute local food shortages and is able to deliver at least some food to those areas in time to prevent the worst famines. There are, of course, exceptions to this: the Ethiopian famine was little known about until it was too late (Rivers et al., 1976), but in December 1977 the FAO were publishing advance warnings of further food shortages likely in the sub-Saharan countries of West Africa. These advance warnings came as a result of the rainfall monitoring programme established by the FAO in 1972 which reported that the monsoon rains for the summer of 1977 had been weak and erratic.

Unfortunately, the world's population increase is very far from uniform, and in the developing countries as a whole was nearly 3 per cent per annum between 1965 and 1976. Food production per capita (Figure 5) has

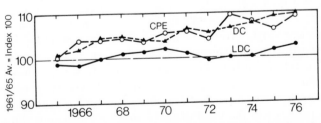

Figure 5. Food production per capita. DC = developed countries; CPE = centrally planned economies; LDC = developing countries. Source: FAO, *Production Year-books* (1976, 1977)

been fairly static in the developing countries. A steady increase in the later 1960s, when food production was outstripping population growth, was reversed in the early 1970s returning to the levels of food production per capita of the 1961–65 period. In most developing countries the period since 1976 has shown another upswing in food production per capita but, with all the efforts and investment of the green revolution, food production is still delicately balanced and continuing massive investment efforts are clearly needed just to keep pace with population growth. The spectre of Malthus's basic assumption of geometric increase in population and linear growth in food supply is still very real in many developing countries where population policies have had little effect and where there has been little food production increase. The average annual rate of growth of the population in Bangladesh is estimated at between 2.8 and 3.2 per cent, and 45 per cent of the population are under fifteen years, whereas food production has averaged only 2.5 per cent annual increase over the past eleven years. Other estimates put this production increase very much lower (World Bank, 1978a). The food production/consumption gap in such countries can do little but grow wider in the long term.

Although overall food production in the developed countries showed the smallest rate of increase, because population growth is now very small in such countries, food production per capita has grown fast. As the developed countries' capacity to absorb this increased production is limited (income elasticity of demand for food is as low as 0.2 to 0.1 (Heidhues, 1976) in the developed countries) they can be expected to export food at an increasing rate to continue to supply some of the shortfall in food production in the developing countries. However, the costs, both of purchase and shipping, of such quantities of food will grow very large and may in the future become the factor limiting the ability of the developed world to supply the food needs of the developing.

Production Potential

Production increases may result from either increases in the amount of cultivated land or, with multiple cropping, cropped area, or from yield increases. World cereal yields per hectare have risen more or less steadily from about 1150 kg/ha in 1950 to 1950 kg/ha in 1976. The 1970s have shown an increasingly erratic pattern of yield changes and there was some early evidence of a reducing rate of increase on a world scale. However, better years in 1976 and 1977 have served to return yields to more or less the trend of the previous twenty years and there has been no world-scale downturn in production per hectare. Although similar crops may be grown throughout the world the yield of these crops are strikingly different under different circumstances. In the major cereal-producing areas the yields of all cereals vary from highs of 3507 kg/ha in the United States and 3101 kg/ha in Europe with up to 4779 kg/ha in the Netherlands, to lows of 1215 kg/ha in

India and 979 kg/ha for Africa as a whole. In the case of rice alone, if the yield of all the developing countries together (1968 kg/ha) could be raised to a half of the present rice yields in Japan (5503 kg/ha) the increased production would amount to about 74 million tons a year. This is more or less equal to the predicted deficit of food grains in the developing countries by the year 1985.

In the case of wheat, where production is rather more equally divided between the developed, less developed and centrally planned countries of the world, there are similar contrasts in yields. The developing countries as a whole show yields of 1414 kg/ha in 1976 and the developed world 2239 kg/ha, again with a high of 5437 in the Netherlands.

One of the determinants of high yields of cereals and other crops is fertilizer application (Figure 6). Japan's very high yields in cereal production are matched by the highest fertilizer application rates in the world. On the other hand, the great variation found within the European countries alone indicates that there are other factors involved. The yield of cereal crops in Switzerland is not very different from that in the Netherlands, but the latter is achieved with over twice the rate of fertilizer application. Norway's cereal yields are only two-thirds those found in the United Kingdom but the fertilizer application rates are higher. Clearly there are many other factors at work including climate and soil, the labour intensity of agricultural production, the size of farm, and land-holding systems which may all be correlated with yield and fertilizer use. Increases in yields are not likely to be accounted for solely by increases in fertilizer availability and application, although these may be expected to be major controlling factors. Table 5 illustrates the response rates to fertilizer application in different developing countries.

With high application rates there will be diminishing returns—'it is likely that the conversion ratio (fertilizer to crop yield) is becoming less favourable and that a given rate of increase in food production probably requires an increasing rate of plant nutrient application' (Allen, 1976). Such diminishing returns from increased fertilizer use are not likely to be of significance for many years to come in most developing countries as present application rates are so low. Consumption of chemical fertilizer per hectare of arable land and permanent crops in the developing countries rose 244 per cent between the average of 1961–65 and 1975 but was still only 19.6 kg/ha in comparison with 100.4 kg/ha in the developed economies and 185.2 kg/ha in the developed countries of Western Europe. Africa is the region with the lowest fertilizer application rate of only 5.6 kg/ha in 1975 (FAOa, 1977). In such circumstances diminishing returns are not a significant problem.

Fertilizer availability may be a serious constraint on agricultural production in parts of the Third World again in the future as it has been in the past. Cycles of fertilizer production appear to be clearly established, with periods of overinvestment, oversupply, and low price, followed by

24

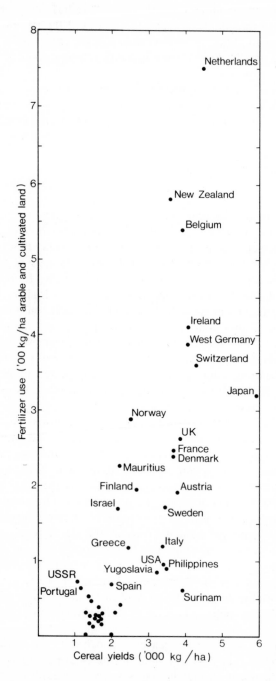

Figure 6. Fertilizer application and cereal yields, 1975. Source: FAO, *Production Yearbook* (1976); *FAO Fertiliser Review*, (1976)

Table 5. Rice yield response to fertilizer

Country	Yield per hectare without fertilizer (kg)	Increase in yield per kg[a]		
		Nitrogen (kg)	Phosphate (kg)	Potash (kg)
Burma	1432	4.7	2.6	1.0
Sri Lanka	1476	5.2	5.4	1.0
Bangladesh	991	10.5	7.1	3.3
Ghana	749	9.1	9.1	6.1
India	1230	9.9	6.5	—
Iran	2049	7.6	8.2	1.2
Thailand	1172	9.0	8.5	3.2
Vietnam	1271	5.4	3.0	0.7
South Korea	2350	8.0	0.5	2.3

[a]Increases result from the application of 30 kg/ha except in South Korea where the application level is 60 kg/ha.
Source: Timmer (1976a).

periods of underinvestment in plant later followed by shortage and high prices. Recently this cycle was accentuated by the oil crisis and, although the FAO expect that fertilizer will match demand until the early 1980s, future fluctuations appear likely. Also, actual application rates in particular circumstances have little relationship with production alone, as price is critical. The price of oil as the basic feedstock for fertilizer production means that fertilizer will not be cheap in the future except in those countries lucky enough to have their own supply of a suitable fuel. Bangladesh's supplies of natural gas are invaluable in this respect. West African countries on the fringe of the Sahara, 2000 miles or more from the sea, are unlikely to be able to produce their own fertilizers. Because import costs will be so high more research work is necessary on alternatives to chemical fertilizer application in these remote areas.

The second major contributor to yield increases has been the development of new seed varieties and hybrids. Plant selection and breeding to provide different strains of now familiar crops has been continuously developed since the earliest years of settled agriculture based on cultivation. The introduction of high-yielding hybrid corn into the United States has been plotted and monitored by many authors (for example, Griliches, 1960a). It is the developing world where the plant breeders have had their most dramatic impact. With ever increasing population there is a need to improve levels of food production in those areas of the world where yields have been more or less static, under the same systems of cultivation, for centuries. Norman Borlaug and his colleagues working in Mexico, first developed high-yielding varieties (HYV) of maize (Jesús Cutié, 1975; Winkelmann, 1976). These new

c

Table 6. Fertilizer/yield response for Indian wheat

	Nitrogen application rates (kg/ha)				
	20	40	60	80	100
Increased yields (kg/ha)					
HYV wheat	780	1400	1963	2406	2742
TV wheat	298	472	588	[a]	[a]

[a]Limited further increase or possible decrease.

varieties, joined first by HYV wheat (Borlaug, 1968) and then rice, developed at the International Rice Research Institute in the Philippines, have a major advantage over traditional varieties. They are short-strawed dwarf plants so that any extra nutrient the plants receive from fertilizer application goes not into producing a long stalk but rather a larger head of grain. If fertilizer is added in any quantity to traditional varieties they grow tall and become lodged. Once lodged the crop tends to rot and is difficult to harvest. Yield increases in response to different fertilizer application rates have been estimated for Indian wheat by the FAO and recorded in Allen (1976) (Table 6). Generally, as an equal amount of potash and phosphates as nitrogen are required, the marginal crop yield/fertilizer response ratio is between 8 : 1 and 12 : 1 at about 70 kg of plant nutrient per hectare. In addition the new varieties have a shorter growing season which increases the possibility of an additional crop in the space of one year. As many local varieties of seed, adapted to highly specific local circumstances, had to be replaced by a very limited number of the new varieties, they had to be adaptable over a wide range of latitude and altitude.

Progress with the new technology, which involved not only the new varieties of seed but also a package of farm management proposals including fertilizer and irrigation application, was very rapid at first. This new technology was usually more or less free to the recipient countries and their farmers, made available as part of aid programmes from the Rockefeller and other Foundations. It has been argued that such aid was designed to benefit, first and foremost, the developed countries by providing an outlet for their technological industries selling fertilizer and fertilizer manufacturing plants, tractors, irrigation machinery, etc. (George, 1976), but there is little doubt that the green revolution, as this particular package of agricultural development proposals became known, was a very attractive proposition to those countries facing a growing food deficit in the 1960s. It is also arguable that it would have been in the best interests of the United States to have the developing world as dependent as possible on US supplies of wheat and other grains as this was also the time of huge US surpluses.

By the 1972–73 crop season there were estimated to be 15.7 million ha of HYV rice planted, about 20 per cent of the total area of that crop, and 16.8 million ha of wheat, about 35 per cent of all wheat production. By this time rice developments were accelerating and many more successful varieties (e.g. IRRI 22) were being developed so that by 1975 HYV rice area, at 21 million ha, had surpassed wheat. Maize developments were less important as it is a less significant developing world cereal crop, but the new varieties achieved considerable local importance in Mexico and some East African countries. It is possible to make a very crude estimate of the overall benefit, in terms only of increased cereal production, of the adoption of the new HYV seeds. Assuming a rather pessimistic increase in yield of 500 kg/ha on about 40 million ha planted to the new varieties, the increased production is 20 million tons. In 1975–76 total world food aid in cereals amounted to about 7 million tons and the developing countries together imported about 30 million tons of cereals in 1975.

Judged by any standards India's performance in wheat production in the late 1960s was remarkable (Vyas, 1975). From 1966–67 to 1971–72 wheat production increased from 11.4 million tons to 26.4 million tons. If the trends prior to 1966 had continued, using existing varieties of seed and continued improvements in irrigation, wheat production might have been raised to about 16 million tons. The additional 10 million tons can be attributed directly to the new HYV seeds. The arrival of the new technology for wheat in advance of other cereals meant that wheat, which contributed about 16 per cent of all cereal production in India in 1964–65, increased in importance to 28.3 per cent in 1971–72. In the six years up to 1971–72 the area of high-yield-variety wheats increased from 541,000 to 7,439,000 ha or from 4.2 per cent to 39.1 per cent of all land planted to wheat. The wheat lands of India were particularly suited to this new technology, having a fair degree of topological and climatological uniformity. Progress was remarkably rapid. In 1963 four Mexican varieties of wheat were introduced into India for early production experiments. The results of these early trials led to the import of 250 tons of *Sonora* 64 and *Lerma Rojo* 64 in 1965. The latter variety showed the best adaptability to the range of physical circumstances in India, and the summer of 1966 saw a further import of 18,000 tons of seed, enough to plant 292,000 ha in the first year of commercial production. There was some early consumer resistance to the small-grained red Mexican wheats and this was reflected in a price differential between it and the traditional *Deshi* varieties, but subsequent developments have reduced this resistance and the price differential.

At first general yield increases, using HYV seeds of wheat and rice and the correct applications of fertilizer and irrigation water, were remarkable. Four times or even up to six times the average grain yields of the country would be recorded from experimental plots. However, when the technology was transferred to the real world, performance was rather less impressive though it was substantially better than with traditional varieties of seeds. Under experimental conditions the plants were never stressed, they were given fertilizer at the best possible times in the best possible amounts and the same was true for irrigation water. This was hardly likely to be the position in real farming situations even with the best farming practices. Vyas (1975) found for Indian wheat lands:

> partly because of the non-availability of adequate water supplies from public irrigation system, the HYV adopters in many areas could not give adequate irrigation. Administration of the canal system often brings water to the farmer when he does not want it and makes water completely unavailable when needs are critical. . . It was observed that farmers irrigated their wheat only four times, while the recommended number of waterings was six.
> Practically all the studies of HYV have concluded that the use of fertilizers is much below the recommended levels. . . The application of fertilizers ranged widely from 15 to 137 per cent of the recommended doses in 1967 and 12 to 102 per cent the following year. In the Purnea district of Bihar the utilisation of fertilizer between 1964–65 and 1968–69 jumped from 62 to 900 tons. This nearly 15 fold increase, however, does not mean that the farmers applied fertilizers at the recommended level. If they had done so, the consumption would have been nearly 2,700 tons.

There has been a predictable decline in the yields of HYV rice and wheat (Table 7). Such technological developments would tend to be concentrated at first on the best farmers and on the most suitable land. With time and increasing use of the innovation, both of these would change for the worse and yields would be expected to decline. In addition, the HYV wheats are not suitable for the colder and drier areas of, for example, Afganistan and Pakistan, and the deeply flooded areas of Asia await the development of suitable high-yielding varieties of rice. Local varieties of deep-water rice are adapted to fast growth. Keeping up with the rising flood waters the plants can grow 76–100 mm in one day and can achieve lengths of 3 to 4 m.

Table 7. Declining yields of HYV wheat and rice

| Crop year | HYV yields (times higher than traditional varieties) | |
	Wheat	Rice
1966–67	2.87	2.58
1967–68	3.70	2.18
1968–69	3.49	2.05
1969–70	3.68	2.26
1970–71	3.44	2.27
1971–72	3.50	2.03
1972–73	2.35	1.76
1973–74	2.59	1.71

Source: Wade (1974).

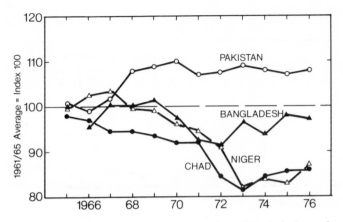

Figure 7. Food production per capita, Bangladesh and
Pakistan, Niger and Chad. Source: FAO, *Production
Yearbooks*

Bangladesh alone has about 2 million ha of deep-water rice, making up
about 20 per cent of the total rice area and 16 per cent of the production
(Islam, 1977). The dwarf varieties of rice are quickly innundated and once
the water has risen above the ears of grain for any length of time the crop
is lost. As an example the early arrival of the monsoon rains, or
exceptionally heavy rainfall in the March/April period can cause problems
for the irrigated HYV Boro crop in Bangladesh.

The timing of the HYV seed developments in the mid 1960s caused
intercountry differences in food production. In 1967 the food production
records of the east and west wings of Pakistan, later to become the
separate states of Bangladesh and Pakistan, started to diverge (Figure 7).
Two important factors here were the suitability of the new HYV wheats to
Pakistan and the insignificant role which wheat played in the total food
production of Bangladesh. By the early 1970s the divergence was very
marked. This divergence, and the large amounts of overseas aid to
Pakistan which helped to make it possible, was one of the imbalances
between the two wings of Pakistan which led to the war which created the
State of Bangladesh. In the Sahel, also unsuitable for large-scale wheat
production, the green revolution has had little effect. Indeed in the two
countries, Chad and Niger, illustrated in Figure 7, food production per
capita started to decline at the same time as that in Pakistan was
improving.

The effects of the green revolution are now declining. The increased
food production per capita achieved in Pakistan between 1966 and 1968
continued at a decreased rate until 1970, but has now apparently stabilized
at more or less the rate of population increase and the overall food
availability is no longer improving. The green revolution gave no more

Table 8. Indian food crop yields before and including the green revolution period

Crop	Yield trend rates of growth (% per annum)	
	1949–50 to 1964–65	1949–50 to 1973–74
Wheat	1.27	2.99
Rice	2.13	1.72
Cereals	1.76	1.85
Food grains	1.52	1.65
Non-food grains	0.85	0.88
All crops	1.34	1.40

Source: Veeman (1977).

than a short breathing space in the race between food production and population increase. Veeman (1977) concludes that in retrospect the green revolution has had little overall effect on food crop yields in India. Making allowance for drought years he finds that the trend rate of increase in cereal production was little different for the period including the green revolution years than for the period before it. Although the rate of increase in wheat production had increased, it had fallen for rice. As rice is a more important crop for India than wheat the rate of increase of cereal production for India was only very little higher between 1949–50 and 1973–74 than between 1949–50 and 1964–65 before the new seeds arrived (Table 8). The years 1975 to 1977 were good production years for wheat and rice and the position now looks less pessimistic. Such calculations are very sensitive to the choice of period and base year.

We have seen that the new seeds rely not only on suitable fertilizer application but also on good water management. The world's irrigated area increased by 20 per cent between the average of 1961–65 and 1975 to 227 million ha. Fifty-two per cent of the extra irrigated area was in the less developed countries and 37 per cent in the centrally planned economies. There are, however, difficulties in interpreting data on the irrigated area. Recording of the irrigated area tends to be inaccurate in many countries. Often the area recorded is the design area of the irrigation schemes in operation and little or no account is taken of mechanical breakdown, incomplete operation or the rate of loss of irrigated land through waterlogging and salination. In most arid and semi-arid lands soil deterioration due to salt accumulation is common. Perhaps as much as 50 to 60 per cent of previously non-saline soils in arid lands have been rendered saline through irrigation (Kovda, 1971), and irrigated lands are degraded at about 125,000 ha a year (Sharp, 1972). Water delivery systems to farmers may not be managed in relation to the needs of individual farmers (Reidinger, 1974) and as we have seen this is one of the reasons why the new HYV seeds do not achieve the high yields on farms that they manage on experimental plots. The efficiency of water use in irrigation schemes varies between 25 and 50 per cent and in certain situations in developing countries may be very much lower (Doorenbos, 1975). Even in the western states of the United States the water-use efficiency is no more than 40 per cent. But the value of irrigated production is probably as high as all other production together (Kovda, 1971) and the potential irrigated area in the world, if all available sources of irrigation water were used to the full, has been put at 470 million ha (Buringh *et al.*, 1975). Such an area, if it could be utilized, would have a very dramatic effect on the world's food production, though land loss through salination and related problems is currently close to the annual rate of increase in irrigated land.

Operating together or separately, seed developments, fertilizer application and irrigation have played the major part in providing increased food crop yields over the last twenty years. Table 9 shows how yield and area changes have contributed to production increases. In general, yield increases have been substantially larger than area increases and have been growing at a faster rate. An average annual growth rate of 2.7 per cent for cereals in the developing countries results from a 1.1 per cent increase per annum in area harvested and a 1.6 per cent increase in yields from that increased area.

Growth in harvested acreage comes about in two ways. In many tropical and subtropical countries, where the growing season can last throughout the year, more than one crop is technically possible. Irrigation and flood control allow crops to be grown where previously the land was idle or as fallow either through too much water or too little. The winter, or dry season, in many monsoon climates, particularly in much of India and Bangladesh, is the season when solar energy is at its highest and if irrigation water can be provided a highly successful dry season crop can be

Table 9. Irrigation and a dry season rice crop in Bangladesh

Year	Area irrigated ('000 ha)	Area planted to HYV Boro paddy ('000 ha)
1969–70	1089	241
1970–71	1202	357
1971–72	1078	331
1972–73	1247	453
1973–74	1334	606
1974–75	1484[a]	679
1976–77	1218	492

[a]FAO estimates for 1975 = 1500.
Source: *Statistical Yearbook of Bangladesh* (1975), and Government of Bangladesh (1978).

raised. The median monthly rainfall in Bangladesh between November and February varies between 0 and 6 mm, compared with between 302 and 439 mm in June to September, and maximum temperatures vary between 25 °C and 28 °C. The provision of irrigation to allow an extra crop during this season has been closely matched by the growth of the dry season paddy crop (Boro) most of which has been of high-yielding varieties (Table 9). In countries where there is more than one rainy season the potential for double or treble cropping is higher and can be met with less investment in irrigation.

The potential for multiple cropping can be met with not only irrigation but also other inputs, although irrigation may be the most important. Labour availability, draft power, fertilizer, and credit to exploit these possibilities are important. The cropping intensity, (land harvested/arable land) is 90 per cent in Asia, 67 per cent in the Near East, 69 per cent in East Africa and 57 per cent in West Africa. These data on cropping intensities should be interpreted with caution as not only are the statistics gathered under very different circumstances in different countries and with greatly varying accuracy, but the role of fallow land, particularly in Africa, gives the impression of low ratios, whereas the land which is cultivated in any one year may be multiple cropped. It is also important to note in passing that multiple cropping is different from intercropping. The former implies more than one growing season on each plot of land, the latter more than one crop type from each plot of land in one growing period.

Multiple cropping and intercropping may be practised together where crops have different harvesting dates and the growing seasons can overlap as in the Taiwan example (Figure 8). The cropping seasons do not often coincide completely with a calendar year and cropping calendars are drawn up usually for periods of up to year and a half during which time three crops may be produced. In Bangladesh, for example, wet season paddy (Aus) may be planted in May and harvested at the end of August on land that is not deeply flooded. In early September the same land may be planted to a winter crop of tobacco, wheat, or mustard which will be harvested from late January to early March, depending on the choice of crop. This crop will then be replaced by jute which will be harvested in late August in time for a further winter crop to be planted and then replaced by a summer crop of rice. The choice between jute and rice in any one year may be determined more on the basis of the relative prices of the two crops and on the degree to which the farmer is able to grow cash crops than from any consideration of crop rotations. Different cycles will be present on different quality lands, depending largely on the depth of the annual flooding to be expected. Johnson (1975b) provides a very detailed crop calendar for Bangladesh showing cropping patterns on several qualities of land.

The second, rather slower, way to increase harvested area is to bring new land into cultivation. There are few cases where this involves strictly

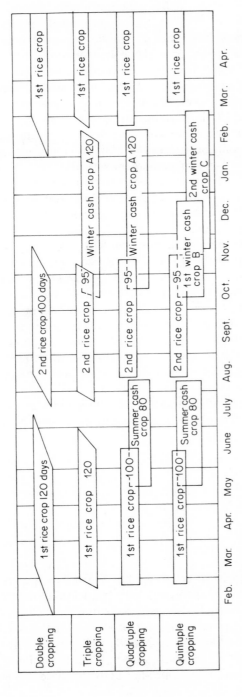

Figure 8. Multiple cropping systems in Taiwan. *Key to crops.* Winter crop A: wheat, barley, buckwheat, maize, soybean, sweet potato, rapeseed, field pea, tobacco, flax, green manure crop (green bean), broccoli, cauliflower, Chinese cabbage or tomato. Winter crop B: native cabbage. Winter crop C: wheat, maize, broccoli, cauliflower, Chinese cabbage or fieldpea. Summer crop: Oriental pickling melon, Japanese cantaloup, jute, sweet potato, soybean, green manure crop or native cabbage. Source: Dalrymple (1971)

speaking new land, the draining of the Dutch polder lands, and the bringing under cultivation of the deltaic lands of active deltas as in the Ganges/Brahmaputra delta in Bengal. It is most unusual for there to be potentially arable land where there is at present no system of agriculture at all. Most of the potential to increase the cultivated area will require a change in the system of agriculture from pastoralism or slash and burn cultivation. In the latter case large areas of the land's surface may appear to be unused but it is actually under some system of fallow, perhaps for a very extended period, which is fulfilling the function of fertilizers and leguminous crops under more advanced systems of cultivation and returning fertility to the soil. Such areas of shifting cultivation are being reduced as the pressure on land for permanent settled agriculture becomes greater. The forest lands of South-East Asia are changing in this way at a very fast rate. The increase in arable land, both realized and the potential, is best seen as an increase in the intensity of use rather than the bringing into productive cultivation of new land.

At present about 1400 million ha are cultivated, that is, about three times the land area of Europe and about 10 per cent of the land area of the globe. This cultivated area represents about 0.35 ha per person but it is far from uniformly distributed, with the cultivated land area per person ranging from 1 ha in Australia and New Zealand to 0.23 ha in Asia. There is not a complete match between the distribution of arable land and the distribution of the capability to produce food, as the arable land is of differing quality and also non-arable land is capable of producing large quantities of food products, especially in North and South America and in Australasia.

Attempts to estimate the potential increase in the world's arable area are beset with difficulties. Estimates of the total cultivatable land have to take into account:

(a) the problem of fallow periods under existing and future systems of cultivation;
(b) the potential realistically available water supplies and the technology to extract and utilize this water; and
(c) the potential for double or multiple cropping on the same land area. Few estimates of the available arable land make explicit reference to this factor.

Estimates of the total potential arable land in North America range from 463.0 million ha (Revelle, 1974) through 495 (OECD, 1976a) and 546.0 (de Hoogh et al., 1977) to 626.7 (National Research Council, 1977). It is not difficult to see that when estimates are produced for the whole world such differences will be considerably magnified. The OECD, perhaps most sensibly, gives no estimate for the whole world as 'the definition of exactly what constitutes arable land varies somewhat between these estimates (for different regions) according to the severity of climatic, terrain and soil constraints that have to be imposed'. Precise comparisons between countries and regions are not possible. Not unexpectedly, estimates which have been made for arable reserves for the world vary by a factor of two.

For example the National Academy of Sciences (National Research Council, 1977) estimates 1979.5 million ha, the President's Scientific Advisory Council in 1967 and Revelle (1974) provide middle ground estimates of 2750 and 2819 million ha respectively, while the highest is de Hoogh *et al.*, (1977) with 3687.0 million ha. It seems that the world's arable area could be at least doubled with a degree of technological effort (Blakeslee *et al.*, 1973). The potential, however large it may finally turn out to be, is not equally divided among the world's regions. Table 10 presents some estimates of arable reserves in different parts of the world as an illustration. All sources agree that it is in Africa and South America that the bulk of the potential for new arable land exists. The FAO (1970a) estimates that only about 11 per cent of the potential is used in South America and 22 per cent in Africa against 87 per cent in Asia. The OECD estimates show less extreme differences but they are of the same order. Asia has by far the largest and fastest-growing population and therefore we can expect the maldistribution of arable land per person to become more extreme as new arable land is developed. Increase in arable area as a source of increased food production is of little significance or comfort to areas like Bangladesh or Java. Taking into account the potential for multiple cropping, Revelle (1974) estimates that the net cultivated area

Table 10. Arable land reserves (million ha)

	Latin America	Africa	Asia	Oceania	North America	Europe	USSR
Arable land cultivated (base year)	119[a]	214[a]	467[a]	47[b]	230[c]	141[a]	225[d]
Potential arable	570	733	628	107	495	141	270
Arable as % potential	21%	29%	74%	44%	46%	100%	83%
Net cultivated area[e]	760	977	837	143	660	188	360

[a]Base year 1970.
[b]Base year 1970–71.
[c]Base year 1971.
[d]Base year 1973.
[e]After Revelle (1974) assuming double cropping on one-third of the potential arable area.
Source: OECD (1976a).

could be increased to 4230 million ha and de Hoogh *et al.* (1977) estimate that the potential agricultural production of the world could increase a staggering twenty-four-fold using existing technology over all the world's agricultural land.

To a large extent such projections are purely academic exercises as their usefulness depends on ability to realize this potential. The social and physical obstacles are immense. Many people have postulated that the costs of this utilization will preclude its realization and this is one of the premises of the Limits of Growth Model (Meadows *et al.*, 1972). It is however, not necessary to consider the capital-intensive technologies of the Western world as the only alternative available for the development of this arable potential. Labour-intensive methods would allow much new arable land to be developed at much smaller real cost (Ruch *et al.*, 1976). The physical problems should not be overlooked; according to the FAO for the savanna grasslands of Africa:

> It would be extremely unwise to underestimate the difficulties of the savannas. The great excess of precipitation over evaporation in the summer causes severe leaching, while the intense desiccation in the dry season may lead to the formation of a hardpan that impedes movement of water and root penetration. From the pastoral point of view, a long, dry season which exhausts the cattle in their search for water and nutriment is followed by a short period of abundant food, but the rapid growth results in the grasses quickly becoming tough. Here again a tremendous amount of research and patient experimentation with soil management, machinery, crops, pastures and fodder preservation, as well as investments for conservation of water, are necessary before these lands can be rendered productive.

The problems are no less acute in the utilization of the apparently luxuriant equatorial forests of Latin America. It is now well understood that the clearance of forrest cover exposes the soil to rapid leaching and erosion and that, without either large inputs of artificial fertilizer and/or extensive fallow periods, these areas will remain productively arable for only a very short time. There is also the very real possibility of long-term climatic change brought about by extensive forest clearance.

In conclusion, because of the difficulties of bringing new land into cultivation and because of the loss of irrigated arable land through salination and waterlogging, and such problems as the desertification of much of the world's dry land margins, most of the world's increased food supply, at least over the next twenty-five years, will come from increased yields on the world's existing arable land rather than any major increase in the total arable area.

Farming Systems

It is clear that food and agricultural production vary very considerably throughout the world in response to different physical and economic circumstances. This variation is in both the crops grown and livestock reared and also in the systems of production. The methods used and the yields obtained make the growing of wheat in Pakistan very different from the growing of wheat on the American prairies, and the small fields thinly scattered with mustard plants in Bangladesh in the winter bear little resemblance to the specialized cultivation of that crop in eastern England. Crop cultivation can be labour or machinery intensive, can be irrigated or rain-fed, can be based on settled agricultural methods, or on shifting cultivation with fallow periods.

Most agricultural research is crop orientated rather than concentrating on the system of agriculture within which the crop is produced. In many ways this is one important reason why the green revolution in practice has been less successful than on experimental plots. The research effort went into the breeding of new varieties of plants for the production of single crops and little attention was paid directly to improving the agricultural system within which these new crops were to be grown. The typical small farmer in the developing world and elsewhere manages a complex farming system.

A number of commodities are produced both for family subsistence and for a cash sale. Animals are almost always present, as a source of power, food, fuel, income, and fertilizer (National Research Council, 1977). The farming systems adopted throughout the world have evolved over time as a result of interactions among soil, water, and the climatic base, together with human capabilities and economic factors such as capital and markets (Ruthenburg, 1971).

Research concentration on single crops is not surprising because of the very great variety of agricultural systems. Any research to improve the efficiency of a system may be highly specific to only one small region. A particular system on a farm and in a region will have developed in response to the local physical environment in all its facets and the growth of population. The present intensity of production will be related to the man–land ratio. Distance to market may be a factor both through the physical problems of marketing goods and the effects which distance has on the price and the profitability of production. Also, at least in the developed economies, there is evidence of regional specialization controlled by economic forces of price and comparative advantage. Cultural factors will also be locally important, sometimes in the most obvious ways such as the virtual absence of pigs from most Moslem countries. Grigg (1974) stresses also the historical evolution of agricultural systems as one of the most important explanations of present patterns. Man has cultivated the surface of the earth for many centuries and only in the recent past has he made substantial technological changes in his methods of cultivation.

Climate and Agriculture

Although it is certainly possible for man to overcome almost any environmental circumstances to grow different crops, provided there is the financial incentive to make the necessary technological investment, there are very few factors in food and agricultural production which have a more significant effect throughout the world than weather and climate. The National Research Council has defined weather as referring to 'events, such as temperature and precipitation, occurring within a two-week period, while climate is associated with events occurring over longer time spans' (National Research Council, 1976). Climate is the summation or average of the weather in a particular place. Weather and climate affect agriculture on both a long- and a short-term basis. The crop damage resulting from a typhoon is essentially a local short-term effect which does not have any long-term effects on a region's agricultural production. This is despite the considerable local disruption and damage which may result from such a typhoon as in Bangladesh in 1970 and South India in 1977. Climate, on the other hand, being the summation of weather conditions, has a great and obvious influence on all forms of agriculture.

Climate affects agriculture by placing geographical limits on various forms of agricultural production; setting crop limits as a result of long-run average precipitation and temperature conditions. We may regard these controls as more or less stable. The various crop limits in the world do not change much, and if they do these changes are spread over several years and may result as much from the introduction of new crop varieties which are less climate sensitive as from alterations in climatic conditions. The number of frost-free days and the growth of cotton, the length of the growing season and the ripening of maize, the supply of water and the production of rice (van Liere, 1974), the control provided by temperature on the growth of tea and coffee—the list of such controls is endless. Most of the world's grain production is in the middle latitudes where summer temperatures average between 21 °C and 24 °C. The grain belts are limited at lower latitudes by high summer temperatures and at high latitudes by the length of the growing season (Thompson, 1975). As grain is the world's most important food, climatic conditions in these middle latitudes are of vital significance.

Such climatic controls provide limits to the world's major agricultural regions, provide potential for double or multiple cropping, irrigation and different forms of agricultural production. But these limits, like all geographical boundaries, are far from absolute, and changes are not abrupt but gradual. The changes are gradual because the features of the climate controlling the production are not constant but vary from year to year. One moves from a location where the production of a crop is successful three years out of three, to one where the crop fails one year in three, to one where the crop is hardly ever successful. The success or failure of a crop is itself hardly ever absolute, very rarely is there total loss or the theoretical maximum yield. A broad transition zone may be expected in which production depends on the attitude to risk on the part of the farmers. Is the chance of a crop failure a matter which would be a temporary setback which would be more than recovered in later years, or is it far more serious than that? In general one might expect these climatic limits to be more clearly defined in circumstances where the risk of crop failure is to be avoided. In many developing countries, with the majority of the population farming at or below subsistence levels, one crop failure spells disaster. The production of food crops must be as near a certainty as possible. In commercial production, with capital reserves, the risks can be higher and the climatic limits less absolute, whether the production is in the developed or the developing worlds. In commercial agriculture the climatic margins may be expected to be wider or narrower depending on the marketing circumstances of the crops being produced. As price rises so the limits of production are pushed out into previously uncultivated land or land use changes from one crop to another. Thompson (1975) and the

Table 11. Climate and agricultural production in the United States

Crop	% Change in production brought about by a 10% increase in precipitation		
	In dry years	In normal years	In wet years
Corn[a]	2.8	2.2	1.1
Wheat[a]	2.3	2.3	2.5
Range production[b]	8.5	8.5	8.5
Soybean[a]	3.0	3.3	3.6

[a]Main producing areas.
[b]West of 100°W. longitude.
Source: personal communication based on National Research Council (1976).

Change in precipitation (%) assuming a 1 °C drop in temperature	Change in wheat yields (bushels per acre)					
	North Dakota	South Dakota	Kansas	Oklahoma	Illinois	Indiana
−30	−2.62	−1.88	−2.10	−3.09	+4.24	+4.12
−20	−1.81	−0.71	−1.06	−1.83	+3.41	+3.06
−10	−0.56	+0.29	−0.11	−0.90	+2.38	+1.98
+10	+1.89	+2.33	+1.49	+0.04	−0.25	−0.25
+20	+3.07	+1.47	+2.61	+0.03	−1.86	−1.40
+30	+4.30	+1.39	+2.73	−0.29	−3.68	−2.58

Source: Thompson (1975).

National Academy of Sciences (National Research Council, 1976) provide evidence that there would be considerable benefit from both a cooling of summer temperatures and an associated increase in rainfall in most of the corn, wheat, soybean, and range lands of North America (Table 11). Most of these crops are being produced beyond their climatic ideal because of market prices of the commodities. As we shall see, government policies have a great deal to do with prices of agricultural commodities and government pricing policies can have the effect of encouraging production beyond the 'normal' climatic limits.

Risk is present in agricultural production because climate is not static but fluctuates. Crops can fail one year and be a success the next. If the effects of these climatic fluctuations could be predicted then the crop limits would also fluctuate as farmers adjusted to the predicted climatic conditions of that growing season. As these year-to-year fluctuations in climate cannot be predicted with any accuracy, risk-taking becomes necessary. That such fluctuations in climate, from year to year or over longer cycles, affect agriculture is unquestionable. 'In many areas of the world variability of the climate is the rule rather than the exception' (National Research Council, 1977), and Mayer (1975) mentions that in almost every year since the Second World War there has been a famine in some part of the world which could be attributed to such climatic fluctuation. 'The unfavourable weather of 1972 and 1974 in middle latitudes and the failure of the monsoons in India and the sub-Sahara over the past several years have caused greater recognition of weather and climate in relation to food supply in the world' (Thompson, 1975).

We are not only concerned with fluctuations around a norm but also with the vital question of longer-term fluctuations in the norm. Does the short-term climatic fluctuation take place around a set of mean climatic characteristics which are also changing? Is there any indication that the climate of the next twenty years will be generally less favourable to the world's agricultural production? This might be either by a deterioration in temperature or rainfall conditions, or by increasingly more erratic climatic conditions but around the same mean, which will affect crop boundaries and production even if the mean climatic position remains unchanged. As this book is concerned primarily with government policies for dealing with change, it is pertinent to concentrate on some of the evidence for recent climatic change and its effects on agricultural production.

Until very recently there was a tendency among agricultural economists to take weather and climate as a set of randomly fluctuating variables which could not be explained but which could be ignored because the position beneath these random fluctuations was stable. Such analysis of climate as was carried out concerned its relationships to short-term variations in yield (Waugh, 1967) which 'ignores the most important aspect of the subject' (Allen, 1976). On the basis of this belief, the climate of the decades ahead could be predicted to wield the same influence over production as in the past (FAO, 1970a). By the early 1970s the weather was no longer considered a significant factor in grain production, at least by the USDA (Thompson, 1975).

There has recently accumulated a considerable body of evidence that the climate of the 1960s had two characteristics which enhanced this sense of complacency:

(a) it was better than the average for the century in certain key grain-producing areas; and
(b) it was much less variable from year to year than before or since.

As corn accounts for about two-thirds of the total cereal tonnage produced in the United States the climatic conditions in the corn belt have been particularly significant in anticipating future grain production. Both Thompson (1974; 1975) and McQuigg (1974) have tried to isolate the effects of climate from technological changes on crop yields. Using multiple regression techniques the effects of changes in climate can be studied

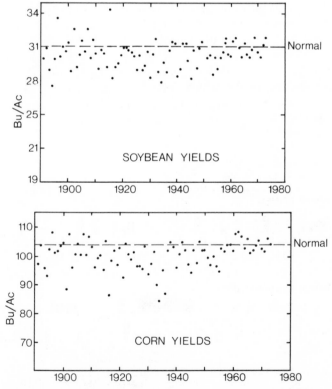

Figure 9. Simulated soybean and corn yields in the United States corn belt, assuming constant technology levels. Source: Thompson (1975)

holding technology, in the form of fertilizer application and mechanization, constant. Doing this for technological levels of 1973 (Thompson) and 1945 (McQuigg) shows the remarkable stability and favourability of the period from 1956 to 1973 in the yield of corn and soybeans (Figure 9). Thompson (1975) estimates that the effects of weather and climate fluctuations are underestimated by this analysis by about 50 per cent, but the pattern produced is very clear and is useful in comparing the period 1956 to 1973 with that before and since.

Thompson (1975) found no similar run of favourable years for the Great Plains area, but Schneider (1974) presents data for rainfall and temperature in five wheat-growing states (Figure 10) which shows that the last fifteen years have generally had above-average rainfall and below-average temperatures. The contrast with the 'dust bowl era' is particularly striking.

The National Academy of Science's study (National Research Council, 1976) finds that Russian grain lands both east and west of the Volga river are climatically variable, with this variability reaching a peak in the period 1930 to 1940. Both areas show markedly less variability in the decade ending 1972. It is significant that the year 1968 formed the basis of the 1971 to 1975 five-year plan period and helped an overestimation of the grain production potential in the USSR in 1972. This overestimation, and the Russian government's method of dealing with it, was one of the reasons for large Russian grain purchases from the United States and the huge price rises for grains which followed (see Chapter 8). It is also significant that the marketing policy of the United States, expressed through the USDA, was largely based on Russian grain production

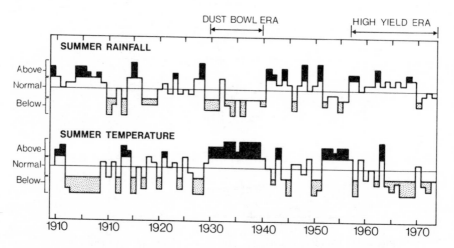

Figure 10. Summer rainfall and temperature conditions in the United States wheat belt, 1900–75. Source: Schneider (1974)

performance between 1962 and 1972 when improved yields were put down to technological improvement in the agricultural sector in the USSR. As with the grain yields in the United States, at least a part of this improved Russian agricultural performance resulted from favourable climatic conditions during that period. A recent Central Intelligence Agency study of the effects of climate on USSR agriculture is less optimistic than the USDA has been in the past since it bases its predictions on a longer period than the one covering the climatically more favourable years used by USDA (Shapley, 1977).

The decade of the 1960s induced a false sense of security with regard to climate and agricultural production. In part at least this must have been helped by the acute agricultural overproduction problems of the United States. It did not look as if the United States would ever return to a situation where potential production fell below or even close to demand. Despite this, any climatic study undertaken in 1970 would have put a high probability on the United States returning to less favourable conditions. The disastrous years of the 1930s were not so far away.

There is mounting evidence of cycles of change with both long time scales of hundreds of years and much shorter cycles of fifteen to twenty years. It is possible that cyclic changes in agricultural yields are associated with sunspot activities (King *et al.*, 1974; Allen, 1976). Allen concludes that the double sunspot cycle provides the best basis we have of interpreting past fluctuations in wheat and feed-grain yields in the high plains and the Mid-west of the United States. However, the connection with sunspot cycles is insufficiently established (National Defense University, 1978), and it has proved possible to correlate many things with sunspot cycles where the causative link is less obvious.

Longer-term trends are also identifiable. The world is currently in a warm interglacial period which began about 10,000 years ago. This followed from the glacial maximum about 18,000 years ago when much of North America and Europe was covered with ice. The period AD 1100 to AD 1400 was relatively warm and this was followed by the little Ice Age of AD 1400 to about AD 1850 when winter fairs on the frozen River Thames in London were regular events. From 1850 to 1940 there was a warming in the Northern Hemisphere of about 1 °C and since then a further cooling trend has been detected (Lamb, 1976). There remains controversy concerning prospects for any long-term cooling or warming of the earth's climate, but climate is no longer taken as static or randomly variable in agricultural planning. The 1977 US Agriculture Act contained the following reference: 'The Secretary shall conduct a comprehensive study of the effects of changing climate and weather on crop and livestock productivity . . . this shall include . . . the possible impact of changes in climate and weather conditions on the Nation's economy and future food and feed availability and prices'. Overall there is fairly conclusive evidence that climatic conditions for agriculture over the next twenty years will not be as favourable as they have been over the last twenty. Also, we can say that some at least of the improved agricultural performance of all countries over the last twenty years has been the result of favourable climatic conditions and that we can expect the rate of increase in agricultural production to slow down in the future for that reason alone. We should take heed of this in making predictions of agricultural production in the future and not fall into the same trap as did planners in the United States and the USSR in the early 1970s.

Climatic control over agriculture is far from deterministic. The great expansion of wheat lands in the USSR in Khruschev's New Lands policy of the 1960s has spread production into Kazakhstan and Siberia to the Chinese border. Although a period of favourable climate may have allowed this development it certainly did not cause it. It was a political decision and one which, because of the apparently increasingly erratic climate at this dry margin of production, is giving rise to severe production fluctuations and associated planning problems. Attitude to the risks provided by climatic fluctuation are conditioned by the price of agricultural commodities and the alternative types of production available. Many of these factors are controlled by governments for essentially political reasons. Whatever the physical controls on agricultural and food production, the role of governments in determining prices and trade and production policies will be equally if not more important. World agricultural production did fall sharply in 1972 and cereal production more sharply in both 1972 and 1974 (Figure 1), but both of these falls left production far above the level of two years previously. These production falls of no more than a few per cent on a world scale, but very much larger for individual countries, largely resulting from climatic factors, were not severe enough in themselves to account for the dramatic movements in the food commodity markets during this time. We are not in a position to ignore climate in agriculture, but we can to some extent mitigate its effects and limit its control by recognizing the risks that it creates and compensating for these through prices and strategic food stocks. The physical circumstances for agricultural production provide one of the justifications for government interference in agriculture. There are many other justifications. Equally, there are many other reasons apart from climate which explain fluctuations in agricultural production and demand. These will be the subject of the following chapters.

CHAPTER 3

Government Intervention in Agriculture

Introduction

Although the physical environment may exert considerable, even perhaps the ultimate, control over all forms of agricultural production, national governments and some international organizations such as the European Community exert at least a comparable influence. Food policies and agricultural policies are two overlapping subsets of overall economic policy and this chapter will deal with both side by side. They have achieved prominence recently as a result of policies which have at times given rise to unsaleable surpluses or 'mountains', as well as an increasing realization of the international political and economic power that can be wielded with any available food surplus. It is not only the organization of oil-producing states who have obtained publicity and interest recently through the operation of a supplers' cartel. Past secretaries of state for agriculture in the United States have stated publicly that food is a potential weapon in the realm of international relations. It seems most unlikely that future food surpluses will be entirely disposed of for philanthropic reasons without the donor countries continuing to have an interest in the political, economic, and military development of the countries in receipt of this surplus. One of the most important reasons for government intervention in the agricultural sector is this international political role played by food, although originally perhaps this role was a somewhat fortuitous spin-off from intervention brought about for other reasons. Such bargaining power will automatically result from a maldistribution of the supply and demand for agricultural produce. This maldistribution is becoming more marked, with production per capita in developed countries outstripping that in the developing countries. The economic and political influence will be strongest over those countries which have least bargaining power, for example countries whose economies rest on export of primary products, especially those like jute and rubber which are easily substitutable. For these countries the terms of trade are especially bad and getting worse. The oil-producing countries, with rapidly rising personal incomes and more sophisticated food demands, make up a major group of food-deficit countries and will make up one of the world's largest markets for beef and dairy production in the United States and the European Community. This agricultural trade will become a bargaining counter to the energy supremacy of the OPEC countries. The international scene puts a new perspective on national policy, a perspective which will gain increasing importance. Such issues as the distribution of food aid from the United States (Chapter 7) and the relationship between the grain sales from the United States to Russia and the growth of *détente* between those two countries are examples of the present international political importance of food.

It would be very surprising if government intervention was not a significant factor in agricultural production as it is no less universal than climate. There is no country which does not in some way influence directly its agricultural sector. In the centrally planned economies of Europe and Asia this interference is obvious, overt and in some cases all but total. The production and consumption processes are managed by central governments acting through local organisations, and private initiative in both production and consumption may be non-existent. Such extremes are unusual. In the USSR small-scale private production can exist alongside the state-run collective farms (Symons, 1972), and the Chinese system allows some local initiative in agricultural and other production.

In the United States, the world's main example of the *laissez-faire* free enterprise society, the government has had a major stake in the management of the agricultural sector of the economy since the early 1930s. Government intervention continues even in the smallest national economies. The government of Tonga exerts considerable control over the production, processing and export of coconuts and copra. Although a production of only 17,000 tons of copra estimated for 1976 and 125,000 tons of coconuts, is minute on a world scale, on the national scene it represents the only important foreign exchange source after tourism and its role in the national economy is therefore considerable.

Government intervention in agriculture may appear to be out of all proportion to the size and importance of that sector measured in terms of the number of producers, size of the output or its importance to the gross national product of the countries concerned. Obviously the reasons for this intervention are many and complex and they are interrelated. Unravelling them is a difficult process and can be difficult to represent in a logical, causative order. We will first look at the scope of this intervention and then at the reasons for, and methods and effects of, its occurrence.

Scope of Government Intervention in Agriculture

Production, consumption and trade are three closely interrelated aspects of any national economic system. If a set of government policies are defined for any one sector they will influence the other two. Often, for example, policies will be enacted to influence production and this will effect consumption through effects of the production policy on prices, and may affect trade through the creation of additional production which cannot be consumed within the country. Perhaps the production policy objectives will be reached by protecting home production from cheaper imports with tariff barriers or other trade controls. Alternatively, a set of government policies enacted to see a reasonable distribution of food among all income groups in the population implies that food supplies have to be adequate to meet this demand and this may require further government action on the production side and/or to encourage further food imports.

Agricultural policies, concerned mainly with production of agricultural goods both food and non-food, are a subset of national economic policies which will be concerned to divide the nation's resources among the various sectors of the economy and to manage this economy according to the political ideals and objectives of the government. Food policy will be concerned with the production of food and in that respect will be a subset of agricultural policy. It will also concern the consumption of food and its distribution among all sectors of the population, and in this way extends beyond agricultural policy. Both are overlapping sets within the larger set of national economic policy.

The reasons for government intervention, the methods of that intervention and the consequences of it may be divided into production factors, consumption factors and trade factors. The production, consumption, and trade reasons for intervention are interrelated and production reasons can give rise to methods of intervention which refer to consumption and to trade. Similarly, these methods, once adopted, have effects on production and trade as well as on demand. We will unravel this, looking at reasons for intervention and the methods of intervention in this chapter and the effects of intervention largely in the next.

Reasons for Government Intervention

Production

Most attention is this chapter will be paid to the production reasons and methods for government intervention. They form the largest part of most government programmes. Distribution and trade questions will be developed more fully in Chapters 6 and 7. Agricultural production has a number of characteristics which differentiate it from production in other sectors of the economy and have made it necessary or expedient for governments to intervene. In most of the developed economies this intervention is thought necessary to ease the farming population over the great changes and adjustments which have characterized and so modified the industry over the last half-century. Agriculture, at least in the developed world, has seen a greater amount of change in the last 100 years than over its entire history.

The first characteristic which differentiates agricultural production is that it is the result of the activities of a large number of individual producers. In the simplest of economic terms most forms of production take place in circumstances where a producer's actions may modify the market significantly and where market changes can be rapidly reflected in production. This interconnection between producer and market is facilitated where there are few actors on the production side. Generally, production elasticity is large as the communication between the market and the producers is immediate and the actions of one group have a direct effect on the other.

The same is far from true in agriculture. The great number of independent producers means that such direct communication is made difficult or impossible. Production movements by a single farmer from one crop to another make up such a minute proportion of overall national or international production that the effects of this change on the market and the price will be non-existent. Most economic production models incorporate the assumption that the producers have a perfect knowledge of the state of the market. With limits defined by seasonal and regional production fluctuations this is a reasonable assumption for farmers, but problems arise over knowledge of the actions of all other producers selling in the same market. Whereas in industrial production it is not too difficult to discover what rival companies are doing or planning to do, perhaps for several years in advance, because of necessary long-term investments, the same is not true in agriculture. It is not possible to assume that all producers operate knowing what all other producers are doing and are going to do in the future and this is aggravated by the geographical spread of producers (Brandow, 1969). The locational problem of beach ice-cream vendors is an example of where two sellers operate not only in a knowledge of what the market is but also of what the competitors serving that market are doing, so necessary adjustments can be made immediately. Thus the equilibrium position is reached where the market is logically divided between two or more ice-cream sellers. A large number of small-scale agricultural producers operate in response to what they see as the market forces of the future, but they operate and make their assessments independently. Thus the tendency is for all producers to over-react to the likely market situation. Such independent reactions to market demands, or rather perceived market demands, can be exacerbated by fluctuations in production conditions produced by the environment. The wheat farmers of the United States reacted to the exceptionally high prices in the mid 1970s by planting more area to wheat. This planting was facilitated by the removal of production controls by the United States government. Thus, the fall in price in 1976 and 1977 was the more dramatic in its effects because of the increased production stemming from a large number of independent reactions to the state of the market and the encouragement by the Department of Agriculture to produce more.

More extreme examples can be postulated. Pigs and vegetables are examples of many agricultural products which have cyclical production fluctuations resulting from weather changes, the lags in the production process between decision to produce a certain crop and the harvesting of that crop, and the price effect of farmers' reactions to markets. Imagine a cycle where the first year is particularly poor climatically for the production of potatoes, much as 1975 was in the United Kingdom with severe summer drought. The following year many farmers will consider it worth planting some of their farm area to potatoes, and some individuals may undertake very large shifts in production. Partly as a result of this demand the price of seed potatoes will be high, but such an investment looks worth while in terms of the likely returns. We will then expect to see the following production season characterized by a larger number of producers and many of the existing producers planting a larger area (Figure 11). If the second year remains poor for the production of potatoes the price will fall somewhat as a result of the increased supply, but if it happens to be a good year, with plenty of rain at the right time, as 1977 was in the United Kingdom, the production of potatoes will dramatically

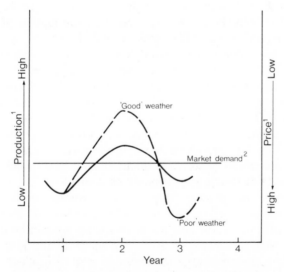

Figure 11. Agricultural production cycles. Idealized production cycle for an agricultural commodity. 1. For simplicity price is shown as the inverse of production. 2. Market demand constant assuming a zero price elasticity of demand. Weather conditions can accentuate the cycle which results from independent producer reactions to the market

increase. This alone will cause the price to fall substantially and this will be reinforced by consumer resistance to potatoes built up during the period of high prices. Some proportion of these consumers will not return to potato-eating even when the price has fallen. The elasticity of demand for such staple food is fairly close to zero and the market is not able to absorb the increased production even with a very low price. During this second year a number of producers will lose money because of the high price of seed potatoes and the low returns to that investment. The following year, year three, production will fall as producers change to other crops, and may fall sufficiently sharply to raise prices again and provide the incentive for increased production in year four. So the cycle of under- and over-supply and high and low prices will continue, accentuated by weather fluctuations. Individual producers are not aware of the actions of their fellows and there is no orchestration of the overall policy of the farming population. An external agent is needed to manage the supply of such agricultural commodities for the good of the consumers as well as the producers. The government has often been such an external agent.

The need for supply management is especially acute for commodities which cannot be stored effectively, but the demand for which is more or less constant throughout the year. Almost all agricultural production is highly seasonal but demand rarely is. The best example of such a product is milk. The production of milk is highly seasonal while domestic consumer demand for fresh milk remains more or less constant. To avoid seasonal price fluctuations both the production and the consumption of milk has to be managed in some way. The most effective way is to ensure that production in the winter is at least sufficient to meet the domestic demand for fresh milk and to channel the necessary summer excess production into manufacturing of other dairy produce. Where the seasonal agricultural commodity can be transported considerable distances seasonal over- and under-supply can be overcome by trade which allows, for example, New Zealand apples into the United Kingdom during the spring and early summer when the UK producers have none to sell except from storage. Most of the price effects of seasonal fluctuations in non-perishable produce can be smoothed out through storage and controlled release to the market.

Despite storage by producers, processers, wholesalers, and retailers, situations of seasonal over-supply and shortage still occur. Storage capacity is expensive and is geared at best to the available production in an average year. A good year's harvest, or probably more likely a series of good harvests, can overstretch storage capacity and lead to product deterioration and falling prices, even if there should turn out to be sufficient world demand for the product. News pictures of overflowing grain silos in the wheat belts of the United States abounded in 1977.

The problems of seasonal oversupply and seasonal shortage are very much more severe where the market is less well organized as in most developing countries. A normal year's production can stretch the marketing, transportation and storage facilities to the utmost and, as they are less well able to cope with adverse weather, crop losses will be higher than in developed economies. In addition the weather itself, perhaps in the form of the Indian monsoon, can be more damaging to the harvested crops. Seasonal price fluctuations will be more pronounced in developing countries with unsophisticated marketing channels. This in turn has a greater effect on the producers with little or no access to credit, very primitive or non-existent on-farm storage facilities, producing an important food some of which they will need to feed their families. Such producers are more or less forced by circumstances to sell immediately after harvest when the price is at its lowest because of the abundance of supplies and difficulties with drying, storage, and transport. The crop as sold may be in poor condition with a high moisture content reducing the price still further. The producer may then be forced to buy back some of the same produce later in the season to meet the needs of his family for food, when the supply is scarce and the price is high. Thus, seasonal fluctuations in price have a double impact on producers in the developing countries as they are buyers as well as sellers, each at the least profitable time. Seasonal price fluctuations for major food grains may be extreme in Bangladesh (World Bank, 1978a). They reach a peak in July, in the middle of the wet season, and a trough in December after the most important of the rice harvests is in. For example, the market price for paddy in December 1976 was about $2.67 for 37 kg and by April the following year it had doubled (FAO, 1977b).

Such a situation does not imply that government must intervene, indeed it is just in many such developing countries that the government organizations and expertise are lacking for detailed market management (Lele, 1976). Alternatively, the producers can be encouraged to form co-operative organizations to increase their bargaining power with purchasers and, if seasonal price fluctuation is great, to make storage facilities economically viable which may well not be the case on an individual farm with a small production. The co-operatives can realize economies of scale by arranging storage, packing and marketing as well as perhaps the purchase of necessary inputs for production. These are often subject to just the same bottlenecks resulting from a highly seasonal demand as are the products of agriculture. Such farmer co-operative organizations are common in European agriculture. It is, however, much more difficult for farmers to organize themselves, obtain the necessary credit facilities and set up the organizational structure in the developing countries. Where such co-operatives do exist they tend to be dominated by the larger and better-educated farmers making up the rural élites to the exclusion of the great majority of producers. (Government of Bangladesh, 1974; Islam, 1978). Such a position not only benefits the already well off but positively disadvantages the majority of producers as the marketing channels become even more dominated by the élites. In general, in developing countries co-operative organizations have been more successful in dealing with various forms of cash crops than with food grains. The market for cash crops is simpler, with fewer outlets because of the need for processing, and because the crops are sold for cash there is an easier connection between the production and the provision of credit (Lele, 1975). Even in most European countries it has been necessary or expedient for governments to intervene to actively encourage the formation of such co-operatives and to ensure equal access to their resources. Such intervention is more critical in developing countries, although unfortunately in most cases the governments do not prevent the selective membership of co-operative organizations. Co-operative efforts require a change in social outlook away from individual or family self-reliance towards community development and to be successful may require the break-up of long-standing established networks between producers, traders, and money-lenders. The success of co-operative organizations in reaching the small farmers and the sharecroppers of the Third World is likely to be limited.

Producers would be in a better bargaining position over the sale of agricultural goods and the purchase of agricultural inputs if there were more, and more competitive, supplier and purchaser organizations. Over time, the number of these bodies has shrunk faster than the number of producers. In the developed market economies at least, the producers are faced with a smaller and smaller number of large conglomerates, food-packing companies and seed merchants who increasingly regard farmers as but one link in a vertically organized business which may include production, processing, packing and retailing as well as the supply of the necessary inputs for production. The largely disorganized producers are faced with a highly organized and informed small body of purchasers. Many governments have attempted to lessen this imbalance through the creation of marketing boards set up to help farmers organize their marketing.

The ultimate in vertical organization of agriculture is contract farming. In its extreme form the farmer is doing little more than leasing his land and his labour to an organization which is controlling the inputs and outputs, the production methods, and the profit margins. Such contract production is common in certain types of livestock production, especially pigs and poultry. It is also common where the food-processing and packing plants have to ensure a tight control over production rates to match the processing and packing capacity of their plants. Vegetable freezing falls into this category. The freezing company must ensure a constant supply of freshly harvested vegetables to match the freezing capacity of the plant. Contracts are drawn up between the producers and the freezing company. The company determines the planting and the harvesting dates and the production methods. The harvesting is often contracted for separately as the machinery is highly specialized and harvesters will work on several farms. Such contract production can work to the farmers' advantage, perhaps by allowing them to become established as producers without a large capital investment (Allen, 1972). But the unequal bargaining power of the two parties to such contracts provides the opportunity for exploitation, an opportunity which has certainly been taken on occasions.

In the centrally planned economies, where government control over agriculture as with other sectors of the economy is more or less complete, the producers are very much in the position of contract farmers hiring their labour (land is usually held communally by the state) in much the same way as the factory worker is hired. The returns for labour are often in kind or, in China, in the form of work units, which can be exchanged for goods within the commune. In such cases government intervention is at a maximum although this is mainly in the interests of supply management rather than maximizing or providing a fair rate of return to the agricultural producers. This latter goal may be a secondary objective and a consequence of such comprehensive supply management.

In the developing countries the purchasers are less well organized and there are few centralised corporations involved in food processing and marketing. There are notably exceptions to this in cash crop production, particularly the production of bananas and other fruits and coffee and tea, but the statement remains true for most staple food crops. Of course, a large number of purchasers does not mean that there will be effective competition, as the spatial extent of agriculture may encourage local and regional monopolies even with a large number of independent purchasers.

Despite this possibility there is evidence that existing rural marketing channels in developing countries are efficient mechanisms for transmitting a fair price through the various markets to the farm gate (Jones, 1970, 1972; Lele, 1971; Pinthong, 1978). It is argued that there is more or less free entry into the market for traders and therefore that intertrader competition is strong. There has been a tendency in political circles to regard the various middlemen between farmers and consumers as profiteers, preventing the benefits of high consumer prices reaching the producers. It is an argument that is not confined to the developing world but was used, for example, before the establishment of the various agricultural marketing boards in the United Kingdom. There have been a few examples of attempted take-overs of the food trade by government in the Third World, for example, the Indian government take-over of the wheat trade in 1973, but the evidence suggests that the government operations have higher margins than the private trade (Lele, 1976). While this may be true there are a number of complexities which make an assessment of the impact of private traders on farm prices more difficult.

1. Firstly it is difficult to measure the real farm-gate prices for food commodities. One complicated case arises in Thailand where the marketing of paddy from the farm to the trader is arranged by volume while the trader sells to the rice mills by weight (Pinthong, 1978). The farmer is

prevented from selling direct to the mill by the small quantities which he has available for sale. The trader's margin is dependent on the accuracy with which both he and the farmer guess the relationship between volume and weight which is dependent on the moisture content, proportion of broken grains, stones, etc. In other circumstances the farmer may not actually sell his grain for cash at all but rather may use it for the repayment of debts incurred with the trader, or other farmers. The price and interest rates are therefore intimately connected and the arrangements made may prevent the sale of the crop and the repayment of the debt in cash. Furthermore, the debt itself may have been incurred in kind, in the form of food, when the prices were high and the debt will be repaid in kind when the prices are low. Interest rates are difficult to calculate in these cases, but have been found to be as high as 300 per cent (Government of Bangladesh, 1978a). Finally the farmer may use some of his food crop for the payment of labour, although at times of low food prices during harvest labourers will prefer payment in cash; this option may not be made available to them where there is no labour shortage. Farm-gate prices are so difficult to assess accurately that the trader's margins calculated often have little validity. A Thai study found these to be between 4.39 and 10.39 bahts per kg of rice, but the data base for this assessment was fairly weak (Pinthong, 1978). In such circumstances it is tempting to rely on the assumption that trade is competitive as there are so many traders and that therefore the trader margins are small and farm gate prices fair.

2. A further factor, however, is that the effective competition for the trade of a particular farmer may be minimal. Although there are many traders they are serving a very large number of farmers, each of which has only a minimal amount for sale at one time, perhaps only what he can carry to the market in a basket on his head. The small farmer has little on-farm storage, and limited processing and drying facilities may mean that he is forced to sell in small quantities as the harvest proceeds (Government of Bangladesh, 1978a). Not only is he limited by storage but also he usually has no vehicle and is therefore limited by his human carrying capacity and that of his family. Sales must keep pace with harvest by head-loading to the markets. Although primary markets are densely distributed, at least in the densely populated developing countries like India and Bangladesh, time will be valuable during the harvest period and in fact in Bangladesh up to a half of the goods reaching even the smallest primary markets came through intermediaries, most of whom were itinerant traders buying at the farm gate and selling in the primary markets (Tarrant, 1979). In these circumstances the effective competition for the farmer in a small isolated village will be limited. Also, where there are credit arrangements made between the farmers and the traders, at harvest time the farmer will have no choice as to which trader he sells his produce.

This effective monopoly may continue for several seasons as the trader establishes a pattern of providing other services to the farmer apart from the purchase of his production, and indebtedness continues. It is possible that the competitive structure of the marketing system will be greater if there is a possibility for substitution among crops. Where a farmer is free to switch from one crop to another, and to a parallel market structure for the new crop, improved competition may mean that farm-gate prices are a reasonable reflection of market prices.

3. Finally, there is the question of seasonal price fluctuation and storage capacity. Small farmers must sell their produce after harvest and buy back food during the rest of the year. In a Bangladesh study (Government of Bangaldesh, 1978a) small farmers sold an average of 17 per cent of their production but bought back the equivalent of about 25 per cent. Large farmers, by Bangladesh standards with over 4 ha of cultivated land, sold 26 per cent and bought only 1 per cent. Seasonal price fluctuation means that the small farmers are buying dear and selling cheap. Although Lele (1976) has argued that there is little evidence that passing the storage function from the traders to the farmers would be to their overall long-term benefit, where seasonal price fluctuations are great, and in Bangladesh they appear to be getting larger (World Bank, 1978a), the costs of storage and losses incurred (Greeley, 1978) would almost certainly be less than the seasonal price differential. Improved storage and more gradual sales would also relieve congestion in marketing and transport channels which provides one of the reasons for the seasonal price fluctuations in the first place and raise average farm-gate prices.

On balance it appears rash to assume that the marketing organization in the lesser developed countries generally are truly competitive. The situation is highly complex and worthy of further investigation. It is probable that at least some measure of government intervention in this marketing would be as valuable for the LDCs as it has been for some produce in the developed countries.

It is an oversimplification to consider that all farmers within a country have the same set of interests. While farmers' organizations and lobbies of various sorts imply a uniformity of interest, in reality this is far from true. Grain farmers were those who, together with some co-operation from cotton producers, organized the 1977–78 'strike' in the United States with frequent public demonstrations against low grain prices. Although the operation was known as the farmers' strike it did not by any means represent all farmers' interests. Some farmers use the produce of others in their own production processes. Thus the livestock producers of the United States use over 60 per cent of grain produced as a basic input for fattening livestock. They are obviously most interested in lower prices for feed grains while the grain farmers are interested in the reverse. These conflicts of interest between different types of farmers and the other interconnections between the many facets of agriculture provide a further reason for government intervention in this sector of the economy.

Disequilibrium in Agricultural Production

Many agricultural economists have commented on and analysed what appears to be a constant disequilibrium in agriculture in the food surplus countries of the developed world where the returns to labour, land and machinery investments are consistently lower than in other sectors of the economy and, with falling relative product prices in agriculture, there are no comparable shifts of tnese assets out of agriculture and into other sectors of the economy. Economic returns to agriculture started to plummet in the early 1930s. Taking the 1929 wholesale price index for agricultural products as 100, by 1932 it had fallen to 46 in the United States, 42 in Canada and 35 in Argentina. In the tariff-protected countries of Europe the fall was less dramatic, to 83 in France, 70 in Germany and 55 in the more free trade economy of Britain. The parity ratio, the ratio of prices paid by farmers to the prices they receive, fell from over 110 in 1917 in the United States to just over 50 in 1932 (Figure 12). Thereafter it began to climb as a result of government support and the effects of wartime demand for agricultural products, but from 1950 onwards it had fallen again, with a brief rise in 1973 and 1974 in response to high world prices of grain. The effects of recent high rates of inflation are much greater at retail levels than at the farm gate and this has helped recently to widen the gap between the price changes of farm inputs compared to farm outputs (Cochrane and Ryan, 1975). Disequilibrium is caused by the fact that this situation does not lead to a sufficient shift of productive resources out of agriculture.

The main feature of this disequilibrium is a more or less chronic tendency to produce more goods than can be absorbed by the market, both domestic and world, at prices which cover the costs of production. At times of falling farm prices the logical economic behaviour is to reduce production as resources usually put towards agricultural production are transferred to other sectors of the economy where returns to investment are higher. Not only does this production reduction not occur but it has been postulated that at times of really depressed farm prices production actually increases as returns per unit production fall. Each farmer tries to make enough money to cover his fixed costs of loan repayments on machinery and land. Such increased production serves only to lower prices still further and make it even more difficult for farmers to meet their costs. Hathaway (1959) has argued that most of the production increases on such occasions could be put down to the results of better-than-average weather and production did not increase as a result of deliberate actions on the part of farmers. For whatever reasons gross agricultural production, while it did

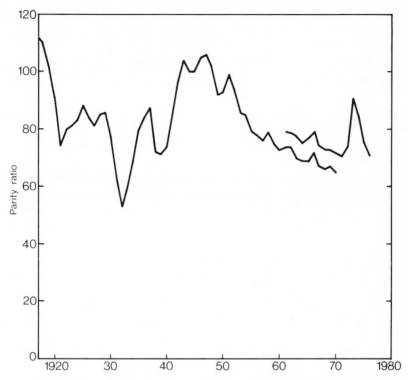

Figure 12. United States parity ratio. Ratio of prices received to prices paid by US farmers: 1917–70 from Johnson and Quance (1972); 1961–77—FAO, *Production Yearbooks*. The ratios are calculated in different ways in the two sources. USDA (1976) agrees closely with FAO, *Production Yearbooks* for 1961–74. The FAO data are not adjusted to take into account farm programme payments—such an adjustment would generally raise the parity ratio by about four percentage points (USDA, 1976)

not rise during the Depression, fell hardly at all between 1929 and 1932 while industrial production fell by 37 per cent. This implies that adjustment of agricultural output is less easy than in the industrial sector. Figure 9 indicates that this was not a period of good weather for agriculture, in fact the reverse.

Certainly, more complex reasons have to be sought for the disequilibrium in agriculture.

1. Firstly there is the nature of the demand for agricultural goods. As incomes and prosperity have increased in the developed world in this century there has not been a concomitant increase in the demand for food. Although there are differences between rich and poor people, once incomes are high enough to ensure a reasonable diet, the income elasticity

of demand for food of all sorts declines and for starchy, unprocessed foods reaches more or less zero or may become negative. Income elasticity of demand for agricultural produce in aggregate has been estimated in the United States as between 0.15 and 0.20 (Hathaway, 1963). 'There remain higher income demand elasticities for processed and/or tasty high protein foods and/or low calorific fruits and vegetables and very high income-demand elasticities for products incorporating services which save consumer labor' (Johnson and Quance, 1972). The increasing demand for high-protein foods, particularly beef, will partly compensate for a lack of rising demand for direct consumption of cereals and cereal products. However, this has a small effect on the overall price of cereals as there are alternative feeding methods. At times of high cereal prices large numbers of animals are raised on forage crops, turning back to cereals as and when the price falls. Johnson (1975a) estimates that 56 per cent of US livestock are reared on pasturage rather than on cereals. In general, demand for agricultural produce, especially cereals and dairy produce, has not kept pace with the ability to produce them. This ability has shown remarkable developments in the last forty years.

2.   Production increases on farms in all developed economies have been made possible partly by increasing specialization. Johnson (1957) identifies specialization between the farm and the non-farm sectors, specialization between farm regions and between farms within regions. Farmers increasingly rely on outsiders to provide inputs and to arrange marketing. The provision of power and fuel is now almost totally external to farms in most developed economies. Except for a few fringe examples, the mixed farm where animals provide fertilizer and are fed on home-produced feed is a declining farm type. Such a change has allowed a concentration of resources into single types of production and productivity has increased. There are counter-moves towards so-called organic farming and more complete crop rotations to help preserve soil structure, but these remain limited. Specialization within farming regions allows economies of scale in supply and marketing which in turn continues to encourage further farm specialization.

3.   Technological development in agriculture in the United States and in the agriculture of many other developed and centrally planned economies has been spectacular. Moreover, it is an irreversible change. Once the tractor replaced the horse and new hybrid seed corn replaced earlier varieties it was not economically possible to revert to earlier methods. Thus, Cochrane (1958) has argued that this provides the main reason for the inability of agricultural production in the United States to adjust downwards to match demand. The index of farm outputs in the United States rose from 55 in 1917 to 120 in 1968, while the input index rose only 22 points. Productivity therefore increased greatly (Johnson and Quance, 1972). There are critics of those who put too much store by past increases in productivity (Griliches, 1960b), but even allowing for these

criticisms, which mainly concern undervalued inputs, productivity increases remain very impressive. One of the most spectacular productivity changes has been brought about by the release of land previously used for producing food for farm and non-farm animals. Hathaway (1963) shows that in 1920 37.5 million ha of crop land were devoted to feeding horses and mules used on farms, and an unknown but substantial area used for feeding non-farm draft animals. By 1960 about 4 million ha were used for this purpose. Thus the product of one-quarter of the crop land of the United States was shifted, mostly to the production of goods for human consumption. Johnson (1975a) shows that grain consumption per capita fell by nearly one-third between 1909 and 1939 as a result of a reduction in the number of work animals. This change was irreversible and a once-and-for-all change, although spread over a long time period and paralleled by other technological developments such as chemical fertilizer, insecticides and new varieties.

It is not sufficient to limit our discussion to the view that technological change has provided the reason for production to outstrip demand. We have to understand why farmers adopted the technology which seems in retrospect to be against their corporate interests with the greatly increased production in most years leading to oversupply and reduced prices. The first explanation for this adoption must be that the technological developments have been more or less free to the farmers and they have been actively encouraged to adopt them by government extension workers and commercial companies. That is not to say that tractors were free of charge, but rather that the development costs of such technological changes were very small to each farmer. Also, seed developments were not paid for directly by the farmers. Hybrid seed corn varieties were not more expensive that their predecessors and Rogers (1958) has plotted their diffusion through the United States corn-growing areas. The individual farmer pays little if anything of the development costs of such improvements, most are the results of work in government-financed research stations. New seed varieties which make up the mainstay of the green revolution in the developing world were developed at research stations financed by international organizations and agencies. The seed costs alone were little higher than for the traditional varieties, although the yield increases to be expected from the new varieties were considerable.

The second reason for the adoption of technological change was outlined by Cochrane (1958) and developed by Hathaway (1963) and Johnson and Quance (1972). Cochrane's original thesis was that, as farmers cannot individually influence the market prices for the commodities they produce, they adopt the new technological developments to increase output. Although total costs are not likely to be reduced, output is often greatly increased so the cost per unit of output is lowered. Early adopters are therefore successful in increasing profits, but as the total output increases so the price falls and other farmers are more or less forced to follow suit just to *maintain* their income levels as before. Thus, Cochrane calls this process the 'treadmill of technological advance'. Others have discussed the shortcomings of this thesis (Hathaway, 1963). The main economic argument is that factors of production in the form of labour, machinery and land should move freely in and out of agriculture depending on the relative prices of agricultural produce. That this free movement only takes place into rather than out of agriculture has formed the basis of an explanation of overproduction developed by Johnson and Quance (1972).

4. This explanation is based on the difference between the acquisition costs and salvage values of agricultural inputs. It extends the idea of Cochrane that farmers are trapped into adopting technological change although there may be no long-term overall benefits. Salvage values are lower, sometimes effectively zero, than acquisition costs, and assets (land, and capital) become trapped in the agricultural sector because their real opportunity costs once adopted are very low or nil. These assets will be acquired as long as their marginal return is positive, but they are then trapped by falling prices. The extent to which different inputs are trapped depends on their relative salvage values.

Fertilizers are flow inputs, acquired frequently and used once only. They are therefore the most responsive of all agricultural inputs to agricultural product price changes. Timmer (1976b) has shown that fertilizer application rates are very responsive to the price of rice in the main rice-growing developing economies. Agricultural machinery has a low opportunity cost—combine harvesters once acquired by a farmer have little or no use outside the agricultural sector. Attempts have been made, usually abortive, to use machinery developed for other purposes in agricultural production, but there have been no attempts the other way. Once sold such machinery tends to continue in use in the agricultural sector, although not necessarily on the same farms, until it becomes so old that its use is no longer a net marginal benefit. But, as machinery has to be replaced relatively frequently its sale is responsive to agricultural product prices, although much less so than fertilizer. Such goods are easily trapped by falling prices. During the period of high grain prices in the United States between 1972 and 1975 farmers responded by purchasing new machinery, the net benefit of which was often considerable at the time. Often this machinery was bought on credit. Such machinery has little or no salvage value outside agriculture and some of the agitation for higher guaranteed crop prices in 1977 was the result of the continuing costs of such assets in the face of declining returns.

Farm land may have limited salvage value outside agriculture. The sale of land for urban development is limited by land use zoning and by other planning legislation. Also the demand for new urban land is limited during downturns in the national economy and it is generally during such downturns that agricultural product prices are at their lowest. Most economic depressions are seen as being led by agriculture, at least in the United States. Urban land use as an alternative to agriculture is also limited geographically. A small market for agricultural land may be found for conservation, and land may be leased to the government as a part of a conservation reserve. Land can also be switched from one form of agricultural production to another, although the capital costs of such a switch may be prohibitive and major shifts from livestock production to arable farming can only be undertaken rarely. Increasing specialization and technological development have made switching land from one form of farm production to another increasingly difficult. Therefore, in times of low product prices the salvage costs of farm land may be very low. It may be transferred within the agricultural sector, with farmers becoming tenants of larger companies, but in times of severe economic depression much land is abandoned. Such a process was common during the dust-bowl era in the United States, when the economic returns to farming continued below input costs and the banks foreclosed on the farmers' loans. The effects of the high grain prices recently was to put up land prices in the United States as farmers tried to expand their productive area to respond to the high prices. Mortgage repayments on this acquired land became increasingly difficult to make as grain prices fell. The land so acquired could not be transferred to other, non-agricultural, uses or sold within the sector without considerable capital losses. The resource was therefore trapped within agriculture.

Of all the inputs to agricultural production labour has the lowest rate of return to investment. Opportunities for alternative employment are few and far between, especially in downturns of the business cycle when general levels of unemployment rise. At the smallest scale of the family farm where the operator employs little or no labour other than this own, labour is inseparable from the land and machinery and is already at an irreducible minimum. Although many small farmers are able to supplement their incomes by part-time employment off the farm the salvage value of agricultural labour is low because the skills acquired in agriculture are not required in other sectors. The lack of appropriate skills and experience becomes increasingly serious as the age of the labour increases and the gap in earnings between someone redeployed from agriculture, and one who started in another sector, widens. Although it is difficult to conceptualize the acquisition costs of agricultural labour, Hathaway (1963) relates it to the opportunity of alternative employment at the time of entering agriculture. This may be quite low, but the salvage value of a later transfer out of agriculture is even lower.

Machinery, land and labour resources are therefore effectively trapped in agriculture. Taken on to increase returns per unit cost in times of high product prices these resources have little value outside agriculture and they continue to be devoted to agricultural production, even though the economic returns to their continued use may be very small or non-existent.

The reaction to this situation should be an adjustment over time with less labour resources in agriculture and a reduction in overall production to match demand. Low wages and profits in agriculture should reduce the number of small uneconomic farms and farm amalgamation should continue until returns to agricultural investment match those in other sectors of the economy. Most forms of government intervention in the agriculture sectors are ostensibly to ease this process of adjustment although, as we shall see, nine times out of ten the methods chosen for such intervention have tackled the symptoms not the causes of the problem. They have been designed to tackle the short-term problem by maintaining high prices in agriculture not the restructuring necessary (Wilson, 1977). In many cases there may be hidden reasons for slowing down or limiting the effects of adjustment of factor use in agriculture (Heidhues, 1976). Many governments have an ideological commitment to the family farm. In the United States the family farm is seen as a major source of security and continuity to the American way of life. This stems essentially from the Jeffersonian political philosophy enshrined in the Homestead Act of 1862 (Green, 1975). As a result it receives mention in much of the agricultural legislation and in Presidential messages to Congress. For example, President Eisenhower in a message to Congress in January 1956 said '. . . more than prices are involved. In America, agriculture is more than an industry; it is a way of life. Throughout our history the family farm has given strength and vitality to our entire social order. We must keep it healthy and vigorous'. Similarly the 1977 Food and Agriculture Act contained the following section: 'Section 102A: Congress hereby specifically reaffirms the historical policy of the United States to foster and encourage the family farm system of agriculture in this country. Congress further believes that any significant expansion of non-family owned, large scale corporate farming enterprises will be detrimental to the national welfare' (House of Representatives, 1977). By the same legislation the Secretary of Agriculture was instructed to report annually to the Congress on the status of the family farm in United States' agriculture.

Much concern is shown both within the United States and outside about the growth and power of agribusiness (George, 1976). To some extent the references to the importance of family farming in the United States' legislation is a reaction against large corporations which is reflected in much anti-trust legislation. To some extent also we might see government reaction against corporate farming as another example of the ambivalent attitude to the 'farm problem'. Economic forces leading to the movement of factors, particularly labour, out of agriculture leads to farm amalgamation into larger and larger units. The financial resources necessary for this amalgamation will encourage corporations into farming as a logical end state of this adjustment process. Government moves against this change lead inevitably to policies such as price support which will mitigate the effects for farmers of failing to make the adjustments to factor inputs which are economically necessary.

Farming remains a relatively labour-intensive operation and there are few, or possibly even negative, economies to scale after farm size increases beyond that which can be conveniently managed by two or three men (Britton and Hill, 1975; USDA, 1978a). Even if it were true that corporate ownership of farm land was rapidly expanding, for *operating* purposes this land will often remain divided into smaller units, probably of a size which could reasonably be run by a farmer and his family. It is therefore important to distinguish between land ownership and farm operation when considering the role of agribusiness in actual farming, rather than in the processing, storage, and marketing operations which are clearly dominated by such corporations. Unfortunately little up-to-date information is available for the United States although the USDA has an extensive land-ownership survey in progress. In 1969 Census of Agriculture is the most recent source available. Commercial farming, defined as holdings with a farm income of $2500 per annum or more, accounts for only 60 per cent of US farms, and 80 per cent of the total marketed agricultural production comes from only 20 per cent of the farms. The percentage of off-farm income rises from 8 per cent for farms with more than $100,000 sales to 93 per cent for non-commercial farms (USDA, 1975a). The overall pattern of ownership of these commercial farms is shown in Table 12.

Table 12. United States farm ownership, 1969

	Commercial farm operation[a]					
	Owned and operated				Owned and rented out	
Category	Area (millions of ha)	%	Category		Area (ha)	%
Individuals	163.2	43.9	Farm operators		16.2	4.4
Partnerships	36.4	9.8	Individuals, estates, partnerships		109.3	29.4
Corporations	19.8	5.3	Corporations		6.5	1.8
			State, federal and Indian lands		20.2	5.4

TOTAL   371.6   100%

[a]Farms with sales of $2500 or over—in 1969 60% of all farms.
Source: USDA (1975).

Table 13. Methods of co-ordinating production of selected agricultural commodities, 1970 estimates

| | Corporate | Contracts | | Producer | Open |
| | | | | | |
Commodity	Vertical integration (% of production)	Individual producers (% of production)	Producer bargaining associations (% of production)	Producer co-operatives (% of production)	Open markets (% of production)
Sugar-beets	2	—	98	—	—
Sugar-cane	60	23	—	17	—
Fluid grade milk	3	15	—	80[a]	2
Broilers	7	85	—	5	3
Processing vegetables	10	69	9	7	5
Citrus fruits	30	14	3	38	15
Turkeys	12	42	—	17	29
Potatoes	25	24	13	8	30
Deciduous fruits and nuts	20	—	8	30	42
Eggs	20	20	—	15	45
Fresh market vegetables	30	21	—	5	44

[a]Includes producer bargaining associations.
Source: USDA (1975).

Corporations are of little significance, owning only 7 per cent of all farm land, 75 per cent of this is farmed by the corporations and the remainder rented out to others. There were 21,513 corporations active in farming about 1.2 per cent of all farms in 1969. The impact of corporate land holding on the agricultural sector is more significant than these relatively small numbers imply as this land is concentrated in the larger farm size groups, which have a disproportionate share of commercial farm sales, and is concentrated in particular areas and on particular forms of production.

Over 90 per cent of the corporations were 'closely held' with less than ten shareholders; these often started as family farms or partnerships and are usually now family-owned corporations. Of the remaining 1797 corporations which together account for 2.9 per cent of commercial sales, significant concentrations are found in Hawaii, Florida and California where they account for 55 per cent, 10.7 per cent and 6.2 per cent of commercial farm sales respectively. Corporation farms are least significant in the corn and wheat belts where they typically account for 1 per cent or less of commercial sales. More of the large corporations are involved with feed-lot programmes for beef and calves than any other type of farming, with poultry operations second in importance and ranching a close third. The importance of corporation farms in Florida and California reflect their importance in vegetable, fruit, and nut production (Table 13). The relative importance of corporation farms to all operations varies substantially from type to type. Thus, although a number of cattle-raising operations are corporate owned, there are an overwhelming number which are not. The importance of contractual production reflects the increasing role of agribusiness short of direct land ownership, this is especially true in broiler production and processing vegetables.

The individual family farm accounted for less than 60 per cent of all farms with sales of over $100,000 a year. Partnerships made up 25 per cent of this group and corporations 16 per cent. The importance of large farms in terms of absolute numbers, net farm revenue and the value of land owned, has increased greatly since 1960 and particularly since 1969 (Table 14). There is no reason to believe that the significance of corporation farms has not increased accordingly. The change is particularly significant in terms of net revenue from farming where the farms with sales over $20,000 make up only 28 per cent of all farms but account for 77 per cent of the net revenue in 1976 (Figure 13).

The question of farm size and ownership has recently become increasingly important where there are federal-financed irrigation projects. The Reclamation Act of 1902, by which federal financing is arranged for the supply of irrigation water in the form of interest-free construction loans and subsidized water prices, was intended to distribute irrigation water to small family farms. An individual owner was permitted to irrigate 64.8 ha with project water, or 130 ha as a husband and wife team. The rules as laid down by this legislation have been extensively abused and have been

Table 14. Number of farms, net realized income and value of owned real estate by farm size in the United States, 1960–76

| | | Size class ($ sales per annum) | | | | | |
| | | % of all farms | | | | | |
Year	⩾100,000	40,000–99,999	20,000–39,999	10,000–19,999	5,000–9,999	2,500–4,999	<2,500
1960 1	0.6	2.3	5.7	12.5	16.7	15.6	46.4
2	6.4	11.2	16.5	22.8	19.0	10.7	13.4
3	8.0	12.4	16.2	20.8	16.4	9.6	16.6
1965 1	1.1	3.7	8.4	13.8	15.1	13.7	44.2
2	10.0	16.0	20.3	21.6	13.8	7.1	11.2
3	11.3	15.1	18.0	18.3	12.9	8.0	16.4
1970 1	1.9	5.9	11.0	13.2	13.6	14.4	40.0
2	16.6	21.1	23.7	15.9	9.1	5.1	8.5
3	15.0	17.3	19.0	15.0	10.4	8.3	15.0
1975 1	5.0	10.3	11.5	11.2	11.2	11.7	39.1
2	37.9	23.0	14.9	7.9	4.5	2.7	9.1
3	29.8	22.8	15.0	9.7	6.5	5.2	11.0
1976 1	5.6	11.0	11.5	10.9	10.7	11.3	39.0
2	39.4	23.2	14.1	7.2	4.1	2.5	9.5
3	31.7	23.5	14.4	9.0	6.0	4.8	10.6

1 = Number of farms.
2 = Realized net income.
3 = Value of real estate.
NB: Not all rows may sum to 100 per cent because of rounding errors.
Source: USDA (1977a, 1977b).

the subject of many recent investigations by the Department of the Interior and the USDA (USDA, 1978a). Nearly 4.5 million ha of irrigable land is under federal water projects in seventeen western states; 930,000 ha in 6,041 ownership units are estimated to be irrigable but in excess of the authorized entitlement to irrigation water. Although 200,000 ha of this was eligible for project water under special rules, 47 per cent of the remainder actually received irrigation water in 1976. Interestingly, 40 per cent of the crop production on this land is of produce which is subject to existing federal price-support policies. In California alone there were forty-two owners receiving irrigation water on 308,307 ha which are ineligible by the statute. The next largest state total is 9,165 ha in Colorado divided among ninety-eight holdings.

Large land-holding and farm operation has been common in the westlands area of California and in the central valley for many years. Before the federal water projects only the very large landowners could afford to use well irrigation and, with the arrival of the federal water with

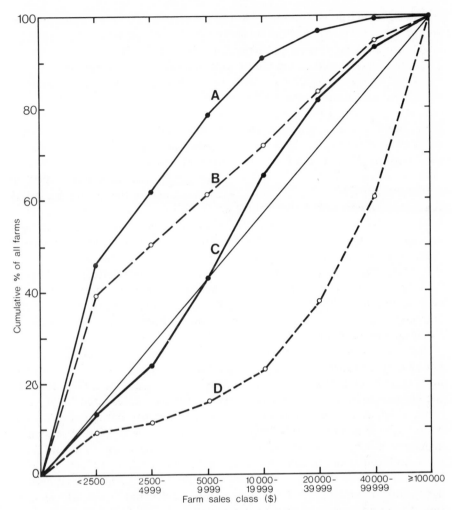

Figure 13. Number of farms and realized net income by size of farm: United States, 1960 and 1976. **A** = number of farms 1960; **B** = number of farms 1976; **C** = realized net income 1960; **D** = realized net income 1976. Source: USDA (1977a, b)

the rules loosely enforced, these large holdings have been able to irrigate greatly increased areas with vastly increased turnover resulting. The Southern Pacific Land Company alone is indicated as owning 43,420 ha in 1976. As a result of recent court decisions new rules of ownership are being enforced which require owners to reside within 80 kilometres of their land and limit the area irrigated for each owner to terms close to those of the original Act. Land in addition to this entitlement may be irrigated with federal water for ten years provided that the owner agrees to sell under conditions approved by the Department of the Interior at the end of that time. The most important of these conditions of sale is that the land should be sold at its pre-irrigation price. This action emphasizes the continuing importance of the family farm operation in US legislation.

Overall the average size of farm in the United States increased from 86.2 ha to 162 ha between 1950 and 1978 while the number of farms has declined from 5.6 to 2.7 million. This gives a measure of the extent and the rapidity of adjustment in agriculture in response to the economic forces outlined in this chapter. Table 14 indicates that there is till a long way to go. Many of the non-commercial farms, and a number of the commercial ones also, are run by people for whom profit maximization is not an important consideration. Farmers who have owned their land for some years are not concerned about the consequences of rising land prices. They have no large mortgages to pay off. When the costs of operating the farm become too high, or when the farmer becomes too old to continue operations, the farm will be sold. The purchaser then has to ensure that the returns from that farm more than cover the invested capital. It is at such times that the possibility of amalgamation and corporate ownership become significant. Not surprisingly the farmers participating in strikes and demonstrations in 1977–78 were the younger ones who have substantial mortgage commitments recently acquired.

With the decline in the number of farms has gone a decline in the numbers of the farm population; from 15.6 million in 1960 to 8.3 million in 1976 (US Departments of Commerce and Agriculture, 1977). In 1920 the farm population numbered over 30 million and represented 15 per cent of the population. The fall in numbers of the farm population, after a short period of rising numbers following the Second World War, was steady, averaging 4.8 per cent per annum in the 1960s. Between 1970 and 1974 the rate levelled off to only 1.2 per cent annual decline, reflecting higher agricultural prices and a slowing in the rate of economic adjustment in agriculture. Following 1974 the decline has accelerated again. At the same time the employment of this farm population has shifted from agriculture to other sectors. In 1961 30 per cent of the farm resident labour force was employed in non-agricultural employment. By 1976 this proportion had risen to about 50 per cent and the farm and non-farm employment of the farm population had converged. In general, farm numbers, farm size distribution, and farm employment in the United States have all reflected adjustments to the economic forces of the 'farm problem'. These adjustments have not gone so far as to give rise to a very significant involvement of corporations in actual farming although there are important exceptions to this.

A recent study of ownership of farm land in the United Kingdom (Harrison et al., 1977) shows that about 7 per cent of the farm land is owned corporately but much of this land is of the best quality. No major changes are predicted over the next twenty-five years. As with the United

States the small involvement by corporations in farming does not imply a lack of a major restructuring in agriculture. Between 1955 and 1975 the UK agricultural labour force declined by 50 per cent while the agricultural net product increased by 75 per cent. These changes were particularly noticeable in certain enterprises. For example, two out of every five dairy farmers went out of production while milk output increased from 9.8 to 13.6 billion litres and the average herd size per farm increased from 17 cows to over 40 cows (Dexter, 1978).

In Switzerland in 1902 and 1921 agricultural protection policies were enacted after national referenda. One reason for popular acceptance of costly farm support policies (remembering that women, the major food purchasers, did not have the vote at that time) has been attributed to the general public's view of farmers as a stabilizing influence in opposition to the socialistic tendency of the industrial labour force and also to a general respect for the quality of life on peasant farms (Tracy, 1976). A similar commitment to the family farm was evident on the opposition to the Mansholt Plan for the restructuring of European agriculture designed to reduce the costs of EEC agricultural support through policies of farm amalgamation, farmer retirement and the diversion of much European land from agriculture to forestry and other non-agricultural uses. In certain areas like northern Sweden, western Ireland, and parts of Italy and France, agriculture may be the only way of providing for the survival of local culture and languages by allowing the maintenance of a viable rural population in these areas, sufficient to support local schools and other government and commercial operations. Thus, an important government policy objective may be to halt the economic adjustment in agriculture (OECD, 1973–75).

The Political Influence of Farmers

By few measures is the farming sector as important as its political influence. The political influence of agricultural production and of farmers goes beyond the economic factors and the ideological role played by the family farm that we have considered so far. The United States, the United Kingdom and most of Europe are no longer characterized as agricultural economies. Many times more people are employed in manufacturing and service employment than in agricultural production. In addition the number of farmers and farm-workers have fallen rapidly, far more rapidly it would seem, than their political influence. In the democracies the political significance of farmers, despite their small numbers, is a result of a combination of:

1. the electoral system and the geographical distribution of the farm vote;
2. the increasing importance of minority groups in times and circumstances

where the balance of political power is close and minority or coalition governments are common;
3. the organizations and lobbies of the farmers themselves;
4. the role of agricultural production in the GNP, balance of payments and self-sufficiency of countries which affects both the developing and developed countries.

As a result of some or all of these factors there may be a 'country party' specifically made up of rural and farm interests. We shall look briefly at each of these factors in turn.

1. Although the great majority of the population of most developed countries is employed in manufacturing and service industry, the rurally employed sector is much more widely distributed geographically and, despite several reform efforts, the system of constituency representation means that the rural population continues to have a disproportionate importance. In the United States this is particularly true at the state legislature level and in the Senate, which makes up its membership on a geographical rather than on a demographic basis with two senators from each state. The twelve states where agriculture provides more than 5 per cent of total personal income between them command sixty-four electoral votes in the Presidential election process. Breimyer (1977) discusses the role of wheat farmers in influencing congressmen from states where the farm vote is significant. In the United Kingdom there are recognized rural constituencies where the significance of the farm vote is important. Wilson (1977) draws attention to the fact that most Parliamentary seats are won on the basis of a small majority. The farm vote in any such constituency does not have to be even as large as this majority to make it worth while for politicians to court it. Although it is unlikely that the farm vote would swing from one party to another in its entirety on the basis of farm policy alone (other political factors affect farmers just as they affect other sections of the population), Wilson suggests that, as voting behaviour appears to be becoming more volatile and majorities smaller, small swings could be of great significance. A swing of 30 per cent of the farm family votes away from the winning party would have changed the result in twenty constituencies in the United Kingdom election in 1974 and a change of twenty seats would have altered the nature of a government in 1950, 1951, 1955, 1964, and after the two elections in 1974. Therefore, such a minority as the farmers is hardly insignificant. In the United States the farm vote is more open to competition than in the United Kingdom with its traditional allegiance between the farmers and the Conservative Party. Party identification is not strong in the US except in the South, and Campbell et al., (1964) conclude that many farmers vote in accordance with their impressions about the likely outcome of promised farm policies. In addition, in contrast to the position in the 1950s, farmers are now seen

as one of the most politically active groups in the United States, standing second only to white-collar urban professional people in political participation measured in terms of letter writing and voting behaviour (Lewis-Beck, 1977). In conclusion, farmers' votes may be small in number but they are politically significant, and therefore politicians tend to take them seriously as a group, and to react to their problems.

2. This political importance is more significant at times of close elections or coalition governments. The United Kingdom has had small majority or minority governments for nearly ten years. President Carter beat President Ford to the White House by a close margin in 1976. The *Economist* (1977), reporting on the role of Germany in the Common Agricultural Policy of the EEC, commented as follows:

> Mr. Josef Ertl has been Germany's farm minister since 1969. German farmers love him . . . Mr. Ertl wields disproportionate influence in the German Cabinet, . . . partly because he is one of only four ministers from the Free Democratic Party whose support is essential for Mr. Schmidt's government. The Free Democrats, in turn, depend on farmers' votes for at least four of their seats in the Bundestag.

3. The farmers themselves are organized to a greater or lesser extent to exploit and advance this political influence. But the extent to which the organizations established in their name are successful in this is doubtful. Wilson (1977) concludes that in the United States, supposed to be the home of interest-group politics, the farmers' organizations are very ineffective at representing the real views and interests of their members and thereby influencing farm-orientated legislation. This is left to the congressmen and women, on the floor of the House and the Senate, and in the House and Senate Agriculture Committees. There are four main farmer organizations in the United States; the American Farm Bureau Federation (AFBF), the National Farmers' Union (NFU), the Grange, and the National Farmers' Organization (NFO). It is hard to differentiate the members of these groups in terms of crops or geographical location, but between them they represent no more than 40 per cent of the farming population. The more affluent farmers tend to be members, especially of the more liberal organizations. Wilson (1977) gives us a detailed history and political analysis of each of these organizations. In summary, the largest, the AFBF, is essentially a political organization with extreme Republican views which leads to a stance recommending an end to all government interference with the free operation of market forces in agriculture. This could hardly be said to represent the views of a majority of farmers, especially in times of low prices. The leadership is heavily involved in wider conservative causes well outside the field of agriculture. In contrast the NFU has a more liberal political position, agrees that government should step in to remedy the shortcomings of the market place in agriculture, has its strengths in the Mid-west, especially in North

Dakota, and generally supports the Democratic Party and its policies. Because the Democratic Party has had a majority in Congress since 1954 the NFU has more political influence than the AFBF, but its relationship to the government is weak. Neither the NFU nor the AFBF employ experts and they are not consulted by government in a technical way. Both large organizations, claiming to represent agriculture, are not generally accepted in this role because of their widely differing political stances. The other two organizations of farmers are smaller and of even less significance. The farmers' 'strike' of 1977–78, repeating a similar militant posture of withholding production as was first advanced in the Mid-west during the Depression, was a grass-roots organization. Most participants appeared to be members of the AFBF and/or the NFU, but they reflected the often stated view that farmers joined such organizations for the group services offered, especially the concessional group rates for medical and other insurance, rather than as a method of exerting political influence.

In the United Kingdom, the National Farmers' Union (NFU) for England and Wales has a membership of about 80 per cent of all full-time farmers and operates as an adviser to the Ministry of Agriculture, Fisheries, and Food (MAFF). Its most important role is during the preparation of the annual review of agriculture with MAFF which recommends the support price policies for the following year. The NFU was first involved in this consultation in 1944. The role of the annual review has been reduced but not eliminated by the final transition of the UK into full EEC membership. The NFU tries for, and in general succeeds in maintaining, an apolitical point of view rather as an extension of the Civil Service, to advise and persuade government regardless of the political party in power. Wilson concludes that in order to continue to appear to be useful in this role, the NFU has to present a reasonable and conciliatory front, even going so far as agreeing with certain proposals which go against farmers' interests in order to protect its position as the confidant of the MAFF. In a way, therefore, the farmers' organizations in the UK and the US fail for the opposite reasons. In the US they are too political and cannot be taken as objectively presenting policy advice on behalf of farmers. In the UK the NFU is too apolitical and, to protect its position in the decision-making process, cannot truly be considered to be a farmer's advocate. Farmers' organizations have been influential in many other countries, particularly the Swiss farmers' union in the Agriculture Act of 1951 and elsewhere in Europe (Tracy, 1976).

In both the UK and the US perhaps the most consistent advocates of farmers' interests have been ministers and secretaries of agriculture. Both have behind them a vast bureaucracy with resources to prepare material for their legislative bodies in a way which is difficult to question and to dismantle. These powerful government individuals and their departments are representing farmers, admittedly moderated by other political considerations, to their legislative chambers. President Nixon, in his 1971 message to Congress, proposed a substantial reorganization of government which would have involved the disbanding of the USDA and spreading its various responsibilities among four new 'super departments' which would have looked after Human Resources, Community Development, Natural Resources, and Economic Development. There were objections raised from other departments which would lose their identity, though there were many people in favour of such reorganization. However, this was one issue which combined all the various farmers' organizations and spokesmen against the loss of an effective government voice for farmers. Shortly after the appointment of Secretary Butz to the USDA nothing more was heard of the proposal.

The real strength of the farm lobby remains with the politicians who are concerned about the farm vote as well as with those politicians who are committed to an administered society. The 1977 Food and Agriculture Act in the United States is a good illustration of how farmers' interests are represented within the US Congress. Log-rolling has long been a feature of the American legislative process. In this Act it reached a peak, although in all probability it will turn out to be only a minor one. The very title of the Act implies that it is a combined measure between the production and the distribution aspects of agriculture. The essential feature of the political bargaining in the Congress was that some of the rural members would support a liberalized food stamp programme in return for a fairly generous farm price support programme. Food stamps had first been linked to the Agriculture Act in 1965. Although it is possible to see the US food stamp programme as a demand-boosting exercise which should help maintain prices for producers, this is clearly not the motivation behind the Act: the two parts are distinct and separate, placed together to make the package acceptable to the Congress. Although the detailed agricultural proposals will be considered later, the rudiments are that support prices for wheat were raised from $2.29 a bushel in the fall of 1976 to $2.90 for the 1977 crop and to $3.00 for the 1980 crop. The House had originally proposed $2.65, but in the conference between the House and the Senate over the Act was persuaded to settle for the Senate's higher figure. There were other proposals for corn, cotton, rice, and for on-farm storage loans, but the wheat price was the political front runner. The maximum size of payments to an individual farmer was raised from $20,000 to $40,000; the existence of such limits had been the result of pressure from urban congressmen and the doubling of the limit was a retreat for them. Such payment limitations had first been proposed in 1968 and finally agreed in 1970. The main argument used against them is that such payments are necessary to encourage reduced production. Such reduction will not occur if the large farmers are excluded from this full compensation. In return for this easing of payment control food stamps were to be available to poor consumers, most of whom are in the northern cities, without a requirement to purchase equivalent amounts of food with their own resources. Also food stamps are to be made available for the first time to people on strike.

4. Finally, the political importance of farmers is increased because they make a contribution to the national economy in an area which has been shown to have great strategic importance in the past and increasing economic and political significance today. With certain exceptions like New Zealand, agriculture makes but a small contribution to the gross national product of developed countries. Despite this it is usually large and important enough to form an essential part of a managed economy. Although the ideological positions of political parties in different countries may vary widely from a belief in centralized planning to a belief in the free play of market forces, the extent of government management in agriculture is surprisingly similar. As agriculture is more important in the gross national product in developing countries agricultural planning could be expected to play a more central role; however, it is one of the weaknesses of government in many such countries that until recently scant attention has been paid to the agricultural sector. An important part of managing the economy is consideration of questions of the balance of trade and the food security. In the United Kingdom during the Second World War the agriculture sector, both production and consumption, was closely managed to increase self-sufficiency following the Atlantic blockade. Today farmers are increasingly conscious of the important role they play in national economies, especially in either producing for export or producing to substitute for imports, either way improving the balance of payments. Such importance is stressed in official publications of the type of *Food From Our Own Resources* (HMSO, 1975) and the issue will be raised again in Chapter 7.

In conclusion to this section on the production reasons for government intervention in agriculture it is important to remember that it is always easier to continue existing legislation than it is substantially to change it. There are several examples of this legislative inertia inside and outside the agricultural sector. The United Kingdom joined the EEC even though its agricultural policies were very different from those in the UK. Despite the wishes of the Labour government following 1974, changes in the agricultural policies of the EEC have proved very hard to make. Agricultural policies enacted to meet the very real problems of the Depression years in the United Kingdom and in the United States have continued ever since, slightly modified by each successive piece of legislation, but fundamentally unchanged. The programmes proposed by the 1977 Food and Agriculture Act in the US are little different from those proposed and ultimately enacted after the Depression. The technical job of making major legislative changes in agricultural or any other field are very difficult and the political job is much harder, especially where government majorities are small and/or party support in legislative voting patterns is not the established norm. Wilson (1977) concludes that the inertia in Britain was the result of a lack of questioning about policy. The size of the agricultural subsidies was controlled but their existence was never challenged. In the United States the policies were constantly questioned, especially at the fundamental level of whether government should be involved in agriculture at all, but no one was able to change the legislation. As we shall see in Chapter 8 it was outside factors which allowed changes, albeit temporary, rather than internal decision-making.

For a combination of all the reasons outlined in the above sections farm legislation makes constant reference to equality of economic opportunity for the farming community.

> The objectives of agriculture is to provide consumers with high quality food and fiber at reasonable prices, improved the productivity of basic land resources, and contribute to higher levels of human nutrition and living. The reward for these contributions must be an income that will provide the opportunity for a constantly rising level of living for farm people fairly related to that of other large productive groups of the nation (Secretary of Agriculture, Benson – address to the Central Livestock Association in St Paul, Minnesota – quoted in Cochrane and Ryan, 1975).

This is little different from the terms of the 1936 Primary Products Marketing Act in New Zealand which stated: 'A farmer should be assured of a sufficient net return from his business to enable him to maintain himself and his family in a reasonable state of comfort'.

Consumption

Price and supply management in agriculture can be motivated by consumer interests as well as by producer interests. Although there are only a small number of direct purchasers of agricultural produce the whole population are the ultimate consumers. Therefore, in terms of numbers, the lobby strength of consumers would be expected to be greater than that of the smaller number of producers. However, until relatively recently the interests of consumers have often been directly equated with those of the producers. In the United States at least, the free play of the market and competition were widely assumed to be in the best interests of both producers and consumers. At a most basic level, however, the two groups are obviously in conflict. The conflict is more imaginary than real in the developed economies where a large proportion of the final cost to the consumers of the food product is absorbed in processing and packaging. Rising world wheat prices had only a small effect on domestic bread prices in the developed world in 1973–74. In the lesser developed countries, however, where food consumption is mainly of unprocessed staples, the conflicts between consumer and producer groups are much sharper and the political decisions as to whether to assist and protect consumers or producers are more difficult.

A cheap food policy based on imports can be made acceptable by a system of deficiency payments to home producers to compensate for low market prices. Conversely, where high producer prices are maintained, subsidies may be necessary to encourage consumption. Where domestic production is high enough to meet domestic demand, consumers may be protected from high world prices by tariff controls and export taxes. Production, trade and consumption policies are obviously interconnected, with sometimes the consumer and sometimes the producer being the most influential in policy-making.

In recent years in many developed countries consumer interests have come to the fore. This has partly been the result of activities of a number of individuals and their established organizations in advocating the rights, and pushing the influence, of consumers as a group. Such consumer groups belong to a large family of such organizations which have become concerned with the rights and interests of groups not previously adequately represented. In the early days the activities of consumer groups were confined to safety and quality questions, but as inflation progresses and the influence of such organizations also increases, more and more attention is placed on prices. The United Kingdom government has a Cabinet-level Minister for Prices and Consumer Affairs, and even the United States Department of Agriculture has a strong consumer lobbyist as an Assistant Secretary. This latter appointment was a matter of some concern to farmers. The political significance of consumers is now considerable. Consumer interests are largely the province of legislators from urban areas who represent the largest concentrations of population. These groups can then combine with legislators from rural areas, each supporting each others' policies, because they do not directly affect each other. Thus the food stamp issue can be linked to agricultural price support. As food stamps are paid for from general government revenues not by the food producers through lowered prices, this support is politically possible. Indeed it can be argued that the food stamp programme should raise demand so both consumers and producers could actively support it. In contrast, other programmes, in developing countries, to raise consumption by lowering prices where such policies rely either on the domestic procurement of food at controlled prices or on food aid shipments, can seriously affect prices and therefore incentives to producers and this will be discussed in more detail under food aid (Chapter 7). In general, the balance of political strength in less developed countries lies in the urban areas despite the generally greater number of rural population. The urban population is geographically closer to the centre of power and contains more government employees and members of the armed services. Subsidized food distribution in most developing countries is an urban phenomenon.

There are four main reasons for governments to be concerned with agricultural and food policy from the point of view of the consumers:

1. The most general reason is a need to reduce the effects of domestic inflation. This is especially important in those countries where food bills make up a substantial proportion of a family's budget. General food subsidies will be very costly for government expenditure, but the political significance of food prices and domestic inflation is considerable, even in the centrally planned economies. The Polish government has twice had to deal with food riots which followed government attempts to raise food prices to levels which more nearly covered their production costs.

2. The second reason is to control the price of certain basic food commodities such as milk and bread or rice. The objective here is to reduce the effects of price rises and to ensure sufficient consumption in such a way that the wealthy do not benefit more than the poor. Price elasticities of demand for basic food decline as incomes rise so that a reduced price for basic commodities will benefit the poorest of the population more as it will have a greater effect on their consumption patterns. On the other hand, this type of selective food subsidy is an inefficient way of reaching those in need as all sections of the population can benefit from the low prices. The overall costs of such food subsidies can be large. In the United Kingdom the cost of subsidies for milk, bread flour, butter, cheese, tea, and household flour in the financial year 1975–76 was £547 million. These subsidies have since been removed.

3. The third objective may be to provide subsidized food to selected groups of the population specifically in need of additional food or cheaper food. Most of this needy section of the population can be reached by providing food stamps so that a proportion of social security, unemployment benefits, or other types of government-financed income supplements can be paid in the form of subsidized food. Alternatively, other programmes may be devised for those sections of the population in need of additional nutrition, for example free school meals, subsidized milk to families with small children or other specifically targeted supplementary feeding programmes to the nutritionally vulnerable. Such objectives and the resulting programmes are common in Third World countries, organized usually by international agencies.

4. Finally, a government objective may be to provide subsidized food to other sections of the population who cannot be considered to be in nutritional need but who the government wishes to reach for other reasons. In many developing countries the effects of inflation will be felt most severely in the towns and cities where there are concentrations of wage earners with little opportunity to grow any of their own food. Many of these wage earners will be government servants, in administration, the police, the armed forces and so forth. One way of controlling wage rates in this public sector is to provide a proportion of the income of such people

in the form of subsidized housing and subsidized food. Other reasons for wishing to concentrate on such areas for the distribution of ration food or food subsidies is that these areas provide the main *concentrations* of population and distributive channels are relatively easy to establish. It would obviously be much more difficult and costly to set up a food distributive network outside the market sector over extensive rural areas. Finally, since urban areas of the Third World are the most sensitive politically, national governments may be particularly anxious to supress criticism by subsidizing food to certain groups in the towns and cities.

Trade

Very few countries exist independently of international trade in agricultural and food produce. Although the export side of the food trade is dominated by a very few countries (Brown, 1975), food and agricultural imports are vital to a large number. As we have already seen trade policies may be a part of, and/or a consequence of, production policies through the need to control cheap imports. It may also be a part of consumption policies by preventing or controlling exports to a more lucrative world market or by encouraging imports of cheap food. There are two additional reasons which are rather more independent of direct production and consumption considerations:

1. Where there is actual or potential surplus production governments may wish to encourage exports. These may be commercial or on concessional terms or even free in the form of food aid. Many of these matters will be raised in more detail in later chapters, but the two most important reasons for such encouragement are, firstly to remove surplus production and maintain producer prices at home, and secondly, to improve the balance of payments position of the country by boosting exports. Exports by value of agricultural goods from North America amounted to $27,990 million in 1976, substantially more than the costs of agricultural imports (Figure 14). The value of agricultural exports from all developing countries exceeded the value of agricultural imports, but the position is very different when we look at exports and imports of cereal crops (Figure 15). North America, with only 20 per cent of the world's cereal production, had 59 per cent of the world's exports. The developing countries with 30 per cent of the production had only 11 per cent of the exports. Such trade makes considerable impact on the economies of both the importing and the exporting countries. During the early 1970s the commercial exports of cereals from the United States at the current high world prices, made a significant contribution towards that country's balance of trade. An USDA report to Congress, originated by a member of President Nixon's White House staff, stressed the importance of agricultural exports to the American economy. To encourage those

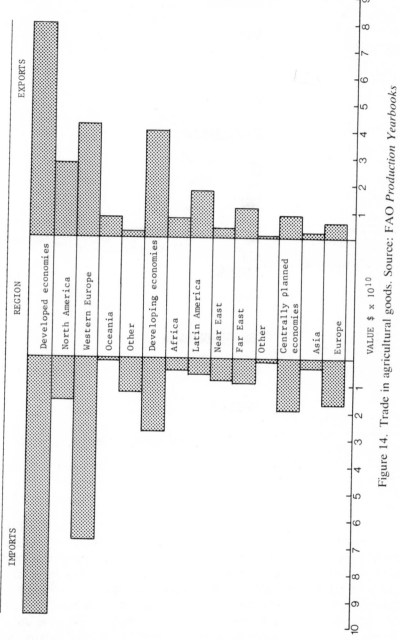

Figure 14. Trade in agricultural goods. Source: FAO *Production Yearbooks*

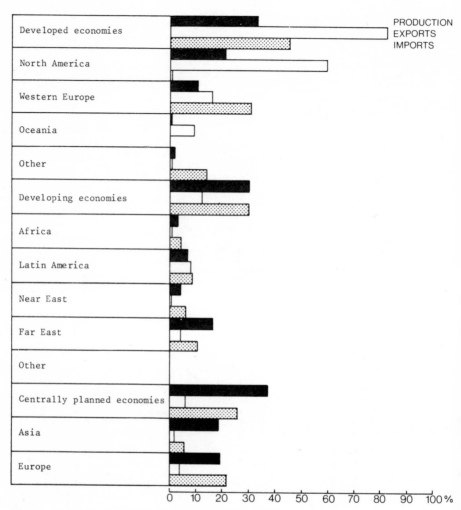

Figure 15. World production and trade in cereals. Source: FAO, *Production Yearbook* (1976); FAO, *Trade Yearbook* (1976)

exports, trade liberalization was considered essential. '. . . the benefits . . . are substantial. The potential gains are threefold; a substantial improvement in the balance of payments; an important reduction in government expenditure; and a significant increase in net farm income' (Congressional Record, 1973). Thus, trade liberalization and agricultural exports became the cornerstones of the Nixon/Butz policies for United States agriculture. Trade liberalization was a virtually impossible dream at that time, but soaring world demand for food allowed the export side of the policy to go ahead with all speed. Later in the 1970s cereal surpluses again built up in the United States, exports declined and world prices fell.

The United States trade gap widened as agricultural exports were no longer sufficient to counterbalance the increasing costs of imported oil requirements.

Thailand is one of the few developing countries with substantial exports of food crops. Although rice exports declined from 45 per cent by value of all exports in 1955 to 17 per cent in 1971, the export of this commodity is still a major contributor to the national economy, as well as to government revenue. Rice exports amounted to 1.8 million tons worth $409.6 million in 1976. Most of this trade goes to nearby countries particularly Japan, Taiwan, Hong Kong, Singapore and Malaysia (Tongpan, 1974).

One of the problems which governments and private traders have to face is that export markets for primary agricultural produce are notoriously unstable. This instability is the result of an accumulation of all the reasons for production instability in the surplus and in the importing regions which we have already discussed. The effects on the exporting countries are magnified by the product specialization and by market specialization. As with Thailand, the export markets for most countries are confined to limited geographical areas within which there is unlikely to be much intercountry variation. The resulting price instability severely limits the usefulness of the export earning potential, especially in those developing countries which may have little other support for the economy. Recommendations have been made to such countries to diversify their products and their markets to try to compensate for price fluctuations in product markets (Soutar, 1977).

2. National governments, especially those of the newly emergent nations of the Third World recently free of colonialism, are concerned about questions of economic dependency. The nature of the world cereal trade (Figure 15) suggests that many importing countries are dependent on North American cereals, a dependency which has been increasing (Brown, 1975). This dependency has to exist regardless of the political alignments which the importing countries may wish to make. Thus, India, for example, has been forced on many occasions to continue importing grain from the United States, even if diplomatic relations between the two countries have been rather strained, as they have been in the recent past.

This type of dependency leads to government programmes striving towards self-sufficiency in food production. This policy may not make a great deal of economic sense, where the comparative advantage of food-exporting countries should be exploited, but it makes political sense in such a vital commodity as food. In times of war, national security may well require that food security is considered paramount and national food policies are enacted to ensure sufficient home production and limited consumption because of restricted trade. In the mid 1920s in Italy preoccupation with national security and food self-sufficiency took an extreme form. Mussolini regarded the necessary importation of one-third of the total national wheat requirement as a strategic weakness and

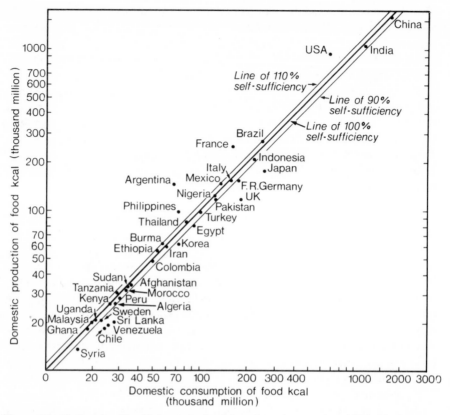

Figure 16. National self-sufficiency in food in selected countries, 1970–72. Source: O'Hagen (1976)

enacted production and price programmes to reduce it. Wheat production was increased but at the expense of livestock production as pasture was converted to arable land. Overall self-sufficiency increased little (Tracy, 1976). Three billion of the world's 3.7 billion live in countries which are at least 95 per cent self-sufficient in kilocalories (O'Hagen, 1976), but this is deceptive as 95 per cent self-sufficiency in a country the size of India means an enormous import requirement (Figure 16). Of all the policies which make up the Common Agricultural Policy of the European Community the one concerned with self-sufficiency has been the most successful (Bergmann, 1977; MacKerron and Rush, 1976). This is largely because these policies do not conflict with, and indeed are often a consequence of, price support policies directed to the maintenance of producer incomes. In the case of many agricultural commodities production has risen way over the self-sufficiency targets (Table 15), although this degree of self-sufficiency was substantially reduced when the EEC

Table 15. EEC self-sufficiency in food

Commodity	% self-sufficient		% change
	1956–60	1971–72/1973–74	
Wheat	90	112	+24
Barley	84	112	+33
Maize	64	68	+6
Rice	83	102	+23
Sugar	104	116	+12
Wine	89	101	+13
Cheese	100	103	+3
Butter	101	120	+19
Eggs	90	100	+11
Poultry meat	93	101	+9
Vegetable oils and fats	19	27	+42

Source: Commission on European Communities, *The Agricultural Situation in the Community*, 1975 report, Table 1/9.1.

expanded from six to nine member countries including the food-deficit United Kingdom.

Economic dependence can be just as marked in industrial goods as with food. The industrialization programmes in India under the second five-year plan were designed to make that country more self-sufficient in manufactured goods as well as to expand non-agricultural employment opportunities. It has been argued that Nigeria would exert more political influence in the rest of West Africa if the oil revenues were used to establish an industrial base while continuing to rely on imported food supplies. Despite this argument food self-sufficiency appears to have a strong emotional appeal and this is one reason why trade liberalization in food commodities has proved to be so difficult within international negotiations (see Chapter 9).

With such a complexity of interlocking reasons for government action in the agricultural sector in ways which affect consumers and producers it is not surprising that government intervention is so universal. In the following chapters we will look at the methods of intervention and their effects.

CHAPTER 4

Agricultural and Food Policies

Introduction

The overproduction problems of agriculture in the United States and Europe were outlined in the last chapter. These, plus reasons of consumption and trade, help to provide the explanation for government intervention policies. This chapter will outline the methods of intervention and their effects with examples from a range of countries. For reasons which should become clear trade policies will not be considered separately but as integral parts of production and consumption policies.

The starting position for all government intervention in agriculture can be illustrated by Figure 17. Here the demand and the supply curves for basic food produce of a developed country at time T are indicated by curves D and S. In developed economies we might expect the elasticity of supply to be greater than that of demand for basic farm produce. For simplicity the demand and supply curves have been shown as straight lines. Actual demand/price and supply/price relationships will be more complex. Supply elasticity is particularly difficult to deal with in this type of simple equilibrium model. Supply response must be lagged. Price changes at one moment affect supply, not immediately, but after a complete production season. Even longer lags are probably more significant especially in developing countries where price incentives may be expected to encourage investment in technological change which may make the long-term supply elasticity very much greater. As price incentives will not produce the same response from all farmers, production elasticities will be greater among those adopting new technologies and average supply response will depend on the importance of the production of these early adopters to total supply. If government policies are used to increase demand or supply they are unlikely to do so equally over the whole range of price. In this, and all future such diagrams alternative demand and supply curves are drawn parallel for simplicity, ignoring possible differential effects over the price range. Taking note of the shortcomings, the simple equilibrium analysis proves a useful way to illustrate the mechanisms and effects of government policies.

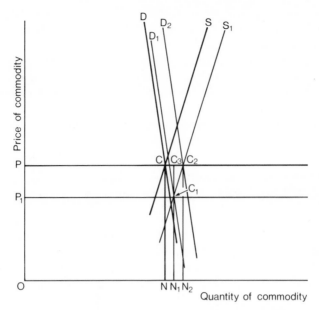

Figure 17. Agricultural demand and supply regimes

The combination of the demand and the supply curves gives an equilibrium price P and a gross return to all producers of the box O, P, C, N. At time $T+1$ technological development has allowed supply to expand so that the supply curve shifts to the right to S_1. Population and affluence have also increased and so the demand curve also shifts to the right, but by a smaller amount to D_1. Population growth in developed countries is generally low and increased affluence does not give rise to an equal increase in the demand for basic agricultural commodities but rather an increased demand for those which have a greater manufacturing component and which save consumers time and effort. The resulting equilibrium price falls to P_1 and gross producer returns are reduced to O, P_1, C_1, N_1. This position presents a number of government policy options which will be listed here and examined in the context of country examples in later sections.

1. The government keeps out of the agricultural sector and allows 'normal' economic adjustments to take place. Agriculture adjusts to the lower product prices by a transfer of resources out of the sector and by farm amalgamation. The effects of this policy alternative could be very extreme, but because of all the reasons discussed in Chapter 3 we have no real world examples to quote as this alternative has not been followed in recent years by any government.

2. Efforts can be made to increase demand, hopefully to D_2 so that price levels return to P and the gross revenue to producers grows to O, P, C_2, N_2.

Demand could be raised by finding additional export markets, the use of 'extra' production for food aid shipments or by boosting demand from home consumers.

3. Supply can be limited, thereby pushing the supply curve S_1 back towards S to such a point that it intersects the new demand curve D_1 at the price level P or at a price level which is considered to give adequate returns to farmers.

4. A combined policy of expanding demand and limiting supply can be followed, to give a sufficiently high price to make returns to farming 'reasonable', however this may be defined in practice. The demand and supply curves will intersect within the triangle CC_2C_1 and the price level will be between P and P_1.

5. The new equilibrium price P_1 can be maintained, but the returns to farmers can be increased by income supplements or by input subsidies or both. Assuming no change in demand curve D_1 and supply curve S_1, these income supplements or input subsidies may be targeted to have a gross value equivalent to box $P_1PC_3C_1$ or the additional gross benefit which would have accrued to farmers had they sold their existing production at the higher price P.

6. Some combination of policy alternatives (4) and (5), involving a measure of supply, demand and price management, direct income support to producers and input subsidies. This complex type of policy is what has evolved over the last forty-five years in Europe and North America.

Policies in the United States

Talbot (1977) identifies three main types of agricultural policy in the United States, each of which he characterizes with the name of the politician which he feels has been the best exponent of that policy. The first, the essentially non-interventionist, the Hamiltonian, has recently been followed by Secretary Butz and President Nixon. Butz, at the Senate hearings on the 1975 Agriculture and Anti-Depression Act expressed this policy as ' . . . the collective daily economic judgements of millions of our people under a relatively free price system is superior to a system of government control . . . as we have had for forty years'. This attitude is common within the Republican Party, exemplifies the right of free enterprise and is the political stance adopted by the American Farm Bureau Federation. In contrast are the Jeffersonians, represented by the late Senator Humphrey. At the same Senate hearing, Humphrey said ' . . . we should move towards a balanced national food policy . . . which provides adequate income- protection for farmers' stabilized farm commodity supplies and prices; develops strategic food reserves and supports an expanding export market'. The agriculture sector of the economy is seen as too complex and important for the best interests of most of the people to be served by the free market. The third policy stand is characterized as Madisonian and involves government by resolution of sectional and often regional interests. If allowed to operate freely such government by lobby is regarded as in the best interests of most of the people and allows such political techniques as log-rolling in legislative procedures. In practice, the ideological positions adopted in the United States are either Jeffersonian or Hamiltonian, non-interventionist, or interventionist, while the methods have tended towards the lobbying for, and matching of, various sectional interests. Over the last forty-five years the United States; agricultural policies have changed from intervention to non-intervention and back again to intervention. Although politicians may take the credit for these changes, external circumstances, especially the export demand for grain, have probably been the major factors causing these oscillations.

There have been numerous historical outlines of agricultural and food policies in the United States (for example, Hathaway, 1963; Cochrane and Ryan, 1975; Halcrow, 1977; Wilson, 1977) and so this outline will be brief, concentrating on major policy shifts rather than on a detailed analysis of the political progress of each legislative change. Although there were many wide-ranging examples of political intervention in agriculture in earlier times, the origins of modern policy are found in the period following the First World War and especially during and immediately after the Depression years. The technological development of the 1920s, especially the freeing of productive land following the outmoding of the various farm power animals, at the same time as export demand for United States' agricultural produce was low, led to the first serious signs of the chronic overproduction problem of agriculture. Various proposals were put forward in the 1920s, including the McNary–Haugen Bill which sought to establish a government agency to buy agricultural produce to maintain prices at home and then to sell these acquired goods overseas at whatever price could be found. This and other efforts were rejected by Congress or the President, but were resurrected in the 1930s, when farmers were so affected by the Depression.

The Agricultural Marketing Act of 1933 set the pattern for US agricultural policy for the next forty years by establishing the principle of loan and support prices. The Commodity Credit Corporation (CCC) was established with two programmes:

1. For storable products—grains, tobacco, and cotton—a loan was made available to growers depending on the size of their production. The loan price was calculated according to a base level of prices for the 1910 to 1914 period. Later this base was changed to the average price received by farmers over the previous ten years. Producers were then free to sell at or above the agreed loan price. If this did not prove possible before the product started to deteriorate the CCC took the produce in payment for the loan, the loan price becoming the purchase price.

2. The CCC was empowered to purchase immediately products for which on farm storage was difficult (eggs, turkeys, butter, and beef) if the farmer was not able to sell for a price higher than the loan price.

The CCC was instructed to dispose of produce it accumulated in ways which did not reduce the home market price still further, preferably by selling overseas or ultimately even by destroying stocks if they became too large or started to deteriorate.

The Second World War then intervened and boosted demand for United States' agricultural produce as it had in the First World War, but the memories of the post-First World War crash in agricultural prices were fresh and the CCC started to act soon after the war was over. The problem (Figure 18) was that although supply was cut back from S to S_1 through various measures for removing land from agricultural production and demand was boosted through exports and US aid policies to D_1, the equilibrium price remained below the loan rate established by the CCC (P_L). Thus the loans became the purchase price of a large quantity of produce and stockpiles began to build up. The CCC acquired that portion of the production which represented the difference between the quantity produced and the quantity demanded by the market at the established loan price, or $N_1 - N$. Gross returns to farmers are represented by the box

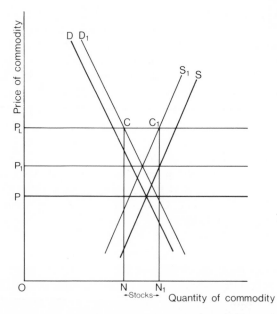

Figure 18. Supply and demand schedules for United States agriculture. (*NB*: Supply and demand elasticities have been exaggerated in this diagram)

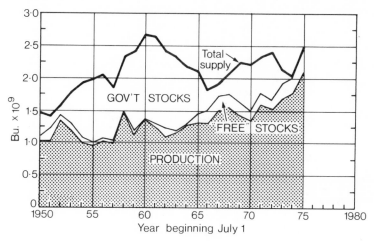

Figure 19. United States wheat production and stocks, 1950–75.
Source: USDA (1975a)

O, P_L, C_1, N_1, of which the government through the CCC, paid N, C, C_1, N_1. CCC commitments, relatively low in 1952, had quadrupled by 1954 (Figure 19), and stocks of wheat approached 1 million bushels.

Various attempts to remedy this situation were tried in the 1950s, but remedies with any real chance of success ran into a variety of political troubles, mainly from Republican Congressmen from farm areas. In 1954 a major American food aid programme was started under Public Law 480 (PL 480) which allowed the shipment of surpluses to developing countries on a variety of concessional terms. The aims of this law were essentially the disposal of surpluses from the United States. Aid to the developing countries was at first little more than a convenient excuse for this disposal. This law remains in force, although substantially modified by later legislation which has served to alter the PL 480 focus towards development aid. (This will be explored more fully in Chapter 7.) In the mid 1950s the soil bank was established to take land out of production where such land could be used for conservation purposes. Although the conservation measures were very necessary, again the prime objective was to try to solve the overproduction in agriculture by reducing the supply.

There were various attempts at this time to make the loan and price support rates flexible to adjust them to production levels and reduce the government stockpiles. Although the loan rates were reduced, relatively weak efforts at production control allowed production to expand from S to S_1 in Figure 20. The quantities acquired by the CCC increased $(N_1 - N)$ although this was acquired at a lower unit cost P_L. Nobody gained from this situation. The stock levels increased and the loan support price was lowered so that the farmers' gross revenue now fell to O, P_L, C, N_1. This situation continued until the early 1960s when a policy change was

E

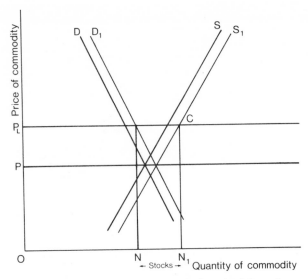

Figure 20. Supply and demand schedules for
United States Agriculture, Post-1955

proposed by President Kennedy and Orville Freeman, his Secretary for Agriculture. The essence of this new policy was to control supply. It had been made clear by the happenings of the previous ten years that price control would not work without excessive cost to government unless supply could be limited. Limited supply could maintain the market equilibrium price high enough for the farmers without the direct intervention of the government in the market place. Efforts at intervention shifted from the market to production. Supply control plus demand expansion would between them push up prices and the CCC loan rate could be set at or below this new equilibrium and no government accumulation of stocks would be necessary. In Figure 21 supply expands through technological developments to S_1, but is controlled through government programmes to S_2. Demand grows from D to D_1 largely as a result of exports and PL 480 sales, and the loan price P_L becomes the open-market price. Unfortunately, the various schemes for production limitation based on compulsory reduction in planted area and production quotas failed to pass the Congress and a referendum of wheat producers turned down the proposals. As a result the production limitation policy retreated to a system of payments for voluntary withdrawal of land from production rather than the production quotas favoured by the administration. The policy was less than successful and CCC stocks continued to exist, although with little increase in size. To some extent the situation was improved by the lifting of the ban on exports to communist bloc countries, particularly Russia; oddly enough in the light of later developments, one of the main opponents of this particular change in policy was Richard Nixon.

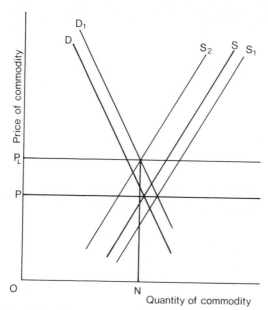

Figure 21. Supply and demand schedules for United States Agriculture, Kennedy–Freeman plan

The present shape of United States agricultural policy was forged originally by President Johnson and passed into law with the Food and Agriculture Act of 1965. This Act combined the urban food stamp programme with common legislation for the major commodities of wheat, cotton, rice, feed grains, dairy produce, and wool, into a single piece of legislation and was intended to run for four years. This amalgamation of legislation was a major achievement and it relieved the Congress of frequent consideration of agricultural matters every session. The principles included some old policies and some new. Demand expansion was to be encouraged by a food stamp programme at home to increase consumption by the urban poor and by active promotion of exports abroad, both commercial and concessionary (Figure 22, D to D_1). Supply controls continued through the operation of voluntary limitations. Direct payments to farmers were made on the basis of this land retirement programme and also as direct income supplements when the market price fell below an agreed target price. But the main difference from previous years was that the government was to make no efforts to maintain the market price at high levels by the purchase of unwanted commodities—rather the farmers were to be compensated for low market prices directly and the selling price of farm commodities was to be the equilibrium price established by the increased demand and limited supply (P_1). Stock levels were not added to. The policy was helped and made

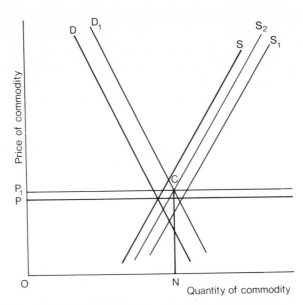

Figure 22. Supply and demand schedules for United
States Agriculture, 1965–77

cheaper for the government by the unprecedented demand for United
States' food crops on a world market, especially from India after a number
of bad harvests following droughts in the mid 1960s. At times the
production controls were withdrawn to allow this export demand to be
met, but they were reintroduced at the end of the decade as export
demand fell with improved weather conditions in South Asia and the
increasing yields following the introduction of green revolution technology,
especially in the wheat-growing areas of India. In good years for export
demand the demand curve moved to the right beyond D_1 and the supply
curve could be moved towards S_1 while still maintaining the same market
prices. Gross returns to farmers included both the box O, P_1, C, N and the
direct payments made for co-operation with the production limitation
programmes and the deficiency payments if the equilibrium price fell below
a specified target price.

The traditional economic view is that world demand for a country's
exports will be elastic as the world demand is very large in relation to a
single country's supply (Breimyer, 1978). This was certainly true for
United States' grains during the early 1970s. During the food crisis of
1973–75 the demand curve for food produce shot far to the right and,
even with all the supply restraints off and all idled land in the United
States being utilized, prices rose to unprecedentedly high levels. Thus,
Secretary Butz was luckier than his predecessor Hardin under Nixon as he
could claim that he, as a Republican, had removed government control
from agriculture and at the same time farm incomes had risen to the

highest levels ever, exports of US agricultural produce were booming and the farm problem was solved. As we have indicated, this success had more to do with external than with internal matters and the euphoria was short-lived. Indeed, there was considerable opposition at the time to the policies which had allowed massive grain sales to the Russians while domestic and world food prices rose to all-time highs and food security provided by stocks and idled land dwindled.

As with the food crisis of the 1960s this period was followed by good harvests in most parts of the world and good levels of grain production in most grain-importing countries. As a result, with the supply brakes off in the United States, and farmers encouraged to plant 'fence row to fence row', overproduction again became a problem and stock levels built up. The costs of agricultural support again became a budgetary embarrassment at the same time as the fall-off in exports was leading to severe balance of payments problems. The 1977 Food and Agriculture Act returned to the position of 1965 with food stamps, exports and aid boosting demand while supply limitations again came into force. Wheat production was reduced by 5.7 million ha which is equal to the wheat production area of the United Kingdom and France together. One difference over the 1965 period was that stock levels are now considered valuable to stabilize the world commodity markets and to provide emergency reserves to meet serious local food shortages in the world. To prevent severe pressure on government storage facilities on-farm storage was encouraged. CCC loans are now available for on-farm storage of produce between three and five years and payments are made to farmers to cover the costs of these loans. If the price of the stored commodities rises to more than 175 per cent of the current support price levels the farmers have to repay the storage costs and loan interest to the CCC. The government hopes that eventually between 300 and 700 million bushels of grain will be so stored and perhaps more, depending on the International Wheat Agreement's future decisions on grain reserves.

There was also an important change in the food stamp policy which allowed recipients to buy food with the stamps without a requirement to make a set level of purchases from their own resources. As a result the demand curve should not be shifted quite as far to the right as was previously the case, as some of the food stamp purchases will replace a proportion of the purchases previously made in the open market. The extent of this effect is not yet known, but we might expect the consequences of the 1977 Act to appear as in Figure 23. Demand will increase only slightly from D to D_1 partly because of a reduced export demand, at least in the short term, and partly because of the changed food stamp policy. Supply restrictions, plus perhaps the effects of the farmers' strike, will continue to reduce the production to S_1. The equilibrium price will rise to P_1. Any government acquisition of stocks for food security will allow the target price to be set at P_2 with stock acquisition at $N_1 - N$. Part

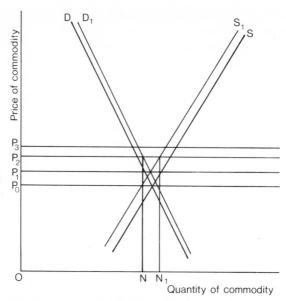

Figure 23. Supply and demand for United States
Agriculture, post-1977

of this stock level will be held by farmers. It is probable that P_2 will still not be as high as the established target price for wheat which was set at $2.90 a bushel for 1977 and $3.00 for 1978. Government expenses of the agriculture programme will therefore be threefold:

(a) the costs of the stock purchases, storage, and storage loan costs;
(b) the costs of the voluntary supply restriction programme; and
(c) the costs of direct farmer payments if the target price P_3 is not reached by the market price P_2.

The 1977 Act is therefore even more of a compromise than previous legislation; it contains attempts to moderate price effects for consumers, support prices for producers and maintain some security stocks.

Policies in the European Economic Community

As in the United States, agricultural policy in Europe started with a fairly simple attempt to tackle one aspect of the problems of agriculture and became successively more complex with time until modern policies embrace most aspects of the problems as we have discussed them.

In the early 1930s the economic depression in the world affected European agriculture in the same ways as it did in the United States. The reaction in Europe to falling world market prices was to raise tariff barriers to cheap world imports to protect the agricultural production of the home countries. Although the United States started this tariff war with the

Hawley–Smoot Tariff of 1930 the effects of the falling world prices were greatest in the major exporting countries and this was aggravated by the increasing tariff policies in many of the major importing countries. Tracy (1976) indicates that the wholesale price index of farm products, with 1929 levels set at 100, were 46 in the United States by 1932, 42 in Canada, but 83 in France, 70 in Germany and 55 in the United Kingdom. The magnitude of the price effects was the inverse of the strength of the protectionist policies. Even though tariffs were introduced in the United Kingdom in 1932, produce from the Empire countries was excluded and the effects of the tariffs were therefore reduced. As prices continued to fall, tariff policies alone were not sufficient to protect the interests of farmers and import quotas of various sorts were necessary. By 1933 a minimum price for wheat was fixed in France, and the excess grain procured by the government at this minimum price was dumped overseas by export subsidies, serving in a small way to depress the world market prices even further and increase the need for protectionism at home. Finally, by 1935, the planting of further areas of wheat in France was forbidden and therefore in four years France had run the whole gamut of import tariffs, quotas (sometimes effectively set at zero), minimum price support and subsidized exports and finally production controls.

An even greater degree of control and intervention was organized at this time in Germany under the influence of the rising Nazi regime. As with the United States the policies enacted to meet a particular crisis in Europe, especially in France and Germany, proved very difficult to dismantle when the need diminished. Although the economic problems of the 1930s were replaced by rising demand, soon overproduction in Europe was to become as much a problem as it was in America, and the Economic Community was to act in very similar ways to attempt to manage this.

Following the Second World War the policy in France and Germany was to expand production after the disruptive effects of the war. Much aid under the Marshall Plan was used to re-establish European agriculture. By the mid 1950s European agriculture had moved into overproduction and measures to support prices to maintain income levels for farmers were increasingly difficult and costly to enact. Therefore, production controls again became important with export subsidies and import restrictions. This was the origin of the Economic Community Common Agricultural Policy (CAP).

Every year the prices of the main agricultural commodities produced in the EEC are agreed by the Council of Ministers. If the market price falls below the agreed level the EEC, through the organization of the European Agricultural Guidance and Guarantee Fund (EAGGF), intervenes in the market by buying the commodities necessary to support the price at the agreed level. Dealings are rarely made direct with farmers (as with the CCC in the United States), but rather through major wholesalers. The EAGGF, therefore, can accumulate large stocks if it is necessary to support price to any extent. Such stocks are disposed of by an export subsidy, or as food aid, or converted to other products not in oversupply. For example, skimmed milk has been used to add to cattle feed and surplus wine converted to vinegar. Such conversions require a heavy subsidy, but do serve to reduce stockpiles. For most commodities EEC prices are established above world prices and so it is necessary to control imports. Imported food goods are taxed sufficiently to bring their market price up to the support price, or market price if higher, in Europe. Similarly, if the EEC price is below world price export levies have be created to discourage the shipment of EEC produce to more lucrative world markets. There are more complex aspects of the CAP, especially concerning intercountry financial transactions, which will be developed later in this chapter.

Represented in the same simplified diagrammatic form as the United States policy, the CAP works as in Figure 24. The basic demand and supply schedules are indicated by D and S and the resulting equilibrium price by P. Demand is increased by policy instruments to D_1. Food subsidies and food stamps are not favoured in the EEC for reasons which will be outlined below and so the demand curve is moved only very little as a result of export subsidies and food aid policies. Also, supply restrictions for most agricultural commodities are not very effective and supply expands to S_1. The equilibrium price falls to P_1. This level is below

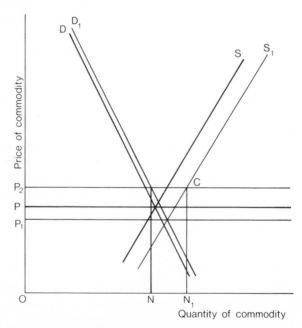

Figure 24. Supply and demand schedules for EEC
agriculture

the price levels operated to support agriculture in Germany and France before the establishment of the EEC. Market intervention by the EAGGF buying in the open market to maintain prices at the agreed level of P_2 means a surplus of supplies over demand $N_1 - N$ which accumulates as EEC stocks. Gross returns to farmers O, P_2, C, N_1 include a substantial direct contribution from the EEC agricultural budget. This is the position which we might regard as normal in the EEC. However, during the world commodity price jumps of 1973–75, this state of producer protection moved sharply to one of consumer protection for most agricultural commodities.

As world prices rose, Community prices remained pegged at P_2 (Figure 25). To prevent the export of the Community's production to the more attractive world markets export levies were introduced to make up the difference between P_w, the world price, and P_2. Because of the world shortages of grain at that time the demand curve for EEC produce moved far to the right and this would have pushed up prices to world levels without this interference. On their existing production farmers lost incomes equal to P_2, P_w, C_3, C while, had their production levels been allowed to react to the real world prices as occurred in the United States, gross farm

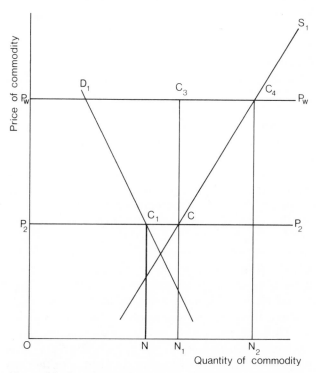

Figure 25. Supply and demand schedules for EEC agriculture. 1973–77

incomes would have risen to O, P_w, C_4, N_2. Therefore in the space of a couple of years the pendulum swung from producer protection to consumer protection and the stocks of most commodities were disposed of to world markets. The pendulum has now largely swung back and commodity accumulation is considerable again. As EEC production was not permitted or encouraged to respond in full to the upswing in the world price the effects of the price falls following 1976 were less dramatic in the EEC than was the case in the United States.

A study of the difference between Figure 24, the normal EEC position, and Figure 23, the present policy position in the United States, shows why a food stamp policy or similar can work in the United States but would be largely self-defeating in the EEC. It has often mystified the populations of European countries that prices are so high for most agricultural goods, with a consequent reduction in demand, yet there are accumulations of large stocks while there is certainly unmet demand available at lower prices. This is particularly true for butter and other dairy produce. Why not dispose of the surplus production by offering it free or on a concessionary basis to the needy populations of Europe as well as in food aid shipments to overseas developing countries? This question has become more insistent when subsidized sales are extended to other countries which are not considered in need in the same way. Particularly aggravating in this respect were the sales of butter to the USSR at prices well below the European market levels.

Now, if food stamps are distributed to enable consumers to buy more in the market the demand curve moves to the right to D_1 (Figure 26) and then back again to the left by the amount that the subsidized sales, or free food, takes away from what would have been the normal demand. The final demand curve is D_2. Whatever the final position of D_2 it will have moved somewhat to the right of its original position, increased the overall demand, allowed the market price to rise somewhat, and therefore reduced the extent of necessary government intervention in the market to provide price support for farmers. Although government expenditure has not been reduced overall, it is divided between consumers and farmers. This movement of the demand curve will presumably be greater if the food stamp sales can be made entirely additional to normal sales, although this restriction on the food stamp distribution was removed in 1977.

In the EEC the situation is different. The demand curve can be shifted to the right as a result of food subsidies of any sort, but this cannot increase the total effective demand because the EEC intervention agencies are *already* buying this surplus production so that the effective demand is already at D_4. Thus the effect of subsidized sales from the stockpiles within Europe is to reduce aggregate demand and therefore widen the gap between supply and demand even further, creating a further need for EEC intervention and the accumulation of more stocks. Demand will reduce to D_3, equal to the difference between D_1 and D_2 or the amount that the food

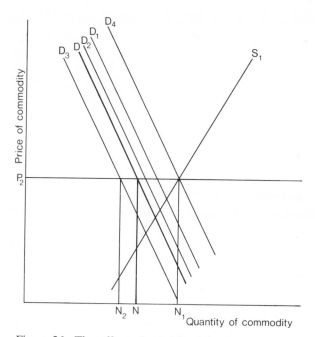

Figure 26. The effect of subsidized food sales in the
EEC and the United States

stamps would reduce normal demand in circumstances where the EEC
were not buying up the surplus production. EEC stocks will rise to $N_1 -
N_2$. This cycle could only be halted by ensuring that food distribution to
the needy in Europe was entirely additional to normal demand and this is
almost impossible to do. Food distribution programmes have been tried in
the EEC, but they have been very limited and short-lived.

The United Kingdom and the EEC

The United Kingdom did not join the European Economic Community
until 1 January 1973 when the original six members were expanded to
include Britain, Denmark and Ireland. One of the earliest stumbling blocks
to British entry had been the Common Agricultural Policy. The different
history of agricultural policy in Britain, and differences with major
European countries, encouraged original British proposals in 1956 for a
Free Trade Area encompassing the countries which later formed the EEC,
but which would have specifically excluded all agricultural commodities.
Finally, after at least two abortive efforts, British attempts to gain entry to
the EEC were successful only after the Conservative Government had
accepted the CAP in its entirety. The government recognized the central
importance of the CAP to the EEC and concentrated on arrangements to
be made during the transition period which was to run between 1973 and

1978. By 1978 Britain was to be a full member of the EEC and subject to its rules with regard to agricultural policy as with everything else.

Guaranteed prices had been introduced into British agriculture for wheat, oats and potatoes under the special circumstances of the First World War. Unlike the major exporting countries where wars have generally boosted demand and allowed some relaxation of government intervention, in importing countries, especially the United Kingdom which in 1914 produced less than a third of her total food needs, the situation was reversed and strategic needs led to strenuous efforts to encourage home production. After the war, following heated debates, guaranteed prices were withdrawn except for sugar-beet which as a new and protected crop rapidly expanded in area (Watts, 1971).

The 1930s saw two developments following from the world economic situation. The first was that, for the first time during peace, guaranteed prices were introduced and these prices were to be met by deficiency payments. The government made up the difference between the agreed price for commodities and the market price current at the time of sale. Such payments were made for wheat in 1932 and other cereal crops in 1937. The second development was a lot of discussion about the shortcomings of the marketing systems for agricultural commodities. The cause of low incomes in the agricultural sector was seen largely as stemming from inefficient marketing channels where there were a large number of producers. The solution to these problems was product marketing boards which would organize marketing on behalf of all farmers. If a majority of the producers of a particular agricultural commodity agreed to the establishment of a board then one was to be set up and all producers, whether or not they had originally been in favour of it, were bound by its organizational structure and rules. Such boards were to control supply, price and, if necessary, hold stocks. These controls could not work without import restrictions and these were introduced in 1933. Such marketing boards were established for milk, potatoes, pigs and hops. Marketing boards have continued in existence ever since, although the commodities covered have altered from time to time. In practice their main role was in the realm of price support and subsidy distribution rather than in market reorganization (Tarrant, 1974).

Meanwhile deficiency payments continued for most other agricultural commodities. By the end of the Second World War annual price reviews were established whereby the Ministry of Agriculture, Fisheries, and Food (MAFF), in consultation with the National Farmers' Union, fixed support prices for most agricultural commodities annually. In principle, the policies of the UK were not very different from those in the European countries which were to form the EEC. In practice, they were different in two important ways. Firstly, the general level of guaranteed prices was very much lower in the United Kingdom. Various agreements allowed many foodstuffs to enter the United Kingdom from countries in the

Commonwealth and this depressed market prices. Budgetary limitations meant that support prices could not be fixed far above the import price levels for these commodities. Secondly, the method of payments to farmers was different in the United Kingdom. The EEC adopted a direct market intervention policy, while the UK stayed with the deficiency payment method whereby the market price was unaffected. The former policy involved import restrictions while the latter was created because import restrictions were not possible while Commonwealth preference continued. Although the principle of government intervention to maintain adequate levels of farm incomes was common to all of Europe, the methods chosen were bound to be different as a result of existing trading agreements.

Following entry to the EEC, policies in Britain changed until, by 1978, they had adjusted almost entirely to the European methods. Very few concessions were granted although the milk marketing boards were allowed to continue. The policy changes involved not only substantial internal transformation but also the breaking of preferential trading connections with the Commonwealth countries. By coincidence the transition period coincided with the unprecedented price rises of agricultural goods on world markets and so the effects of the transformation were not as traumatic as they might otherwise have been. The Commonwealth trading partners for the most part found little difficulty in opening up new markets elsewhere. New Zealand dairy produce, no longer allowed duty-free access to the UK market, when in increasing quantities to Japan. Canadian wheat was at a premium on world markets as a result of a world shortage and special arrangements were made for Commonwealth sugar following the ending of the Commonwealth sugar agreements (Nagle, 1976). In the United Kingdom, although prices rose for many foodstuffs as a result of the change of policy, we have already seen that the EEC policies in the mid 1970s were often protecting consumers from high world prices more than they were cushioning producers from low prices. As a result the food price rises in the United Kingdom were smaller than might have been expected for many commodities.

British policy changed from campaigning for lower prices within the Community to efforts to moderate the rate of increase in guaranteed prices. In particular, during the period of the Labour government's 'renegotiation' of the terms of British entry after 1974, concern was expressed lest the EEC policies had a ratchet effect; raising prices to world levels when they were exceptionally high and then being unable to adjust them downwards as the world markets fell (Marsh, 1975). In fact, the period during which EEC prices were lower than world prices was short-lived and was true only for some important commodities, particularly grain. By 1977 EEC prices were again above world levels.

Another factor external to agriculture has greatly helped in the transformation of policies which followed from full British membership of the EEC. Between the start of 1973 and 1977 the pound sterling was devalued on world currency markets by over 40 per cent. To understand the significance of this fall it is necessary to understand the method the EEC has adopted to finance agricultural trade within its borders. When the CAP was first established all agricultural prices were expressed in a common currency called 'units of account'. The exchange rates between the currencies of the individual member countries and the units of account was determined by the Council of Ministers. In practice it takes a unanimous decision of this Council to change the rates of exchange. As a result the adjustments in these exchange rates have lagged considerably behind changes in the international monetary exchange rates. In effect, therefore, in each member country of the EEC there are three currencies: for example, in the United Kingdom there is the pound sterling, the units of account for the sale of UK agricultural commodities in the rest of the EEC, and there is the green pound which represents what the pound sterling is worth in exchange for units of account.

What should happen is as follows: suppose that in 1974 a ton of wheat was valued at 100 units of account. At that time this would have meant that a German farmer would receive about DM240 and a UK farmer about £40 for a ton of wheat. On the international exchanges assume that the pound was worth DM6 and so trade was free. The UK farmer would be no better off selling his wheat in Germany than in England, and similarly the German farmer would have been at no advantage in selling to the UK. By 1977 we assume that the pound has been devalued by 50 per cent and the Deutschmark revalued by 20 per cent so that the exchange rate has changed from DM6 to the pound to DM3.2 to the pound. If the green currency exchange rates had adjusted fully the ton of wheat might still sell for 100 units of account, but this would be worth only DM192 to the German farmer and £60 to the UK farmer. Again, trade would have been free as the German farmer selling in Britain would have received £60 which he would have been able to convert to DM192, or the same as he would have received if he had sold at home. This adjustment in the green currencies would have involved a fall in prices to the German farmer and a substantial rise in price to the farmer in Britain. This latter rise would have been reflected in higher consumer prices in Britain. Thus, there are political reasons why both countries would be reluctant to adjust their green currencies fully in line with their domestic currencies.

What happened in fact was that the green Deutschmark did not revalue to the full extent and the green pound lagged far behind the falls in the pound sterling (Figure 27). Thus in mid January 1978 German farmers were paid 7.5 per cent more than they should have been and UK farmers 29.2 per cent less. In this situation it would have been very advantageous for UK farmers to sell their produce in Germany where they would have received 36.7 per cent more than selling within the United Kingdom. As the whole idea of the EEC was to allow free trade within the member countries without unfair advantages this situation had to be prevented. The

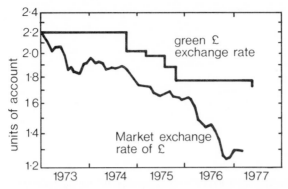

Figure 27. De-valuation of the green pound and the pound sterling. 1972–77. (By early 1978 the gap had closed as a result of a devaluation of the green pound and a strengthening of the pound sterling)

EEC evolved the monetary compensation amounts (MCA) to tax or subsidize sales across international borders to return to the position of no advantage. Thus, UK sales to Germany were taxed by 36.7 per cent and German sales to the UK were subsidized to the same extent. As long as this gap existed consumers in the UK were receiving cheaper food than would have been the case if the EEC policies had worked as they were first intended without the necessity for green currency. In fact the Treaty of Rome makes it clear that the free trade rules were only a step in the direction of more complete political union and that monetary union would be the next step. If there was complete monetary union within the EEC there would, of course, be no case for MCA and all farmers would receive the same price and all consumers pay the same price. Such monetary union seems as far off as ever, and until it comes about there will remain scope for price differences and political reasons for continuing them.

At the end of January 1978 the green pound was devalued, reducing the MCA for the UK to 19.4 per cent and allowing higher prices for UK farmers. France and Italy also devalued their green currencies at about the same time (Table 16). Over the previous few months the pound sterling had recovered somewhat on the international money markets and so the gap between the value of the pound sterling and the green pound closed considerably. Domestic food prices rose in those countries which devalued their green currencies and the total EEC bill for MCA was reduced by about £100 million (*Economist*, 28 January 1978). However, these increased consumer prices will reduce demand, increase EEC surpluses and thereby the total EEC costs. It had been argued that the total costs of the overvalued green pound to the EEC had been minimal despite the large MCA, because the large UK domestic market was using more EEC food as a result of the lower prices and that this increased consumption was

Table 16. Monetary compensation amounts in EEC member countries, 1977 and 1978

Country	MCA December 1977	MCA February 1978
Germany	+7.5	+7.5
Benelux	+1.4	+1.4
Denmark	0.0	0.0
Ireland	−2.1	−2.1
France	−19.4	−16.4
Italy	−24.4	−18.0
Britain	−29.2	−19.4

NB: These represent the differences between the national currencies market exchange rates and their exchange rates to monetary units of account through which all agricultural produce are traded. Thus, Italian wheat selling in Benelux is subject to a tax of 24.4 + 1.4 = 25.8 per cent.
Source: *Official Journal of the European Communities.*

saving the costs of adding to the mountains of unwanted production within the EEC.

Whatever the arguments, between 1973 and 1978 the UK consumer had been considerably cushioned against rising food prices resulting from entry to the EEC. The twin circumstances of rapidly rising world food prices and devaluation of the UK currency made the adjustment of joining the EEC easier than it might have been. In addition we have seen that the cheap food policy had been eroded ever since the 1930s and the reasons for its existence have declined in importance. The UK policy of cheap food imports had been supported by the exports of manufactured goods to Commonwealth countries and to the rest of the world. Since the early years of the Industrial Revolution the UK comparative advantage had lain with the export of manufactured goods. This comparative advantage has disappeared and British industry in many sectors looks distinctly uncompetitive in world markets. This has increased the comparative advantage of UK agriculture and has seen a shift towards an increased self-sufficiency in British agricultural production. Membership of the EEC and the adoption of the CAP which has as its cornerstone increased self-sufficiency and import saving, has not really involved such an extreme policy shift on behalf of the UK as might at first have seemed to be the case.

As so often happens, it is factors external to agriculture which have had a significant effect on agricultural policy. First, we have seen how external factors allowed United States policy to change, at least for a time, to non-interference and the working of the free market. Secondly, the EEC shifted from farmer support to consumer support as a result of the exceptionally high world prices at the same time. Finally, the UK consumer costs of entry to the EEC have been affected by the multitude of factors which led to a devaluation of the UK currency on world markets.

Consumer Subsidies

Most government intervention on the part of producers is found in the developed world while most extensive examples of consumer subsidies are in the developing world. Three policy extremes can be adopted, although in practice in most developing countries one finds some combination of these.

The Bangladesh Example

The first possibility is where the consumer subsidy is made available in the form of sales of basic foodstuffs through a system of national government sales to selected individuals at a reduced price. The necessary produce for this distribution is derived from imports and does not affect the domestic supply curve. Government food distribution in Bangladesh involves the sale of limited amounts of subsidized grain and other commodities to specified categories of consumers. The government of Bangladesh refers to this subsidized food distribution as 'rationing' but, although the amounts available to each individual are limited, it does not involve rationing in the strict sense as open-market purchases are unrestricted. The source of grain available for this distribution is mostly imports over which the government has a monopoly. Local procurement has been tried on a compulsory basis in times of shortages, but this only encourages widespread evasion and smuggling of the crop to India. It also seems likely that the market price of produce not passing through government channels increased more than it would have in the absence of such withdrawals (Lele, 1976). In recent years (Table 17) procurement has been voluntary and, as the market price of rice has fallen, an increasing amount has been purchased by government agents. In 1976–77 about 21 per cent of the total ration supplies were procured locally through voluntary schemes. In 1977–78 this government procurement acted fairly effectively as a mechanism to support a floor price for producers. The procurement price was announced well before the planting season and procurement centres were able to buy in excess of 500,000 tons, helping to decrease the seasonal fall in prices normally occurring at harvest. None the less the policy remains primarily a mechanism for obtaining food grains for distribution in the ration system.

The distribution of subsidized food grains is very biased towards the urban population while the rural population, which makes up about 90 per cent of the total, receives little more than 20 per cent of the available food. The definition of urban is also rather restrictive and thus the proportion of the subsidized food going to the urban population is underestimated. The main recipients of the subsidized food live in the seven most important urban areas which together make up the statutory rationing scheme. Each person in these cities is entitled to a ration of rice, wheat, edible oil, and salt each week at prices fixed often considerably

Table 17. Bangladesh : food-grain production and ration distribution

Year	Net production ('000 tons) (a)	Ration offtake ('000 tons) (b)	(b) as % of (a)	Statutory %	Modified %	Relief %	Other %	Imports	Domestic procurement ('000 tons)
1965/66	9,329	986	10.6	NA	NA	NA	NA	923	93
1966/67	8,526	958	11.2	NA	NA	NA	NA	1,100	8
1967/68	9,943	887	8.9	NA	NA	NA	NA	1,019	22
1968/69	10,127	944	9.3	21.5[b]	58.2[b]	6.7[b]	13.6[b]	119	9
1969/70	10,731	1,169	10.9	17.9[b]	68.3[b]	1.2[b]	12.6[b]	1,547	9
1970/71	9,972	1,294	13.0	15.9[b]	59.0[b]	17.7[b]	7.4[b]	1,146	6
1971/72	NA	1,734[a]	NA	16.2[b]	50.2[b]	24.3[b]	9.3[b]	NA	NA
1972/73	9,018	2,618	29.1	17.8	60.8	7.9	13.5	2,782	52
1973/74	10,646	1,727	16.2	29.0	45.0	3.1	22.9	1,651	71
1974/75	10,102	1,764	17.5	26.7	32.8	9.1	31.4	2,260	138
1975/76	11,511	1,676	14.6	21.5	29.5	13.5	35.5	1,440	415
1976/77	10,500	1,473	14.0	NA	NA	NA	NA	810	316
1977/78	12,000[a]	NA	NA	NA	NA	NA	NA	1,849[a]	530

[a] World Bank estimates.
[b] These data should be taken as approximate only as different sources give different total ration offtakes.
Sources: Gavan (1977); World Bank (1978a).

below the current market price. Although the coverage is not as complete as the scheme implies, in 1974–75 about 27 per cent of the food distribution was issued through the statutory scheme. It is one reason why the urban areas appear so attractive to the rural poor, especially during the wet season when there is little employment on the land. However, many of these migratory poor do not obtain a ration card. The second level of the ration distribution is the modified ration scheme which in theory covers most of the rest of the country. In practice the twin constraints of limited supplies, transportation, and storage difficulties means that the distribution is decidedly patchy. The amount distributed is supposed to be the result of discussions between the local government officials concerned with the needs of the local population and the Ministry of Food which is concerned with the available supply. The amount finally delivered to the local area is divided among the population according to the family income level based on taxation assessment. There is rarely enough available to go beyond the poorest of the income categories—those who pay no tax at all. The supplies available in the larger urban areas of the modified ration scheme are fairly steady but the rest of the country has highly variable supplies and little advance notice about availability. At best under the modified ration scheme supplies are available only twice a month and the allowances are set at the same level as in the statutory areas so the overall supply per household is half that in the latter areas. Rarely is even this target reached. A further category of rationing is the special groups of government employees, who obtain the full statutory ration when they live outside the statutory ration areas. Also included are the police, army, hospitals, student hostels and prisons. Finally the Ministry of Relief distributes food grains in times of national disasters, such as floods and cyclones, and also makes wheat available for payment of labourers under food for work projects which are undertaken mostly in the winter, the dry season.

The total offtake from the ration system varies greatly from year to year depending on fluctuating needs and available supplies. This fluctuation is catered for by two processes. Firstly, the quantities available per card holder are altered. Between February 1975 and August 1976 the ration was 1.417 kg, between October 1976 and March 1977 it rose to 3.719 kg and is currently 2.790 kg per adult per week (children's rations are half that of adults). Because of the importance of imports for the supply for this distribution system, and some external pressure to reduce the amount of rice distributed in this way (see Chapter 7) one-third of the ration is currently in the form of wheat. The second adjustment to variable supplies is made by varying the amount available under the various ration schemes. Modified rationing is the most variable and large numbers of people move into and out of the ration scheme, depending on the availability of supplies. The general trend in the quantities distributed under modified rationing is downwards which balances growth in the 'other' category, of that going to special groups of people, especially government employees.

In 1976–77 the total ration offtake was equal to about 13 per cent of total consumption and the World Bank (1978a) estimates that such ration food reached between 15 and 20 million people although actual numbers reached are not recorded. As expected from such a distribution system the beneficiaries are largely urban people and the urban bias is increasing. The ration food appears to raise the consumption of the low-income groups in urban areas from below the consumption levels of the same income groups in rural areas to a level somewhat above. The question of the urban bias must be considered in the context that the average calorie consumption of low-income groups in urban areas is below that in rural areas because of the possibilities in rural areas for most families to grow some rice. Also, urban people have higher costs for fuel and shelter. On the other hand urban populations have a reduced need for food because of reduced physical activity. The value of the ration, represented by the difference between the ration and the market price of the subsidized food, represented between 20 and 30 per cent of total family expenditure in the lowest income groups of the urban population.

In terms of the diagrammatic analysis we have considered throughout this chapter the original demand and supply curves (S and D) are indicated in Figure 28 and the resulting equilibrium price is P. Supply and demand elasticities are difficult to estimate. Technological developments make

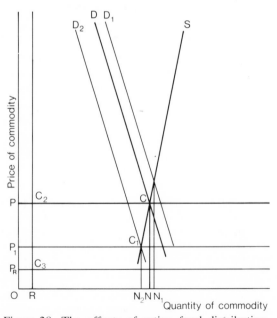

Figure 28. The effects of ration food distribution
on supply and demand

long-term supply elasticities potentially very much larger than in the short term (Gavan, 1977). Demand elasticities are in some respects even more difficult to estimate as they are known to vary very much between income groups, and the distribution of different income groups in the country will make considerable differences to the overall elasticity function arrived at. In Bangladesh some demand elasticities have been calculated in Table 18.

The ration distribution is represented by R and the ration price by P_r. The ration distribution is in reality some function of market price. One would expect the amount distributed through the various ration outlets to rise with increasing market price, but the relationship in practice is rather weak and for illustrative purposes the ration has been shown as having zero elasticity. The ration system of distribution inreased the demand to D_1 through an income effect. Where food expenditure makes up a high proportion of the consumer's total budget, lowering the price of a proportion of food demands has the same effect as raising the income of that section of the population in receipt of the ration. When incomes are raised more food will be bought. But in the commercial market place the ration food distributed decreases the demand by some amount larger than the income effect in just the same way as food stamp sales would do in the EEC. The final demand curve moves to D_2. The ration distribution cannot be entirely additional consumption, even in the very poor sections of the population. They would have bought some food in an open market situation or starved, and so only in very extreme circumstances can ration distributed food be considered additional in its entirety. Where the ration

Table 18. Price elasticities of demand for food for different income groups: Bangladesh

Household expenditure group (takas/month)[a]	Rural households	Urban households[b]
0–99	−0.70	−0.18
100–149	−0.54	−0.13
150–199	−0.45	−0.16
200–249	−0.38	−0.14
250–299	−0.34	−0.14
300–399	−0.28	−0.12
400–499	−0.23	−0.09
500–749	−0.19	−0.09
750–999	−0.14	−0.04
1,000–1,499	−0.11	−0.03
1,500–1,999	−0.06	−0.01
2,000+	0.00	−0.01
All rural	−0.22	−0.07

[a]25 taka = £1.
[b]Elasticities in urban areas are lower because of the effects of the ration distribution.
Source: Gavan (1977).

distribution is supplied by imports the demand curve moves to the left from D_1 by the same amount as is imported. Thus, $N_1 - N_2$ equals $R - O$ which equals the imported quantity. Price to the domestic producers falls to P_1. Although the magnitude of these shifts in demand and price may be disputed there is no doubt that they must take place to some degree, as the ration system in Bangladesh is specifically designed to replace some of the existing demand from urban consumers. Government employees are given the ration privileges partly to avoid increasing wages and a large section of this population is already sufficiently well off to meet their food demands on the open market. Under these circumstances the ration system must replace a substantial part of the existing demand, especially perhaps for high-quality rice. Gross returns to farmers therefore fall to O, P_1, C_1, N_2. Consumption rises from N to N_1 as a result of the income effect but this will be noticeably less than the size of the ration distribution OR.

Assuming that the import price is the same as the original equilibrium price P the costs of the programme to the government will be the difference between the import price of the food P and the ration distribution price P_r times the quantity distributed or P_r, P, C_2, C_3. If, as in the case of Bangladesh, the imports are mostly effectively free in the form of food aid, then the government has a gain of O, P_r, C_3, R, but a subsidy still exists in the form of the opportunity costs of the foregone revenue of selling this food aid on the open market (P_r, P, C_2, C_3). In addition to the political and other benefits which may accrue from the ration distribution itself, this additional income may be used for general development or budgetary purposes. The benefits of such food aid shipments will be set against the loss of incentives to producers through lowered prices (see Chapter 7). In recent years the ration price has been raised to close the gap with market price and, again as a substantial proportion of recent food imports have been on a concessionary basis, overall government income has risen (Table 19).

Table 19. Ration and market price for rice in Bangladesh

Year	Retail price[a]	Ration price
	(Taka per maund)[b]	
1969–70	44.78	30.40
1970–71	45.30	30.00
1971–72	57.10	30.00
1972–73	89.20	40.00
1973–74	167.95	40.00
1974–75	252.20	60.00
Dec. 1975–Feb. 1976	127.10	70.00
Feb. 1976–	127.20	90.00

[a]Average price medium-quality Bangladesh rice.
[b]25 taka = £1 and 1 maund = 37 kg.
Source: Ahmed (1977); World Bank (1978a).

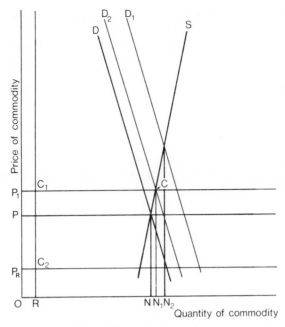

Figure 29. The effects of domestic procurement
policies on supply and demand

Where such imports are too expensive in terms of foreign exchange,
and/or not available in the form of food aid on free or concessionary
terms, any ration distribution has to be met by domestic procurement. The
effect of such policies is in many ways not unlike the position in the United
States and for many years the government of India has been operating a
system which is a compromise between domestic procurement to supply
the ration shop system and imports. The totally domestic procurement
policy to supply a ration shop distribution of subsidized food can be
illustrated by Figure 29. The ration distribution R and price P_r creates a
new demand which pushes the demand curve to D_1, but as a proportion of
this was being met previously the demand curve falls back to D_2. The
difference between D_2 and D is the income effect of the ration distribution,
and the quantity $N_2 - N$ has to be met from domestic procurement, even
though the domestic consumption rises by only $N_1 - N$. The effect of this
increased demand is to raise prices to P_1 and gross producer income to box
O, P_1, C, N_1 of which the government pays P_r, P_1, C_1, C_2. Such costs may be
very considerable. Possibly by raising domestic prices above world market
prices this policy may be more expensive than an import policy, although
cheaper in foreign exchange. In addition the 'normal' consumer, not
eligible for the ration, has to pay the increased domestic price. Also, all
consumers will have to pay the increased price for the remainder of their
needs which are not met from the ration distribution. The subsidized sales

have therefore to be paid for by government expenditure and by the 'normal' consumer. On the other hand, the increased domestic prices provide an incentive to domestic producers and may encourage sufficient production to lead towards self-sufficiency in food. The balance of the final policy between imports and domestic procurement will depend on many factors including the political attractiveness of the alternatives and the availability of aid and foreign exchange.

The Case of India

The present Indian system of government intervention in the interests of consumers started during the Second World War to prevent profiteering by traders when supplies were limited following the involvement of Burma in the conflict. Its origin was in Bombay but it rapidly spread to other states and was intended to supply certain categories, particularly government employees, industrial workers and the military with food at reasonable prices. This was arranged through a government-established network of fair price shops where food was made available to qualified persons. These people were identified by ration cards indicating the amount each was entitled to, depending on size of his family. The fair price shops were not intended to meet all the food needs of these consumers but to ensure a basic minimum at a subsidized price. This operation was intended to control price rises in the open market. During the Bengal famine of 1942–43 the fair price shop system was extended into full statutory rationing which limited the total purchases of all consumers. By 1947 statutory rationing covered 857 urban areas with a total population of about 160 million. This essentially remained the two-pronged attack of the Indian government aimed at controlling food prices: controlled prices and, at times, controlled consumption. The fair price shops have remained in operation since that time and statutory rationing has also been introduced in years and/or places of particular shortage.

Rationing continued more or less uninterrupted until 1952–53 when, after two good crop years, supplies were adequate and rationing was removed. In the late 1950s supplies continued plentiful and the fair price shops continued as a regulator of retail price levels. By 1964–65 prices were rising fast again and rationing was reintroduced and this continued through the lean production years until 1970–71. Again good harvests boosted supplies, even through a poor year in 1972–73 when government food stocks were utilized to avoid rationing, but continuing drought and a shortage of imports in 1974–75, plus the depleted stock levels, led to rapidly rising prices which the fair price shops were not able to control. Rationing was reintroduced for a while, but the cycles of shortage and abundance have continued and rationing has now been abandoned in all but a few cities as abundant harvests and overflowing stocks are again a feature of Indian food supply. The present position is that statutory rationing is in force only in Calcutta, Bombay, and some industrial towns, and the fair price shops are becoming more numerous and are encouraged to sell to all comers with or without ration card privileges.

Supplies for these shops have come from two sources, internal procurement and imports. Internal procurement has been organized by limiting interstate trade in food grains. By preventing interstate trade these controls allowed grain prices in the surplus regions of India to be held down, at least during poor harvest high price periods. Government purchasing took place at these depressed prices and the grain was shipped for sale in the deficit states through the fair price shops. The central government issues the grain at an issue price to which the states then add a tax to cover the state level expenses of storage and distribution. This becomes the price to the fair price shops which then add a sales commission. From the central government level downwards the scheme is supposed to be self-financing. In years of plentiful supplies, i.e. 1977, restrictions on interstate trading are lifted. In some cases, notably the State of Kerala, this source of supply has been supplemented by a compulsory levy on local production, though other methods of local procurement have been adopted by various states from time to time. Imports have been a major contributor to the fair price shop distribution. This was especially true during the years of massive PL 480 shipments of wheat from the United States. In 1956–57 agreements were signed for shipments of 3.1 million tons of wheat and 0.19 million tons of rice under PL 480 terms and this contributed to the ending of statutory rationing that year. Again, in 1961, agreements were made for the shipment of 16 million tons of wheat and 1 million tons of rice over the following four years. During this period government procurement could be limited and interstate trading was liberalized.

Throughout this post-war period both the fair price system and rationing (when in force) were largely confined to the urban areas. In years of plentiful supplies there was much talk of the need to expand the system to the rural areas, but very little effective action proved possible. This urban bias, as in Bangladesh, is made the more unfortunate by the fact that not only do the vast majority of the poor live in rural areas but they are increasingly dependent on the market for food with declining payments for labour made in kind (Parthasarthy, 1976). There were and remain several reasons for this lack of rural coverage.

1. During periods of statutory rationing it is not possible to attempt to ration the consumption of producers, only the landless rural labourers without access to their own production can be affected. Thus the schemes would have had different effects on the two sections of the population, would have lent itself to black market dealing and would have been very difficult to administer. This difficulty is increased if the many different types of producers are considered. Sharecropping and other systems of

land tenure mean that there will be a whole range of producers from those who meet all their own needs and sell a proportion of their production, to those who are able to grow but a fraction of their own needs. The same difficulties are evident in meeting the needs of the rural poor in Bangladesh.

2. Rural areas have lower population densities than the urban areas. The range of fair price shops is limited by the walking distance of the potential customers. It is probable that the demand within such a catchment area would be too small to allow for viable operation of a fair price shop, especially in the north of the country and during the harvest season when the call on such shops would be limited. Low profit margins from the commission on the sale of fair price grain would lead to temptations for black market dealing. Although government distribution of grains could be organized combined with distribution of other commodities in short supply, such as sugar, oil, and batteries, this has only been tried in limited areas.

3. Rural areas, especially with a limited demand, would have been difficult to supply frequently. The allocation to a particular shop might arrive once a month, at a date which varied from month to month. The typical rural poor have little cash, relying on short-term credit arrangements for small food purchases made frequently. The existing small multifunction shop is geared up to this demand by supplying milled grain, ata, and other needs, in small quantities. The price difference between the fair price shops and the open market would have to be considerable to allow the rural poor to deal in larger quantities at a time. Alternatively, the profit margins for the fair price shopkeeper would have to be larger to allow him to provide the sort of service that is provided by the existing rural shopkeeper. Without rationing it seems likely that the available supplies within the fair price shops would be purchased by those who have the capital to buy large quantities at a time, leaving those in the most need without effective access to the system.

Only in the State of Kerala is the fair price system virtually complete in its coverage. This state has long suffered from a food deficit, relying on Burmese trade before the war and latterly on government-run, interstate trade to supply the fair price shops. Ration cards entitling their holders to use the fair price shops are issued to all households except those classified as full producers of food. Only some 3 per cent of households are so regarded, indicating that the classification of 'full food producer' is a stringent one. The contribution of the fair price shops was particularly significant during the last half of the 1960s as interstate trading restrictions meant very high prices for food in the open market. As this state is so short of food the fair price system had to work to prevent widespread starvation. Overall today the contribution of the fair price shop sales is relatively small, especially since tapioca production has increased rapidly as a substitute food crop for rice (Table 20). In 1971–72 the fair price

Table 20. Food grain production, trade and ration offtake, Kerala State, India

Year (1)	Net production of rice excluding procurement[a] (2) ('000 tons)	Offtake of rice and wheat from ration shops (3) ('000 tons)	Imports of rice on private trade account (4) ('000 tons)	Net availability of cereals (2) (3) (4) (5) ('000 tons)	Net production[b] of tapioca (6) ('000 tons)	Rice equivalent of tapioca (7) ('000 tons)
1961/62	879	249	776	1904	2019	918
1962/63	956	207	769	1932	2019	918
1963/64	987	199	805	1991	2019	918
1964/65	981	541	453[c]	1975	2210	1005
1965/66	821	1187	(51)[d] —	2008[e]	2477	1126
1966/67	893	1061	(56) —	1954[e]	2728	1240
1967/68	907	1007	(77) —	1914[e]	3358	1526
1968/69	1017	1011	(78) —	2028[e]	3265	1484
1969/70	979	956	(94) —	1935[e]	3733	1697
1970/71	1053	866	(83) 400	2319	3694	1680
1971/72	1113	926	(70) 450	2489	4343	1974

[a]Net production equals gross production minus 12.5 per cent for seed, wastage, etc.
[b]Net production here equals gross production minus 20 per cent for export and industrial uses of the tapioca.
[c]Only to October 1964.
[d]Figures in parentheses indicate the quantities procured during the year, but they are included in the figures for offtake. The differences between offtake and procurement, if any, represent drawings from the central pool.
[e]Not including imports of rice on private trade account because such imports were virtually stopped during these years.
Source: U.N. Dept. of Economics and Social Affairs (1975).

shops contributed about 20 per cent of total food consumption, although a much higher proportion of the consumption of the poorer households (U.N. Dept. of Economics and Social Affairs, 1975).

In Kerala, the poorest 30 per cent of the households obtain about two-thirds of their total food needs from the fair price shops and the rest was probably made up with tapioca and food payments in kind. In addition there is an extensive school feeding programme in the state. In the poorest households it is likely that this programme substituted for other food consumption rather than added to it. Most of the food supplies for the fair price shops come from outside the state, from government procurement and imports, but Kerala is one of a very few states which has tried to enforce a local procurement scheme based on a production levy. Each farm is classified according to size and according to the average yield of paddy over the preceding five years in the district within which it is situated (Table 21). The size of the levy on production should vary from 30 to 80 per cent of production depending on the size of the holding, but as Table 21 shows, in fact very little has been procured in this way. One reason is that land is divided into very small pieces, often within the same

Table 21. Rice levy for ration distribution, Kerala State, India

Area of paddy holding	Quantities to be sold to the procuring authority		
	In group 'A' taluks	In group 'B' taluks	In group 'C' taluks
(1) 0–2 acres	—	—	—
(2) 2–5 acres	3 quintals per acre for every acre in excess of 2	2.5 quintals per acre for every acre in excess of 2	2 quintals per acre for every acre in excess of 2
(3) 5–10 acres	As for (2) for the first 5 acres; 7 quintals for every acre in excess of 5	As for (2) for the first 5 acres; 5 quintals for every acre in excess of 5	As for (2) for the first 5 acres; 3.5 quintals for every acre in excess of 5
(4) 10 or more acres	As for (3) for the first 10 acres; 9 quintals for every acre in excess of 10	As for (3) for the first 10 acres; 7 quintals for every acre in excess of 10	As for (3) for the first 10 acres; 5.5 quintals for every acre in excess of 10

Notes:
1. The same rates apply for each of the three paddy crops grown in a year.
2. The taluks are classified on the following basis taking into account the mean yield of the crops for the five years immediately preceding the crop to which the levy applies:
   Group A: Taluks with a mean average yield of more than 2500 kg/ha.
   Group B: Taluks with a mean average yield of more than 2000 kg/ha, and up to and including 2500 kg/ha.
   Group C: Taluks with a mean average yield up to anc including 2000 kg/ha.
Source: U.N. Dept. of Economics and Social Affairs (1975).

family, to avoid the levy so paddy land and paddy production are widely under-reported to reduce or avoid levy payments.

Isenman and Singer (1975) conclude that food aid shipments to India between 1955 and 1971 had little effect on domestic prices, except on a few occasions. The outcome of the Indian policy during this period has been a balance so that imports filled the net increase in demand and domestic procurement made up for the substitution of ration demand for commercial sales and the equilibrium price was more or less maintained. Figure 30 shows that during the period 1962 to 1966 when food grain imports were growing fast, public distribution of food grains was growing faster while production was more or less static. Domestic procurement was made possible by limiting local demand through internal trading restrictions and the ration was supplied by a combination of domestic procurement and imports. From 1966 to 1972 imports fell away to almost zero, while the fair price shop distribution fell much less fast. Thus the domestic procurement part of the policy grew while production increased. Isenman and Singer show that the relative domestic food grain prices were the same in 1971 as they were in 1966, and so a good balance was apparently maintained during this time between imports and domestic procurement without substantial effects on domestic market price and domestic production. Since 1972 production has levelled off while the ration increased, requiring additional imports, but in 1976 production

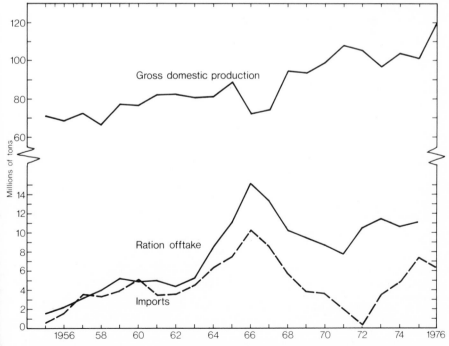

Figure 30. Production, ration and import of food grains, India, 1955–76

increased again necessitating less imports. This picture is not complete, of course, because of the lag effects of storage from one year to another, but it serves to confirm that, in general, the procurement and import balance was about right for most of the last twenty years.

The previous two main consumer-orientated policies have been to supply subsidized sales to consumers through inputs and through a mix of imports and domestic procurement. The third option for a food subsidy policy, which is included simply for completeness, is a policy of having no imports while maintaining domestic market prices at their original levels and subsidizing food sales. In this rather unlikely case the government meets a proportion of the domestic demand at reduced prices but leaves the extra demand this creates unfilled by not allowing prices to producers to rise. Thus the increased demand stemming from the ration distribution $N_1 - N$ in Figure 28 is not met. Such a policy requires total control over the agricultural sector and is probably most closely approximated in the centrally planned economies like Poland where prices for some food commodities are controlled below equilibrium prices, often below production costs, and the excess demand is left unfilled and is evidenced by long lines at food shops. Under these conditions smuggling and black market food dealing may be rife. The efficiency, and the effects of, these producer- and consumer-orientated policies will be examined in the next chapter.

CHAPTER 5

The Effects of Government Policies

Introduction

Any examination of the effects of government policy in agriculture is complicated by the often conflicting effects of these policies on different groups; for example, producers and consumers, poor consumers and taxpayers, large and small producers, the owner occupier and the tenant farmer, the cash tenant and the sharecropper. The impact on these groups and the various subdivisions of each may be reinforcing or contradictory. Artificially supported prices may encourage the producers at the expense of the consumers and taxpayers, but many consumers are also small producers, especially in developing countries where a large proportion of the population are employed in agriculture. Thus, the effects of policies for one or the other group are difficult to unravel. One of the greatest difficulties is the attribution of value to policies (Johnson and Quance, 1972).

Although it is not possible to be totally objective this chapter attempts to show the effects of different policies without dwelling on whether these effects are good or bad in any absolute sense. Instead, policies will be examined in terms of their objectives. How successfully does food price control lead to increased consumption and improved nutrition? How successful have policies been in maintaining the incomes of the farming population in relation to the rest of the community? Such analysis cannot be based entirely on economic principles. In the past many economists 'have reached the erroneous conclusion that an economy which reached competitive equilibrium would be the best of all possible economies' (Johnson and Quance, 1972). Most recognized that some redistribution of assets and benefits might produce a better economy but it is difficult to define how or even if such an alternative is superior. One of the special problems to which there is no answer is that many of the different results of government policies cannot be measured in the same units. Money, purchasing power, and savings are relatively easy units of economic measurement, but non-monetary considerations, such as the quality of life of the farmer, have always been important in the formulation of agricultural policy. It is very difficult to place a cash value on the benefits accruing from improved standards of nutrition. To be sure there are economic benefits which aid economic development (Berg, 1973), but there are equally important considerations such as the quality of life of the people concerned, the freedom from hunger, the improved resistance to disease, the joys of seeing a family survive in health instead of accepting a high infant mortality rate.

Some of the more direct effects of government policy have already been considered, for example, the increased self-sufficiency of the European Economic Community after the initiation of the Common Agricultural Policy and the increases, and later decreases, in United States carry-over stocks of food with changing government attitudes to the management of the agricultural sector of the economy. In this chapter we will examine first the income effects for the farmer of price and production control policies, concentrating largely on the United States as an example. Particular attention will be paid to the income distribution effects of such policies and also policies to subsidize inputs to agricultural production. Similarities exist between the concentration of benefits on the large US farmers and the advantages which the green revolution has given to the larger farmers in the developing countries. After the effects of consumer-orientated policies have been briefly examined the nature of the conflicts between the consumer and producer policies will be explored. Finally the overall budgetary costs of agricultural programmes will be examined in relation to the political and economic importance of the sector as outlined in Chapter 3.

Producer Effects

Farm Incomes

One of the major objectives of government policy in the agricultural sector is to maintain incomes for agricultural producers in the face of the economic forces we have discussed which are tending to reduce the returns to agricultural activity. Often these policies are designed to halt, or to at least limit, the effects of these forces, leading to a declining farm labour force and to an amalgamation of farm holdings.

Farm incomes can be considered 'reasonable' in relation to past income levels, reasonable in relation to production expenses or reasonable in relation to incomes in other sectors of the economy. To eliminate the effects of changes in production expenses realized net incomes in the agricultural sector are examined (Figure 31). These net incomes to farmers in the United States are shown in constant 1967 dollar values by weighting each year's value by an index value for the prices paid by farm families for living items that year. Farm production items are omitted as they are

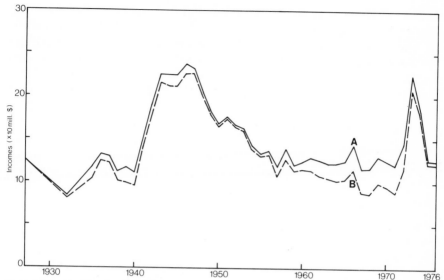

Figure 31. Realized net farm income to all farm operators with/without government payments: United States, 1927–76. **A** = net income; **B** = net income without government payments. Prices expressed in constant 1967 dollars using index of prices of family purchases made by farm operators. (1927 figure average 1925–29; 1932 average 1930–34). Source: USDA (1977a)

included in the calculation of net farm incomes. For comparative purposes this same index is used throughout this section to convert financial data to 1967 constant values. The low net income to farmers in the 1930s showed little recovery until the increased demand during and after the Second World War boosted prices and net incomes in the agricultural sector more than doubled. After the war income levels declined steadily until 1959–60 from which time they remained more or less constant until the rapid rise in 1973 which briefly raised them to levels typical of the wartime period. These gains were short-lived, however, and net income in the farming sector in 1976 was back at a level typical of the 1960s. Inflation of course means that the actual income level was much higher than the 1960s, but in terms of purchasing power the agricultural sector was no better off. Taken as a whole, government payments to agriculture from 1933 to 1959 made little significant difference to net farm incomes. From 1959 to 1971, however, a different pattern emerges. Net farm incomes without government payments continued to fall throughout this period except for brief respites in 1966 and in 1969 in response to improved world market prices. However, the net government payments increased during this period to hold net incomes more or less constant. The difference between the two curves for this period is a measure of the success of the government policies in their objectives of maintaining incomes in agriculture. The contribution of government payments during the price

F

rises of 1972–74 and post-1974 have remained minimal. The mounting costs of government intervention programmes in the 1960s was halted by the effects of the world market changes and the increased demands for American food produce. The costs of food stamp programmes are not directly included in these data but, to the extent that they have raised demand and prices during their operation, their effects are included in the lower of the two graphs.

Another object of government intervention has been stated as the smoothing out of the effects of price fluctuations on farmers' incomes by government purchasing in times of low price and government sales in times of higher prices. This smoothing can hardly be said to have been achieved. Very rarely is the direction of change in net farming incomes without government payments reversed by including these payments. The periods between 1938 and 1939 and between 1963 and 1964 are the only examples. Even in 1966, when world agricultural prices rose so also did government payments, thereby far from smoothing out the fluctuation, accentuated it. In general, government payments seem to have followed the market fortunes of agricultural net incomes and have occasionally emphasized trends. Strict deficiency payments to farmers would have raised incomes in poor price years and left them unaffected in high price years. However, throughout the 1960s substantial payments were made to keep farm land out of production. The payments received in any one year were not affected by the market price of the produce grown on the remaining land, they merely added a more or less constant amount to realized net incomes.

However, this analysis has concentrated on net incomes to the entire agricultural sector. The number of farms declined throughout the period, from 6.8 million in 1935 to 2.7 million in 1978. Both the net commercial incomes and the government payments were allocated among fewer and fewer farmers. Moreover, we might expect the number of farms to decline most sharply following years with low prices and low net incomes. This should reduce the apparent post-war decline in farm incomes and produce a closer match to changes in the incomes of the non-farm sector. Figure 32 shows the net farm incomes with and without government payments divided by the number of farm operators each year. The difference between this figure and the last is considerable. The net income per farm operator declines much less dramatically after the war as the reduced income is divided among fewer farmers. In the post-1959 period income per farm rises slightly even without government payments. With these payments net farm income per operator rises more or less constantly throughout this period. As the increased government payments are going to fewer operators the gap between net incomes with and without these payments widens more sharply over this period than in the previous figure.

Finally, how did the farm population fare in comparison to the rest of the population? Are the net income rises during the 1960s, which were the

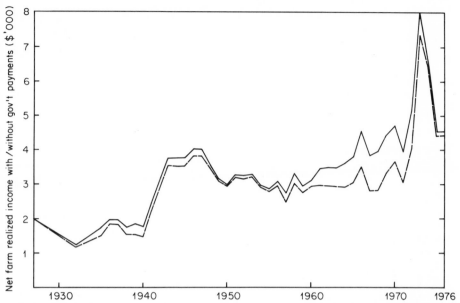

Figure 32. Realized net income per farm operator with and without government payments: United States, 1927–76. Expressed in constant 1967 dollars using index of prices of family purchases made by farm operators. Source: USDA(1977a)

direct result of government payments, enough to make the incomes of the farm population compatible with those in the non-farm sector? Figure 33 shows the per capita net disposable income of the farm population as a percentage of that of the non-farm population (curve **A**). Before the Second World War, during the economic depression, farm population net incomes were generally less than 40 per cent of incomes in other sectors. Farm incomes include the value of farm commodities directly consumed on the farm. This difference was despite the early government efforts to support agriculture. During the war years this ratio rose and reached nearly 68 per cent in 1948. The post-war decline in farm incomes was relative as well as absolute, with small reversals in the trend in 1951 and 1958 reflecting years with higher net realized incomes in agriculture. The period 1959 to 1971 shows a steady improvement in the income standing of the farm population rising to the highest levels of almost 75 per cent in 1969–71. Briefly, farm population incomes rose ahead of other sectors in 1973.

This picture is confused by two related factors. Firstly an increasing proportion of the farm population makes its living totally off the farm, commuting from the farm to employment mostly in the towns. Secondly an increasing proportion of *farmers'* net income is derived from non-farm employment. To obtain a better idea of net returns to *farming* as distinct from the total income of the *farm population* the yearly values are

124

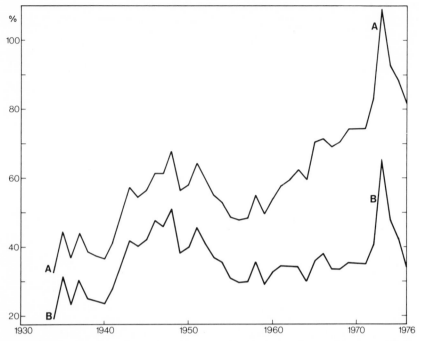

Figure 33. Per capita disposable income for farm and non-farm populations: United States, 1927–76. **A** = per capita income from all sources, farm population as per cent of non-farm population; **B** = a weighted by ratio of farm to non-farm income of the farm population. Source: USDA (1977a)

weighted by the ratio of farm income to non-farm income of the farm population. So in 1970 for example, the per capita disposable income from all sources of the farm population was 74 per cent of that of the non-farm population. But the net income per head of the farm population was $1336 from farm sources and $1483 from non-farm sources. Farm income made up only 47 per cent of total net income to the farm population in that year. This reduces from 74 per cent to 35 per cent the ratio of income from farming compared to income in other sectors of the economy. The difference between the two curves in Figure 33 is considerable. The declining proportion of farm incomes derived from farming means that returns to farming alone remained more or less static during the 1960s despite the increasing government efforts to the contrary. Prior to 1960 the ratio falls more or less uniformly as the ratio of farm to non-farm income of the farm population changes from 31 per cent in 1935 to 51 per cent in 1948 and fell to about 30 per cent in 1959. The rising income status of the farm population during the 1960s was largely the result of increasing non-farm employment. Only in 1973–74 did *farming* incomes rise briefly and then only to 65 per cent of incomes in other sectors.

Over this period, therefore, government payments can be said to have contributed to raising farmers' incomes, but generally by amounts sufficient only to maintain the standing of the farm population, not to improve it. All the efforts of the United States government must be counted as of limited significance in terms of their declared objectives. There is no doubt that the incomes of farmers would have *declined* relative to other sectors without such policies and we will examine the extent of this probable decline at the end of this chapter.

Income Distributional Effects

Farm payments by the United States government have been closely related to the size of production of the farm units. The purchasing activities of the Commodity Credit Corporation in the 1960s, buying the production which could not be disposed of at the target price, meant that government payments were directly related to the size of the farm production. Similarly, payments for retiring a proportion of a farmer's land will be higher the larger the farm. Such payment methods must be concentrated in their effects on the larger farms and the small, poor and marginal farms receive little benefit from this massive government involvement in agriculture (Schultze, 1971). In many ways such government programmes operate in contradiction to their objectives to compensate for the process of economic adjustment which tends to concentrate the economic benefits of farming on to the larger and more efficient farmers. Government payments are similarly concentrated. In a perverse way, therefore, such government payments can be said to be working for overall economic efficiency by encouraging farm enlargement. This is hardly the stated objectives of the policies, especially with the political commitment to the small family farm in United States legislation. In 1960 farms in the two smallest income classes (with less than $5000 annual sales) accounted for 62 per cent of all farms but for only 24 per cent of farm income and 26 per cent of all government payments. In contrast, farms with annual sales of over $40,000 made up only 3 per cent of all farms, 18 per cent of farm incomes and 15 per cent of government payments to farmers. In 1968 there were some very large individual payments (Table 22) including three, incredibly, in excess of $1 million. Despite policies to limit the maximum size of payment per farm (see Chapter 3) the position has become more polarized since 1960. In 1976 the two smallest classes of farms accounted for 50 per cent of all farms, 12 per cent of farm income and only 10 per cent of government payments. In contrast the two largest classes made up 17 per cent of all farms, 62 per cent of farm income and 62 per cent of government payments (Figure 34). The larger farms have increased in number over the period, but the proportion of government payments to these farmers has increased faster. The increase in the size of permitted maximum payments per farm under the 1977 Agriculture Act will lead to further development of this position in the future.

Table 22. Distribution of US producer payments[a] (excluding wool and sugar programme payments), 1968

Size of payment	Producers			Total amount of payments[b]		
	Number	% Distribution	Cumulative % distribution	Million dollars	% distribution	Cumulative % distribution
Less than $100	281,413	11.9%	11.9%	$13.6	0.4%	0.4%
$100 to $199	258,762	10.9	22.9	38.3	1.2	1.6
$200 to $499	543,822	22.8	45.7	182.8	5.7	7.3
$500 to $699	244,819	10.3	56.0	145.4	4.6	11.9
$700 to $999	257,576	10.9	66.9	216.3	6.8	18.7
$1000 to $1999	397,360	16.8	83.7	555.8	17.4	36.1
$2000 to $2999	154,187	6.5	90.2	376.0	11.8	47.9
$3000 to $3999	79,591	3.4	93.6	274.6	8.6	56.5
$4000 to $4999	46,359	2.0	95.6	206.9	6.5	63.0
$5000 to $7499	52,908	2.2	97.8	319.1	10.0	73.0
$7500 to $9999	21,342	0.9	98.7	183.6	5.8	78.8
$10,000 to $14,999	17,290	0.7	99.4	208.2	6.5	85.3
$15,000 to $24,999	10,320	0.4	99.8	194.5	6.1	91.4
$25,000 to $49,999	4,611	0.2	100.0	153.5	4.8	96.2
$50,000 to $99,999	1,010	c	100.0	66.7	2.1	98.3
$100,000 to $499,999	255	c	100.0	41.2	1.3	99.6
$500,000 to $999,999	6	c	100.0	3.9	0.1	99.7
$1,000,000 and over	3	c	100.0	7.0	0.2	99.9
Total	2,371,634	100.0%		$3,187.3	100.0%	

[a]Includes payments under the following programmes for: cotton, feed grain, wheat, milk indemnity, agricultural conservation, emergency conservation, Appalachia, crop-land conversion, conversion reserve, and crop-land adjustment.

[b]The sum of individual percentages and individual total amounts of payments may differ from the totals shown because of roundings.

[c]Less than 0.05 per cent.

Source: Walter W. Wilcox, *Economic Aspects of Farm Program Limitations* (Washington, DC: Library of Congress, Legislative Reference Service, 6 November 1969). After Cochrane and Ryan (1975).

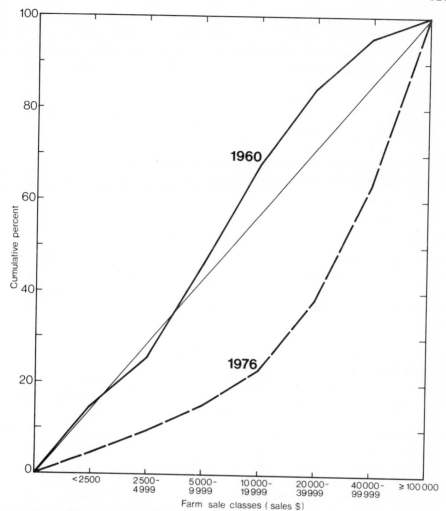

Figure 34. Distribution of direct government payments by size of farm: United States, 1960 and 1976. Source: USDA (1977a)

Concern for the income distributional effects of government policy has led to investigations concerning the use of federal irrigation water and the limitation on the size of farms allowed to receive this in the future (Chapter 3). However the new regulations are considerably more lenient than the original legislation and it seems likely that very large farms will continue to be able to receive federal water for a considerable time to come. All other government payments, so long as they are based on production rather than income, will tend to benefit the large farmers rather than the small. It can be argued, of course, that this really is the objective as, to encourage investment in agriculture, the return should be proportional to the size of the investment and government should ensure that the large investors are receiving this adequate return. However, this is one further example of the conflicts inherent in agricultural policy. The protection of farm *incomes* would be best dealt with by *income-support* policies while *investment* protection is best provided by *production-related payments*. Such payments have certainly encouraged a continuing restructuring of US agriculture. As the number of farms has declined the average farm size has risen, more or less doubling from 86 ha in 1950 to 162 ha in 1978. Although government payments have tended to maintain or raise agricultural incomes generally (Figure 32), because a large percentage of these payments go to the larger farmers, they have possibly speeded up the economic adjustment of the agricultural sector.

Production Controls

The government policies of income support that we have examined so far in this chapter have been an aggregate of price support and attempts to control and limit production. Production limitation alone has a number of special problems, one of which is the distribution of benefits among farmers of different sizes.

In the United States, production limitation has operated in one of two ways. Firstly, there has been a long-standing conservation programme, withdrawing land from production for soil and water conservation reasons. Figure 35 shows that the conservation programme has been in progress since almost the earliest days of government intervention and between 1956 and 1968 the soil bank was particularly important, requiring considerable payments in the late 1950s. Secondly, farmers have been encouraged to withdraw a proportion of land from the production of crops which are in oversupply and for which the government is anxious to see stable or rising prices. This policy has worked in two ways. Either the farmers have been given direct payments to withdraw this land, the amount of the payment depending on the area withdrawn, and/or the farmers become ineligible for price-support payments if they do not participate in crop-land withdrawal programmes.

His speciality was growing alfalfa, and he made a good thing out of not growing any. The government paid him well for every bushel of alfalfa he did not grow. The more alfalfa he did not grow the more money the government gave him and he spent every penny he didn't earn on new land to increase the amount of alfalfa he did not produce. Major Major's father worked without rest at not growing alfalfa. (J. Heller, *Catch 22*, Simon and Schuster, New York, 1955).

In the United Kingdom there are production controls on the growing of sugar-beet in order that production should be geared to the processing capacity of the sugar-beet factories. The area is planted under contract and only the contracted area is bought by the factory. In this case the

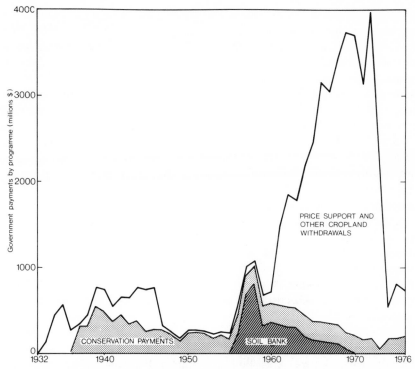

Figure 35. United States government agriculture payments by programme.
Source: USDA (1977a)

production controls are not designed to maintain prices but to prevent wasteful production which could not be processed. Similarly, the production of vegetables for freezing and for canning is usually controlled by the processing factories through production contracts. Also in the United Kingdom the production of potatoes has been limited through the operations of the Potato Marketing Board, and this operation has been designed to limit production and maintain a reasonable price. The price elasticity of demand for potatoes is very small so, without a measure of control, unmarketable surpluses would easily result after good growing seasons. In this case the area planted to potatoes by each farmer is subject to a quota established by the Board.

The first problem with these production policies is that a farmer asked to, or required to, retire say 20 per cent of his wheat land will retire the least productive land and will concentrate his efforts on the land remaining. Average yields on the remaining productive land will increase, not only as it is naturally the best land but as it now receives all the farmer's attention and probably a higher fertilizer application. A reduction in area of 20 per cent of wheat land will lead to a much lesser reduction in wheat production. Statistical evidence for this is difficult to accumulate because of the effects of extraneous variables, particularly the weather, but what there is appears conclusive (see, for example, USDA, 1956). Also, unless the regulations require that this idled land is not used for any other form of production, similar crops may be substituted for the crop the production of which is to be limited. Thus, policies to control the production of wheat in the early 1960s led to an increased production of feed grains. In these circumstances the farmers benefit twice or three times over: from the higher wheat prices, possibly from direct payments for production limitation and also from the increased production of the substitute crop or crops. The problems with overproduction of alternative crops led to changed legislation requiring that land withdrawn from one form of production be left idle or in pasture only. The 1977 Food and Agriculture Act indicates that land in set-aside programmes may be used for other purposes provided that these do not increase the costs of any government price-support programmes. Crops for which there is a potential demand are allowed on this land. Specific mention is made of hay and sunflower seeds.

The second problem with production limitation policies is that, if payments are made directly for retiring land in proportion to present levels of production, the larger the farmer the larger the payments. Also, the large farmers will receive greater total benefits from the rise in product prices which the artificially created shortage has caused. Therefore, especially where there are direct payments for land idling, the large farmers benefit twice over and the farm income gaps between the large and the small widen.

The third, and the most difficult, problem of production controls is the provision of a strong enough incentive for land retirement without compulsion. The individual farmer's position is very similar to the 'prisoner's dilemma' faced by individual property owners in an area of potential urban renewal. Two neighbouring owners can benefit by renovating their properties as values will rise. If both renovate the values will rise more than if one does and the other does not. The shabby appearance of the second property will reduce the value of the first. On the other hand, one will benefit from doing nothing if the other renovates as property values in general rise with the improved appearance of the neighbourhood and the evidence of the potential for improvement. Each then is a prisoner of the other's action or inaction. One will gain from the other's actions without any change on his part, and so neither can reap the benefits of complete renovation unless their actions are co-ordinated by some outside agency whose organization allows all investors to benefit from a general improvement of the whole area.

It is not difficult to see how this relates to farmers and production control. The benefits of reduced production will be higher prices. If a farmer can contrive to maintain his production level while all others reduce theirs, he benefits from higher prices on his original level of production. To prevent this happening the production control must either be legally enforced, as with the Potato Marketing Board in the United Kingdom, or the incentive to comply must be greater than the incentive not to do so. The latter requires very fine judgement. If the farmer is receiving direct payments for production limitation, such payments plus the expected increased price for the remaining production must exceed the price he would expect to get if he maintained or even increased his production. Again we return to the principal dilemma of agricultural production, that it is controlled by millions of individual operators, farming independently of decisions made by other producers.

Even if there are no direct payments for land idling the problem is no less complex. The position in the United States at the start of the 1978 planting season was that the United States Department of Agriculture wished to see a reduction of 20 per cent in the wheat-growing land and a 10 per cent reduction in the area planted to feed grains. Farmers will not receive the deficiency payments between the market price and the target price for these crops unless they have reduced their productive area accordingly. But the original 1978 target price for wheat of $3.00 and for feed grains (corn) of $2.10 a bushel is low in relation to the market prices which have been reached over the last four years. Farmers have to speculate about how low the *market* price will be, determined in part by how much all their colleagues reduce their production, and what will be the profit from the reduced production at the target price against a full production at the market price. This would be a difficult enough problem for agricultural economists and can be little more than guesswork for most farmers. The concensus at the start of the 1978 season was that the incentives to reduce production were not sufficient as the target price for grains was too low. Probably much less than the hoped-for 20 per cent reduction in productive area will be achieved. The position was complicated by the threats of the striking farmers who are intending to stop production on a much larger scale than is intended by the USDA, thereby pushing prices up towards the parity levels. It is difficult to assess the effects of this policy, but there are great problems in obtaining a common action from sufficient farmers to make it effective.

In many ways using land to control production is anachronistic (Breimyer, 1978). Land costs make up only a small percentage of total inputs to agriculture, even with the recent rapid escalation in land prices. Balance sheets prepared by the USDA (1977b) show that payment on land mortgage debts amounted to only 2.3 per cent of total production expenses in 1960 and this had risen to 4.9 per cent by 1976. In contrast, the costs of feed had stayed at about 17 per cent of total costs and depreciation on farm capital had risen slightly from 16 to 17 per cent of total costs. Fertilizer costs had risen from 5 to 7.5 per cent and fuel costs had also risen, both relatively and absolutely. Breimyer suggests that fuel could be used as a mechanism for production control just as effectively as land.

During the Arab oil embargo, and resulting fuel shortage in the United States, supplies to agriculture were maintained at 100 per cent because of the concurrent world food shortage. Would it not be possible to reduce fuel availability to the agricultural sector in times of food oversupply? High natural gas prices are possibly already limiting the use of natural gas-powered irrigation systems in part of the south-west of the United States. In general, such fuel rationing would effect the large, heavily capitalized farmers more than the small family farm and might therefore be more acceptable to the Jeffersonian supporters in US agricultural policy.

This argument leads logically to a consideration of government payments to farmers based on production costs. In theory this is an ideal method of agricultural support as the payment levels are increased where production costs per unit are high, and reduced elsewhere. The incomes to the agricultural sector can then be made more uniform over the whole range of production conditions from the easy to the marginal. Although land prices, and therefore mortgage costs, will reflect these production conditions we have already seen that they provide only a small part of overall production costs. Such policies are horrendously difficult to formulate and, although tried briefly, have not survived for long. The difficulties lie both in measuring production costs and in ensuring that inefficient producers are not encouraged to the disadvantage of the efficient. To some extent all artificially maintained prices support the inefficient producer and allow the marginal farmer to continue to produce. Gearing payments directly to production costs would probably provide even more protection for the inefficient. In some cases this might be a specific government objective, but it seems unlikely that general government policy will be successfully linked directly to production costs, despite the theoretical attractions of such a policy.

The financial effects of all government policies to support the agricultural sector are funnelled almost exclusively into the value of land (Gaffney, 1965). This was hinted at in the reaction of Major Major's father when he bought more and more land in response to government payments (p.123). A proportion of the government payments are allocated according to the amount of land owned and this, plus the fact that land is the prime asset of agriculture, means that land prices will reflect the level of government support. Thus, when government payments are high, and compensating for falling incomes in agriculture, we will expect to see land prices also holding up or rising. Figure 36 relates the value of farm land per hectare in the United States at 1967 prices to the realized total net income per farmer, also at 1967 prices. Between 1960 and 1965 farm income rose as a result of government payments, and land prices followed the rise closely. From 1966 to 1971 government payments made up a more or less uniform proportion of total farm income, and these incomes fluctuated with high points in 1966 and 1969 and lows in 1967 and 1971. With some lag, land prices halted their rise, even falling slightly to a low in

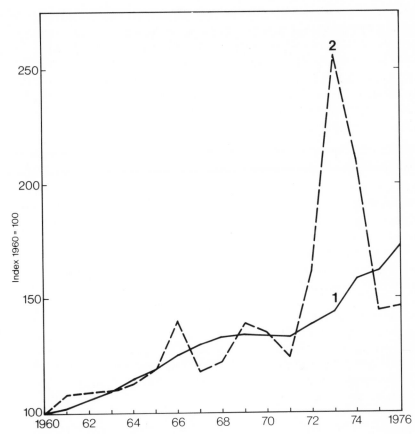

Figure 36. Value of United States farm land and total net income per farm, 1960–76. **1** = value of farm land per hectare (1967 dollars); **2** = total net income per farm (1967 dollars). Source: USDA (1977a)

1971. From 1972 onwards the rise in land values was responding to world prices and greatly increased net incomes rather than to government payments. The steepest rise in land prices occurred between 1973 and 1974, reflecting the sharp rise in net incomes between 1972 and 1973. It is significant that farm land prices in 1975 and 1976 had only reached the level of the trend line established during the period 1961 to 1968. 'As high as farm real estate values have soared they still hardly represent more than a capitisation of the USDA budget, not to mention the $2 million charged to foreign aid that really belongs in the agricultural budget, plus public works charged to the Interior and the Army' (Gaffney, 1965). There are many other factors influencing land prices, but government payments and the contribution that they make to net realized incomes in the farming sector appear to be important.

Not only did most of the government payments benefit the large farmer during the 1960s, but the secondary effects on land values made it increasingly difficult for new entries to the profession without considerable capital investment and borrowing. As land values rose so did the average size of farm and the likelihood of corporate investment in agricultural land. The capital gains from such investment were good and continued to be stimulated by government policies. The size of the required investment made it increasingly difficult for the individual to start farming or to expand an existing operation.

Input Subsidies

Although policies of price support based on production costs have had little success there are a great variety of programmes of government payments subsidizing agricultural inputs. The motivation for such payments is rarely to increase the net margins of farmers but rather to encourage investment and thereby foster change and modernization in agriculture. Such policies, especially in developing countries, are used as a stimulant to agricultural production rather than an income support, although they do also have a net income effect. Policies to encourage change and development in agriculture encompass the provision of credit, fertilizers and other inputs at less than market price, education and agricultural extension services, various encouragements for farm amalgamation, as well as less direct policies such as government encouragement for the formation of co-operatives for purchasing inputs and marketing produce.

As with policies of price support and production limitation, the effects of such actions are not uniformly distributed over the farming population. The more of a particular subsidized input which is used the more the farmer benefits from the subsidy programme. Although input subsidies can be, and often have been, carefully targeted towards particular groups of farmers, the income distributional effects of such policies can be considerable, especially in developing countries. Most of the green revolution can be considered as a government-subsidized investment improving the inputs to agriculture, and increasing food production.

In the developed world a whole range of input subsidies is used. In the United Kingdom over £300 million was spent in 1975–76, or about 17 per cent of the total agricultural budget, on subsidizing inputs. Unlike other major sectors of agricultural expenditure only a small proportion of such moneys (about 6 per cent) was derived from European Economic Community sources (Table 23). The subsidies in the UK relating to cattle could be considered as production rather than inputs, encouraging in that year the conversion to beef production, but they have much the same effect as other input subsidies. In the United States input subsidies made up at least 15 per cent of total agricultural programme expenditure, excluding the costs of education. The total costs of input subsidies of all forms in the US in 1975 was about $1700 million. In New Zealand, a

Table 23. United Kingdom budgetary appropriations for agricultural inputs, 1975–76

Purpose	£ millions		
	Gross amount	Income	Net UK amount
Capital grants	64.29		64.29
Brucellosis eradication	25.47		25.47
Land drainage	14.09		14.09
Farming less favoured areas	17.29	6.04[a]	11.25
Agricultural training	10.66		10.66
Research	31.43		31.43
Advisory services[b]	33.01		33.01
Dairy herd conversion	11.35	4.54[a]	6.81
Calf subsidy	53.26		53.26
Beef subsidy	7.41		7.41
Other services and costs[c]	108.39	20.55[d]	87.84
Total	376.65	31.13	345.52

[a]From European Agricultural Guidance and Guarantee Fund.
[b]The work of Agricultural Development and Advisory Service (ADAS).
[c]Includes administration, vaccine provision, land purchase, etc.
[d]From sales and from the EAGGF.
Source: *UK Budgetary Appropriation Accounts* (1975–76).

country traditionally seen as having a largely unsubsidized agriculture, out of total payments of $NZ189,775 million to agriculture in the 1978–79 budget $NZ115,730 million or 61 per cent were input subsidies of one sort or another. The most important is $NZ89,705 million devoted to fertilizer and lime price, application and transport subsidies.

In contrast, the EEC policies are concentrated on price support and only a very small proportion of expenditure goes for input subsidies and for the restructuring of agriculture. Total EEC agricultural payments are distributed through the European Agricultural Guidance and Guarantee Fund (EAGGF) but 96 per cent is allocated to the price guarantee services. Out of a total budget of 9607 million units of account (UA) in 1977, 6188.7 million, or 64.4 per cent was spent on agriculture. Nearly 5000 million of this was spent by the EAGGF of which only 212 million went for guidance purposes. Between 1964 and 1974 the majority of this guidance expenditure has been allocated to land and water improvements, mainly drainage projects and the amalgamation of scattered holdings of farm land (Table 24). The major share of these payments have been made to Italy, Germany, and France (Table 25). Germany, particularly seems to have received a disproportionate share of this fund in relation to the number of farmers and to the area of agricultural land. However, the crude percentage of the number of farmers and the amount of farm land does not tell the whole story of the need for restructuring in agriculture. With the exception of the much smaller country of Belgium, Italy and Germany

Table 24. EEC agricultural guidance expenditure, 1969–74

Sectors	1975 projects			1964–74 projects		
	No.	Aid[a]	% of aid	No.	Aid[a]	% of aid
Land and water improvement	122	32.5	15.3	1786	491.4	38.9
Milk	61	20.6	9.7	539	189.7	15.0
Vine products	86	36.1	17.0	504	146.1	11.6
Fruit and vegetables	40	13.5	6.3	528	97.4	7.7
Meat	69	31.9	15.0	484	110.2	8.7
Fisheries	112	13.8	6.5	128	33.1	2.6
Cereals	24	7.6	3.6	123	34.6	2.7
Forestry	43	8.2	3.9	132	33.9	2.7
Olives	17	3.8	1.8	165	32.2	2.5
Animal feed	19	6.0	2.8	67	18.8	1.5
Flowers and plants	3	1.3	0.6	38	11.2	0.9
Eggs and poultry	3	0.2	0.1	64	9.4	0.7
Seeds and nurseries	13	2.1	1.0	50	8.6	0.7
Research and information	10	2.6	1.2	38	5.8	0.5
Sugar	—	—	—	2	0.8	0.1
Others	70	32.4	15.2	116	40.5	3.2
Totals	692	212.6	100.0	4704	1263.7	100.0

[a]UA millions.
Source: *Official Journal of the European Communities* (1975).

have the highest ratio of farmers to farm land which does indicate a larger need for guidance expenditure than in, for example, the United Kingdom. The data for Britain, Ireland, and Denmark are not strictly comparable with those for the original six members of the EEC because of their later membership.

Table 25. National shares of the EEC guidance funds, 1964–75

Country	Payments ('000 UA)[a]	% of payments	% of farmers in EEC (1975)	% of farm land in EEC (1975)
Italy	471,773	31.7	38.1	19.0
Germany	376,538	25.3	18.9	14.2
France	303,104	20.4	24.4	33.6
Holland	106,069	7.1	3.5	2.4
Belgium	96,233	6.5	2.3	1.7
Britain	72,891	4.9	5.5	20.2
Ireland	29,767	2.0	4.7	5.3
Denmark	23,531	1.6	2.5	3.3
Luxembourg	6,349	0.4	0.1	0.2
Total	1,486,255	100.0	100.0	100.0

[a]UA = units of account.
Source: *Official Journal of the European Communities* (1975); *The Economist* (28 January 1977).

Input Subsidies for the Green Revolution

In the developing world the largest input subsidy of all has been the green revolution. The technological development of the new seeds which formed the basis of this revolution has been effectively free to the farmers of the developing countries using the seeds (Falcon, 1970). The continuing work of the International Rice Research Institute (IRRI), and other such centres for crop research, is providing more plant varieties to suit particular circumstances. The results of such work are being passed to developing countries and thence to their producers at little real cost. In most developing countries, with farmers retaining a proportion of their production to provide the seeds for the following season's crop, once the first years of production of the high-yielding varieties are over these new varieties are no more expensive than the traditional varieties. The early years of production are usually subsidized through governments and/or through international aid. In addition, the inputs of irrigation and fertilizer necessary for the successful cultivation of the new varieties have usually been heavily subsidized. In fact, although we concluded in the previous chapter that most developing countries have adopted policies of consumer protection through maintaining low prices for basic foods, producers have been helped through extensive input subsidies. The FAO (1974b) has produced an incomplete tabulation of countries according to the extent of government fertilizer subsidy. All countries listed as providing more than a 47.5 per cent subsidy are developing countries. In the developed world high subsidies on superphosphates in New Zealand are reflected in high fertilizer application rates (Figure 6). Subsidies for fertilizer are also high in many centrally planned economies, especially Hungary. Given the well-established relationships between fertilizer application and rice yields, and between rice prices and fertilizer use (Timmer, 1974), fertilizer subsidies in rice-growing developing countries should be particularly effective in both stimulating overall rice production and raising farm incomes. It has been estimated that if only half the recommended dosage of fertilizer were used on half the rice lands of Bangladesh the country would be self-sufficient in regard to its staple foods without any other developments in irrigation, HYV seeds or other inputs (FAO, 1977b). Fertilizer use in Bangladesh is close to being the lowest among all the rice-growing economies. Taking into account double and triple cropping, in 1976–77 fertilizer use was 512,586 tons applied to a total cropped area of 30,441 million acres (Government of Bangladesh, 1978b), or 41.5 kg/ha. Such average figures are of little significance, however, as they include large areas to which no fertilizers are applied.

With such low application rates the yield response to additional fertilizer use can be expected to be high. Bangladesh as a whole is towards the bottom of a fertilizer response curve where significant gains will accrue from both the application of more fertilizer to land on which some is already used, and also from the application of fertilizer to land for the first time. A general input/output relationship for fertilizer to food grains is estimated as 1 : 4.00 (Government of Bangladesh, 1978c). The World Bank estimates 1 : 3.5 and Ahmed (1977):

1 : 3.3 for Boro rice (HYV and traditional varieties aggregated)
1 : 3.24 for Aman   (HYV and traditional varieties aggregated)
1 : 3.05 for Aus   (HYV and traditional varieties aggregated)

Taking the ratio as 1 : 3.5 the increase in fertilizer use from 513,000 tons in 1976–77 to approximately 700,000 in 1977–78 should, had it all been applied to food grains, have increased food-grain production by 654,500 tons. In fact actual production increased by 1.5 million tons, a substantial proportion of which can be attributed to increased fertilizer use.

There are three areas for government action regarding the provision of fertilizer in Bangladesh: supply, subsidy and distribution. Domestic manufacture falls well short of meeting domestic demand. The FAO (1977b) estimate that between 1977–78 and 1985–86 total import demand will be for 160,000 tons of urea and 2 million tons of TSP and MP. Such estimations assume that there will be no repetition of the recent breakdowns of the Bangladesh urea plants. Although between 80 and 85 per cent of imports have been grant-aided in recent years, incurring only transportation and distribution costs in Bangladesh, continued imports of fertilizers will require substantial foreign exchange allocations and continued efforts to persuade donors to change from food aid to fertilizer aid as food production in Bangladesh increases. Such a transfer will not be easy when major donor countries have surplus food supplies to dispose of. Fertilizer surplus is not as politically sensitive as wheat surplus. Bangladesh could be self-sufficient in urea by 1985, but with a deficit emerging after that. There is no realistic prospect of TSP and MP manufacturing capability in Bangladesh to meet the projected demand.

Fertilizers have long been sold at below world market prices in Bangladesh, and recently the cost of this subsidy has been of concern to the government. As the use of fertilizers has increased so also has the cost of the subsidy. In 1962–63 the cost was 17.6 million taka and a recent study (Economist Intelligence Unit, 1977) estimates that this had grown to 520.0 million taka by 1975–76. The Ministry of Agriculture calculates that, even with the fertilizer price rises proposed for 1978–79, the costs of the subsidy will be 1082.1 million taka with a consumption of 750,000 tons. The current two-year development plan for Bangladesh talks of huge amounts of money being incurred by the government in order to subsidize agriculture. The situation is not that simple, however. The FAO study (1977b) concludes that the subsidy is more than returned through the increased food grain produced. While that conclusion is correct for the value of the increased grain production, in terms of government expenditure the position is made more complicated by the receipt, and subsequent sale through the ration system, of food aid. In the short term, ignoring the ultimate repayment of food aid credits, government expenditure will be increased for fertilizers and revenue decreased by the reduced need for food aid and its sale through the ration system. Furthermore, the increased production may lead to increased pressure for domestic procurement and additional government costs. A final complication is that a substantial proportion of the fertilizer consumption is met by imports, 85 per cent of which are received as grant aid, the Bangladesh government incurring only transportation, storage and distribution costs. Thus, for some 60 per cent of the fertilizer sold in Bangladesh the government costs are close to zero and there is a net revenue to the government exchequer from the rural sector amounting to the sale price of this fertilizer. The subsidy on this grant-aided fertilizer turns out to be the opportunity cost of the difference between the market and the subsidized price. Interestingly, there is no hesitation in discussing the ration distribution of food at less than market price as a direct subsidy to consumers, even though the major proportion of the ration offtake is acquired from food aid shipments, the real costs of which are less than the ration selling price. Again the subsidy is the opportunity cost of the revenue lost as a result of government sales at less than the market price.

The third policy area concerns the method of distribution of fertilizer. At present the responsibility for importation and wholesale distribution of fertilizers rests with the Bangladesh Agricultural Development Corporation (BADC). Retailing is organized through a series of licensed retailers who collect from BADC warehouses and sell at a regulated price to farmers. Dealers are allowed a margin or discount per maund depending on the distance between the thana warehouse and the dealer's operation. These discounts have been changed from time to time to provide dealer incentives to increase sales. In times of supply shortage, buoyant demand for fertilizers will encourage sales by dealers at well above the controlled price, limiting the available supply to the relatively wealthy large farmers who have sufficient cash or collateral for credit. Opening up the fertilizer trade to the private sector, coupled with improved supply to establish a free market price by competition, would help transfer the element of government subsidy in the fertilizer price to the farmers rather than to the dealers (FAO, 1977b).

An experimental scheme was started in Chittagong District in September 1978 under which the BADC will sell only from primary distribution points, mainly the port and the urea plant, except in the remote thanas which the BADC expect the private sector will not adjust serve adequately. The BADC will not sell from local warehouses unless the market price rises significantly above the BADC established retail price. The resale price will be unrestricted up to the BADC-administered retail price and anyone will be able to buy from the BADC—the system of licensing retailers is to be stopped. Attempts will be made to provide credit for the fertilizer dealers through the commercial sector and government. It is recognized that this scheme will only work if the supply is adequate to meet demand, both at the primary distribution points and at the village level. If the experiment is successful it will be expanded to cover the rest of the country.

No realistic assessment is possible of the extent of the overall subsidy provided by national governments and the international community, which are part of the green revolution, but the rapidity with which the technology has spread in many parts of the developing world provides an indication of its magnitude. Within six years of the adoption of high-yield varieties of wheat in India, 7.5 million ha were planted to these varieties, 39 per cent of the total wheat area (Vyas, 1975). By the mid 1970s 21 million ha of the high-yield varieties of rice were planted throughout the developing world and only a slightly less total area to the high-yield variety wheats. This was little more than ten years after the initial developments in Mexico. A pessimistic estimate would be that in 1975 the increased world production of cereals, as a result of high-yield variety seeds planted in developing countries, was about 20 million tons, close to the level of grain imports to the developing countries in that year.

At a basic level the subsidized inputs could be said to have been very successful in their main objective of raising agricultural production. Even allowing for weather fluctuations the increased yields were highly significant allowing, for example, Mexico to become a net exporter of grains between 1965 and 1969 (Brown, 1975). Just as with the impact of United States government policies, however, these aggregate data hide significant differences in the effects of the policies on different sectors of the farming population and between different regions in the developing countries. The differences depended largely on the suitability of areas for the new technology (Perrin and Winkelmann, 1976), and on the ability of farmers to adopt the new techniques. We have seen that the United States' policies concentrated the benefits on to the larger farmers. The concentration of the green revolution technology on large farmers was probably even more marked and potentially of even greater significance.

After the early euphoria with the green revolution many writers have expressed reservations about the income distributional effects of the changes (for example: Falcon, 1970; Wade, 1974; Perelman, 1976). Only the main points of such reservations will be covered here; the differential adoption and use of irrigation, fertilizer, and the new seeds by different farming groups and in different regions, to assess the effects of the government policies beyond the aggregate level.

High-Yield Variety Seed Adoption and Use

There is little doubt that high-yield variety seeds were first adopted by the large farmers. They had the capital, the ability to take the necessary risks with a new and untried crop; they were the ones who stood to gain the most from the adoption and they were the ones which the government advisers and extension workers could reach most easily. In addition, the larger farmers had better access to market information. A great deal of evidence to substantiate this is now available from India (Lockwood *et al.*, 1971; Vyas, 1975) and from Latim America (Colmenares, 1975). In Indian states, especially the Punjab, where adoption of the new seeds and techniques was particularly profitable, the smaller farmers quickly caught up with the larger farmers and soon the adoption was more or less total (Table 26). Elsewhere the differences of adoption between the large and the small farms are still evident. In a survey of 188 pure stand maize growers in lowland Columbia in 1972 only 17.4 per cent of the small farms (with less than 2 ha cultivated) had adopted hybrid maize, against 85.1 per cent of the large farmers with over 10 ha of land cultivated (Colmenares, 1975). Not only did the large farmers in developing countries adopt the high-yielding variety seeds more readily but they did so on proportionately larger areas (Schulter, 1971). Finally, in addition to earlier adoption and adoption on a larger proportion of their total farm area, the large farmers obtained a better yield from the HYV seeds planted, at least in India during the early years of the green revolution (Table 27a). In the case of traditional crops almost universally the reverse has been found to be true with yields per hectare being larger, often considerably so, on the smaller farms where intensive use of family labour ensures a high level of care for the crop through all stages from ground preparation to harvesting (Table 27b). The case of Indian high-yield variety wheats reflects a declining importance of labour in relation to other factors of production. The large farmers had better access to other resources necessary for the successful production of the new varieties, particularly to fertilizer, irrigation water, and to expert advice. On the other hand, the case of rice production in Bangladesh shows a different pattern with yields for the new varieties following the pattern of yields for the traditional varieties in being larger on the smaller farms. The percentage of land devoted to HYV certainly rises with farm size but the yields decline. This suggests that access to fertilizer and to irrigation helps to control the area planted to HYV seeds, but that where these are available to the small farmer his yields can be very high.

Proper water control is vital for the successful production of the wheats and rices. Again it is the larger farmers who have best and most reliable access to irrigation water. This is the result of both the relatively large area irrigated under most modern methods and the difficulties of obtaining satisfactory co-operation between small farmers to divide irrigation water. Thus, in the Punjab the command area of a tube well is about 10 ha, close to the ideal size of farm for the irrigated production of HYV wheat under local conditions (Vyas, 1975). Although this problem is less acute where large-scale surface-water projects are well managed, or where small-scale

142

Table 26. Early adoption of HYV wheat in India

Name of study/area	Year	Size group	% of HYV adopters	
1. Bihar	1967–68 (Rabi)	Below 2.5 acres	42	
		2.5–5	67	
		5–10	62	
		10–20	89	
		20–50	100	
		50 and above	100	
		Total		59
2. Haryana	1967–68 (Rabi)	Below 2.5 acres	0	
		2.5–5	4	
		5–10	6	
		10–20	13	
		20–50	28	
		50 and above	31	
		Total		16
3. Punjab	1967–68 (Rabi)	Below 2.5 acres	58	
		2.5–5	68	
		5–10	66	
		10–20	85	
		20–50	92	
		50 and above	100	
		Total		80
4. Rajasthan	1967–68 (Rabi)	Below 2.5 acres	0	
		2.5–5	12	
		5–10	4	
		10–20	20	
		20–50	43	
		50 and above	51	
		Total		30
5. Uttar Pradesh	1967–68 (Rabi)	Below 2.5 acres	25	
		2.5–5	36	
		5–10	41	
		10–20	65	
		20–50	75	
		50 and above	62	
		Total		42
6. All states	1967–68 (Rabi)	Below 2.5 acres	27	
		2.5–5	36	
		5–10	38	
		10–20	53	
		20–50	51	
		50 and above	47	
		Total		43

Source: Planning Commission (PEO) (1968).

Table 27. Yields of traditional and HYV rice and wheat on different farm sizes: India and Bangladesh

(a) Indian studies

Size groups	Yield HYV wheats (quintals per hectare)	
	1967–68	1968–69
<2.5 acres	23.64	22.90
2.5–4.9	22.70	19.27
5–9.9	23.91	20.08
10–19.9	24.72	25.19
20–49.9	28.21	25.74
>50	31.10	26.26

Source: Vyas (1975). (Original units of the study have been maintained.)

(b) Bangladesh studies

Size groups (ha)		Area planted to TV rice (ha)	Area planted to HYV rice (ha)	Yield TV rice (kg/ha)	Yield HYV rice (kg/ha)
0–1.61	(a)	0.89	0.20	392.3	724.3
	(b)	0.69	0.08	362.2	754.5
1.62–4.04	(a)	1.86	0.49	422.5	664.0
	(b)	2.02	0.32	256.5	377.3
>4	(a)	4.74	5.99	377.3	588.5
	(b)	4.62	0.81	332.0	452.7

(a) = Study area Sulla Thana; (b) = study area Nalchiti Thana.
Source: Government of Bangladesh (1978a).

traditional irrigation methods based on surface water are available, the percentage of irrigated land still rises with size of farm. Even where most irrigation remains based on traditional methods as in Bangladesh (Table 28) this involves much labour. Hired labour is most readily available to the larger farmers who can pay either in cash or in food.

The importance of access to both credit and to advisory services is shown by Table 29. The smaller farmers in Colombia received little credit, less visits from extension workers, and had a much lower percentage adoption of both fertilizers and hybrid seeds. The provision of credit alone is more successful in leading to adoption of fertilizers, while visits are more successful in leading to the adoption of new seed varieties. However, access to credit and advice are obviously not the only criteria as the success rate for both these factors is lower for the small farmers than for the large. In 78 per cent of the visits to small farmers no adoption resulted. Either

Table 28. Net irrigated area by source, 1977 estimates:
Bangladesh

	Area ('000 ha)	%
Traditional methods		
Dhone	437	43
Swing bucket	49	5
Dug well	4	—
Total	490	48
'Modern' methods		
Hand pumps	10	1
Shallow tube well	28	3
Deep tube well	54	5
Low lift surface water pump	406	39
Large-scale canals	40	4
Total	538	52
TOTAL	1028	100

Source: Edwards *et al*. (1978).

Table 29. Services to farmers and adoption of fertilizers and hybrid seeds among Colombian maize growers

Size	Farmers receiving	% farmers	No. of farmers	% Adopting			
				None	Fertilizers	Hybrids	Both
Small	None	82	242	84.3	7.4	6.2	2.1
0–2 ha	Credit only	2	7	—	42.9	—	57.1
	Visits only	12	36	77.8	—	22.2	—
	Both	3	10	—	40.0	30.0	30.0
	Totals		295	78.6	8.5	8.8	4.1
Medium	None	71	84	83.3	—	13.1	3.6
2.1–9.9 ha	Credit only	5	6	—	50.0	33.3	16.7
	Visits only	17	20	50.0	15.0	30.0	5.0
	Both	7	8	—	—	25.0	75.0
	Totals		118	67.8	5.1	17.8	9.3
Large	None	47	40	47.5	5.0	25.0	22.5
10+ ha	Credit only	9	8	—	12.5	—	87.5
	Visits only	21	18	11.1	11.1	33.3	44.4
	Both	23	20	—	—	—	100.0
	Totals		86	24.4	5.8	18.6	51.2

Source: Colmenares (1975).

Table 30. Use of fertilizer and rice marketing by size of farm: Bangladesh

Size	% of total fertilizer used[a]	% of cultivated land[a]	% of marketed rice[b]
Small (0–0.83 ha)	33.62	23.30	7.0
Medium (0.84–2.08 ha)	24.31	25.64	11.0
Large (2.09+ ha)	42.07	51.06	82.0

Sources:
[a]Bureau of Statistics. *Master Survey of Agriculture*, Seventh round, Phase II, 1967–68, Dacca.
[b]Agricultural Marketing Directorate, Dacca.

the nature of the visits was different or less effective, or as is more likely, the small farmers had a higher resistance to the changes the new technology involved possibly because of a greater aversion to risks.

In general, the use of fertilizer in developing countries appears to be more uniformly spread over different sizes of farms than are many other inputs. For example, in Bangladesh the use of fertilizer is more uniformly distributed than is the resulting commercial sale of rice and paddy (Table 30). Thus the subsidized fertilizer policy adopted in that country is a more successful way of reaching the small farmers who market only a tiny fraction of their production and who are not much affected by any price support policy. The proportion of total expenditure in small Indian farms (Table 31) spent on fertilizers is much higher than in the large farms. In general, however, it is not a lack of incentive which keeps down production of the new HYV paddy on small farms so much as a lack of access to the necessary factors of production. Land is very unequally divided, in Bangladesh 57 per cent of the population live on 9 per cent of the farm land. Also, access to water and to fertilizer is unbalanced in favour of the

Table 31. Total cash expenditure and expenditure on fertilizers by size of farm, 1967–68, POE study, India

Size group (acres)	Total expenses		Fertilizers	
	HY holding[a]	Other holding (Rupees/acre)	HY holding[a]	Other holding
Less than 2.5	202	28	82	11
2.5–5	215	24	66	7
5–10	227	33	83	9
10–20	215	28	82	7
20–50	270	36	102	9
50 and above	281	45	111	10
All farmers	244	34	92	8

[a]Holding growing HYVs.
Source: Vyas (1975).

large farms. In the case of fertilizer, with a heavy government subsidy, it is not the price but limited supplies which favour the large farmers. Supplies of fertilizer have remained short for many years and have only been widely available to the large farmers with both the transport facilities to reach the scattered government-controlled distribution centres and the influence and possibly the money with which to bribe the distribution agents. In an attempt to provide an element of competition within the fertilizer trade, there have been moves to open up the fertilizer trade to private commerce.

Although fertilizer and seeds are almost totally divisible and there is no minimum size of farm for their successful use, there remain significant differences between the adoption of the green revolution technology by large and by small farmers. These differences are emphasized where irrigation is necessary because of the difficulty of scaling the technology down to the smallest size of farm.

The general proposition behind studies of the diffusion and adoption of new agricultural technologies is that the large farmers adopt the innovation first, but that the small are not far behind as the risks are easily assessed from the experience of the large. In fact, however, in many developing countries the first adopters tend to be the medium-sized farmers. The small ones are not able to innovate and the largest do not have the necessary commercial interest in maximizing profits since ownership of land not food production is the key to social standing. The catching up of the small farmers may be prevented by structural changes in the pattern of land tenure and ownership in favour of those farmers first adopting the technological developments. Thus, although studies in the Punjab do show almost total adoption of high-yield variety wheats after a very few years, at the same time other changes were taking place, particularly an increase in the number of large farmers, so at least some of the progress in adoption must be put down to the demise of the small farmer rather than his adoption of the new technology. Rudra (1971) shows that between 1955–56 and 1967–68 farms between 40 and 60 ha increased their total land by 38 per cent, mostly through acquisition, while farms between 8 and 10 ha increased in land area by only 0.4 per cent. Although this process was under way before the green revolution reached India it was hastened by the arrival of the new seeds and related technology. Byres (1972) quotes many studies which show that not only did the operational size of holdings increase in India but that the tenurial system also changed. This was a change from a feudal sharecropping system to a commercial system where the number of tenants declined (from 583,000 to 80,000 between 1955 and 1964 in the Punjab) and those tenants that remained became cash-paying rather than sharecropping. Where landlords started to operate their own land they employed labourers, but as we shall see in the following section, the labourers were probably fewer in number than the previous tenants.

The green revolution has had significantly different effects in different

Table 32. Adoption of hybrid maize in Colombia

Zone (elevation)	Total farmers surveyed	No. adopting hybrids	% adopting hybrids	Average farm size (ha)
1. 0–1099 m	256	93	36.3	24.3
2. 1100–1799 m	234	41	17.5	16.8
3. 1800+ m	248	16	6.5	2.5

Source: Colmenares (1975).

regions and in different countries, depending on suitability for the production of the new seeds. In South Asia the early development of HYV wheat led to differences in production between the two wings of Pakistan (Figure 7), and between wheat- and rice-growing areas of India. The lack of high-yielding varieties of deep-water rice means that large areas of Bangladesh are not able to take advantage of the green revolution. In Colombia the suitability of the flat lowlands for hybrid maize cultivation shows up in the different adoption rates of the hybrids in the different zones (Table 32). The position is complicated by the multi-collinearity between the physical suitability of the area for the hybrid seeds, average farm size, access to extension services, access to markets and other factors. For whatever reasons, regional and national differences exist alongside differences between different farm sizes. These differences provide one reason for supporting grain prices above the level suggested by increased supply stimulated by the green revolution. The government of Pakistan spent more than $75 million supporting the price of wheat, partly in order to protect the farmers in rainfed areas of the country unable to partake in the green revolution changes (Falcon, 1970).

In developing countries in general, government payments that subsidize inputs to agriculture go primarily to those farmers already advantaged through having access to larger shares of the factors of production, particularly land. By so directing government payments these recipients are further advantaged.

Infrastructure

In the less developed countries investment in rural transport, marketing and storage facilities can also be considered as financial support to agriculture. Investment in rural transport may have many objectives, among which are internal and external security, access for government officials, eased tax collection and many others. Also rural road construction has been used to employ people under food for work projects (Chapter 8). Such projects, along with irrigation and drainage schemes and flood protection, can be designed to use large amounts of labour with very little capital investment. Despite these numerous objectives the principal beneficiaries of rural transport improvement will be both the farmers marketing produce and the traders.

The case for improving rural transport in many developing countries appears to be foolproof. There is much talk, and some evidence, of seasonal bottlenecks in the movement of farm produce to market after harvest, with resulting lower prices to producers and wastage in extreme cases. The poor access to many rural areas is supposed to give rise to large price gradients between producers and final markets and to the exploitation of producers by traders because of the poor flow of market information. Investment in the improvement of rural roads should therefore benefit producers by reducing blockages in the transport system, decreasing seasonal gluts and increasing prices, and benefit consumers by facilitating the regular supply of food from rural areas.

There are considerable doubts about each of these reasons for investment in rural transport. Firstly, many studies have shown that the price gradients between the producers and the consumers are not excessive (Lele, 1976). This question has already been examined (Chapter 3) and some of the possible reasons for low producer prices have been listed. Rural transport does not seem to be a generally significant factor. There are certain local exceptions, especially where the produce is highly perishable. The marketing margins for pineapples grown in Bangladesh may exceed 100 per cent because of transportation difficulties and the short shelf life of pineapples in the monsoon season (Tropical Products Institute, 1976; Government of Bangladesh, 1978a). For most crops, although transport improvements would speed their movement from rural areas to the major urban markets, speed itself is not essential and there are doubts about who would benefit from such improvements.

In South Asia much of the marketing of food produce is not the result of an overall surplus of production. Aggregate national statistics of food production less consumption equalling marketable surplus are confusing (Clarke and Turner, 1977); the qualtities actually marketed will exceed this calculated figure as production is sold after harvest to raise cash to repay debts and the same type of produce is then bought later in the year to feed the family (Chapter 3). The result of this return trading is that the rural transport networks are overloaded with local transactions (Figure 37). In such circumstances, government investment in factors to diminish this double trading of food produce would be an effective alternative to investment in rural transport (OECD, 1976b). The provision of storage at village and farm level (Greeley, 1978) and the availability of credit to both the small and the large farmers, could eliminate as much as 60 per cent of the present movement of food grains along rural transport routes. This released potential would then be available for any increased marketable surplus which will result from the adoption of the green revolution technology.

Figure 37. Marketing movements in Nalchiti Thana, Bangladesh. These are estimated proportions of total annual movements based on sample surveys of traders, purchasers and sellers at a representative sample of markets in the thana. 1 = local buyers some of whom are farmers. Source: Government of Bangladesh (1978a)

Furthermore, such investment would, if properly managed with suitable safeguards, not add to the advantages of the large farmers. On the contrary, it is highly probable that the improvement of rural roads and waterways will benefit only the large farmers and the commercial traders. The reason for this is simple. Without vehicles available to the small farmer the improvement of roads and canals is of little significance. The small Bangladeshi farmer will continue to walk, even if he is walking along a surfaced road suitable for trucks. In the estuarine areas of southern Bangladesh, where almost all transport is on foot or by boat, the straightening of channels will benefit only those with boats. The distribution of vehicles is not equal between farms of different sizes. In one study only 36 per cent of farmers with less than 1.6 ha of land owned boats, while over 70 per cent of those cultivating over 4 ha did so. Such contrasts were even more marked in other areas (Government of Bangladesh, 1978a). The large farmer will move his produce more cheaply to market, and indeed he may now be able to skip the lowest level of market, move up the market hierarchy, and obtain a higher price for his produce. In contrast, the great majority of farmers, with small quantities available for sale and with no transport vehicles will remain dependent on the small local markets. With more distant markets now accessible to a proportion of the large farmers, the local markets will decline in importance. The small farmer will be dependent increasingly on the itinerant trader at his farm gate and a reduced number of traders at the local market.

It can be argued that the traders' costs will have been reduced as a result of the improved transport and these reduced costs will be transferred to the small producers. But there are circumstances where the trade/producer relationships are not truly competitive. (p.55). The decrease in the local marketing as the large farmers move to higher order markets will reduce this competitiveness still further. We see the same patterns with rising mobility in rural areas of the United Kingdom and the United States over the last thirty years. Those without cars are dependent on declining local services for which they pay significantly higher prices.

The general tendency for roads to absorb the bulk of the funds made available for public works, when there are potentially much more productive uses available in agriculture, is in many cases explained not only by the ease with which road construction can be undertaken at short notice but also by the fact that such investment does not generally bring into sharp focus some of the difficult issues which the selection and implementation of schemes affecting agricultural land directly would almost inevitably raise. Moreover, road construction is such a contractor-oriented type of public works that, where decisions of this nature are dominated by considerations of political patronage and administrative corruption, it becomes the preferred investment even when it cannot be justified on any economic grounds at all. (U.N. Dept. of Economics and Social Affairs, 1975).

The benefits of road improvement are reflected in the raised land values of the farms alongside the road and the benefits so measured will be greater for farmers with larger holdings and a higher proportion of marketed output. Overall, government investment in infrastructure improvement, especially rural road construction, will have the same effects of benefiting large farmers more than small. Whereas this may be considered a desirable economic goal in developed countries, it is certainly not the case where the enormous majority of farms in a country are small. Road improvement, in common with most other forms of government action in agriculture, without parallel attempts to allocate rural resources more equitably will lead to land amalgamation and to an increasing proportion of landless people.

Mechanization

Government-subsidized inputs to agriculture in the developing world do not only affect the relative economic strengths of the large and small farmers but also the relative strengths of the farmers and the agricultural workers. This may be something of a false distinction in some countries where farmers are unable to produce enough on their own land and land they may rent to feed their families. The farmer and members of his family may then hire out their labour to neighbouring large farmers. Small farmers are often, therefore, both farmers and labourers (Abercrombie, 1975). In Bangladesh about 30 per cent of the population are classified as landless labourers, a section of the population which is growing fast as a result of both demographic and economic forces. The annual growth rate of the agricultural labour force in developing countries has risen from 0.9 per cent per year in the 1950s to 1.1 per cent in the 1970s. Although this change in growth rate may not seem large, the number of people involved is enormous. It results from the overall growth of the population and from the very limited growth of non-agricultural employment. As this section of the population is usually the poorest and the least educated the growth rate is faster than for other sections of the population. A very substantial proportion of this agricultural labour force is, at least seasonally, unemployed or under-employed. The proportion of the population which is landless is growing due to demographic reasons, because of the demise of the tenant farmer in favour of the hired labourer, and as a result of the amalgamation of farms into larger units.

There is disagreement over whether the consequences of government intervention linked to the green revolution have tended to increase or to decrease demand for agricultural labour. There are factors which encourage and factors which discourage the use of agricultural labour, and which group of factors becomes dominant in any one situation depends on the structure of the rural institutions and the orientation of government services to farmers (Abercrombie, 1975). At least in the short term changes in agricultural techniques attendant upon the green revolution increase the demand for farm labour. The most significant reason for this is that the use of irrigation has often allowed the production of an extra crop or even two extra crops, and therefore the labour demand has increased at times of the year when it was previously low. The extra crop or crops also increases the labour demand in transport, storage, milling, and distribution. Even where extra crops have not been made possible, the yields resulting from the use of the new high-yield variety seeds with fertilizers and improved methods of cultivation have led to greatly increased production, and the bulk of this increase reaches commercial markets. The actual production process needs more labour for such activities as seed-bed preparation, fertilizer application and weeding (as the weeds are just as encouraged by the new cultivation practices as is the grain), irrigation pumping, water control and harvesting. It might be thought from the foregoing that by encouraging the green revolution governments might be helping to increase the growing problem of rural unemployment and the drift of the rural destitute to towns and cities where employment opportunities usually turn out to be illusory.

Unfortunately, there is another side to the coin. Many of the factors stimulating labour demand become, in the right circumstances, a stimulation for farm mechanization and hence lead to a reduction in labour demand. Where multiple cropping is possible speed is of the essence in preparation of the ground and planting of each crop. Similarly, the harvest must be quickly accomplished to clear the ground for the next crop. So, although the total labour demand may increase, it is needed for short intensive periods. Where only one crop is grown the seasonality of the farm labour demand is most acute. This may lead to labour shortage at peak times, despite generally high levels of rural unemployment. Many agricultural labourers have small plots of land of their own and will be needing to harvest on their own land at more or less the same time as they are most needed for the harvest of others. Such seasonal shortage will raise the price of labour. Shortage at peak seasons, plus the increased costs of labour, will encourage mechanization of farms.

There may be other incentives for mechanization. The prestige provided by tractor ownership, the freedom from a seasonal search for labour and from other labour troubles may be sufficient incentive even where mechanization is not economically viable (Rudra, 1971). Mechanization also frees land from fodder production for draught animals. [The effects of this process on food-grain production in the United States was dramatic (Chapter 2).] With increased yields an expansion of food-grain producing land is an attractive proposition. But the loss of animals has other consequences, particularly an increased reliance on usually imported chemical fertilizers, and in countries where firewood is in short supply and hence where dried animal dung is the principal source of energy, a reduction in fuel for cooking (Eckholm, 1975).

Government fiscal policies may actively encourage mechanization. In the early stages there are likely to be few tariff barriers against the import of agricultural machinery. Later the manufacturing companies may be encouraged to establish assembly and ultimately manufacturing plants in the developing countries. Such infant industry will usually operate with active government encouragement, subsidy and tariff protection. Government-sponsored schemes for the provision of rural credit, especially as these generally favour the larger farmers whose land makes suitable collateral for the loans, may encourage the purchase of machinery at low real prices. Production of tractors in one developing country may even be 'dumped' in another to protect the home production (Byres, 1972).

The effects of farm mechanization is to create the need for a small, skilled labour force to use and maintain the equipment. Thus, employment for a privileged few may be gained at the expense of unemployment for the majority. Some employment will be created in the maintenance and possibly the manufacture of machinery, but experience suggests that this will be small. Tractor manufacture employs few people (Abercrombie, 1975). The following simple calculation illustrates how these two opposite pulls on employment work:

Examination of a 10-acre well-irrigated farm in Punjab, with typical cropping pattern and using traditional technology including the Persian wheel as means of irrigation, shows that on an average demand for labour per acre is 51 man-days. With the use of HYV in conjunction with other inputs such as fertilizers, pesticides, etc., the demand increases to 60.1 man-days, resulting from higher yields and inputs. But when we introduce a pump-set, a wheat thresher, a corn sheller, a power cane crusher, a tractor and a wheat reaper, without any change in cropping, the average demand for labour goes down to 25.6 days, i.e. by about 57 per cent. This loss, however, is offset to a large degree by the additional labour required, for the increase in cropping intensity (Billings and Singh, 1969).

However, the farm size structure and government incentives have to be right for the changes coming with the green revolution to lead to a reduction in labour demand. When farm sizes are generally small, mechanization will make little headway unless either technology provides machines appropriate for smallholdings or substantial farm amalgamation takes place (Singh, 1976). At least one study of an area of predominantly small farms shows that both animal and human labour demands are higher on modernized farms (Table 33). In the Punjab, with much larger farms, mechanization has increased fast, but in so doing it has increased both productivity of hired labour and demand (Roy and Blase, 1978). Elsewhere in India where conditions are less suitable (for example irrigated land is a smaller proportion of cultivated land) and providing government incentives are available to the farmer through cheap credit, and to manufacturing industry through tariff policies and subsidies, mechanization will displace substantial quantities of rural labour.

If employment opportunities are substantially reduced then the green revolution may become partly self-defeating. A continued increase in food production is not really the major problem in many developing countries. India in 1976, 1977 and 1978 had considerable stocks of grain (16 million tons before the 1978 harvests) after three successive good production years. Imports were reduced to zero and in certain special circumstances India began exporting food grains. Despite this there was still widespread malnutrition and yet further improvements in production would have done little to remove this. No matter how much food is produced it will have little effect on those who are unable to afford to buy it. By increasing the landless classes and increasing the unemployment in those classes, the green revolution may reduce the demand for food through increasing rural poverty. Thus, as prices fall with increased production and limited effective

Table 33. Animal and human labour needs[a] on traditional and modernized farms in eastern Uttar Pradesh

| | Modernized farms | | | | Traditional farms | | | |
| | Human labour | | Bullock labour | | Human labour | | Bullock labour | |
Farm size	On net area	On gross area	On net area	On gross area	On net area	On gross area	On net area	On gross area
Small	98.36	54.67	30.55	16.98	89.10	53.86	32.26	19.50
Medium	88.60	49.44	26.02	14.52	70.76	49.90	24.58	17.27
Large	87.60	45.65	21.52	11.21	54.87	42.24	18.41	14.17
All farms	88.94	47.61	23.53	12.54	62.21	45.47	21.32	15.61

[a]Days per acre.
Source: Singh (1976).

demand, the incentives for the producers to adopt the new technology also decline. Of course the green revolution changes have not *caused* the increased rural income disparities, these result from the social structure of rural areas which concentrates land and influence in the hands of a few. Government policies have emphasized these disparities.

Rural employment has not only to be maintained but also increased sharply to keep pace with the increasing size of the rural labour force. One way of increasing rural employment and agricultural production in the developing countries is through reallocation of the resources of production, particularly land. Given the political difficulties of any such reallocation, short of some type of revolution, it is tempting to concentrate only on the aspect of the problem which concerns the food gap between production and consumption demands, assuming some ideal consumption rate per capita. Theoretically, by the 1980s these gaps should be very large for many developing countries (IFPRI, 1977a) and must be filled largely by increased home production. Domestic food grain production can best be stimulated in the short-term by a concentration of government aid on the large farmers who are well equipped to make the necessary changes and investments. It is hoped that this increased production will stimulate demand for other goods and services, machinery, fertilizer, consumer goods, etc. which will stimulate other sectors of the economy and provide employment not only for those displaced from agriculture but also for the growing rural population (Mellor, 1976). The enormous number of such people presents severe problem for the operation of such a development process and to this must be added the generally low labour demand of modern manufacturing industry. With few actual examples to quote, the best overall development policy for the agricultural sector, or for the economy, of a developing country remains more a matter of ideology than economics.

Government policies which concentrate on large farmers and displace a rural labour force are perhaps justifiable and acceptable in developed economies where the agricultural sector is relatively small. The same cannot be said so readily for the developing countries, especially those with a large number of small farmers. Although large farmers may be better able to raise the necessary food production in the short term, the solution to the apparent conflict between growth and equity lies with policies of aid to small farmers. With equal access to resources, the yields of the small farmer are higher so the economic benefits of a more equitable policy will ultimately be larger. Unfortunately, where supply is limited and various key inputs (e.g. fertilizer or irrigation) are subsidized, black market prices will operate to the advantage of the large farmers. Clearly, input subsidy must be coupled to supply improvements to enable the production potential of the small farmer to be utilized.

There remain substantial differences of opinion concerning the overall benefits of the green revolution. These are best summarized by two contrasting quotations.

Agricultural research pays handsomely in developing countries . . . it is essential that agricultural economists develop better guidelines to help the production scientists establish research strategies to reduce the adverse consequences of increased production. Until these strategies are formulated we have no choice but to pursue the simplistic goal of increased food production. To do otherwise is to risk the disaster of world famine (Jennings, 1974).

and

. . . it [the green revolution] cannot but rapidly lead to an extreme polarisation between a small section of big and prosperous farmers in the process of becoming even more big and prosperous, and the vast numbers of small farmers and landless labourers remaining more or less where they are (Rudra, 1971).

Government Encouragement of Different Crops

Government policies of price and production control and input subsidy have had dramatic effects on the distribution of incomes and resources among farmers. It is hardly to be expected that such policies would be equally concerned with all crops. The existence of government support for the production of some crops and not others may accentuate differences in income between different types of farmers. Several mentions have already been made of the different attitudes to high grain prices between cereal and livestock producers. In Third World countries the encouragement and support of cash crop production may be at the expense of food production. Conversely, in a country like Bangladesh, where agricultural exports are almost the only source of foreign exchange, the balance between food production, which in this case means rice, and jute production to earn foreign exchange to pay for imports, including food, is very delicate. With large volumes of food aid available at low or minimal foreign exchange costs, the short-term temptation to go for jute production can be great.

Policies which single out particular crops for special attention must by their nature single out the producers of these crops for attention. A second step in this process, especially where there is little unused land available, is to encourage more astute producers to shift their production to take advantage of the government incentives and support. Government policies would not be working if this shift did not take place. This shift from one crop to another may have significant effects on the diet and nutritional status of the population, though these effects will be unevenly felt by different sections of the population. The best known, and potentially the most important of these changes, has been the shift from legumes to high-yield variety wheats and to a lesser extent rices in the Indian subcontinent. There, in common with most of the developing world, diets are essentially vegetarian, being based on cereals. The protein content of cereals ranges from 6 to 12 per cent. A cereal diet consumed in sufficient

156

quantities may be able to satisfy both protein and calorific needs for most of the population. Significantly, it cannot do so for young children, nursing and pregnant women (Vieira, 1976). Thus, there is an urgent need for supplementary protein and one of the best sources of such protein is the legumes or the pulses. The protein content of pulses is twice that of wheat and three times that of milled rice. In comparison to wheat, and latterly rice, little research effect has been devoted to improving the yields of pulses in the past. The greatly increased potential wheat yields means that the incentives for Third World farmers to shift from pulses to cereals is obvious, provided that cereal prices hold up sufficiently under increased production. Government measures to support prices of cereals during the early years of the green revolution, combined with the more recent developments in the world cereal markets, have helped to encourage the shift to cereals.

Although the area planted to pulses had been falling before the green revolution an abrupt change took place in Indian agriculture following 1966–77 (Figure 38). Until 1966 the area planted to wheat and to pulses and the yields of both crops moved together quite closely, with yields declining in 1964 and rising sharply in 1965. In 1967 the yields of pulses fell but those of wheat rose and, despite the fall in wheat yields in 1973 and 1974, the trend of separation has continued. The pattern of the area planted to the two crops is also predictable. Pulse area fell steadily between 1964 and 1973, but then recovered to more or less the same level as in 1962. The

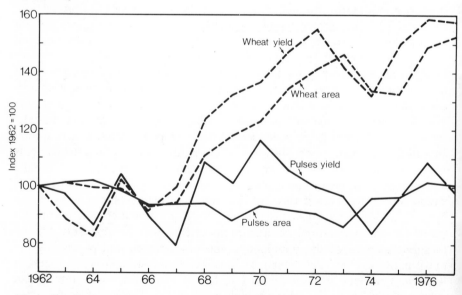

Figure 38. Indian wheat and pulses: area and yields, 1962–77. Source: FAO, *Yearbooks*

area planted to wheat has risen every year since 1966, with the exception of 1974 and 1975. The drop in area planted to wheat in these years understandably lagged one year behind the fall in yields. Similarly, the recovery of the planted area shows a one-year lag. The effects of investment in wheat production is also shown by comparing the yields of wheat in the United States of 2039 kg/ha in 1976 with 1409 kg/ha for wheat in India. On the other hand, United States' yields of pulses is 1325 kg/ha while the comparable figure for India is only 531 kg/ha. The competition between wheat and pulses is obviously most severe in the best wheat-growing area of India. For example, the area planted to pulses in Punjab and Haryana states fell by 1.2 million ha, or 44 per cent, between 1960 and 1969, whereas the decline for the whole of India was only 11 per cent (Berg, 1973).

The case of soybeans is rather special. Soybeans production in Brazil has mushroomed in recent years from 2218 ha in 1971 to 11,227,000 ha in 1976. Yields have also improved from 1,396 kg/ha to 1,750 kg/ha over the same period. This puts Brazilian soybean yield above that of the United States. Unfortunately, although soybeans are an excellent source of protein, Brazilian production is largely for export with the EEC the largest customer (Missigen, 1978). The pulse which forms a part of the diet of most Brazilians is the dry bean, and over the same period the area planted to this crop has fallen from 2,500,000 ha to 1,923,000 ha and yields have fallen from 668 kg/ha to 483 kg/ha. Government policy to develop soybean production for export, especially in the south of the country, has reduced the supply of protein-rich food for the bulk of the population. Although Brazilian soybean yields are higher than in the United States, the yields for all pulses are only at about one-third of the United States level.

The Effects of no Intervention

Before leaving the production effects of government policy we should pay brief attention to a consideration of what might have happened in the agricultural sector without the various policies of price support, production limitation and consumer subsidy. In many cases life would have gone on with very little change for the agricultural producers. The peasant producer in most developing economies remains more or less ignorant of government policies and, with only a small proportion of his production commercially marketed, many such policies are of little relevance. In other respects the effects could be dramatic. We have already estimated by how much the production of food grains in the developing world rose as a result of the green revolution. The increased availability of food and the resulting lowered relative prices must have reduced the level of malnutrition in many developing countries where the production of wheat and later rice is important. Although starvation is largely a result of an inability to purchase food no matter how cheap it is, the increased availability of food helped those with a little money as well as those already wealthy.

In the United States, government intervention policies have been both long-lasting and expensive. Some attempts have been made to simulate what would have been the result of failing to intervene in this way (Robinson, 1960; Tyner and Tweeten, 1964; Ray and Heady, 1974; Nelson, 1975; Cochrane and Ryan, 1975). The studies vary considerably in their assumptions and simulation methods, but they conclude that farm prices would have fallen between 10 and 40 per cent. As production controls are removed production volume rises at first and then falls in response to the decreased prices as the least productive land is removed from production and fewer inputs are used. As production falls so prices can be expected to rise again, possibly to levels at or above the levels existing during government price support. The Ray/Heady study indicates that prices fall by a greater amount than can be compensated for by production increases because of an inelastic demand for farm produce. Farm incomes fall, and in fact in this study never regain their previous levels. Nelson's study shows farm incomes recovering some twelve to fourteen years after the removal of the government programmes and then rising considerably higher than previously. The farmers who survive would therefore be expected to benefit considerably from the removal of the government programmes. However, as Cochrane and Ryan point out, it is pertinent to ask how many farmers will have been able to weather a period of twelve to fourteen years with incomes reduced by upwards of 40 per cent.

Although such studies do help us to clarify the cost of government programmes, such 'what if' speculation is really of little value. The political reasons for the continuation of intervention in most developed economies have been sufficient to ensure its continued existence, with a few short-lived exceptions, despite dramatically falling numbers of farmers and a diminished overall significance of the agricultural sector in the economy. There is little indication that this position will change in the immediate future.

Consumer Effects

In contrast to the effects on producer incomes only a limited amount is known about the effects of consumer-orientated programmes. This is partly because, in developed countries at least, they are more recent, and partly because of the difficulties of isolating the direct effects of consumer-orientated policies. Although such policies may give rise to a better level of nutrition and a more balanced diet, it is also often the case that other changes have been made in, for example, health care, education and housing. All of these will have an effect on mortality and morbidity and the specific effects of improved diets are difficult to determine.

The per capita calorie intake in the State of Kerala is the lowest in India despite the wide availability of the ration food distribution system. On the other hand, general mortality rates and infant mortality rates are among the lowest. In Kerala, hospital and other health care facilities are good and, with one exception, the state has the highest number of hospital beds per 100,000 of the population of all Indian states (U.N. Dept. of Economics and Social Affairs, 1975).

As with the various production and producer income policies there are income distributional effects of consumer policies. A general food rationing or subsidy scheme benefits those not in need as well as those in need. One example, showing the effects of the United States' food stamp policy, has been published by Lane (1978). Food stamps are sold to consumers at less than their face value, the difference between the sale value and the purchase price being varied according to a means test. The average for the whole country is 45 cents for a dollar's worth of food. In a sample survey of Californian recipients of food stamps the average household received an income effect of $8.69 (the difference between the purchasing power of the stamps and the purchase price) and received $3.26 worth more of food than the non-participating households in the sample. The marginal propensity to consume (the amount of each additional unit of income that would be spent on food) is estimated to be close to 30 per cent, a figure approximated by these survey results. It also agrees fairly well with a black market price of about 50 cents per dollar for the food stamps (Clarkson, 1975). The extra food consumed showed up in the improved nutritional status of the participating households, which had higher per capita consumption of protein, calcium, vitamin A, and riboflavin as a result of the food stamp programme. An earlier study (Clarkson, 1975) is less optimistic. Although the programme reaches 15.8 million people and costs in excess of $4 billion it has inefficiencies. The participants tended to purchase more expensive food of lower nutritional value per dollar expenditure. This means that the increased consumption generated has had its largest impact on the food processing industry rather than on farmers. The programme has little or no educational value, is not linked with other supplementary feeding programmes such as school lunches which generally have a higher nutritional impact (Price et al., 1978), and has very great administrative costs, exceeding $228 million in 1976.

Producer and Consumer Policy Conflicts

The separation of agricultural producers from consumers is somewhat artificial. All producers are also consumers and, in many developing countries, most consumers are producers. However, in the developed economies the number of producers is sufficiently small for policy conflicts to exist, and in the developing countries where there is a consumer-orientated set of policies they are targeted at the urban populations clearly distinguishable from the rural food producers.

The nature of the conflict in the policies is clear enough; how to resolve the conflict is more difficult. Producer-orientated policies are designed to improve farm incomes, increase production, or raise both. Although production gains can be brought about by exhortation or by co-operation among producers with various degrees of enforcement, the most successful way is to raise prices. This either provides the incentive to the producers to produce more or compensates for reduced production where this is necessary. Farm incomes can be raised or maintained through direct income supplements, input subsidies, marketing assistance and so forth. But all such policies have to be paid for and there are only three sources of finance in the developing countries and only two in the developed economies. The most direct and obvious is to allow consumer prices to rise. Alternatively such payments can be financed from the central exchequer, or in the case of developing countries from foreign aid. Conversely, if consumer prices are to be lowered by government policy, this implies lower producer prices, or direct government subsidy, or the use of cheap or free food imports. Lele (1976) comments on the irony of the Indian ration system which has in the past been based on a compulsory regional procurement arrangement which the large producers can avoid, leaving the burden of providing cheap food for the often relatively wealthy urban consumer on the poor small farmers.

The discussion of issues of growth versus equity, when examining the producer effects of government policy, can be extended to consider the wider social costs and benefits of policies of agricultural development (Akino and Huyami, 1975). Scobie and Posada (1978) argue that too often the distributional effects of government encouraged technical change and development in agriculture are confined to the production sector alone, paying attention to the effects on large and small farmers, to the exclusion of the urban population and particularly the poor urban population. Examining the introduction of new high-yielding varieties of rice into Colombia between 1964 and 1974 the authors are able to show that the increased production lowered prices and that net benefits to all farmers were negative, despite the greater output. The worst affected were those farmers not able to take advantage of the new technology, the upland small farmers (Table 34a). On the other hand, the net benefits to the poor urban consumer were positive and considerably greater than those to the more wealthy urban consumer because of the higher proportion of rice in the diets of the poor and the importance of food costs in total family expenditure. The lowest three income groups account for 15 per cent of total household income, 52 per cent of households and received 67 per cent of the benefits from the programme. (Table 34b). Although this work ignores a number of important consequences of technological change, particularly changes in employment, it does show that income distributional

Table 34. Annual average distributional impact of the Colombian Rice Research Programme

A

Farm size (ha)	Change in producer surplus plus share of research costs as % of 1970 income	
	Upland sector	Irrigated sector
0–1	−58	−56
1–2	−53	−39
2–4	−60	−25
20–30	−41	−48
30–40	−35	−47
40–50	−30	−45
200–500	−18	−79
500–1000	−21	−69
1000–2000	−19	−49

B

1970 Income level ($ col. '000's)	Cumulative percentage of		
	Net benefits	Households	Household income
0–6	18	19	2
6–12	50	39	8
12–18	67	52	15
18–24	77	64	23
24–30	83	71	29
30–36	88	76	35
36–48	93	82	43
48–60	95	86	51
60–72	96	89	57
72+	100	100	100

Source: After Scobie and Posada (1978).

effects of policies of agricultural change spread wider than over the agricultural sector alone.

An extensive study was conducted by the Food and Agriculture Organization (1975) showing the producer and consumer tax and subsidy elements in government programmes of market intervention in Australia, Canada, Japan, the United Kingdom, the United States and in the European Economic Community between 1968 and 1974. This period is particularly interesting as it includes the dramatic policy turnabouts in many countries following the world food price rises of 1973. During the 1960s government price support measures were generally paid for by high consumer prices. The price rises of 1973 reduced the effectiveness of existing policies as intervention prices, floor prices, target prices and so

Table 35. Producer and consumer subsidy equivalents for wheat, 1968–74

	1968 (%)	1969 (%)	1970 (%)	1971 (%)	1972 (%)	1973 (%)	1974 (%)
EEC							
Producer subsidy	34.3	41.2	39.0	41.6	24.3	−42.1	−29.3
Consumer subsidy	−33.8	−40.1	−38.6	−40.8	−23.2	38.4	29.3
USA							
Producer subsidy	29.2	41.0	43.8	35.9	45.0	6.8	0.1
Consumer subsidy	−21.4	−25.3	−27.8	−24.6	−30.8	1.1	1.3

NB: The difference between the producer and consumer subsidies represents net costs to central government funds.
Source: After FAO (1975).

forth were vastly exceeded in world markets. At the same time many countries initiated policies to protect the consumer against these high world prices and a consumer tax changed into a subsidy. This change was more dramatic in the EEC than in the United States, reflecting the greater degree of insulation from world markets within the EEC. By 1974 consumers and producers in the United States were paying and receiving effectively the world market price for cereals (Table 35).

The Case of Thailand

Thailand is in a unique position as a developing country as a major exporter of food grains, while not being one of the major food-grain producers. The government has adopted policies to tax the export of rice and this has in turn worked to subsidize consumers and increase government revenues, a proportion of which has been spent to subsidize consumers further. The export tax has been borne by the producers and by the export customers. Thailand is an agricultural country with 82.2 per cent of the employed population living on farms. In 1976 30 per cent of the gross national product came from agriculture, though if the processing and selling of agricultural products are included this percentage is considerably higher. A major part of this agricultural production is rice, domestic consumption of which presently averages 161.5 kg per head per year—or over 442.5 g per day. This is equivalent to 1597 kcal and 29.6 g of protein from rice consumption alone, a level of rice consumption that is among the highest in the world. Thailand has been a significant exporter of rice since 1855 when the Bowring Treaty opened up trade with the Kingdom (Corden and Richter, 1967). Exports grew to about 1 million tons per year in the 1920s and have ranged between 1 and 2 million tons annually except for the disruptions of the Second World War (Tongpan, 1974). Generally, exports have been less than 20 per cent of the production, reaching a recent high of 23 per cent in 1972 and falling since that year.

Thailand remains a major world exporter, although the relative importance of rice to the balance of payments of the country has fallen steadily with the rise of other forms of export (Siamwalla, 1975). The majority of the export trade is handled by private traders of which there are probably no more than twenty operating through a number of different companies (Pinthong, 1978). Direct government-to-government trade is only used with those countries which insist on such arrangements, for example, Sri Lanka, India, and Japan.

The rice economy is managed by controlling exports. Through this, domestic availability and therefore domestic price are controlled. The government sets export targets each year and grants export licences to traders. There are three closely related ways in which this export trade is taxed. The first is a simple export tax. The Rice Committee of the Board of Trade draws up a price list for all grades of rice each week, fixing the tax level for that week. The second method of taxation is the rice reserve. Established in 1962 this consists of the mandatory sale to the government of a fixed proportion of the rice exported by each company. This rice reserve has operated in times of short world markets when Thai rice would have been exported to the detriment of the domestic market, or when the domestic market is short because of a poor crop year. It is suspended under conditions of adequate domestic supply. The rice reserve scheme in 1973 required the compulsory sale of 200 per cent of the volume exported by each company, but this proportion had fallen to 50 per cent by 1974. The rice which the government acquires is used to supply the government-run ration shops in Bangkok. As we shall see this provides a double subsidy for the Thai urban consumer as the net effect of the export tax is also to reduce prices. The third method of export taxation is the rice premium. This is notionally a fee for an export licence (Wong, 1978). The premium is legislated as a fee so that it can be altered by the executive without being voted on by parliament. It can be used as a quick and effective export-control mechanism (Pinthong, 1978). The premium was introduced by the Rice Office in 1950 as a fixed sum of money per ton of rice exported and varies with the grade of rice. In times of domestic shortage the premium plus the rice reserve can be raised sufficiently to cause the domestic price to the exporters to equal or exceed the world market price, thereby preventing exports. When such circumstances occur it is hardly surprising that smuggling of rice certainly occurs over the Thailand borders.

The major debate over Thai rice policies concerns the impact of these taxes on the producer, the consumer and the export customer. Are the taxes passed on to the export customer through higher prices or do they result in the exporters paying lower prices to producers in Thailand to maintain the same export price? This depends on the price elasticity of demand for Thai rice on the world market, or the extent to which the Thai exporters can raise prices and still sell the rice. An early view of the export tax was that the government, by organizing the trade, was merely replacing the monopoly previously held by the Chinese traders and the profits were being transferred to the consumer through the ration shops (Silcock, 1970). For this to be the case the world demand for Thai rice would have to be completely inelastic, a set amount can be sold on the world market regardless of the price asked. The world rice trade is of a residual nature, only about 5 per cent of the total production being exported. Because Thailand is a major exporter it may be expected to exert some control over the world price of rice. In addition the rice trade is characterized by direct government-to-government trade, much of it under concessional terms, so that the commercial market is even smaller than the export trade. There are marked regional preferences for varieties of rice, and Thai rice, of high quality, is regarded favourably in many parts of South and South-East Asia (Ingram, 1971; Timmer and Falcon, 1973). For these reasons we might expect demand for Thai rice to be somewhat inelastic, but Baldwin (1974) argues that overall world prices are determined by *demand* and this is in turn determined by world production, of which Thailand represents only about 1 per cent. More recently Setthawong (1977), in an analysis of world rice prices, concludes that the demand for Thai export rice is fairly insensitive to price with an elasticity of -0.269. This is based on the regression equation:

Vol. Thai exports $= 4.088 - 0.269 Price + 0.102 Vol_1 - 0.299 Vol_2$

where *Price* = fob Thai 5 per cent white rice price,
  Vol_1 = volume of US rice exports,
  Vol_2 = vol of Chinese rice exports.
  (All variables are expressed as logarithms).

On the basis of this low elasticity the author argues for increasing the revenue to Thailand by raising the price premium.

Figure 39 shows little relationship between the volume of rice exported and the export price of Thai rice. Although the volume fell between 1973 and 1975 when prices were high, the simple correlation coefficient between the two variables is only -0.20. The export premium follows the export price quite closely, suggesting that it is an important contributor to the export price but the extent to which it controlled export volume is uncertain. It is significant that Thai exports were apparently depressed in 1973 and 1975 when the premium was low. This suggests that the world demand was limited by high prices and that the additional burden of the premium in 1974 had little real effect on export volumes.

We can illustrate the effects of export taxation in Figure 40. In an untaxed situation the domestic supply and demand schedules are shown by S_d and D_d. The horizontal difference between them represents the available supply for export at various prices above P and this is represented by the export supply schedule S_e. Export demand D_e is shown as downward

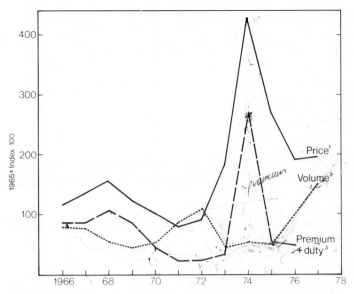

Figure 39. Thailand rice exports volume, price and rice premium, 1966–77. 1 Price=average price of Thai export rice. 2 Volume = total volume of Thai rice exports. 3 Premium + duty = rice premium plus export duties. Source: *Bank of Thailand Monthly Bulletin,* Vol. 18/3 (1978)

sloping, indicating only a slightly elastic demand for Thai rice. The world price P_0 determines the domestic price and the domestic consumption C and production Q. $Q-C$ is available for export and equals $E-O_1$. When the export tax is imposed $(P_1 - P_2)$ a proportion $(P_1 - P_0)$ reduces domestic producer prices. As a result domestic consumption rises from C to C_2 and production falls from Q to Q_2. Available supply for export falls from E to E_2. Additional consumer benefit is provided by the ration shop sales the income effect of which raises the demand schedule to D'_d reducing the export supply. Any reduction in the export tax would raise domestic prices. Renaud and Suphaphiphat (1971) find that a 1 per cent reduction in the export tax would raise domestic wholesale price by 0.77 per cent, confirming that most of the effects of the export tax are passed on to the domestic producers. The Thai domestic rice trade is generally competitive (Pinthong, 1978) and any increase in the wholesale rice price would be expected to be passed on as increases in the farm-gate price. On the other hand the policies bring in considerable government income, in 1960 the rice taxes accounted for 12.0 per cent of total government revenue, and do provide benefit for the urban domestic consumer. Wong (1978) estimates that, despite high export premiums (between 1961 and 1970 the premium was about one-third of the export price) there was a net welfare gain to Thailand as a whole. The taxes provide a considerable burden to the poor farmers and the depressed domestic price has probably reduced incentive

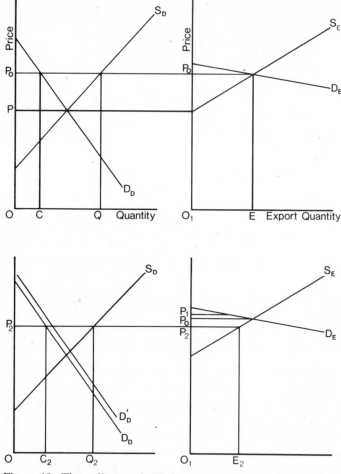

Figure 40. The effects of Thai export taxes on domestic supply and price of rice. Source: after Wong (1978)

to increase domestic production. Paddy yields are low and rice production per capita has remained more or less constant over the last ten years. Although there may be a net welfare gain from the rice policies, the burden for this gain falls unfairly on a generally very poor section of the population to the benefit of the urban consumers. Producer and consumer policies are in conflict and the situation is complicated for Thailand by the importance of the export market as a source of foreign exchange and as a source of government revenue through its taxation policies.

The Case of Bangladesh

Much has been heard, firstly of policies for the elimination of world hunger in ten years and, secondly, of the obscenity of a world which shows the two faces of malnutrition, obesity and starvation, side by side (Eckholm and Record, 1976). One of the reasons that the second exists and the first is an unrealistic objective lies in the conflicts of policies directed at the producer and at the consumer in the Third World. Recent work by Gavan (1977) illustrates so well the exceptional difficulties of implementing policies which can raise consumption by the poorest sectors of Third World communities that it is worth examining in detail. In a country like Bangladesh with a preponderance of rural and urban poor, the essential problem is to make available food at prices which the poor can afford, while not reducing prices to producers to such an extent that production falls, making the policy self-defeating. The nature of the problem has already been presented diagramatically and here we discuss some of the consequences of policies for increasing the effective demand of the poorest sectors of the consumers.

Taking as a standard calorie requirement 1870 kcal per head per day approximately 40 per cent of the rural population and 30 per cent of the urban population are presently receiving less than the minimum requirement. This represents in excess of 30 million people and all indications are that calorific intakes are falling. Taking as a very limited objective the reduction of this number by 25 per cent, various policy alternatives are available. In this simplified case only rice will be considered, although as wheat is the major food grain of aid, the consumption trade-off between wheat and rice is obviously important.

1. The present ration system providing food grains at subsidized prices could be extended to cover a greater section of the population. As the ration system is primarily urban orientated the best way of extending the ration system would be to incorporate more of the rural population.
2. A variant of this is to ensure that the food distribution under this extension of the ration system is directed only at the poor—say to households with incomes of less than 500 taka per month.
3. The government of Bangladesh could sell the grain it has available for the ration system in the open market. The sales would reduce the market price sufficiently to allow 25 per cent of the presently malnourished population to purchase more grain in the market place. This policy of open-market sales has been recommended by the World Bank (1978a).
4. The government of Bangladesh could adopt a system of food stamps whereby the purchasing power of the poor is raised to enable them to purchase food grain in the open market. Food stamps might be restricted to those households earning less than 500 taka per month.
5. A further option would involve the same extension of the ration system as option 1, but domestic procurement proceeds at a sufficient rate to maintain the price to producers at its pre-existing level.

The following evaluation of these policies is made solely in terms of the costs of reaching the desired objective. No account is taken of the administrative and political difficulties and the implementation costs of the policies.

Table 36 summarizes the results of the study, assuming a supply elasticity of 0.3 which is probably somewhat higher than the true producer response to price changes. The additional quantity of food grain required to meet the 25 per cent reduction in the number of undernourished people is directly proportional to the degree of targeting in the policy chosen. Government open-market sales would be available to all and therefore approximately three times as much food grain would have to be released under this policy as would be needed for the food stamp policy. The figure is not higher for the open-market sales solution as the marginal propensity to consume of the poor sections of the population is much greater than for the more wealthy, and therefore lowering the price will affect the consumption of the poor more than the rich. A policy of distributing food stamps would require less additional grain to be available than either of the ration systems as it assumes that the stamps would be available at zero cost while the ration food is subsidized but not free. Since price effects will be related to the size of the additional supply to be imported, the greatest fall in domestic price will be under option 3 where government open-market sales are organized to reduce prices to allow greater purchasing by the poor.

Assuming that the extra imported supplies become available as free food aid, maximum government revenue would come from the open-market sales policy, these increased market sales reducing prices by 14 per cent. It seems unlikely that close to 1 million extra tons of food grains will be available and the long-term disincentive effects of a 14 per cent fall in producer prices on investment in agricultural development would be disastrous. From a government fiscal point of view, however, such a policy has obvious attractions. Extending the ration system, either limited to those most in need or not, is a compromise. Producer price reductions occur but not excessively, and the government budget receives substantial revenue from the ration sales. Perhaps it is not surprising that this is the present policy of the government of Bangladesh. What is highly significant from the point of view of the theme of this section is that any policy which attempts simultaneously to increase consumption and maintain domestic producer prices will be extremely expensive to a government whose resources are already sorely stretched. The food stamp policy as the most closely targeted, even assuming zero cost of imports, would cost the government of Bangladesh 750 million taka, or approximately 25 per cent of the total government revenue from all sources in 1974.

The budgetary pressures for Bangladesh to continue with, and even expand the ration system (Table 36 options 1 and 3) are obvious. The depressing effects on producer prices is one of the reasons for the slow growth in agricultural production. With population increase outstripping

Table 36. Costs of various food policies in Bangladesh

	Policy option				
	1 Extend rationing	2 As for 1 but to low-income households	3 Government grain sales	4 Food stamps	5 As for 1 with domestic procurement
Additional supplies needed (tons)	545,000	430,000	915,000	250,000	300,000
Change in market price (%)	-7.0	-5.0	-14.0	0	0
Government net revenue, Import costs zero (taka $\times 10^6$)[a]	580	460	2,500	-750	-2,000
Import costs at world price (taka $\times 10^6$)	-914	-727	0	-1,439	-2,800

[a] 25 taka $\approx$ £1.
Source: After Gavan (1977).

increases in agricultural production, policies which lower producer prices seem destined to increase the country's reliance on imports and/or food aid. The long-term importance of incentive prices to producers has been often stressed (Lele, 1975), but effectively to maintain incentive prices to farmers the government needs greater control of the price and market system for food grains than it at present possesses.

The conventional wisdom has swung away from an all-out encouragement of the technical fix for food production increases, towards the considerations of equity and the meeting of basic human needs. Although it is theoretically possible to meet both the equity and the growth objectives of development policy, at least as far as the producers are concerned, there are very few Asian countries which pass this test (Falcon, 1978). Policies to reach the poor and the disadvantaged can be devised, but they are usually expensive in terms of financial resources and in terms of skill and management. Perhaps the best that can be hoped for is a package of producer policies to increase production in ways which are as far as possible accessible to all producers. Growth *must* be achieved in order to close or at least to maintain the present size of the food gap in the developing countries. Hopefully, producer policies managed with care will provide a successful middle road between the goals of equity and growth and between the needs of producers and consumers.

The difficulties for developing countries in enacting effective producer policies should not be overlooked. The creation of a minimum support price as a stabilization measure alone requires that the government has effective control over the market, has access to all producers and can control large stocks of grain. Such power is beyond the grasp of many developing countries at present (Lele, 1975). To expect in addition effective policies to help all the poor and disadvantaged is hoping for miracles. The Bangladesh policy alternatives outlined above would meet the nutritional needs of only 25 per cent of the population at present receiving less than the minimum calorie requirement. Yet that minimum is itself very low. Unfortunately, we must conclude that the policy costs and conflicts are so great that any goal for the elimination of world hunger by 1985 must be dismissed as unrealistic.

The Costs of Government Policies

Government policies for intervention in agriculture make for a greater use of resources in that sector of the economy than would be expected under free market conditions. Many such interventions were planned to be transitory, tiding farmers over the adjustment to changed economic circumstances. The measures adopted during the economic depression of the 1930s were supposed to ease the adjustment of the farming sector in Europe and the United States to mechanization and less use of labour. Similarly, consumer subsidy policies in developing countries are presumably seen as temporary expedients, awaiting the rises in incomes and wealth that are hoped to be the product of faster economic growth.

In fact both types of policy are politically very difficult to dismantle. The producer protection initiated in the 1930s has been built upon and modified but not dismantled and we have seen how, from a fiscal and a political point of view, it is difficult for the governments in Bangladesh and India to dismantle the food ration distribution system. The costs of such policies are considerable. In addition to the producer and/or consumer taxes or subsidies there are large payments from central government funds. Such payments fall on taxpayers generally.

An estimate of government expenditure on agriculture in New Zealand for 1978–79 amounts to $NZ267.5 million. In addition there is $NZ15.6 million allocated for agricultural research and $NZ48 million for agricultural development on Crown Lands. There is also the agricultural education budget, loans for land development and a major part of government expenditure on rural roads which should be allocated to agriculture, although detailed figures are not available. Total agricultural expenditure probably exceeds $NZ500 million, which is 60 per cent of the education budget, 56 per cent of the health budget and is in excess of 6 per cent of the total government expenditure for 1978–79. New Zealand is a small country which does relatively little to support its agricultural sector. In 1975 the United States' budgetary appropriations for the USDA were $14,658 million, compared, for example, with $87,000 million for the Department of Defense (US Government, 1976). Table 37 shows both the complexity of payments to agriculture in the United Kingdom and the interrelationship between those payments made through the EEC and those financed from UK sources alone. The situation changes considerably from year to year, for example, the food subsidies were shortly phased out and the EAGGF has now taken over more payments than in 1975–76, but the overall size of the commitment to agriculture and its complexity remains unchanged. Within the EEC some 64 per cent of total financial resources are spent on agriculture and an overwhelming 94 per cent of these are spent on price-support policies.

In addition to these direct costs there are the opportunity costs of the resources which are maintained in agriculture; the returns to these resources are low and this itself provides the main reason for the government intervention in the first place. The country loses the wealth which would be generated by a more efficient employment of these resources. One of the reasons why agriculture in developed countries needs government support is that these resources are trapped, having little or no salvage value. Agricultural labour in particular has a low opportunity cost when national unemployment rates are high. Labour opportunity costs add little to the overall costs of government intervention in agriculture. Capital is a rather different matter. As government payments are capitalized in land, in a sector with relatively low returns to capital, this government

Table 37. United Kingdom payments to agriculture, 1975–76

Expenditure	Amount (£ millions)	Income Source	£ millions	Net MAFF payments (£ millions)
Inputs and production payments (see Table 23)	376.65	1, 2, 3	31.13	345.52
Marketing payments				
Price guarantees: milk	283.6	4	273.6	10.00
sheep	7.14			7.14
wool	1.97			1.97
Intervention buying: Skimmed milk	11.05			
beef	1.05	1	1.66	13.04
to EAGGF	1.65			
other	0.95			
Aids to private storage	8.77			
Animal feed purchase	5.70			
Export/import refund	179.52	3	202.00	0
Import subsidy: sugar	8.01			

Beef premium	89.95	3	49.89	40.06
Food aid purchase (transport)	0.71	2	0.71	0
Butter subsidy	113.98 } 9.51	2	25.26	98.23
Beef subsidy	117.28			117.28
Wholesale horticultural markets	2.53			2.53
Food subsidy: milk	273.68			
bread flour	77.46			
butter	92.55	5	540.27	0
cheese	58.58			
tea	30.15			
household flour	7.85			
Other marketing payments	6.37	1	1.66	4.71
TOTAL	1,766.66		1,126.18	640.48
Total net United Kingdom payments				1,454.35

1. Sales.
2. EEC.
3. EAGGF.
4. Department of Prices.
5. Department of Health and Social Security.

Source: UK Appropriation Accounts.

expenditure would have been better directed to other sections of the economy.

Consumer subsidies raise different issues. Although resources devoted to such policies could have been utilized in other sectors of government expenditure, the benefits of consumer subsidies are difficult to measure. The indirect benefits of improved nutrition in the population may be considerable through the creation of more effective labour, lower health care costs, as well as unquantifiable improvements to the quality of life of citizens (Berg, 1973). These issues will be discussed in the next chapter on nutrition and nutrition planning.

CHAPTER 6

Consumption

Introduction

Production is but one side of the world food equation. It is obvious that as the world's population continues to grow, more and more food will have to be produced to feed the extra mouths. The effects of increasing population have been illustrated by a comparison of world food production and production per capita (Chapter 2). Food consumption is not simply a matter of the number of people in the world. Man has a physiological need for food just as he has for water and for shelter. In fact exposure, at least in cold climates, is the greatest hazard—cold can kill a person in a very short space of time. Man's requirements for water are great, a lack of it leads to death in about two days. Food can be foregone totally by healthy adults for as much as two weeks without lasting harmful effects.

There is a minimum food intake requirement for each person below which that person would not be able to survive. The absolute minimum food requirement for the whole world could therefore be specified as this minimum physiological need times the world's population. In such a calculation account would have to be taken of the different physiological needs of different sections of the population. Age and sex are important in this respect. Such a minimum requirement has no real meaning, however, as the population so fed would be unable to work, grow food or even, in all probability, reproduce itself. Physiological need is better expressed as the minimum food requirement to maintain the world's population in full health. Even this calculation would have little practical value as the world's *demand* for food is very different from the summation of physiological needs. People naturally demand more food than the absolute minimum they require to stay healthy. Not only does this increase the total demand but, more importantly, the nature of this food demand changes. With rising incomes people consume more sophisticated foods, particularly meats. Domesticated meat animals are fed to an important extent on grains which man could and does eat directly. These animals convert the food values of this grain rather inefficiently so overall food consumption rises faster.

If it is true to say that increased income raises the effective demand for food, it is equally true to say that reduced or inadequate income lowers effective demand. Malnutrition is the result of poverty and therefore an inability to purchase the necessary food to meet the basic physiological requirements. In fact it can be argued that the production of food can be stimulated simply by turning the world's latent food demand into effective demand by reducing poverty. An alternative argument is that, by increasing production, wealth is increased and filters down to all sections of the population, this wealth allows the purchase of the extra food now being produced. These developmental planning arguments will be examined at the end of this chapter.

Actual consumption of food is a combination of the needs of the population and their ability to produce and/or pay for food. It is naïve to consider food supply only in Malthusian terms; increasing affluence must also be incorporated into the demand side. As an illustration, Indonesian policies to increase rice production were most successful between 1966 and 1976, raising total production by about half and yields by about a third. But consumption of rice rose even faster, stimulated by rising incomes, at least in the urban sector, and the relative cheapness of rice in comparison to other foodstuffs. When the production increases plateaued in 1973–76, imports of rice had to rise dramatically to meet this continued demand for rice, a demand which grew regardless of the levels of domestic production. By 1977–78, Indonesia imported about $2\frac{1}{2}$ million tons of rice, about one-third of the world's total rice market.

In general, the world consumption figures for food do not lead to optimism. World cereal consumption in 1975–76 was estimated to be 2.7 per cent below 1969–71 levels (Table 38) (IFPRI, 1977a). World cereal consumption data is complicated by differences between countries and the role of livestock in grain consumption. In the period up to 1972 the USSR adjusted grain consumption by slaughtering livestock so as to meet the demand for direct human consumption. Indications are that this slaughtering policy was again rather drastically used in 1975 to mitigate the effects of a poor grain harvest. Excluding reduced consumption in the developed countries, largely a result of reduced livestock production, the centrally planned and the developing countries have shown grain consumption per capita levels recovering by 1975–76 to the 1969–70 and 1971–72 average levels. The static nature of consumption in comparison to production is partially explained by the rising population and is replicated in the production per capita data.

The balance between production and consumption is obviously critical, and world production has increased just fast enough to maintain world consumption per capita lvevels. Average data hide enormous differences between countries. For example, the reduction in grain consumption per capita in North America can hardly be considered as a serious consumption effect; on the other hand in many developing countries where

Table 38. Total grain consumption per capita

Kilograms per year

	1969–70/ 1971–72	1970–71	1971–72	1972–73	1973–74	1974–75	1975–76
Developed countries							
USA	531.7	523.0	549.0	557.6	553.2	496.8	509.3
EEC	821.5	799.4	848.0	870.3	843.1	668.2	719.7
	438.6	436.6	445.4	457.6	457.8	450.7	442.1
Centrally planned							
USSR	354.3	355.5	362.7	362.3	381.3	373.5	354.8
China	706.9	726.4	704.5	709.4	814.1	761.5	650.2
	207.3	210.9	212.8	208.3	212.7	221.4	219.1
Developing market economies							
India	186.1	188.2	185.2	182.8	186.6	182.9	187.5
Bangladesh	167.5	173.7	164.3	162.0	173.1	156.6	165.8
Indonesia	174.1	170.7	165.3	174.7	190.9	188.8	190.3
	136.1	139.2	139.3	141.2	145.0	147.1	145.9

Source: After IFPRI (1977a).

upwards of 80 per cent of income is spent on food, most of it cereals of some sort, the effects of even a very small production shortfall can be immediate and catastrophic. Famines in the Sahel, India, Bangladesh, and elsewhere have become commonplace news. The Western world is probably no longer as shocked as it ought to be by television pictures of emaciated bodies and signs of widespread starvation. Such events take place not as a result of any world shortage of grain, or even in some instances as a result of a real local shortage, but basically because some production shortfall raised prices so that the available supplies are beyond the reach of the poorest sections of the population. The better off continue to eat as much as before. It is not hard to imagine the effects of a doubling of the price of grain on those who are already spending 80 per cent of their income on food. It is indeed fortunate that during the dramatic rise in grain prices in 1973–74 many in the developing world were cushioned by domestic price policies, rationing, food aid, and by a proportion of household domestic self-sufficiency. Such cushioning was not sufficient to prevent widespread malnutrition and starvation. The critical balance of food production and consumption is of more importance in the developing countries, where consumption is normally minimal, and where the population is not able to make adjustments to changing price levels consequent upon changing production. In this chapter we will examine the major factors in the demand for food and how world consumption patterns vary. The chapter concludes with a brief analysis of the planning implications of consumption as distinct from production and the present status of nutrition planning.

Population

There is no doubt that it is population which is the dominant influence in gross world food consumption. The spectre of billions of mouths to feed from the finite physical agricultural resources of the world haunts us all. The apparently geometric growth of population in the face of a linear growth of food supply has been the thesis of disaster since the days of Malthus. It is obvious that the geometric growth of population cannot continue for very long. The world's population roughly doubled in the seventeen centuries after the birth of Christ. At the rate of increase in the world's population found in 1970, it would only take thirty-five years to double the present population. It is possible to predict standing room only on the world's surface in a very short time.

This surrealistic situation obviously cannot happen. What is important are the controls which will prevent it from being reached. Malthus believed that it was to be starvation, disease and warfare over the increasingly scarce food resources which would control the population in an essentially biological manner, with the world's population growing only so fast as could be supported by the environment. Neo-Malthusians see this biological limitation as having been staved off by technological progress whereby increased food yields per hectare, and the use of further cultivatable land, have enabled food supply more or less to keep pace with the population growth—so far. These technological fixes must ultimately be limited, both in terms of the biological capability to utilize the process of photosynthesis, and physically in terms of the finite land area of the globe on which photosynthesis and some form of cultivation are possible.

The question remains whether there is any way in which the human population can or will be limited short of this Malthusian nightmare. The population growth in the world's developed countries is much less than in the developing countries and the critical issue is whether the decline in the growth rate will apply to the developing countries, if so when, and will it be soon enough to ensure a world population which can be reasonably sustained by the world's food supply, short of the 'natural' processes of limitation foreseen by Malthus.

The contrast between the developed countries and the developing countries can be examined in terms of the conceptual framework of the demographic transition. Pre-industrial societies had generally high death rates, so high fertility was necessary to maintain the population. In contrast, advanced industrial societies show both low mortality and low fertility. The demographic transition is this change from high birth and death rates to low birth and death rates. At each end state the population is more or less stable, but in the process of transition death rates have declined in advance of changes in birth rates following use of modern medicine and disease control. At some point following the decline in death rates occurs a decline in fertility. The length of the lag between these two separate declines is of critical importance as the recent boom in world population is the result of declining death rates in the developing world which has not yet been followed by a significant decline in fertility. The decline in death rates was the result of a technical fix, it required the import of foreign technology which did not need to be understood, simply followed. Early work on reducing fertility was based on assumptions of a similar technical fix but 'reducing fertility from traditionally high levels that are buttressed by customs and social norms is not a process constrained only by what is feasible, as was the case in reducing mortality. Effective methods of fertility control have always been known and available in all societies. Fertility transition implies profound social changes rather than merely a change in technology', (Demeny, 1974).

Although there is a fairly close relationship between development status, measured in terms of the gross domestic product, and life expectancy (a better measure than the crude death rate as it is unaffected by an ageing of the population) the relationship between GDP and the birth rate is far less clear (Figure 41). In each case the developed countries form a compact group with low birth rates and high life expectancy. The developing countries show a trend of increasing life expectancy related to increased GDP with Bangladesh as the low point and Argentina as the high. In the

180

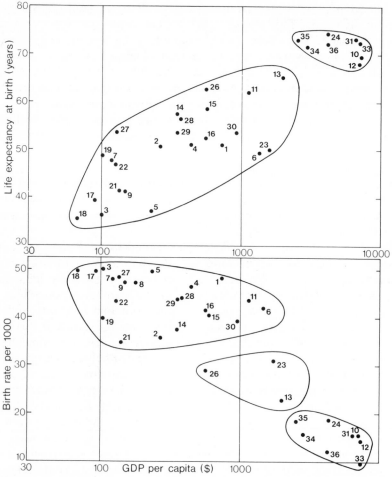

Figure 41. Birth rates and life expectancy compared with GDP per capita for countries with over 15 million population. Key: 1. Algeria, 2. Egypt, 3. Ethiopia, 4. Morocco, 5. Nigeria, 6. South Africa, 7. Sudan, 8. Tanzania, 9. Zaïre, 10. Canada, 11. Mexico, 12. USA, 13. Argentina, 14. Brazil, 15. Colombia, 16. Peru, 17. Afghanistan, 18. Bangladesh, 19. Burma, 20. China, 21. India, 22. Indonesia, 23. Iran, 24. Japan, 25. Korea, N., 26. Korea, S., 27. Pakistan, 28. Philippines, 29. Thailand, 30. Turkey, 31. France, 32. Germany, E., 33. Germany, W., 34. Italy, 35. Spain, 36. United Kingdom. Latest available data are used—normally 1970 or 1974.
Source: United Nations, *Demographic Yearbook* (1975); United Nations, *Statistical Yearbook* (1976)

case of birth rates, however, the trend for developing countries is much less marked and Iran, South Korea, and Argentina occupy intermediate positions between the developed and developing countries. Because there are countries at all stages of the transition does not imply that those countries which have not yet shown any decline in fertility will necessarily do so, although there is a reasonable expectation that, if the correct social and economic conditions can be produced, there will be a decline in fertility. These correct conditions depend at least partly on economic development, but as a high fertility rate delays this development, poverty and high fertility tend to be mutually self-sustaining. In most developing countries children are seen as a net financial investment, in providing wage-earning capabilities at an early age and providing security for a time when the parents can no longer work. With high mortality rates a large number of children have to be conceived to be reasonably certain of a surviving male child. The conditions which will help to reduce fertility are those which provide the population with economic and social security and these are not necessarily related to gross national product or to the traditional economic measures of development. There is some contrary evidence from Indonesia (Hull and Hull, 1977) suggesting that fertility is positively related to economic status. More educated and economically better-off households appear to have more children because of a better survivor ratio of children, a higher disruption of marriage among the poor resulting from divorce and widowhood, a longer abstinence period after childbirth partly associated with a high incidence of breast feeding among the poor and, finally, the poor couples have shorter reproductive lives. These factors will tend to work against the demographic transition resulting from economic development but are likely to be temporary, the fertility rates will take on an inverted 'U' shape, rising at first and then falling with continued social and economic change. Developing countries with reasonably complete population records are showing signs of declining fertility and 'happily, perversely, and extremely contrary to Malthus, we see that throughout the world when people become prosperous they have fewer children' (Kirk, 1972).

The demography of population change is in some senses unimportant from the point of view of food policy. The number of people on the earth at present, plus the slow rate of change in the factors which control population growth, means that significant changes in rates of growth will be unlikely over the next thirty to forty years. The population to be fed from the earth's food supply will more than double regardless of the success or failure of any present efforts to control population growth. The importance of these programmes will not be felt until well into the next century. The population structure of the developing world is dominated by children. As these children reach child-bearing age the population will continue to grow. Only when the age structure reaches maturity will zero population growth be possible. The possible effects of food supply on population growth will be examined later (p.273).

Physiological Food Needs

The physiological food needs of the human body are proteins, energy, vitamins, and minerals. In each case it is possible, with various degrees of accuracy, to specify minimum levels of consumption and so-called safe intake levels (FAO, 1973). As needs vary from individual to individual the safe levels are set to ensure that the great majority of the population obtain at least the minimum level of the required commodity.

In terms of overall nutrition, proteins and energy are the most important ingredients in any diet. Proteins provide the building material for the body, no living matter is without them and, after water, they make up the largest proportion of body tissue. Energy is provided by carbohydrates and fats (and also from proteins) and is measured in calories, the amount of heat needed to raise the temperature of a litre of water from 15 to 16 °C. Alternatively, the energy content of food can be measured in joules, 1 kcal equals 4.184 kJ. The kilocalorie will be used here as it is the most familiar unit in general nutrition usage. A person's requirements for protein and for energy vary according to age, sex, body size and weight, and, at least in the case of energy, to activity and climate. Obviously, before determining the possibility of eradicating hunger in the world, and providing sufficient food for adequate nutrition in future years, it is necessary to calculate the requirements of different populations and to estimate the adequacy of present food intakes. The following section examines the protein and energy content of different foods and the different human requirements, starting with the most complicated of these, proteins.

Proteins

Proteins contain nitrogen in combinations of different amino acids, twenty-two of which are now known to be physiologically important. Proteins in food are broken down into their constituent amino acids, absorbed into the blood, carried to the different body tissues, and there reconstituted into different combinations of amino acids to make up human protein. Proteins form an essential part of the nucleus of each body cell and the combination of the amino acids determines the type of protein, which in turn helps to determine the type of cell.

The protein content of different food varies considerably. It is very high for some fish, up to 90 per cent of the dry weight of shark's fin for example, around 40 to 45 per cent of the dry weight of beef and soybeans and around 10 per cent of the dry weight of cereals (Table 39). Food is not bought in measures of dry weight and the protein content of food as bought is often substantially different (Table 39). The weight as bought will differ from time to time for the same food so the protein content as a percentage of dry weight is normally used as a standard, although confusion can arise as this tends to overstate the protein value of foods, especially of meat and fish. Such crude protein levels give some idea of the protein 'value' of different foods but, as each protein is made up of different combinations of amino acids, and, as the human body requires certain combinations of these amino acids, the nutritive value of the protein in foods is different from the crude protein content.

There are ten amino acids which are generally recognized as essential in

Table 39. Protein content of different foods

Food	(A)	(B)	(C)	(D)	(E)	(F)
	Crude protein level		Amino acid score (%)	Digesti- bility (%)	NPU	Useful protein (% dry weight)
	% as bought	% dry weight				
Egg	13	48	100[a]	97	97	47
Cow's milk	3.5	27	100[a]	97	97	26
Fish (fresh)	19.0	72	100[b]	97	97	70
Beef	18.0	45	100[b]	97	97	44
Soybeans	38.0	41	74[a]	78	58	24
Dry beans	22.0	25	54[b]	78	42	11
Groundnuts	26.0	27	65[b]	78	51	14
Green vegetables[c]	3.0	27	57[b]	65	37	10
Wheat grain	12	14	53[a]	79	42	6
Whole wheat flour	11	12	47[b]	78	37	4
Sorghum	8	10[d]	37[b]	55	20	2
Maize (whole)	10	10	49[a]	70[e]	34	3
Brown rice	8	9	70[b]	75	53	5
Polished rice	7	8	67[a]	84	56	4
Potato	2	9	54[b]	74	40	4
Cassava	2	2	56[b]	74	41	1

(A) From Bogert et al. (1973).
(B) From Bogert et al. (1973).
(C) Determined from limiting amino acid (see Table 40).
(D) From FAO (1973).
(E) Net protein utilization. Amino acid score × digestibility/100. Note this calculation gives slightly different results to those based on rat studies—see for example Scrimshaw and Young (1976).
(F) Calculated as protein % of dry weight × NPU/100.
[a]From FAO (1973).
[b]Calculated from amino acid content in FAO (1970b).
[c]Cabbage is used as an example of a range of values.
[d]From FAO (1970b).
[e]Estimated value.

human diets, four of which are normally shown paired. In addition one further amino acid, histadine, is essential for young children and probably also for adults (Bogert et al., 1973). The remainder of the amino acids which are essential to the human body can be synthesized and do not have to be consumed directly. Protein quality is, therefore, measured in terms of the amount of these essential amino acids. These amounts are compared with a standard, which used to be the balance of amino acids found in whole egg but, normally an improved reference protein is now used which is not directly related to a specific food. In Table 39 the amino-acid balance of this reference protein is compared with that found in a number of different foods. The value of a protein is determined by a comparison of the amount of each of its amino acids with the amount in the reference protein. The lowest ratio found determines the 'limiting amino acid' and the overall value of the protein. The ratio for the limiting amino acid gives the amino-acid score and the percentage of the protein which can be utilized by the body (Table 40). The overall utility of the protein is therefore limited by the most deficient of its constituent amino acids in comparison to the requirements of the human body.

In addition, the different foods have different levels of digestibility and the utilization of the food's protein content is also limited in this way. The 'net protein utilization' is found by reducing the amino-acid score by the digestibility factor (Table 39). In the case of brown rice, for example, the crude protein level is about 9 per cent of the dry weight. Table 40 shows the amino-acid breakdown of this protein and that lysine is the limiting amino acid with a ratio of 70 to the lysine content of the reference protein. Digestibility is estimated as 75 per cent, so 75 per cent of 70 per cent (equals 53 per cent) is the net protein utilization of brown rice. For every 100 g of rice consumed there are therefore only 5 g of utilizable protein (53 per cent of 9). The remainder of the protein present in the brown rice will be converted to energy.

An examination of the amino-acid contents of different foods against the reference protein shows that, although animal products make excellent proteins, an adequate protein consumption can be obtained from a strictly vegetarian diet. Consumption has to be sufficient to compensate for the smaller percentage of the crude protein which is utilized by the body and the low starting levels of crude protein in some vegetable products, especially root crops. A very large amount of cassava will have to be consumed if this is the only item in the diet, as 100 g contains only about 1 g of useful protein. It is in places where the diet is made up primarily of cassava and similar starchy roots that we will expect, and will find, the most severe forms of protein deficiency.

A careful study of Table 40 shows that, because of the role of the limiting amino acid, a diet which is a combination of different food products will yield a higher useful protein level than either of the individual products eaten separately. Provided that the different foods are eaten actually together, or at least separated only by a short time interval, the limiting amino acid of one food can be compensated for by an excess of that amino acid in the other food. This returns us to the importance of legumes in the green revolution changes in Asia. A diet of 100 g of wheat yields 2.09 g of nitrogen and Table 40 shows that this will produce 2192 × 2.09 = 4581 mg of essential amino acids excluding histidine. The amino-acid score determined from the limiting amino acid, which is lysine, is 53 and the digestibility is 79, therefore the net protein utilization is 42 per cent, or 1924 mg of essential amino acids. Similarly, a diet of 100 g of dry beans yields 3.54 g of nitrogen and 9084 mg of essential amino acids. The amino-acid score is 54 and the digestibility is 78, therefore the net

Table 40. The amino-acid content of different foods

| Food | Essential amino acids[a] | | | | | | | | | Total AA | | LIM[c] AA | Reference[d] protein for Lt AA | AAS[e] | N[f] |
	IS	LE	LY	M+C	P+T	TH	TR	V	H	Ess[b]	Total				
Egg	393	551	436	362	618	320	93	428	152	3353	6446	—	—	100	1.98
Cow's milk	295	596	487	208	633	278	88	362	167	3114	6463	M + C	220	94	0.55
Fish (fresh)	299	480	569	253	474	286	70	382	221	3034	6093	TR	60	100	3.01
Beef	301	507	556	249	500	287	70	313	213	2996	6065	V	310	100	2.83
Soybean	284	486	399	162	505	241	80	300	158	2615	6157	M + C	220	74	6.65
Dry beans	262	476	450	119	484	248	63	287	177	2566	5662	M + C	220	54	3.54
Groundnuts	211	400	221	150	555	163	65	261	148	2174	5887	TH[g]	250	65[g]	4.69
Cabbage	193	331	194	135	304	235	66	263	159	1880	4451	LY[g]	340	57[g]	0.26
Whole wheat	204	417	179	253	469	183	68	276	143	2192	6033	LY	340	53	2.09
Wheat flour[h]	232	379	159	224	462	192	68	270	121	2107	6226	LY	340	47	2.05
Sorghum	246	832	126	181	473	189	76	313	134	2569	6023	LY	340	37	1.62
Maize (whole)	230	783	167	217	544	225	44	303	170	2683	6093	LY	340	49	1.52
Brown rice	238	514	237	212	540	244	78	344	156	2563	6327	LY[g]	340	70[g]	1.26
Polished rice	262	514	226	229	503	207	84	361	146	2532	6007	LY	340	66	1.13
Potato	236	377	299	118	422	235	103	292	94	2176	4910	M + C	220	54	0.32
Cassava	175	247	259	170	256	165	72	209	129	1682	4554	LE[g]	440	56[g]	0.26
Reference prot.[i]	250	440	340	220	380	250	60	310	—[j]	2250	—	—	—	—	—

IS = isoleucine; LE = leucine; LY = lysine; M + C = methionine and cystine; P + T = phenylalanine and tyrosine; TH = threonine; TR = tryptophan; V = valine; H = histidine; total AA (ess) = total essential amino acids; total AA = total amino acids. [a]mg/g total nitrogen. [b]Essential amino acids, excluding histidine. [c]Limiting amino acid. [d]Reference protein mg/g nitrogen for limiting amino acid. [e]Amino acid score, %. [f]g nitrogen/100 g. [g]Calculated AAS is different from FAO (1970b) as using the reference protein from FAO (1973), indicates different limiting amino acids. [h]80–90% extraction. [i]Reference protein composition from FAO (1973). [j]Considered essential, but amount in reference protein unknown.
Source: FAO (1970b) unless otherwise indicated.

H

protein utilization is 42 per cent or 3815 mg of essential amino acids. Eaten separately, such a diet yields 1924 + 3815 = 5739 mg of essential amino acids which can be reconstituted into the various body proteins. Eaten together, however, the position is different. The 200 g of food yield 2.09 + 3.54 = 5.63 g of nitrogen. From the information in Tables 39 and 40 we can construct Table 41. The amino-acid content of the combined food shows that the beans are able to make up for some of the deficiencies of the wheat and vice versa so that a comparison to the reference protein shows that the amino-acid score is 75 derived from the limiting amino acid, isoleucine. Digestibility of the combination will be (78 + 79)/2 = 78.5 and the net protein utilization will be 58.9 per cent, considerably higher than for either wheat or beans alone (42 per cent in each case). Therefore 58.9 per cent, or 8049 of the 13,665 mg of essential amino acids in the combination diet, can be utilized, a 109 per cent improvement over 200 g of wheat alone and a 40 per cent improvement over 100 g of wheat and 100 g of beans eaten separately.

Similar improvement can be shown with a combination of beans and rice, although as the amino-acid score of rice is considerably higher than for wheat, the improvements are not as great. Also, pulses are not as likely to be in direct land competition with rice as with wheat. Such dietary combinations are so many and so complex that assessment of all diets in such a way would be impossible, but the above calculations illustrate both the importance of a balanced agricultural production and of nutritional education. Diets can be adequate if foods are eaten in combination, while

Table 41. Limiting amino acids in mixed wheat/beans diet

Food	Essential amino acids[a]							
	IS	LE	LY	M + C	P + T	TH	TR	V
Per 100 g dry beans	927	1685	1593	421	1713	878	223	1016
Per 100 g whole wheat	426	872	374	529	980	382	142	577
Per 200 g mixed mg/g nitrogen[b]	187	454	349	169	478	224	65	283
Reference protein mg/g nitrogen[c]	250	440	340	220	380	256	60	310
Food protein % reference prot.[c]	75[d]			77		88		91

[a]Milligrams.
[b]Nitrogen levels; beans 3.54 g/100 g; wheat 2.09 g/100 g. Therefore, for example, levels in mg/g nitrogen calculated as (927 + 426)/(3.54 + 2.09) = 187.
[c]Mixed wheat/beans amino-acid level as percentage of reference protein amino acid level. Shown only for potentially limiting amino acids.
[d]Limiting amino acid in mixed diet of 50 : 50 wheat and dry beans.
Source: Calculated from Tables 39 and 40.

inadequate if the same foods are eaten separately but in the same quantities.

As protein is a vital constituent of body tissues it is during rapid growth that man's requirements for protein are greatest. After the late teens protein requirements remain more or less static. Apart from the period of rapid physical growth and the conditions of pregnancy and lactation, the FAO/WHO Select Committee on Energy and Protein Requirements (FAO, 1973) found little evidence of circumstances leading to major differences in protein requirements. Stress and heat may increase protein needs by small amounts and heavy physical work will increase the demand for energy and thereby lead to an increase in food consumption, a part of which will be protein, but the Committee concludes that there is little evidence that protein needs are radically altered by physical activity. Certainly wear and tear on the body tissues will be greater and this will increase protein needs for replacement and maintenance, but this is not thought to be very significant.

The most acute form of protein deficiency has been recognized for many years as kwashiorkor (Trowell, 1973). The symptoms were first recognized in West Africa from whence the name derives. Literally translated it means 'first-second' or 'the illness of the first child when the second is born'. It is essentially a weaning disease when the young child is transferred from a diet consisting largely of the mother's milk to one of native foods, often rendered bland by dilution to make it possible for the infant to eat it. Where diets are based on cassava, the protein content of which is very low before dilution, protein deficiency may become evident. Symptoms of kwashiorkor are easily recognized. Often the limbs swell and the hair changes colour—usually to red or white. Children who have recently recovered from kwashiorkor have a band of different colour in their hair, which, before it grows out, provides a characteristic indication of a previous incident of severe protein deficiency.

Safe protein standards have been recently lowered. In the 1950s and 1960s the main emphasis of nutrition research in the developing world concerned protein consumption, but recommended levels were lowered in 1971 (FAO, 1973) by 20 per cent. A critical review of past and present protein standards is provided by Scrimshaw (1976). The FAO/WHO (FAO, 1973) report, now widely used as a standard work, found that the coefficient of variability of protein needs was about 15 per cent from all causes and therefore fixed safe requirements levels at 30 per cent above the average requirement level in the expectation that this would ensure that most of the population had sufficient. Safe protein levels for different ages, body weights and sex are shown in Table 42. The safe levels are expressed in protein of the quality of whole egg and therefore have to be adjusted upwards to take account of consumption of proteins of lower quality. Body growth takes place in spurts so that during these spurts of growth the child's need to protein increases considerably. Protein

Table 42. Safe protein levels

Age	Body weight (kg)	Safe level protein (g prot. per day)	Adjusted safe levels for lower NPU scores		
			80	70	60
6–11 months	9.0	14	17	20	23
1–3 years	13.4	16	20	23	27
4–6 years	20.2	20	26	29	34
7–9 years	28.1	25	31	35	41
Male 10–12 years	36.9	30	37	43	50
13–15 years	51.3	37	46	53	62
16–19 years	62.9	38	47	54	63
Female 10–12 years	38.0	29	36	41	48
13–15 years	49.9	31	39	45	52
16–19 years	54.4	30	37	43	50
Adult male	65.0	37	46[a]	53[a]	62[a]
Adult female	55.0	29	36[a]	41[a]	48[a]
Pregnancy[b]	—	+9	+11	+13	+15
Lactation[c]	—	+17	+21	+24	+28

[a]These figures may overestimate the adult requirements.
[b]During the last six months add figure indicated to normal female requirement.
[c]During the first six months of breast feeding add indicated amount to the female's normal requirement.
Source: FAO (1973).

consumption needs to be matched to growth requirements and will not necessarily closely follow the pattern indicated in this table.

As with the establishment of any such standards very real problems occur in their application to a real world situation. Actual protein consumption in any developing country is likely to be highly skewed with a long tail to the right made up of people adequately, or more than adequately, nourished, but the bulk of the population will consume less than the specified safe level (Figure 42). In the past the FAO has tended to assume that the causes of this skew are too deep-seated to eradicate and that the total protein need must be determined by moving the whole consumption distribution curve, in its present shape, to the right until the great majority of the population are above the safe consumption level. Such a method of specification leads to the establishment of protein targets which are greatly higher than present consumption and have in turn led to such terms as the 'protein crisis'. The new mean consumption level $\overline{P}'_c$ is now far above the safe protein consumption. Joy (1973), in pointing out the difficulties with this method of specifying protein need, suggests that developing countries short of resources had best direct their nutrition planning, not to meeting goals which are far beyond their reach, but to such improvements in the protein levels in the national diets as yield the maximum benefit. Nutrition planning should be linked to the size of the return, not to targets set unattainably high.

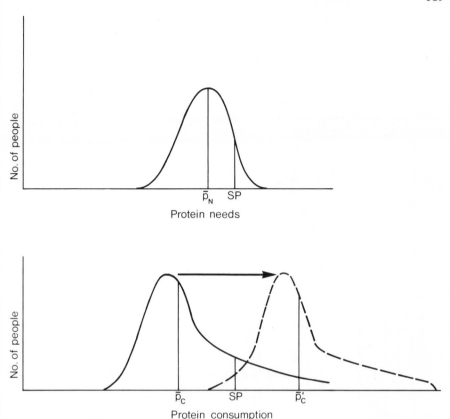

Figure 42. Distribution of Protein need and consumption. $\overline{P}_n$ = average protein need; SP = safe protein level ($\overline{P}_n$ + 2 standard deviations of the need distribution); $\overline{P}_c$ = average actual protein consumption; $\overline{P}_c'$ = average protein consumption after most of the population are above the SP level.

Calories

In the case of protein the level of human requirements are relatively straightforward, but complexity occurs with the different amino-acid make-up of different foods and diets. In the case of calories, the energy content of different foods is relatively straightforward, but it is the specification of the human requirements which adds complexity. The gross energy available in food comes from proteins, carbohydrates and fats, less the digestibility factor. Of this gross energy, the net energy availability for the eater of the food is the gross intake, less the unavoidable losses in urine and faeces. Table 43 shows the efficiency which different food components can be converted into energy. Foods high in fats are a good source of energy. The final column of this table presents the gross energy available in different foods. There is obviously an interrelationship between

Table 43. Energy in different foods

Food[a]	Protein			Fats			Carbohydrate			Total
	g prot.[b] per 100 g food	kcal per[c] g prot.	kcal per 100 g food	g fats[b] per 100 g food	kcal per[c] g fats	kcal per 100 g food	g carbo.[b] per 100 g food	kcal per[c] g carbo.	kcal per 100 g food	kcal per[d] 100 g food
Egg	12.9	4.36	56	11.5	9.02	104	0.9	3.68	3	163
Cow's milk	3.5	4.27	15	3.5	8.79	31	4.9	3.87	19	65
Fish[e]	17.6	4.27	75	0.3	9.02	3	—	—	—	78
Beef[f]	17.5	4.27	75	25.3	9.02	228	—	—	—	303
Soybeans	34.1	3.47	118	17.7	8.37	148	33.5	4.07	136	402
Dry beans[g]	20.4	3.47	71	1.6	8.37	13	64.0	4.07	260	344
Groundnuts[h]	26.0	3.47	90	47.5	8.37	398	18.6	4.07	76	564
Cabbage	1.3	2.44	3	0.2	8.37	2	5.4	3.57	19	24
Wheat grain	14.0	—	—	2.2	—	—	69.1	—	—	330[b]
Wheat flour[i]	13.3	3.59	48	2.0	8.37	17	71.0	3.78	268	333
Sorghum	11.0	2.50	28	3.3	8.37	28	73.0	4.03	294	350
Maize grain[j]	8.9	2.73	24	3.9	8.37	33	72.2	4.03	291	348
Brown rice	7.5	3.41	26	1.9	8.37	16	77.4	4.12	319	361
Polished rice	6.7	3.82	26	0.4	8.37	3	80.4	4.16	334	363
Potato	2.1	2.78	6	0.1	8.37	1	17.1	4.03	69	76
Cassava	—	2.78	—	—	8.37	—	—	4.03	—	—

Source of energy

[a]100 g edible portion. [b]From USDA (1963). [c]From FAO (1973).
[d]Total calculated agrees with USDA (1963) data within rounding errors except in the case of sorghum where the USDA figure is 332 kcal per 100 g.
[e]Cod. [f]Chuck—good US grade. [g]Lima beans. [h]Peanuts with skin not shell. [i]Whole-grain flour. [j]Field corn.
— = not available.
Source: FAO (1973); USDA (1963).

proteins and calories. The protein content of 100 g of brown rice for example, either yields 26 kcal of energy or 3.8 g of useful protein plus 12.5 kcal of energy from conversion of protein not usable as determined by the amino-acid balance of brown rice, or any intermediate combination, depending on the relative needs of the eater for protein or calories. The body's need for energy are met first and so the protein content would only be utilized as protein if sufficient calories are available from all sources.

Energy needs decline with age, not only as a direct result of decreasing physical activity, but because the basal metabolism decreases with age and usually body weight also. The increasing incidence of physically limiting disease and disability is also important. The FAO (1973) recommends a 5 per cent decline in energy needs for each decade between the ages of forty and fifty-nine, a further 10 per cent decline between sixty and sixty-nine, and between seventy and seventy-nine.

In cold climates energy is expended in keeping warm. However, this function is usually fulfilled by clothing and shelter and, if necessary, by increased physical activity. The current FAO standards for energy requirements add nothing for climatic factors as there is no reasonable

Table 44. Recommended energy intakes

Age	Body weight (kg)	Basal metabolic (kcal/day)	Energy requirements (kcal/day)
Children <1	7.3	408.5[a]	820
1–3	13.4	673.4[a]	1360
4–6	20.2	865.0[a]	1830
7–9	28.1	1064.5[a]	2190
Males 10–12	36.9	1285.8[b]	2600
13–15	51.3	1497.8[b]	2900
16–19	62.9	1673.5[b]	3070
Females 10–12	38.0	1270.0[b]	2350
13–15	49.9	1394.0[b]	2490
16–19	54.4	1463.8[b]	2310
Males adult[c]	65.0	1707.5[b]	2700
adult[d]	65.0	1707.5[b]	3000[e]
adult[f]	65.0	1707.5[b]	3500
adult[g]	65.0	1707.5[b]	4000
Females, adult[c]	55.0	1472.5[b]	2000
adult[d]	55.0	1472.5[b]	2200[e]
adult[f]	55.0	1472.5[b]	2600
adult[g]	55.0	1472.5[b]	3000

[a] Average of male and female children interpolated from FAO (1973) data.
[b] Interpolated for body weight from FAO (1973) data.
[c] Light activity.
[d] Moderately active.
[e] 'Reference' man and woman.
[f] Very active.
[g] Exceptionally active.
Source: FAO (1973).

basis for the quantification of the effects of climate which had not already been included in the assessment of physical activity.

The FAO classifies the activity of life styles into four—light, moderate, very active, and exceptionally active—and has determined recommended energy intakes for each (Table 44). These levels are calculated for a reference man and woman, aged between twenty and thirty-nine, weighing 65 and 50 kg respectively. Energy needs rise during pregnancy as basal metabolism rises along with body weight, although in some societies at least, activity rates may decrease: 80,000 additional kcal per pregnancy is the current estimated need for extra energy. Breast feeding for six months requires an additional 100,000 kcal. Widdowson (1976) estimates that women should receive an extra 600 to 800 kcal per day during lactation if they are not to lose weight.

The Protein/Calorie Controversy

Proteins can be converted to calories, but energy cannot be converted to become protein. The body's need for energy is paramount at any one moment. Sufficient energy must be available, at the very least, for the maintenance of basal metabolism. In times of food shortage the body-building function of proteins are foregone in the face of a more urgent need for energy, and consumed proteins are converted into calories. This one-way transfer is the basis of a nutritional controversy about the role of proteins and calories in malnutrition. At first sight most of the undernourished of the world have all the appearance of protein deficiency. They are typically thin, of small stature and have small body mass. Such apparent protein deficiency led to emotive words about a protein crisis and to major efforts towards the production of protein-rich foods, food supplements and the protein enrichment of certain cereals, especially corn. The selective breeding of corn varieties with high lysine contents (Harpstead, 1971) was undertaken to raise the levels of this limiting amino acid, making a larger amount of the total protein in corn available for human nutrition as protein rather than as calories.

Detailed nutritional surveys show that most of the people designated as protein deficient are also calorie deficient and that protein supplementation alone will simply lead to this extra protein being converted to calories to meet immediate bodily needs. This protein supplementation may not be the easiest or the best way of providing the needed extra calories. A survey of 7000 Indian households from four states showed that 50 per cent of those found to have calorie deficiency also had protein deficiency, but that only 5 per cent had protein deficiency without calorie deficiency (Reutlinger and Selowsky, 1976). With such evidence the pendulum of nutritional thinking swung the other way to a concentration on calorific needs. Joy (1973), for example, shows that protein deficiency, without calorie deficiency is most unusual, and that most people who are malnourished actually eat enough protein but that a proportion of this is converted to calories. The curve RR in Figure 43 shows that at higher calorific intake levels necessary protein consumption falls. But if energy intake is less than 35 kcal/kg for adults (2275 kcal per day for the reference male of 65 kg body weight) it matters not how many of these calories are protein calories because the total calories consumption is too low. When eating protein-enriched food an individual might move from X to X_1 on the graph with more calories derived from proteins, but that person remains to the left of the line RR which denotes inadequate nutrition. Wheat already has 5.7 per cent of its calories derived from proteins[1] (point W on Figure 43), and so there is little point in protein enrichment to move it further up the vertical axis. Provided that the population is eating enough wheat to provide sufficient calories to the right of the minimum level of 35 kcal/kg per day, nutrition will be adequate as sufficient proteins are being consumed. The curve SS shows the relationship between protein and calorie consumption for a one-year-old child undergoing normal growth. Again, provided that the child is eating at least 85 kcal/kg body weight per day it is highly likely that the child is obtaining enough protein. One exception would be the so-called sugar

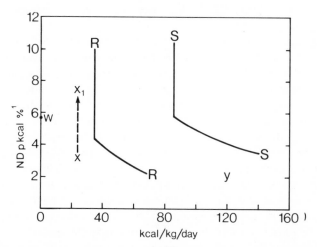

Figure 43. Protein calorie needs. 1 = NDPkcal%. The percentage of the total calories in a diet derived from protein. For example, Table 42 shows wheat having 48 kcal per 100 g derived from protein. Protein 'usefulness' (Table 38) is 37 per cent; 37 per cent of 48 is 18. So 18 kcal or 5.4 per cent of the total 333 kcal derived from 100 g of wheat flour are 'protein calories'. This is different from the figure of 5.7 per cent derived by Joy (1973) using different NPU calculations.
Source: after Joy (1973)

1. The calculation of NDpCal% (net dietary protein calories per cent) varies depending on the method of calculation of NPU. The figure for wheat flour is lower than that used by Joy if the amino-acid scores are calculated using the reference protein as in Table 40.

babies, characteristic of malnutrition in the West Indies where the diet may consist largely of sugar-cane. Calorie intake levels are more than adequate, but they are 'empty calories' as the proportion which are derived from protein is very small. These diets would place the children about point y on the graph and the feeding of supplementary proteins would raise them above, and to the right, of the minimum line SS.

Some have even carried this argument so far as to suggest that improvements in the yield and output of pulses should continue to have a low priority because of the overriding need for cereals. This is erroneous because of the complementary nature of the amino acids of the pulses consumed with the cereals (Johnston, 1978).

The view that, in most cases, protein needs can be met by simply consuming enough of the normal diet to obtain sufficient calories has been criticized by Scrimshaw (1978). Firstly, there is the question of the bulk of food to be consumed to allow for sufficient intake of calories without the use of higher-quality foods. As a simple example, take the case of an Indian small farmer who consumes a diet consisting of 85 per cent rice and 15 per cent legumes. One hundred grams of rice yields 26 kcal derived from proteins. The usefulness of this protein is 53 per cent, so the NDpCal% is 13.8/360 or 3.8 per cent. From legumes (taking as an illustration lima beans) the 71 kcal derived from the protein in 100 g is reduced by 42 per cent (NDP for lima beans) and 29.8 as a percentage of 344 (total kcal derived from 100 g of lima beans) is 8.7. Therefore, the NDpCal% of lima beans is 8.7 per cent. The weighted average NDpCal% of the mixed diet is 4.54 per cent. The weighted calorific yield of the diet is 358 kcal/100 g, therefore, to achieve the recommended 1360 kcal, a one-year-old child will require to eat 380 g of the mixed diet per day. Where food of less calorific and lower protein value is consumed even bulkier diets will be needed. A moderately active adult male will require 838 g of the same diet. If the child or the man is suffering from any disease such a bulky diet is unlikely to be consumed. This is especially true for children at the time of weaning and the malnutrition associated with inadequate diets at this time will be considered in the next section. By way of comparison the average intake of rice in Cambodia is approximately 400 g per head per day for the whole population (Mears, 1974).

Scrimshaw (1978) provides more comprehensive criticism of the statement that calorie consumption levels are more limiting than protein consumption. The protein requirements used by the FAO are calculated as a result of studies carried out on young healthy Caucasian students receiving excess calories, and there is evidence that where energy needs are met to excess, protein utilization is more efficient. In contrast, in most developing countries, where the population is consuming less energy than is required, protein needs are increased as a result of the stress created. Also, longer-term evaluation of diets suggests that higher protein needs and catch-up growth must be allowed for when assessing the real protein needs of young children and adolescents (who still have the opportunity for such catch-up growth). Not only does growth demand itself take place unevenly, but after periods of infection the recovery and catch-up period will increase protein demand.

With a few exceptions, serious malnutrition is the result of inefficient use of proteins because of a lack of energy, so this has taken on the name of protein calorie malnutrition (PCM) to indicate the interconnection of the need for protein and calories (Johnston, 1978). The deficiency disease characteristics of PCM in its extreme form is marasmus which has symptoms of extreme body wastage and the 'skin and bone' appearance which is characteristic of famine throughout the world.

Vitamins and Minerals

Set alongside the energy and protein needs, the other nutritional requirements of the human body appear insignificant. On a world scale deficiency in them is rare. Table 45 lists the necessary vitamins, recommended daily intake and some disorders associated with insufficient consumption. Of particular note is vitamin A deficiency leading to reduced vision and eventual blindness. At least 20,000 children are permanently blinded annually as a direct result of vitamin A deficiency. Only small quantities of retinol or vitamin A are required and it is readily available as carotene in many foods, especially brightly coloured fruits and vegetables. It is also found directly in foods of animal origin, especially fish-liver oil (Table 46). It is estimated that some 30 per cent of sub-Saharan African children are deficient in vitamin A and have totally or partly restricted sight as a result (Bailey, 1975). Cholecalciferal, or vitamin D, is associated with calcium absorption, but the deficiency disease, rickets, is rare except in extreme northern and southern latitudes where daylight is short and in those societies where children and females are confined indoors for most of their lives. Thiamine, vitamin B_1, deficiency causes beriberi and used to have a particular geographic distribution. Following the introduction of steel rollers in rice mills in Asia in approximately 1870, beriberi became a dominant disease in rice-eating areas except where parboiling of rice was common. The parboiling allows the transference of much of the thiamine and other vitamins from the husks of the grain to the kernel before milling (FAO, 1974d). Niacine deficiency is similarly associated with maize-based diets, if not supplemented by other foods. It was common among the poor in the south of the United States following the disruption caused by the Civil War. Vitamin B_{12} is the only essential ingredient of the human diet which cannot be provided by a strictly vegetarian diet. Vegetarians who eat milk products and eggs may be provided with sufficient B_{12}, but megaloblastic anaemia resulting from B_{12} deficiency is common among vegetarian Hindus in India. Human diets must also contain iron, zinc, iodine, and other trace elements (FAO, 1974a). Iron level in rice is far

Table 45. Recommended vitamin and mineral intakes

| | Vitamins | | | | | | | | | | |
| | A | D | B₁ | B | | | B₁₂ | C | | |
Age	Retinol (μg)	Cholecalciferol (μg)	Thiamine (mg)	Riboflavin[a] (mg)	Niacin (mg)	Folic acid (μg)	Cyanocobalamin (μg)	Ascorbic acid (mg)	Calcium (g)	Iron (mg)
Children 6–11 (months)	300	10.0	0.3	0.5	5.4	60	0.3	20	0.5–0.6	5–10
1–3	250	10.0	0.5	0.8	9.0	100	0.9	20	0.4–0.5	5–10
4–6	300	10.0	0.7	1.1	12.1	100	1.5	20	0.4–0.5	5–10
7–9	400	2.5	0.9	1.3	14.5	100	1.5	20	0.4–0.5	5–10
Males 10–12	575	2.5	1.0	1.6	17.2	100	2.0	20	0.6–0.7	5–10
13–15	725	2.5	1.2	1.7	19.1	200	2.0	30	0.6–0.7	9–18
16–19	750	2.5	1.2	1.8	20.3	200	2.0	30	0.5–0.6	5–9
Females 10–12	575	2.5	0.9	1.4	15.5	100	2.0	20	0.6–0.7	5–10
13–15	725	2.5	1.0	1.5	16.4	200	2.0	30	0.6–0.7	12–24
16–19	750	2.5	0.9	1.4	15.2	200	2.0	30	0.5–0.6	14–28
Adult male	750	2.5	1.2	1.8	19.8	200	2.0	30	0.4–0.5	5–9
Adult female	750	2.5	0.9	1.3	14.5	200	2.0	30	0.4–0.5	14–28
Pregnancy	750	10.0	+0.1	+0.2	+2.3	400	3.0	30	1.0–1.2	b
Lactation	1200	10.0	+0.2	+0.4	+3.7	300	2.5	30	1.0–1.2	b
Deficiency disease associated with a lack of ingredient	Impaired vision Blindness	Rickets	Beriberi	d	Pellagra	Megaloblastic anaemia	Megaloblastic anaemia	Scurvy	c	Nutritional anaemia

[a] Commonly referred to as vitamin B₂. [b] If iron consumption normal no extra required.
[c] No specific deficiency disease.
[d] Once thought to lead to small skeletons, this is now known to be associated with protein intake and calcium absorption adapts to need determined by protein level of diet.
Source: FAO (1974a).

Table 46. Vitamin and mineral content of foods

Food	Retinol (international units)	Cholecalciferol[a] (mg)	Thiamine (mg)	Riboflavin (mg)	Niacin (mg)	Folic acid[a,b] (mg)	Cyanocobalamin[a] (mg)	ascorbic acid[c] (mg)	Calcium (mg)	Iron (mg)
Egg	1180	+	0.11	0.30	0.1		Trace	0	54	2.3
Cow's milk	140	Trace	0.03	0.17	0.1		Trace	0.1	118	Trace
Fish	0[d]	[d]	0.06	0.07	2.2		Trace	2	10	0.4
Beef	50[e]	[e]	0.08	0.16	4.2		[e]	0	10	2.6
Soybeans	80	0	1.10	0.31	2.2		0	0	226	8.4
Dry beans	Trace	0	0.48	0.17	1.9	+	0	0	72	7.8
Groundnuts	0	0	1.14	0.13	17.2		0	0	69	2.1
Cabbage	130	0	0.5	0.5	0.3		0	47	49	0.4
Wheat grain	0	0	0.57	0.12	4.3		0	0	36	3.1
Wheat flour	0	0	0.55	0.12	4.3		0	0	41	3.3
Sorghum	0	0	0.38	0.15	3.9		0	0	28	4.4
Maize grain	490[f]	0	0.37	0.12	2.2		0	0	22	2.1
Brown rice	0	0	0.34	0.05	4.7		0	0	32	1.6
Polished rice	0	0	0.07	0.03	1.6		0	0	24	0.8
Potato	Trace	0	0.10	0.04	1.5		0	20	7	0.6

[a]Source FAO (1974a).
[b]Only rich source are green vegetables with traces in milk.
[c]Fruits are the best source—i.e. peeled orange 50 mg per 100 g.
[d]Cod-liver rich source of retinol and cholecalciferol.
[e]Concentrated in liver.
[f]Based on yellow corn—white varieties have only a trace.
+ = present.
Source: USDA (1963), except for note a.

below that in pulses (Table 46), and this provides another reason for the matching development of pulses alongside the green revolution changes in grain (Berg, 1973). Deleterious effects on the vitamin and mineral content of foods can come about through preparation and cooking. For example, the FAO (1948) found that up to 60 per cent of the thiamine (B_1) is removed by the washing of raw rice to remove dust, and a further 30 per cent of the B_1 remaining after the washing can be removed by cooking in excess water. Nutrition planning must not only include the production and distribution of sufficient foods but also an important educational element to ensure that the best use is made of these scarce resources.

Regularity of Diets

Annual average food consumption and/or daily calorific intakes obscure the variation in the diet of individuals within the year. Small self-sufficient farmers can be expected to eat well after the harvest and face a lean period before the harvest. Consumption will vary with the supply. Also, need for energy will vary through the seasons depending on the nature of the farm work to be done, and these needs may be at their highest, for example, for land preparation, when food is relatively scarce. Such farmers often work as seasonal labourers on rural works schemes during the farming slack season, spreading the demand for energy and food more evenly throughout the year, negating some of the advantages of this seasonal employment by increasing the energy food demand. Where payment for heavy physical labour is in the form of food, it is often doubtful that the general nutritional status of the population is much improved. The difference in the calorific need for moderately and very active men and women does much to absorb the extra food energy available.

The effects of seasonal protein shortage can be severe, even in cases where annual average consumption is sufficient. The effects are accentuated if, as is often the case, the season of shortage coincides with periods of disease, with pregnancy or breast feeding. Even short periods of protein deficiency may have permanent effects, especially perhaps on mental development (Klein et al., 1971). In a study of malnutrition among children in the Gambia, McGregor (1976) found marked seasonal differences. From the age of fifteen to forty-seven months, although the average annual weight gain was comparable to United States' standards, weight gain was much smaller in the wet season and in five of the ten age bands considerable weight loss occurred in children. Such evidence of seasonal malnutrition is a complex interaction of changed seasonal supplies of food and enhanced seasonal demand, but the effect of seasonal malnutrition sufficient to lead to weight loss in young children is likely to be great, even when the total annual diet and weight gain are close to the recommended standards.

Malnutrition

The total world food production is more than enough to feed the present population of the world to levels far above the FAO recommended standards. World cereal production alone in 1976 yielded approximately 5 $\times 10^{15}$ kcal for a population of approximately 4×10^9, or well in excess of 3500 kcal per head per day. Such calculations are facile as there is clear evidence that large numbers of people are not receiving an adequate diet. Many estimates have been made of the magnitude of this malnutrition problem, but malnutrition is difficult to measure and only the tip of the iceberg in the form of starvation and famine ever reaches the international media. Clinically severe protein calorie malnutrition rarely reaches above 10 per cent of the population (Cravioto and De Licardie, 1976), partly because it is generally of short duration and partly because of the high death rates which result. When it does occur seriously it generally only strikes one child at a time, partly because that child becomes so sick that its food is released for consumption by the rest of the family. Malnutrition is not limited to those cases recognized as clinically severe and the evidence now strongly suggests that the effects of malnutrition will be considerable even if the symptoms never reach this level.

With steadily refined methods of assessing human dietary needs and measuring world food production and consumption, estimates of the number of people malnourished have declined since 1950 (Eckholm and Record, 1976; Poleman, 1975). None the less the currently accepted figures are still very large. Using FAO standards, nearly two-thirds of the population of the developing countries are undernourished, which represents between 1.2 and 1.3 billion people (IFPRI, 1977a). Table 47 shows that the shortfall of calorie availability over estimated requirement is highest in sub-Saharan Africa (developing countries only) closely followed by South Asia. As the population of the latter is much larger, the overall size of the malnutrition problem is also much greater. It is probable that this study overestimates calorific needs (Johnston, 1978) but the overall

Table 47. LDCs estimated calorie availability in relation to calorie requirement per capita; 1975

	Region (kcal per day)			
	Asia	North Africa/ Middle East	Sub-Sahara	Latin America
Estimated calorie requirement	2210	2450	2350	2390
Estimated calorie availability	2055	2441	2075	2560

Source: IFPRI (1977a).

number of undernourished people in the world must remain almost inconceivable. FAO studies show that in Latin America as a whole per capita energy supplies were 107 per cent of the theoretical safe demand, in the Far East 93 per cent, in Africa 90 per cent and 102 per cent in the Near East. The trend over the period 1969 to 1974 shows considerable stability. Such calculations take into account production, net trade stocks, non-food use, fish, and use by livestock. Although there are considerable errors likely in the calculation of both the needs of the total population and of the available food supply, such food balance sheets do provide a means for the comparison of the nutritional status of different countries. Calorie availability as a percentage of requirements in 1971 was 73 per cent in Tanzania, which was closely followed by Haiti with 76 per cent and Somalia with 77 per cent. Twenty-one of the developing countries listed had calorie availability of 90 per cent, or lower, of requirement and thirty-four of the ninety-three countries had 100 per cent or more of the requirements of their populations.

Even if the estimates of food need used by the FAO and others are too large, as some have suggested, it remains clear that large numbers of people are living at far less than desirable levels of food consumption. There are two consequences of this. Firstly, clinical signs of malnutrition appear, secondly, people make adjustments to lower levels of food intake, by reducing activity, even in extreme cases remaining partly comatose with a slowed metabolic rate. Wide variations exist in estimates of calorific requirements, depending on allowances made for a return to more normal activity rates and for catch-up in physical growth. For example, calculations of the average daily calorific needs for Bangladesh have been as low as 1589 kcal per head per day based on FAO standards, as the stature of the population is generally much smaller than the reference man and woman and assuming that the household cooking and wastage is nil. It is certainly reasonable to assume very low wastage rates in very poor households, but allowing for some catch-up growth raises this daily need to about 1850 kcal. Other estimates have been as high as 2120 kcal per capita (Gavan, 1977). With calculated requirements varying so greatly, and supply not accurately recorded, the overall scale of malnutrition in Bangladesh is not clearly documented. The same problems exist, although to a generally lesser extent, in most developing countries. Such debates on the scale of malnutrition in the world will continue as the methods of measurement are refined, but at this stage it is sufficient to be 'satisfied' with the knowledge that it is widespread and move on to consider some of the consequences.

The most obvious, and probably the least common, effect of malnutrition is that people die. Mortality rates can be related to food stress (Brown, 1976), and obviously in the extreme case of widespread famine, death rates in the population will rise sharply. Using data from the Indian states of Bihar, Orissa and Uttar Pradesh, Brown shows mortality rising from 4.1

per cent to 5.5 per cent between 1970 and 1972 and relates this rise to increasing food stress following the rising price of basic food grains. However, a look at the full picture of all Indian states shows a far less clear relationship between calorie availability per head and mortality (Table 48). One of the most striking states is Kerala with the lowest per capita calorie intake but also with low general mortality rates for the urban and the rural populations, and the lowest infant mortality rate of all Indian states. In contrast, Kajasthan, where the calorie intake is the highest for India, the rural infant mortality rate is twice that of Kerala. A UN report (1975) suggests that there are many other factors involved, particularly education and health care. There are striking differences between the rural and the urban areas, both in the consumption of calories which is lower in the urban areas, and mortality rates which are also lower in the towns and the cities. This is partly the result of lower calorie requirements for the less physically active urban population and partly the result of improved access to what health care facilities and relief food supplies as are available. Notice, however, that despite the fact that the Indian ration system is very urban biased, food consumption remains lower in urban than in rural areas.

Studies of the Chilean free milk distribution system which, in 1958, included all children under fifteen years, accounting for a full 9 per cent of Chile's expenditure on public health, shows that infant mortality rates certainly fell, but it is difficult to relate this directly to the free milk. At the same time as the free milk scheme was in operation there were considerable improvements in other directions; educational achievement, sanitation, and a general rise in the per capita income. It is not possible to establish a direct causal relationship between the extra food intake and declining infant mortality (Hakin and Solimana, 1975). Indeed, the evidence is that consumption of 48 million kg of powdered milk at the height of the programme did little to improve the overall *nutritional* status of the population (Mönckeberg, 1976).

Extensive studies of twenty-six villages including 25,000 people in the Punjab (Rural Health Research Center, 1975) shows that nutritional supplementation is certainly cost effective in reducing child mortality and improving children's weight and growth, but caste differences sometimes had a greater impact on children's health and wellbeing than the various experimental care packages. Also important has been the rising age of marriage of women. The different base years used in the above studies make comparison difficult, but it is clear that there is more than nutrition involved in mortality rates.

Although we may not be able to relate mortality rates directly to nutrition there is a complex relationship between nutrition, health, mental ability, and poverty. There is, for example, a clear synergism between malnutrition and the incidence of infectious disease. Malnutrition reduces resistance to infection (WHO, 1972), and at the same time infectious

Table 48. Calorific intake and general and infant mortality rates

State	Rural			Urban			
	(1972) mortality per 1000 population	(1971) infant mortality per 1000 live births	(1961–62) kcal per capita per day	(1972) mortality per 1000 population	(1971) infant mortality per 1000 live births	(1961–62) kcal per capita per day	(1965) hospital beds per 100,000 population
Andhra Pradesh	17.0	112.6	2184	11.6	63.7	1997	66.4
Assam	18.6	131.4	2354	10.0	72.6	2140	44.0
Bihar	19.0	—	2541	9.7	69.5[a]	2330	33.5
Gujarat	16.4	145.1	2503	11.0	108.7	2115	58.6
Haryana	12.3	64.0	—	8.8	52.0	—	—
Jammu/Kashmir	12.0	74.1	3033	6.5	49.4	2361	92.5
Karnataka	14.3	96.5[a]	—	8.7	64.9[a]	—	—
Kerala	9.4	58.1	1631	7.8	45.0	1554	84.7
Madhya Pradesh	15.1	141.3	2910	11.4	75.6	2162	40.3
Maharashtra	14.5	107.1	2280	9.0	82.2	1916	81.2
Orissa	20.4	132.9	2375	12.1	79.1	2233	44.5
Punjab	13.4	108.0	3076	9.5	71.7	2156	66.5
Rajasthan	18.3	112.8	3147	10.1	74.2	2469	61.9
Tamil Nadu	17.9	127.0	2147	8.9	91.0	1934	47.9
Uttar Pradesh	27.1	100.5	2854	14.8	121.4	2162	34.7
West Bengal	12.0	173.4	2175	10.5	68.9	2040	84.5

[a] 1970.
Source: U.N. Dept. of Economics and Social Affairs (1975).

disease reduces nutritional status by increasing bodily losses of nitrogen as a result of diminished digestion and dysentery (Scrimshaw et al., 1968; Briscoe, 1976). Furthermore, blood and tissue parasites are prevalent in tropical climates and such parasites reduce the nutritional value of the food consumed (Mata, 1972). During periods of infection food intake will usually be reduced, indeed the reaction in many societies to sickness is the feeding of increasingly bland diets, especially to sick children. Such diets reduce nutritional intake which in turn further reduces the child's resistance to the infection.

We have already seen that there is a considerable rise in the nutritional needs of women during pregnancy and lactation. It is corollary that if such nutritional supplementation is not available the effects on the new-born child will be severe. Low child birth weights are associated with malnourished mothers. Adequate growth during the first three months is also associated with an adequate milk supply from the mother.

Malnutrition is also linked with retarded mental development, although the causal links are as difficult to make as between nutrition and infection (National Research Council, 1973). Studies by Klein et al. (1971) show that interconnection between malnutrition and mental development are compounded by six variables: species studied, protein or calorie malnutrition, age of the onset of malnutrition, extent of nutritional reliability, and finally, and possibly most important of all, by the level of environmental stimuli to which the child is exposed. Children tend to be protein deficient early in their life at the time of rapid growth and little activity, and calorie deficient later. Protein deficiency is considered to be more deleterious to mental development than is calorie deficiency. Brain development is especially rapid at a very young age and it is significant that, although the physical symptoms of malnutrition can be overcome and physical recovery can be complete up to about seven to nine years of age, Chilean data suggest that mental ability does not recover after nutritional rehabilitation (Mönckeberg, 1976). Studies have been carried out on the results of both protein and calorie supplementation to pregnant and lactating women and to young children on cognitive development as well as on general physical growth and health status. Multiple regression techniques have allowed some isolation of the effects on mental development (Freeman, 1977). Mental development is known to be related to mental stimulus provided at home, especially in the early years of a child's life. Such stimulation is more likely to be available from a mother who is well nourished (MacCorquodale and de Nova, 1977). A lack of stimulation for the child will not only be a direct result of the nutritional status of the mother but 'it seems clear that poverty effects intellectual development by both social and biological mechanisms' (Mönckeberg, 1976).

The synergism is five-way, including poverty, nutritional status, physical health, and mental health. Family planning should also be included as little progress will be made in tackling any one of these problems alone (Johnston and Meyer, 1977). Whereas it is relatively easy to show an unidirectional positive correlation between, say, nutrition and health, the relationships between all the above five factors are bound together in multiple causation. The temptation for single disciplinary specialists to assume that, for example, infection control will improve nutritional status, reduce the need for large families through a reduction in the infant mortality rate, and thereby reduce the poverty of the people, must be resisted because such reasoning leads to policy implementation based on single discipline solutions, ignoring the multivariate nature of the problems.

The Special Case of Breast Feeding

The most severe cases of malnutrition, especially protein deficiency, appear immediately after weaning when the nutritious mother's milk is replaced by an often grossly inadequate diet. It is only after the first three months that most children in the developing countries depart from the standard growth curve for children in the West (Mönckeberg, 1976). Processes which lead to earlier weaning can be expected to increase this child malnutrition. Human milk has more protein than commercial formulas based on cows' milk and a better balance of the essential amino acids which means that more of this protein can be utilized. The food value of mother's milk is almost complete, the only significant lacks are vitamin D, which can easily be provided by sunlight, and iron. Breast feeding can contribute to the nutritional status of the whole family by a resulting birth limitation which is partly a biological function of the breast feeding and partly a result of social taboos which limit intercourse at these times.

The decline in breast feeding is associated with:

(a) the need for mothers to work, especially in urban areas, and the difficulties and inconveniences associated with breast feeding at work;
(b) related to the first reason is the increased urbanization of the population in many developing countries and the changing role of the family in society;
(c) exposure to advertising and its association with a 'developed' and 'sophisticated' way of life coupled with a plentiful supply of commercial formulas;
(d) a part of the plentiful supply question is the distribution of dried skimmed milk (DSM) from surplus-producing countries, especially in Western Europe.

Berg (1973) shows that the decline in breast feeding has been very dramatic in Chile, where in 1960, 95 per cent of the children were breast fed beyond one year and by 1969 this had fallen to only 6 per cent. The financial costs of transferring from breast to bottle feeding have been estimated as $140 over the first two years of the infant's life, not including the costs of bottles and extra medical care. Against this should be set the costs of extra nutrition required by the mother during this feeding period. With the cost of the manufactured formulas it is not surprising that insufficient amounts are often administered and that the extra medical care required is often lacking. Even more importantly, the formulas are often made up inadequately under unhygenic conditions and over-diluted with polluted water. This is partly a result of unavoidable environmental conditions and partly because the instructions are impossible for the users to understand. Misleading advertising may imply to the uneducated that only small amounts of the 'magic' food are required for healthy babies. Significantly, a study of Guatemala showed that where mothers use boiling water to reconstitute powdered milk the hygiene problems can be overcome even if the reasons for the use of the boiling water are not essentially hygenic but cultural (Kon, 1972).

There is no doubt that some of the multinational agribusiness corporations are to blame for the rapid shift from breast to bottle feeding. Misleading advertising, free sample distribution, and convincing promotion by white, uniformed sales persons appearing similar to nurses, are all factors. Much tighter controls have been recommended, even to the extent of distributing the feeding bottles on prescription only. We might note, in passing, the size of the agribusiness corporations. Nestlé, for example, has gross annual profits which exceed the GNP of Uganda and Tunisia combined (Berg, 1973).

Obesity

Malnutrition, interpreted literally, should include people who are over-nourished as well as those who are undernourished. Just as there are diseases associated with under-nutrition so also there are those associated with overeating. Obesity and consequential heart and other medical problems are an increasing feature of the developed world (Eckholm and Record, 1976). Obesity is found in only two forms of life on earth: man and his pets (Leveille and Rosmos, 1974). Some of the world's population is able to indulge a desire to eat more than their bodies actually require. Obesity is generally inversely related to the occurrence of under-nutrition. Studies in Ecuador have found 21.2 per cent undernourished and 8.4 per cent obese in comparison to Uruguay with only 8.7 per cent undernourished and 30.0 per cent obese (Arteaga, 1976). Obviously, under- and over-nutrition can exist side by side in the world, in individual countries, towns, villages, and even, in extreme circumstances, in the same family. The world's food supply is unevenly distributed and food consumption is even more unevenly distributed as this reflects people's ability to purchase the food which is available. The calculations of overall food supply compared to food need, on almost any scale, are rendered more or less useless by this uneven consumption. This will form the subject of the next section.

Inequalities in Food Consumption

Regional food consumption varies both in the gross amount of energy and protein consumed and in the composition of diets. Total calorie consumption per head in North America is about 3318 kcal per day in comparison with the developing countries of Asia and the Far East with 2082 kcal per head per day. Even greater contrasts are to be found in comparing the protein consumption in different regions. Most of the protein consumed in the developed countries is in the form of beef and other livestock and these animals are partly fed on grain. The consumption of grain per head is much higher in the developed countries than in developing countries, where cereal crops actually form the staple diet (Table 49). Total calorie consumption per head, both direct and indirect, may reach as high as 11,300 per day in North America, a figure which includes the calorific value of the feed given to the animals in the diet. Although the quality of the protein produced may be high, animals are clearly poor converters of energy from the cereal products which they eat (Table 50).

The composition of diets in different countries is related to national and to personal income. The lower the gross national product the greater the proportion of personal income spent on food and the lower the proportion of the diet consisting of animal protein. Berg (1973) compares Ghana in the mid 1960s with a GNP of $160 per head, 64 per cent of personal expenditure spent on food and 17 per cent of protein consumption made up of animal protein, with the United States having a GNP of $3980 per head, 23 per cent of personal expenditure spent on food and 72 per cent of total protein consumption coming from animal protein.

As income remains a major controlling variable in food consumption

Table 49. Grain use and annual income per capita, 1959–61

Country	Annual income per person ($)	Grain used per person per year	
		Direct food (kg)	Total (kg)
Canada	1532	69	840
United States	2288	71	752
Mexico	312	143	202
France	1003	100	422
West Germany	982	82	336
Italy	511	135	333
United Kingdom	1111	82	360
USSR	762	171	445
India	68	135	156
Japan	346	153	210

Source: Heady (1967).

Table 50. Levels of food consumption, 1970

Region	Consumption of foodstuffs (kg per head per year)					(kcal per head per day)		
	Cereals direct	Starchy roots	Meat	Fish	Eggs/milk	Of animal origin[a]	From all foodstuffs	Total consumed[b]
North America	90.3	55.1	109.5	10.7	175.1	1324	3318	11,300
Western Europe	123.6	88.3	68.0	17.6	103.5	1102	3133	9,700
Oceania	106.9	58.8	114.1	6.8	180.7	1498	3262	12,200
Total developed countries	122.6	67.4	74.4	21.3	119.3	1064	3091	9,500
Africa	138.4	177.4	12.8	6.9	19.6	141	2188	3,000
Latin America	126.9	100.8	36.8	6.9	63.9	443	2528	5,200
Near East	185.7	23.4	14.9	2.2	26.8	236	2495	3,900
Asia and Far East	193.7	25.5	4.5	7.8	17.2	124	2082	2,800
Total LDCs	173.3	61.6	12.1	7.0	26.2	189	2211	3,300
USSR and Eastern Europe	207.2	120.3	48.8	18.6	172.4	792	3265	8,000
World	173.8	77.2	29.5	11.5	54.6	425	2480	5,000

[a]450 to 500 kcal of animal origin should cover basic needs.
[b]Total kilocalories consumed, allowing for seven vegetable calories to produce one animal calorie. Such a calculation is crude and varies, for example, from a much lower figure for Australia where most animals are range-land fed to a higher figure for feed-lot fattened cattle in the United States.
Source: Simontov (1976).

great differences exist within the regional data. Simontov (1976) shows that within Latin America the average calorie consumption is 2528 kcal per head per day of which 427 are of animal origin. But within Latin America there is national variation from 1904 kcal and 94 from animal products for Peru to 3039 kcal and 1262 from animals for Uruguay.

Although Latin America may appear to be in overall balance between food consumption and production, disaggregating by national data shows an overall deficit, and disaggregating further by income groups within countries produces even larger deficits (Table 51). The surplus food eaten in one region or by one group of people cannot be offset against shortfalls in other regions and other groups. The same pattern of increasing deficit the smaller the units of disaggregation is evident in all world regions, although to a less dramatic extent than in Latin America as regional and local income differences are less acute. Many other country studies have shown great differences in food consumption by different income groups. A small sample survey in Kerala state, India (UN Dept. of Economics and Social Affairs, 1975) showed kilocalorie consumption per head of only 1513 for those with annual family incomes of less than 100 rupees. Income of between 100 and 250 rupees provided 1760 kcal, between 250 and 500 rupees yielded 2088 kcal, and families with incomes above 500 rupees consumed 2728 kcal per head per day. Similar statistics have been collected from Tunisia and Brazil (Simontov, 1976). Not only does total consumption vary according to income but so also does the composition of the diet. Any additional income available to the poor would be spent almost totally on food and mostly on staple food grains. For the well off, additional income would be spent mostly on non-food goods, and that spent on food would go for 'luxury' foods (Table 52). The significance of

Table 51. Comparison of calorific deficiencies calculated in different ways

	kcal $\times 10^6$			
Region	1	2	3	4
Latin America	0	19	32	74
Asia	202	213	225	283
Middle East	19	32	32	45
Africa	48	56	61	86
Total world	269	314	350	488

1. (Population $\times$ calories available) − (population $\times$ mean calorie requirement).
2. Calculated as 1 for each country separately and deficits summed.
3. (Population in each income group $\times$ calorie consumption) − (population $\times$ calorie requirement) summed over all income groups. Assumes an income elasticity of demand for calories of 0.15.
4. As 3. Assumes an income elasticity of demand for calories of 0.30.
Source: Reutlinger and Selowsky (1976).

Table 52. Allocation of additional rupee expenditure by rural Indians by income group, 1964-65

| Expenditure on: | Average monthly per capita expenditure in rupees | | | | | | |
| | 8.93 | 13.14 | 17.80 | 24.13 | 30.71 | 41.89 | 85.84 |
			(% of additional expenditure)				
Food grains and pulses	55	36	24	15	10	7	2
Milk and milk products	8	11	13	13	12	12	9
Meat, eggs and fish	2	3	3	3	3	3	3
Oils	5	6	5	5	4	4	2
Sweeteners	4	5	5	4	3	3	1
Other food	2	6	8	9	10	12	17
Total food	76	67	58	49	42	41	34
Total non-food	24	33	42	51	58	59	66

Source: Berg (1973).

such studies is that the excess calories consumed by the well-off sections of the population, either directly or as a result of consuming a greater proportion of animal products, cannot be offset against calorific shortfalls in the poorer sections of the population. Such an offsetting is assumed in all national and other forms of aggregate data presentation. Brazilian data show that national food consumption figures are in excess of a reasonable minimum nutrition standard, but that a considerable nutritional deficit exists resulting from inadequate diets of the poorer sections of the population (Table 53). The overall excess kilocalories amount to 89 per head per day but, if excess eating of the rich is not transferred to the poor, the actual kilocalorie deficit for the country is about 12,339 million per day, which is equivalent to approximately 1.26 million tons of cereals per

Table 53. Calorie consumption by income group, Brazil, 1960

| Annual family income (new cruzeiros) | Population ('000) | kcal per day (mill.) | kcal need (mill.) | Deficit/excess[a] | |
				Per capita (kcal)	kcal (mill.)
<100	3,583	5,172	8,778	−1006	−3606
100–149	4,873	8,847	11,939	− 635	−3092
150–249	12,235	25,940	29,976	− 330	−4036
250–349	10,197	23,378	24,983	− 157	−1605
350–499	11,145	28,293	27,305	+ 89	+ 988
500–799	12,884	34,958	31,566	+ 263	+3392
800–1199	7,198	22,689	17,635	+ 702	+5054
1200–2499	6,840	23,022	16,758	+ 916	+6264
2500+	1,986	7,800	4,866	+1477	+2934
Total	70,941	180,099	173,806	+ 89	+6293

[a]Calculated on the basis of 2450 kcal per head per day.
Source: After Reutlinger and Selowsky (1976).

annum. This is 8.4 per cent of the total Brazilian annual cereal production in 1960—the year for which consumption data are available. Although these data are now outdated, the income distribution in Brazil has become more skewed and the resulting overall food deficit larger.

Such calculations require consumer surveys to discover how much each income group in the country spends on food of various kinds and such surveys are naturally expensive to conduct and not usually particularly reliable. A convenient alternative method has been demonstrated by Reutlinger and Selowsky (1976). The authors set income elasticity of demand for kilocalories as 0.15 and 0.30, thereby hoping to bracket the actual elasticity value. The kilocalorie consumption of each income group in the population can be specified by the equation of the general form:

$$C = a + b \log x$$

where C is the calorie consumption, x the income and b is defined by the income elasticity. The familiar Reutlinger/Selowsky diagram vividly illustrates the interaction of income and nutrition. Taking the whole of Latin America (Figure 44) mean calorie consumption is about the FAO requirement of 2390 kcal per head per day. Despite this, a very substantial calorie gap exists as so much of the population is below this average consumption. In circumstances where detailed household consumption data are available the same diagram can be drawn without making assumptions about the income elasticity of demand for calories (Figure 45). Using their analysis Reutlinger and Selowsky have computed that worldwide there is a

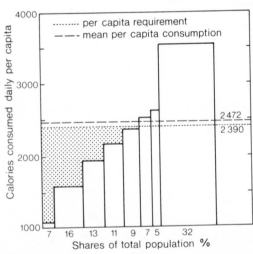

Figure 44. Calorie consumption by income group: Latin America, 1965 (calorie income elasticity set at +0.30). Source: Reutlinger and Selowsky (1976)

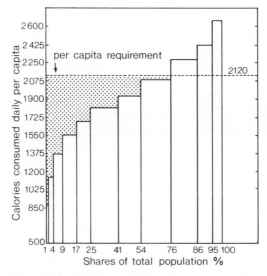

Figure 45. Calorie consumption by income group: Bangladesh, 1973–74. Source: Gavan (1977)

calorie deficit of 350,000 million kcal or approximately 100,000 tons of grain per day. This amounts to about 4 per cent of the total world grain production. However, it would not be possible to target any such extra supplies directly and exclusively to those in need, some amount of any extra food would be bound to 'leak' to sections of the population which are already well enough fed by the FAO standards. It would seem necessary, therefore, to raise this figure of 36.5 million tons per year to at least 50 million. An easy to apply rule of thumb, which seems to take into account most of the results of differing income distribution on food consumption, is to add 10 per cent to the average calorific requirement specified by the FAO and multiply this by the population of the country concerned.

A major criticism of this type of analysis has been that is assumes that the requirements of the population are uniform over large sections of the world. Payne (1977) concludes that these requirements are set too high and, certainly in India, the use of uniform standards over the whole subcontinent and over all income groups, regardless of occupation and physical stature, overestimates the total calorie deficit (Johnston, 1978). Despite this criticism the methodology has proved most valuable as it was the first major attempt to show the effect of income distribution on food demand. The more extreme the income distribution the greater the average calorie consumption will have to be to ensure that the majority of the population will be above a reasonable minimum.

Intra-Family Food Consumption

Poor families with inadequate diets are caught in a nutritional trap. It is rarely possible to provide the extra food needed by pregnant and lactating women and by young children, especially at weaning, even if these needs are understood. If employment for some family members is possible, wages will be low and the amount of food that these wages will buy will be small. The extra physical activity involved in the employment has to be bought with extra food consumption on the part of those working. A 55 kg man, changing from light activity to being very active, will need an additional 660 kcal per day (FAO, 1973), roughly equal to 180 g of rice. Family feeding order, designed to maintain the working capacity of the workers in the family unit, will often deny a reasonable share of the food to the women and the children, even though the former at least may be involved in heavy physical work in the home. This feeding order, partly the result of the necessity of the men continuing work to earn food or to grow food and partly as a result of social custom (Berg, 1973), helps to continue the cycle of malnutrition through the women and children.

In addition, there are important food taboos which may deny certain foods to women and children just when they are needed, even assuming that such food is available. We have already seen that often the reaction to infection and disease in the young is to feed them more and more bland food, often in conjunction with a violent purgative, which compound the effects of the infection, increase the body losses of nitrogen, and hasten death. Almost all cultures seem to have food taboos which deny certain foods to children, even when in good health. Pregnant and lactating women are also subject to such taboos. Paradoxically, they seem to apply particularly to protein-rich foods which nutritionally would be very valuable but which are thought to damage the child either physically or mentally. A great range of such food taboos and customs exist (Berg, 1973).

Food needs are relatively easy to define as they are a function of physiology and activity. Although there may be disputes about the actual level of need in different circumstances, the range of possible variation is quite small. Food consumption is far more complex. It is a function of needs, supply, price, income level, and social factors, often impossible to quantify. Consumption will vary in a predictable way in response to each of these factors, but the interactions of all factors are difficult to untangle. This complexity makes clear that the simplistic goals of eradiction of poverty, starvation, or a limitation of population growth, are unachievable if tackled as separate issues. We are left with a clear impression of a world which produces enough food to feed its population, and in all probability will continue to do so in the future, but the food distribution is such that a substantial proportion of the population is inadequately fed and a great number are close to, or are actually, starving.

The Future Demand for Food

The most significant variable affecting the future demand for food must be population growth. We can expect at least a doubling of the demand for food by the end of the century as the world's population doubles. There are three additional factors of importance when assessing future food demand:

1. Changing age structure. One of the important determinants of calculated total food needs is the proportion of the population at different ages. Again three factors are important here. Declining death rates in developing countries lead to an increased ageing of the population and thereby to an increased food need. Secondly, if conditions can be made suitable to encourage declining fertility then the rate of overall population increase will eventually decline, but the resulting stable population will have an older age distribution. Finally, reduced infant mortality seems likely to delay this aging process until, and unless, this reduction is matched by a decline in fertility as a result of the better survival rate for children. The aggregate effect of a maturing of the age–sex population pyramid on food needs will be considerable. A simple example of Japan can illustrate this. In 1954 Japan's population was 88.92 million and by 1974 this had increased to 110.05 million or by 24.6 per cent. Table 54 shows this population broken down by age and sex and the calorific requirements of the population at the two time periods based on the FAO standards. The sex structure of the population had not altered significantly, but its ageing meant that total calorific requirement increased 25.5 per cent, somewhat faster than the population. To isolate the effects of age alone a number of simplifying assumptions are made, in particular that there is no change in the physical stature of the population and/or the purchasing power of the people. Also the effects of the war on the population structure of Japan complicates the effects of the falling birth rates on the ageing of the population. None the less, the effects of the age structure of a population on food demand are real enough, and when examined on a world scale, would amount to a very considerable demand for food additional to that which arises from a simple increase in the population.

2. Changing income structure. Figure 45 showed how calorie consumption is related to income in Bangladesh. If this income distribution changes then the future demand for food will increase faster or slower than the rate of population increase, depending on whether the population becomes generally better or worse off. Present calorie consumption by the richest 5 per cent of the population is well over twice that of the poorest 5 per cent. If the general pattern of income distribution remains the same, but economic growth allows an across-the-board increase in personal incomes, this will increase food demand faster than simple population growth but less fast than if some of the inequalities of income can be

Table 54. Age–sex distribution of population and calorie needs: Japan, 1954 and 1974

1954

| | Males | | | Females | | | | |
Age	Population (millions)	kcal required per head[a]	Total kcal required (millions)	Population (millions)	kcal required per head[a]	Total kcal required (millions)	Total population (millions)	Total kcal required (millions)
>1	0.883	820	724	0.840	820	689		
1–4	4.133	1,360	5,621	3.961	1,360	5,387		
5–9	5.297	2,010[b]	10,647	5.102	2,010[b]	10,255		
10–14	4.895	2,750[c]	13,461	4.775	2,420[c]	11,556		
15–19	4.363	3,070	13,394	4.274	2,310	9,873		
20–44	15.095	3,000	45,285	16.480	2,200	36,255		
45–64	6.753	2,850[d]	19,246	6.840	2,100[d]	14,364		
65+	1.959	2,700[e]	5,289	2.641	2,000[e]	5,282		
Total	43.378		113,668	44.914		93,661	88.293	207,329

1974

>1	1.054	820	864	0.992	820	813		
1–4	4.105	1,360	5,583	3.873	1,360	5,267		
5–9	4.487	2,010[b]	9,019	4.281	2,010[b]	8,605		
10–14	4.116	2,750[c]	11,319	3.944	2,420[c]	9,544		
15–19	4.108	3,070	12,612	3.966	2,310	9,161		
20–44	22.574	3,000	67,722	22.735	2,200	50,017		
45–64	9.891	2,850[d]	28,189	11.469	2,100[d]	24,085		
65+	3.665	2,700[e]	9,896	3.781	2,000[e]	7,562		
Total	54.010		145,204	56.039		115,055	110.049	260,259

24.64   25.53
% change 1954/74

[a]Based on FAO (1973)—moderate activity.
[b]Average of 4–6 and 7–9-year-old requirements.
[c]Average of 10–12 and 13–15-year-old requirements.
[d]Assumes some reduction in activity.
[e]Assumes light activity.
Source: United Nations, *Demographic Yearbooks* (1955 and 1975); FAO (1973).

reduced. At the same time, increasing affluence not only creates demand for more calories but also for different foods, particularly high-protein meats, which are calorie expensive in production.

3. Increasing urbanization. As populations increase so an increasing proportion of those populations become urbanized and possibly absorbed into the industrial and service labour force. Generally, food needs are reduced through a reduction in the amount of heavy physical labour, although evidence (Table 55) is biased by the different age–sex structure in urban areas reducing food needs and by the fact that actual consumption may have little or no relationship to actual need. Although the overall food demand may be reduced by increased urbanization, a higher proportion of that food has to be purchased as the proportion of the population which is at least partly self-sufficient is reduced. Urban living also requires more expenditure on clothing and shelter than is required in the countryside. Actual food demand, therefore, in contrast to need will be constrained by the ability to pay.

Population increase will increase food demand. This demand will be further increased by an aging of the population and by increased affluence. Working in the reverse direction will be a reduced need, and possibly demand, as a result of an increasing amount of this increased population being urban. The balance of all these factors in future food demand projections is exceedingly complex, and in practice only population increases are considered in any detail (Chapter 9).

Table 55. Urban and rural calorie consumption by income group: Bangladesh, 1973/74

Income group[a] (taka)	Urban			Rural		
	Grain	Other	Total	Grain	Other	Total
			(kcal)			
0–99	1160	120	1280	770	110	880
100–149	1250	170	1420	1000	140	1140
150–199	1350	140	1490	1220	140	1360
200–249	1470	150	1620	1380	170	1550
250–299	1530	170	1710	1470	200	1670
300–399	1610	200	1810	1620	200	1820
400–499	1620	240	1860	1700	230	1930
500–749	1720	300	2030	1830	280	2110
750–999	1780	410	2190	1960	350	2310
1000–1499	1840	450	2290	2070	380	2450
1500–1999	1900	490	2390	2190	510	2700
2000+	1850	730	2580	2120	530	2650

[a]25 taka = £1.
Source: Gavan (1977).

Planning and Policy Questions

Nutrition is traditionally seen as a welfare rather than a development problem (Berg, 1973). Direct planning for nutritional improvement has been, and often still is, regarded as unnecessary. If calorific intake is a function of income, then planning policies which take care of income should take care of nutrition.

Most planning commissions still equate growth with the development of capital stock and expenditure on human resources, with consumption rather than investment. Seen in this light malnutrition is an indication of under-development, the solution to which lies in the very process of development for which capital accumulation is necessary. With development the problem solves itself. To address malnutrition explicitly or 'prematurely', is a wasteful diversion of scarce resources, and hence counter-productive in the long run (Field and Levinson, 1975).

Even if the extra income can be provided through the process of development there is no guarantee that it will be spent on food for those most in need of it. The extra income can be diverted to other necessities and alternative consumer goods (Berg, 1973). The straightforward economic development argument runs that by increasing agricultural output, and alternative employment opportunities which are a consequence of this output, incomes and savings are raised alongside GDP. Policies which attempt to achieve a better nutritional status of the population, especially the poorest of the population, are less effective at improving the financial ability of this section of the population to feed itself. The alternative view is as follows:

In development plans effective nutrition programs deserve support even if they do not contribute to raised national incomes provided that they do contribute to improved lives for the majority of the people. Fortunately perhaps (as development is dominated by economists) more so than for most health factors, improved nutrition can be shown to have a favourable effect on both per capita income and improved quality of life for people (Latham, 1976).

Low nutrition status leads to low labour productivity and to a small or non-existent accumulation of wealth (Reutlinger and Selowsky, 1976). Studies of those employed on rural works programmes have found evidence of malnutrition and low productivity associated with the resultant lack of energy, low weight-for-height ratios and anaemia (Latham and Brooks, 1977). Of course, improved nutritional status can improve the capability to work but not necessarily the actual output, which depends on motivation and reward as well as capability (Latham, 1976).

Viewed in this light, nutrition is as much of a legitimate investment in economic development as is mechanization, irrigation, and fertilizer in terms of its potential for increasing output (Schultz, 1961). The links between malnutrition and mental retardation and with continuing incapacity of future generations, working through the malnutrition of mothers, make nutrition planning and action even more urgent. Finally, and by no means least important, with almost inconceivable numbers of people in the world suffering, it is ethically unacceptable to many to leave such people to their plight awaiting the due process of economic development, the effects of which are by no means certain (Schuftan, 1978). There is adequate evidence that growth of GDP leads to an increasingly skewed income distribution so that the poor do not benefit from the growth of the economy and may be further disadvantaged (Berg, 1973).

Extending the ethical argument somewhat further many have argued that to overeat in the developed world is morally reprehensible while millions starve in the developing nations. While it is certainly medically foolish to overeat, the connections between overeating in the West and starvation in the developing countries deserves a closer look. Superficially, the saving of grain resulting from eating less meat in the developed world would be considerable. A 10 per cent reduction in the consumption of animal products in the developed countries would provide enough grain to eliminate the calorie deficiency of all the developing countries (Simontov, 1976). There are, however, three main difficulties with this type of argument. Firstly, it assumes that the grain would be distributed in the developing countries in such a way as to be effective in relieving calorie shortages *when and where they occur*, whereas the point has been made many times that it is generally not a shortage of grain which leads to malnutrition. Secondly, such a concept would involve about 120 million tons of grain. This would be difficult to ship and to distribute and would have very pronounced effects on production incentives in the developing countries. The resulting drop in production may reduce supply and increase demand for further grain shipments from the West, thus starting a spiral of increased reliance on supplies from the developed world. Thirdly the impact of reduced grain consumption in the developed world needs examination. Reduced consumption alone, without any mechanism to divert the grain to alternative markets, will simply lead to reduction in production (Johnston, 1975a). There would be less incentive for further development of seeds and less incentive to maintain adequate stock levels. To maintain production in the face of declining domestic demand would require an extensive and very expensive government purchasing programme for shipment to the developing countries. Such a process will not follow automatically from a reduction in domestic production. In fact the latter, operated alone for even the most altruistic of motives, is likely to reduce supply of grain to the developing world in the long term.

Furthermore, Johnson makes the important point that 56 per cent of the cattle feed used in the United States is pasturage not cereals, and even where cereals are used, usually these are coarse grains not directly equivalent to food grains used for human consumption in the needy developing countries (although possibly such food grains could be grown on the same land). Estimates of 1 kg of beef requiring up to 20 kg of cereals are far too high, taking into account the pasturage feeds. The real figure is nearer 1 kg of beef to 4 to 5 kg of grain. On the other hand, the most sought-after premium grade beef in the United States, which is liberally marbled with fat, is the result of feed-lot production, requiring at least 10 kg of grain per kg of beef. Such beef is high in saturated fats and therefore in all probability medically harmful as well as expensive in grain use. Overall there is no direct relationship between overeating in the developed world and malnutrition in the developing countries and it is an unfortunate economic reality that the world's food problem has no such simplistic solution.

CHAPTER 7

Aid and Trade

Introduction

Despite a generally high degree of food self-sufficiency in most countries the production and consumption of food are very rarely in balance. Long-term surplus or deficit must be made up either by adjustments in demand or by entering world trade. Short-term fluctuations can be evened out by the adjustment of stock levels. There is a quantitative difference between agricultural crops in general and staple food crops. Most producers of, say, coffee, tea, or rubber, produce vastly more than the domestic consumption can absorb. Such countries exploit their comparative advantage by exporting the bulk of such production. The balance of production and consumption of staple food crops is generally much closer. Secondly, the emotional appeal of self-sufficiency is much greater for staple food crops, encouraging increased domestic food production and a decreased reliance on world trade. If a country's food production shortfall is large a sufficient reduction in food consumption may not be an option without widespread starvation, and such a country will have to rely on world trade. If the country is a poor one some or all of this shortfall may be made up of food aid. Such shipments are made available at various terms of credit or grant, depending on the extent of the need and the state of the world market for the commodities in question. Similarly, those countries able to produce a surplus of staple foods may ship this surplus through normal commercial channels or by food aid. Frequently, commercial channels for staple foods have not been able to absorb all the available supplies and the producer countries have resorted to aid for food disposal. Many food-deficit countries cannot afford to join commercial markets even though there may be a considerable food need, so the aid channels become essential to them as well as to many surplus countries.

In so far as a country is self-sufficient in food production it is free to pursue its internal production and consumption policies independently of other countries. Conversely, policies can be pursued to ensure this independence of other countries as either suppliers or markets. In the

220

majority of cases, however, where countries cannot, or choose not to, achieve this independence of world markets, the internal agricultural and food policies chosen interact with those in other countries. If there were no routes for the disposal of agricultural surplus through commerce or aid, the agricultural policies of the United States would have been perforce very different and production controls would have had to be far more rigid to have maintained price levels at an acceptable level. There is no doubt that food aid policies adopted by the United States during the 1960s delayed consideration of policy alternatives at home to deal with surplus production. Similarly, the policies of the importing countries are affected by the existence of surpluses elsewhere in the world, perhaps encouraging, perhaps just permitting, policies which ignore or pay little attention to domestic food production. Also, countries which operate various protectionist devices to insulate both consumers and producers from world market conditions, affect these world markets by limiting their size. Such limitations in the size of the world trade in food means that the price effects of production changes are amplified and the effects of these changes are felt by only a limited number of countries. This is critical for the importing developing countries when world food prices rise. Such rises as occurred in 1973–74 were greater than would have been the case if the EEC, for example, had not decided to protect its consumers by imposing an export tax on EEC producers (Johnson, 1975a). This chapter will stress the interactions between different national policies, some deliberate through political leverage exerted by food-surplus countries over food-deficit countries and some less overt.

In 1976 world cereal production was 1477 million tons of which 166 million, or 11.2 per cent, were traded (world exports and imports are not exactly equal because of the effects of grain in transit). Of this 166 million tons traded, 7.4 million, or 4.4 per cent, were delivered in the form of food aid under various concessional agreements. Although the proportion of world production which is available in the form of aid does not seem large it should be remembered that 7.4 million tons would be capable of feeding in excess of 20 million people reasonably adequately for one year.

Cereals are not the only agricultural export, they contribute only 18.7 per cent by value of world agricultural exports. Cash crops account for the majority of agricultural exports by value, but the fact that cereals are the world's major staple food means that their importance is paramount in terms of national and international food policy. In 1976 cereals made up 47.3 per cent by value of all agricultural exports from North America, but only 0.8 per cent by value of all agricultural exports from the developing countries of Africa. Cereals comprised some 95 per cent of all the food aid shipped in 1976.

The world pattern of cereal trade was outlined in Chapter 3. North America and the developed countries of Oceania between them export about 109 million tons of cereals out of a world total of 166 million tons. Western Europe is the exception in the developed world with a net import of cereals. With the exception of Latin America, close to being in overall cereal trade balance, the developing countries are major importers of cereals. The developing country regions of Africa and the Near East import about 15 per cent of their production and the developing countries of the Far East import about 7.9 per cent of a vastly larger production. The centrally planned economies are also importers of cereals. In 1976 the USSR and her Eastern European neighbours imported 35.8 million tons of cereals, or 12 per cent of that year's production in those countries. World cereal trade depends almost totally on North America. Of all world cereal exports, 84 per cent come from the developed countries, 65 per cent from North America, and 49 per cent from the United States alone. As many developed countries, especially those of Western Europe, import as well as export, these percentage figures would be higher for net trade balance (Brown, 1975).

Examination of food crop exports over the ten years 1966–76 confirms that the present position is the result of a continuing trend (Figure 46). Compared to a 1966 base year, developed country exports have risen steadily, except for 1974, to double the 1966 level by 1976. In contrast exports from the centrally planned economies and the developing countries have risen more slowly and the centrally planned economies have shown a declining trend since 1974. In contrast Figure 47 shows that for all three groups of countries imports have risen more or less steadily over the period. The sharpest rise and the most erratic trend is evident for the centrally planned economies.

Since the Second World War the developing countries have changed from being net cereal exporters (14 million tons 1934–38 average annually) to being net importers (Table 56), a trend which in some countries was but

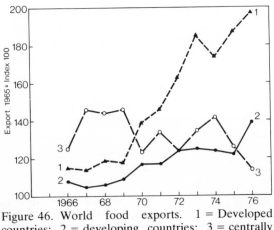

Figure 46. World food exports. 1 = Developed countries; 2 = developing countries; 3 = centrally planned economies. Source: FAO, *Production Yearbooks*

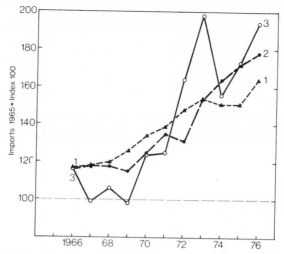

Figure 47. World food imports. 1 = Developed countries; 2 = developing countries, 3 = centrally planned economies. Source: FAO, *Production Yearbooks*

briefly interrrupted by the results of the improved yields from the green revolution. Mexico, for example, was more or less in trade balance for cereals until 1964, from 1965 to 1969 the improved yields allowed exports in excess of 1 million tons per year, but the improvement was short-lived as increased population and demand plus poor harvests in the early 1970s returned Mexico to being a grain-deficit country (Figure 48). The increased

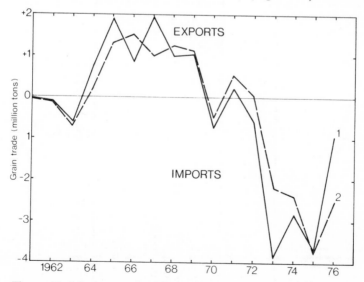

Figure 48. Mexico grain trade. 1 = FAO data, 2 = USDA data. Source: USDA data, Brown (1975); FAO, *Trade Yearbooks*

Table 56. World grain trade

Region	1934–1938	1948–1952	1960	1970	1971	1972	1973	1974	1975	1976
					(millions of tons)					
North America	+ 5	+23	+39	+54	+54	+71	+98	+76	+88	+96
Latin America	+ 9	+ 1	0	+ 4	+11	0	– 3	– 1	– 4	–10
Western Europe	–24	–22	–25	–22	–26	–20	–21	–22	–20	–25
Eastern Europe and the USSR	+ 5	0	0	– 2	– 2	–18	–24	– 7	–20	–30
Africa	+ 1	0	– 2	– 4	– 6	– 3	– 6	– 7	– 9	– 9
Asia	+ 2	– 6	–17	–37	–34	–35	–47	–48	–47	–45
Australia and New Zealand	+ 3	+ 3	+ 6	+ 8	+12	+12	+ 7	+ 7	+11	+11

Source: 1934–38, 1948–52, 1960: Brown (1975); 1970–76: FAO, *Trade Yearbooks*.

Table 57. Net imports of cereals in selected developing countries
('000 tons)

Country	1961–65	1970	1971	1972	1973	1974	1975	1976
India	5380	4159	2441	290	4140	5219	7493	6489
Bangladesh	761	1571	1164	1638	2906	1703	2349	1471
Pakistan	756	365	121	579	555	554	709	403
Indonesia	995	1421	1012	1179	2607	1722	1339	2348
Philippines	678	510	1046	1402	1004	817	824	901
Malaysia	786	777	651	673	721	827	612	775
Sri Lanka	802	1100	790	811	1001	951	1164	926
South Korea	694	2205	3204	3394	3283	2677	3126	2783
Thailand	−2329	−2437	−3449	−3907	−2153	−3383	−3165	−4297
Burma	−1551	− 614	− 781	− 507	− 127	− 281	− 272	− 586
Hong Kong and Singapore	872	1147	1314	1301	1127	1003	1130	1376

Source: FAO, *Trade Yearbooks*; OECD (1976a).

grain deficit of developing countries of Asia is confirmed by Table 57. Trade of cereals in India showed a steady climb in net imports from 0.5 million tons in 1955 to a high of over 10 million tons in 1966, followed by a rapid fall to less than 0.5 million tons in 1972 and an equally rapid rise to 7.5 million in 1975. A succession of record-breaking harvests eliminated Indian imports in 1977. Even in countries where production and yields run at very high levels the amount of imports have had to rise to cope with increased demand. Japan has long been an importer of cereals, but in 1971 imports at about 15 million tons per year came level with production and have continued to rise while production has held steady. Western Europe's import requirements have remained very stable, but the USSR and Eastern Europe have shown a fluctuating but generally rising demand, especially after 1972.

Trade

In a perfectly free, and economically logical, world, trade would result from comparative advantage. The world's agricultural goods would be produced where the ecological circumstances were most favourable, perhaps extending outwards to less favourable land if the size of the market warranted it. Reality is very far from this ideal situation and both production and trade are distorted by government policies, by bilateral and multinational trade agreements and by concepts and policies of national self-sufficiency. In the case of some crops, the production of which is tied to certain ecological zones and demand is more widespread, the separation of production and consumption does lead to trade which is based on comparative advantage. It is obviously possible to produce coffee in the United States, but at a vastly greater expense than to import this coffee from Brazil, Colombia, and from elsewhere, meanwhile growing more suitable crops in the United States and perhaps exporting these to coffee-growing countries. Colombia imported 30,167 tons of wheat and wheat flour in 1976, mostly from the United States, and exported 377,300 tons of coffee, again largely to the United States. Coffee has a comparative advantage in Colombia as does wheat in the United States and this fact is reflected in the trading patterns between the two countries. There is no alterative crop which can be grown outside the subtropics which can be substituted by the consuming country. Trade is the only feasible way of meeting the demand. Out of a total of 3.6 million tons exported annually (1976) 3.5 million are exported by developing countries and the majority of these exports are to the developed countries.

The case of sugar is very different. There are two contrasting crops, both of which can be used to create the same product. Sugar-cane is essentially a tropical crop and sugar-beet is a temperate crop, but both can be refined to create sugar. As the greatest demand for sugar, thanks to the food-processing industry, is in the developed nations, the tropical sugar producers are in competition with the temperate beet farmers. Government policies in the temperate countries ensure that home production is maintained. With the exceptions of Japan and the United States which produce both crops, the world's major sugar importers are also the major beet producers while the exporters are the cane producers (Table 58). The complexity of this situation is confounded by national and international policies with regard to sugar production and trade.

In the nineteenth century France and Germany exported sugar produced from beet to the United Kingdom market. This reduced the import of cane

Table 58. Sugar production and trade, 1976

Country	Imports[a] (million tons)	Sugar-beet[b] production (million tons)	Sugar-cane[c] production (million tons)
Major importers			
Algeria	0.36	—	—
Morocco	0.24	2.36	—
Canada	0.90	1.16	—
USA	4.14	26.70	26.12
China	0.62	8.40	—
Iran	0.31	4.80	—
Iraq	0.39	—	—
Japan	2.43	2.31	1.81
Korean Republic	0.31	—	—
Malaysian Peninsula	0.33	—	—
Europe	5.43	138.13	—
USSR	3.76	98.60	—
Major exporters	*Exports*		
Mauritius	0.55	—	6.60
South Africa	0.67	—	19.22
Cuba	5.76	—	51.00
Dominican Republic	0.98	—	10.25
Guatamala	0.32	—	6.55
Jamaica	0.23	—	4.00
Argentina	0.29	—	16.10
Brazil	1.20	—	103.19
Guyana	0.30	—	4.10
Peru	0.26	—	8.90
China	0.57	—	44.74
India	0.91	—	142.71
Philippines	1.47	—	25.50
Thailand	1.12	—	19.00
Europe	3.40	—	—
Australia	2.20	—	23.80
Fiji	0.25	—	2.33

[a]Countries with more than 230,000 tons exported or imported; total raw sugar equivalent.
[b]Other major producers are Chile, 2.07 and Turkey, 7.60 million tons.
[c]Other major producers are: Mexico, 33.80; Colombia, 20.00; Venezuela, 5.50; Bangladesh, 5.98; Indonesia, 15.09; and Pakistan, 25.50 million tons.
— Denotes no or small production.
Source: FAO, *Trade and Production Yearbooks* (1976).

sugar from Caribbean producers. The first international attempt to organize the world sugar market came in 1903 with the Brussels Sugar Convention. Price control and quota mechanisms were used to regulate the sugar market in the interests of the cane and the beet producers and the consumers. Such controls continue in modified terms today. The world sugar market is effectively split into three parts, in each of which different prices operate. For producer countries there is domestic production, there is the world free market which accounts for under 60 per cent of the world's sugar trade and there are a series of bilateral and multilateral sugar agreements between importers and exporters.

In the United States the Sugar Acts date back to 1934 when a compromise was reached between domestic and foreign producers and domestic consumers which allowed relatively cheap cane sugar from developing countries access to the American market in a limited and controlled way. A total import allowance was subdivided between importers. Domestic production controls were imposed to allow for those imports of cheaper sugar. In 1973–74 the world price for sugar increased dramatically. For reasons discussed more fully in the next chapter, the US Administration was anxious to increase agricultural exports and so President Nixon and Secretary for Agriculture Earl Butz removed all domestic production controls, drew attention to the market opportunities presented by the high sugar prices and finally placed a maximum quota of 7 million short tons on the import of sugar from developing countries. As with the case of wheat the period of sugar shortage and high prices ended after a short time and by mid 1978 there was a world sugar glut, domestic production controls were reimposed and the Administration was again torn between the conflicting demands of the LDC producers, the domestic beet producers and the consumers for a low-priced product.

In 1949–51 the first Commonwealth Sugar Agreement was signed between the UK as a major importer and the sugar-cane producers of the Commonwealth. Agreed quantities and prices were fixed every year with all exporters. Prices for LDC producers were supplemented by a special payment which varied inversely with the world market price. Thus the Commonwealth producers had the advantage of both a guaranteed market and prices which, for the major part of the period of this and subsequent agreements, were above world market prices. This special payment was financed by the UK sugar consumers who paid a weighted average price of the domestically produced sugar-beet, the Agreement price and the world market price. The domestic price was still below that in the EEC where the domestic beet producers were more protected from world supplies. For this reason UK membership of the EEC brought the Commonwealth Sugar Agreements to an end. In fact the last Agreement had been more or less destroyed by the price events of 1973–74 when the world price rose to six times the current negotiated Agreement price. The EEC policy for sugar is the same as for other agricultural products. Except during 1973–74 the EEC intervention price has been higher than the world sugar price. The Lomé Convention allows the limited import of sugar from certain developing countries.

Other special agreements for the sugar trade exist between Cuba and other communist countries and between the USSR and other countries and also among some African countries. Of the remainder of the world market about 85 per cent comes under the International Sugar Agreements. These, signed in 1968, 1973 and 1978, are designed to regulate the sugar market by setting floor and ceiling prices. The current Agreement sets these at 12 and 21 cents per pound delivered in New York. Such commodity trade agreements, attempting to reconcile conflicting interests, have a history of working only while the world supply position is relatively normal. Where the same product is grown in the developed as well as the developing countries, world supply shortage will disrupt agreements as with the Commonwealth Sugar Acts and the US Sugar Acts in 1973–74.

A great many of the world's developing countries are dependent on the export of agricultural goods but, as in the case of sugar, most developed countries have elaborate trade barriers to protect their own agricultural and industrial sectors (Jones, 1976). Even where agricultural produce is imported into developed countries it is usually in an unprocessed form and the processing industries are protected by tariffs. The exporting developing countries are denied the value added resulting from the development of their own manufacturing industries. A small but significant case in point is the protection provided for the jute industries of Aberdeen in Scotland against imports of processed jute products from India and Bangladesh. The political importance of the jobs of the small number of jute workers in Scotland has been of greater significance than the development opportunities increased manufacture of jute products would have provided to India and to Bangladesh. Jute is many times more important to the economy of Bangladesh than it is to Britain, but the protection continues to be provided.

In most issues of national food policy there are alternatives, and one or more of these alternatives have implications for production and/or consumption in other countries and on their food policies. The countries of the world have not only become more interdependent with regard to food production and supply, but also with regard to policies enacted to influence production and supply. For example, the policy alternatives open to the United States in the 1950s and 1960s, when presented with an obvious and expensive food production surplus, were to limit production, to increase exports, or some combination of both. If the export alternative had not been available, production limitation would have had to have been much more dramatic in its effects. The export policy was possible and exports, both commercial and as aid, had far-reaching consequences on the importing countries and on their food and agricultural policies, which in turn would have been different if the imports had not been available. We shall see in a later section how the policies of the government of India were strongly influenced by imports, commercial and grant-aided, from the United States. If the United Kingdom was unable to rely on imported food there would be a greater emphasis on policies of self-sufficiency. Such took place during the Second World War and again more recently when, with the world grain price rise, there was an awakening interest in the possibilities of more food from domestic resources (HMSO, 1975). The elimination of alternatives obviously shifts policy priorities.

Even chronically food-short countries such as Bangladesh have real policy alternatives which are affected by the terms of trade for the commodities produced and consumed in that country. Jute and jute goods make up 87 per cent of all exports and provide the only real commercial source of foreign exchange. However, jute competes directly with rice for land and, to a much lesser extent in a generally labour-surplus country, for labour. It also competes for other agricultural inputs in short supply, particularly fertilizer. Bangladesh has a substantial food-grain deficit and the question arises should the government encourage more jute production and rely on further rice imports, or should food grains be encouraged to the exclusion of all other crops until the food deficit is covered? The same sort of question is raised, although generally to a less prominent extent, in many developing countries where there is a cash crop alternative to food crops. For Bangladesh the answer is provided by the size of the world jute market, including any government restrictions on imports imposed by other countries, and also by the relative earning power of farm land and labour devoted to jute production compared to rice. Jute is grown in the wet season from April to September on land which would otherwise be planted to the Aus or wet season rice crop. After harvesting the jute plant is soaked, retted (the fibres being separated from the stalk), in August to November, then baled and shipped to the export ports. A proportion is taken to the jute mills and converted to sacking and other jute goods for domestic and overseas use. A recent World Bank Report (1978a) estimates that 1 ha of jute, grown by traditional methods, would 'earn' in foreign exchange sufficient to import 1.63 tons of rice at market prices prevailing in 1976. This same amount of rice would have required 1.9 ha of traditional Aus paddy production (Table 59). To provide equal returns to jute and rice, the price ratio has to be in excess of 1.00 as jute production has a larger labour requirement. Furthermore, as improved varieties of rice are successful and research on improved methods of production has proceeded further than for jute, the ratio of jute to rice prices must rise if jute is to remain competitive against improved rice production. The report estimates that the ratio has to be 1.25 for traditional rice and jute production, rising to as much as 2.86 for traditional jute production compared to the use of optimal technology for rice production. This adds to other, domestic, reasons for the government to reduce the market price of rice, making jute competitive and at the same time reducing the incentives to the adoption of the latest technologies for

Table 59. Jute/rice competition in Bangladesh

| | 1976—per hectare | | |
	Production[a] (tons)	Price $US[b] per ton	Value ($US)
Jute			
Traditional	1.235	460	568
Improved	1.655	460	761
Rice			
Traditional	0.840	350	294
Improved	1.408	350	493

[a]Yields less 10 per cent seed and wastage.
[b]Jute fob Chittagong and Chalna. Rice cif Chittagong for Thailand 25–35 per cent broken.
Source: After World Bank (1978a).

rice production. On the other hand there is a limited world market for Bangladesh jute, estimated at about 400,000 tons annually by 1985 (compared to 375,000 tons per year 1973–75 average), so there is little scope for a policy for the *expansion* of jute acreage.

The development philosophy of meeting basic human needs in Bangladesh, concentrating on the needs of the poorest sections of the population, might seem to support the increased production of food grains in preference to cash crops. In Bangladesh the production of this 400,000 tons of jute for export is earning badly needed foreign exchange, providing more rural employment than an equivalent production of rice and helping to keep the consumer price of rice low. Provided that the price of rice is not set so low as to inhibit further investment in rice production it is hard to see that such cash crop production, limited by the state of the world market, is anything but to the advantage of the poorest in Bangladesh. The same situation is not true where the demand for the export crop is buoyant, as for coffee for example, and where returns are so much higher that food crop production may be severely threatened.

Food Aid

Although food aid represents but a small proportion of total food production, and only 4.4 per cent of food exports, it is none the less of very great importance. There are several reasons for this:

1. It goes in large part to countries otherwise unable to pay for commercial imports and may be the only effective way to close the food gap between production and demand, at least in the short term.
2. Because food aid is concentrated on staple foodstuffs, mostly cereals, the effects on farmers in the recipient countries are potentially great as these farmers will be concentrating on staple food production.

3. Food aid may provide an apparently cheap form of aid from the perspective of the donor countries with accumulated surpluses, or the potential for surplus production, already paid for by other programmes of government support to domestic agriculture.
4. Food aid, although perhaps donated for humanitarian reasons, may have far-reaching commercial effects on trade and on production in the recipient country.
5. In common with other forms of aid, food aid has an international political dimension ensuring that it is not distributed according to need, nor according to the ability for the recipient country to pay for it, but, at least in part, for strategic reasons of the donor countries.

Even though trade has political as well as commercial dimensions, aid brings these issues into sharp focus and the remainder of this chapter will explore food aid and its impacts on food policy in donor and recipient countries.

The local, national and international food shortages which have occurred in recent history stimulated various types of relief measures. In particular, Chapter 4 outlined how the Bengal famine gave rise to the public food distribution systems which operate more or less unchanged in India and Bangladesh today. Food for these early relief measures was mostly obtained from within the subcontinent by restrictions on private trade and a channelling of surplus through government procurement agencies. The major difference between the Bengal famine and later famines in India, Bangladesh, or the Sahel is that food for famine relief came mostly from outside the countries affected in the form of food aid. Although famine and starvation are old phenomena in the world, food aid is very recent and reached any considerable size only in the mid 1950s. It is obvious that the existence of food aid has been stimulated by factors other than the needs of the countries suffering from chronic food shortages.

The present era of food aid opened with the passing of the Agriculture, Trade and Assistance Act by the Eighty-third Congress of the United States in 1954, more popularly known as Public Law (PL) 480. Other countries began to make significant contributions following the Food Aid Convention of 1967 and food aid has continued to be arranged through a series of international agreements and organizations while individual countries have continued to organize their own programmes. Early shipments under PL 480 were small, but by 1957 they reached a value of $1525 million. Shipments stayed at a high level until 1965, when the value of United States' food aid started a decline which has since continued. To some extent this decline has been offset by the arrival of many other countries as aid donors. Despite the contributions of other countries, the decline in United States' food aid and the share of total food exports made up of aid shipments (Table 60) was reflected in the receipts of the recipient countries. The average annual cereal imports 1961–63 to the developing countries were 25.1 million tons of which food aid made up 14.3 million tons, or 57

Table 60. Value of commercial and aid food shipments from the United States, 1955–73

	Commercial food exports ($'000)				
	1955–59	1960–64	1965–69	1970–73	Total
Animals and animal products	3,101	3,189	3,641	4,117	14,048
Dairy products	951	744	775	580	3,194
Total grains and preparations	6,199	10,384	13,124	12,882	42,589
Wheat and wheat products	3,558	5,999	6,257	5,640	21,454
Feed grains and products	2,003	3,478	5,364	5,630	16,476
Rice	535	777	1,382	1,350	4,044
Oilseeds and products	2,174	3,479	6,112	9,512	21,277
Cotton	3,426	3,587	2,315	2,116	11,444
	PL 480 shipments ($'000)				
Animal and animal products	938	518	623	413	2,492
Dairy products	740	416	478	312	1,966
Total grains and preparations	3,361	5,032	4,710	2,857	15,960
Wheat and wheat products	2,343	3,980	3,520	1,581	11,424
Feed grains and products	747	672	549	342	2,310
Rice	252	378	570	761	1,961
Oilseeds and products	541	580	540	425	2,086
Cotton	1,429	843	558	448	3,279
Totals	19,090	25,753	31,597	35,420	111,860
	PL 480				
	6,529	7,265	6,640	4,301	24,736

Source: USDA (1974).

per cent. By 1970 this percentage had fallen to 38 per cent and it continued to fall through the 1970s to approximately 16 per cent in 1976. This shows a relative as well as an absolute decline in food aid shipments (Table 61). Some of this decline in aid has been paralleled by a concentration on those countries most in need. In 1976 the countries which the FAO defines as most seriously affected (MSA) in Africa received 31 per cent of total food imports in the form of aid, the Far East figure was 31.4 per cent and the average of all MSA countries received 28.5 per cent of these imports as aid.

Table 61. Cereal imports and cereal aid shipments to developing countries

	Imports	Aid	% Aid
	(millions tons)		
Average 1961–63	25.1	14.3	57
1970	33.5	12.8	38
1971	36.6	12.7	35
1972	34.5	11.8	34
1973	45.6	9.6	21
1974	48.8	7.7	16
1975	54.4	8.4	15
1976	49.6	8.0	16

Source: FAO, *Trade Yearbooks*; *Food Aid Bulletins*.

The decline in the importance of food aid during the 1970s was not paralleled by total development assistance. This rose from $7822 million in 1970 to $16,607 million in 1975 and so food aid declined also relative to development assistance throughout this period. In the United States where food aid has loomed large in absolute terms and in its share of US total development assistance, the picture has also changed. In 1970 food aid accounted for approximately one-third of the $3157 million in development assistance. By 1975 this proportion had fallen to 21 per cent of the total of $4742 million. The relative importance of the share of food aid in total development aid in different donor countries varies considerably. The most important, but not the only, criterion is the existence of a real or potential food surplus in the donor country.

The majority of food aid has been and remains cereals and cereal products (Table 62). Total grains and grain products made up 65 per cent by value of United States' aid under PL 480 between 1955 and 1973, while total grain shipments, both aid and commercial, made up only 38 per cent of total agricultural shipments by value. Aid shipments of cereals have been more variable than commercial shipments, falling from 54 per cent of total shipments in 1955–59 to 22 per cent in 1970–73. Wheat has been the major grain shipped and rice, although a much smaller share of the total, has recently increased in importance. This is significant as most of the food aid recipient countries are rice consumers. During 1976 the total government food aid shipments, notified to the World Food Council, were worth $1384 million with a continuing dominance of cereals, and wheat in particular—6.2 million tons of wheat and 1.2 million tons of other cereals were notified and only 0.3 million tons of all other commodities. The domination of cereals is just as striking whether measured by weight or by value. Despite this the United States and the EEC have been responsible for the shipment of non-food agricultural goods. Between 1974–75 and 1977 shipments of edible oils more than doubled from 113,000 tons to 250,000 tons, and skimmed milk shipments also rapidly increased from 121,5000 tons to over 200,000 tons over the same period. Food aid shipments are closely related to the sur-

Table 62. United States PL 480 shipments, 1955–73

	% By value				
	1955–59	1960–64	1965–69	1970–73	Total
Animals and animal products					
(1)	16.24	12.38	11.52	11.62	12.56
(2)	14.36	7.13	9.38	9.59	10.07
(3)	30.23	16.24	17.10	10.02	17.73
Dairy products					
(1)	4.98	2.89	2.45	1.64	2.86
(2)	14.56	10.24	11.67	13.49	12.91
(3)	77.83	55.96	61.63	53.85	61.50
Grains and preparations					
(1)	32.47	40.32	41.53	36.37	38.07
(2)	51.48	69.26	70.93	66.44	64.53
(3)	54.22	48.46	35.89	22.18	37.48
Wheat and wheat products					
(1)	18.64	23.29	19.80	15.92	19.18
(2)	35.89	54.78	53.01	36.75	46.19
(3)	65.85	66.35	56.26	28.03	53.25
Feed grains and products					
(1)	10.49	13.51	16.98	15.90	14.73
(2)	11.43	9.24	8.27	7.96	9.33
(3)	37.27	19.31	10.24	6.08	11.92
Rice					
(1)	2.80	3.02	4.37	3.81	3.62
(2)	3.85	5.20	8.59	17.69	7.93
(3)	47.08	48.62	41.25	56.37	48.48
Oilseeds and products					
(1)	11.39	13.51	19.34	26.86	19.02
(2)	8.29	7.98	8.14	9.89	8.44
(3)	24.90	16.66	8.84	4.47	9.81
Cotton					
(1)	17.94	13.93	7.33	5.97	10.23
(2)	21.88	11.61	8.41	10.43	13.26
(3)	41.70	23.51	24.12	21.20	28.65
Total					
(3)	34.20	28.21	21.01	12.14	22.11

(1) Percentage of total commercial plus aid.
(2) Percentage of total aid.
(3) Aid percentage of commercial plus aid.
Source: USDA (1974).

pluses in the donor countries, and surpluses are not confined to cereals.

The major donors of cereals aid are indicated in Table 63. The world total declined from 1970–71 into the crisis years of 1973–74 and has climbed again since. Because of the domination of the United States in total cereal

Table 63. Cereals and cereal products food aid, 1969–79
('000 tons)

Donor country	1969–70	1970–71	1971–72	1972–73	1973–74	1974–75	1975–76	1976–77	1977–78	1978–79[a]
Argentina	27	10	13	2	10	20	—	22	34	23
Australia	216	225	215	259	222	330	261	231	255	325
Canada	663	1,608	1,093	887	486	594	1,034	1,176	1,000	1,000
EEC[b]	1,356	983	978	986	1,202	1,391	933	1,151	1,514	1,287
Finland	15	13	—	25	17	24	25	33	47	14
Japan[c]	395	753	731	528	350	182	33	46	132	225
Norway	14	9	8	—	—	—	10	10	10	10
Sweden	38	65	8	56	65	312	47	115	92	75
Switzerland	35	45	27	21	33	29	35	33	17	32
USA	10,008	9,105	9,259	7,025	3,198	4,712	4,284	6,147	5,700	6,400
Other	—	10	231	319	59	751	193	134	392	400
World	12,767	12,826	12,563	10,108	5,642[d]	8,345	6,855	9,098	9,193	9,791

[a] Indicated figure for year from budgetary allocation or commitments.
[b] Includes member country contributions.
[c] In some years calculated from value of cash payments.
[d] Excludes food loans from USSR to Bangladesh and India to be repaid in kind.
Source: Food Aid Bulletin, No. 3, July 1977, and Food Aid Bulletin, No. 3, July 1978.

aid most of this decline can be attributed to a decrease in shipments from the United States. Interestingly, although the policies adopted in the EEC during the difficult time of 1973–74 provided protection for the EEC consumers by imposing export taxes on EEC producers of cereals, these same policies also allowed an increase in food aid shipments from the EEC. In 1970–71 the EEC share of world cereal aid was 8 per cent against 71 per cent from the United States. In 1973–74 the EEC share had risen to 20 per cent and the share of the United States had fallen to 54 per cent. The latest available data show the EEC share as 14 per cent and the United States' share as 66 per cent. The EEC contributions are made up partly of those contributions which originate with the EEC Council and are paid for from central funds, and partly from the individual member countries, which retain the right to allocate food aid according to their own resources and to their own donor criteria. Nearly 60 per cent of France's food aid, independent of the EEC, goes to African countries and 40 per cent of Germany's food aid goes to South and South-East Asia. The member states' contributions make up about 40 per cent of the EEC food aid. The trend in Canadian shipments has followed almost exactly that of the shipments from the United States. Australia's contributions have remained remarkably constant but Japan's aid, calculated recently in terms of the purchasing power of cash contributions, has fallen, partly as a result of the world increase in cereal prices.

PL 480

Part of the original Agricultural Trade Development and Assistance Act of 1954 read as follows:

> It is hereby declared to be the policy of the Congress to expand international trade . . . to promote the economic stability of American agriculture and the national welfare, to make maximum efficient use of surplus agricultural commodities in the furtherance of the foreign policy of the United States and to stimulate and facilitate the expansion of foreign trade in agricultural commodities produced in the United States.

This quotation and the title of the Act state the objectives of the first legislative move by the United States to provide food aid. While some of the emphasis has changed the fundamental objectives as expressed by this legislation remain true today. Originally, the Act was supposed to operate only for three years, by which time the surpluses were supposed to be expended (Mettrick, 1969). Production controls would prevent the renewed accumulation of surpluses and the major rationale for the Act would be removed. As it was first enacted, it is clear that PL 480 was intended as a mechanism for the removal of surpluses accumulated from the operations of the Commodity Credit Corporation, in a manner which would not adversely affect the United States and particularly its agricultural exports and could be used to the benefit of United States foreign policy. PL 480 provided a means whereby surplus agricultural commodities, *in excess of the usual marketings* of such commodities, could be sold through private channels. This emphasis on the development of commercial agricultural trade has always been present in food aid legislation (USDA, 1977c) for food aid was to be used as a pump primer, developing a taste for, and marketing channels for, agricultural exports from the United States. However, foreign policy matters have also remained important criteria for the disposition of aid, and food aid has been no exception. In 1974, when most of the developing countries were in extreme need of food aid, the United States shipped nearly half of its total food aid to South Vietnam and to Cambodia. In September 1974 Bangladesh was 'requested' to stop its jute trade with Cuba as recipients of PL 480 shipments were not allowed to trade with countries blacklisted by the United States. Food aid was clearly used here to exert political leverage over a relatively trifling matter to the United States, but one of some importance to Bangladesh (McHenry and Bird, 1977).

Despite the continuity of all the themes expressed in the original legislation there have been significant changes in the wording and the purpose of the food aid legislation. The Act set up three titles under which food was to be distributed. Title I was the commercial channel. Originally the food was to be sold to the recipient countries for local currency. This currency was accumulated by the United States in the recipient country and used partly to defray US expenses in that country with the agreement of both sides. By 1958, however, US gold reserves were low and a concern for the balance of payments encouraged a change from sales for local currency to dollar credit sales. Large accumulations of local currency had occurred, especially in the major recipient countries like India, which could neither be repatriated to the United States nor be satisfactorily spent in the recipient countries. As the money was not rapatriated, and only a fraction of it actually spent, United States food aid can be effectively regarded as a gift to many recipient countries. Dollar credit sales were consolidated into Title I, and by 1973 had totally replaced local currency sales (Table 64).

Title II involved the donation of food to countries with food shortages. The food aid under this title was, and remains, the responsiblity of various voluntary and international agencies who take over the allocation and distribution in the recipient countries. Such food aid is used for school meals programmes, for food for work schemes, and other attempts at supplemental feeding. For Title II shipments the recipient country is expected to pay for the within-country distribution, but the ocean freight is paid for by the United States. In the case of Title I shipment costs are added to the dollar credits. The Cargo Preference Act (PL 480, Eighty-third Congress) requires that at least 50 per cent of the PL 480 shipments take place in ships carrying the flag of the United States, and the recipient countries are reimbursed the extra costs of using these ships. This 'ocean freight differential' cost $1.1 billion from the start of the programme to September 1976 (USDA, 1977c). Title III was established to allow for the barter of US food for strategic goods needed by the United States and available in the food-needy coun-

Table 64. Value of United States agricultural shipments under different PL 480 titles

Year	Title I Sales for local currency (million US $)	Title I Sales for dollar credits	Title II Donations	Title II %	Title III[a] Barter (million US $)	Total PL 480 (million US $)	PL 480 % total agricultural exports
1955	73	—	187	48.6	125	385	12.2
1956	439	—	247	25.1	298	984	28.1
1957	908	—	216	14.2	401	1,525	32.2
1958	657	—	224	22.8	100	981	24.5
1959	724	—	161	15.8	132	1,017	27.3
1960	824	—	143	12.8	149	1,116	24.7
1961	951	—	221	16.8	144	1,316	26.6
1962	1,030	19	248	16.6	198	1,495	29.1
1963	1,088	57	263	18.1	48	1,456	28.7
1964	1,056	48	270	19.1	43	1,417	23.3
1965	1,142	158	238	15.2	32	1,570	25.8
1966	866	181	267	19.8	32	1,346	19.9
1967	803	178	267	21.0	23	1,271	18.6
1968	723	300	250	19.5	6	1,279	20.0
1969	346	427	265	25.5	1	1,039	17.8
1970	309	506	241	22.8	—	1,056	15.7
1971	204	539	280	27.4	—	1,023	13.2
1972	143	535	380	35.9	—	1,058	13.1
1973	6	661	287	30.1	—	954	7.4
1974	—	575	292	33.7	—	867	4.1
1975	—	762	339	30.8	—	1,101	5.1
1976	—	615	216	26.0	—	831	3.8
Total 1955–76	12,292	5,561	5,502	21.9	1,732	25,087	14.2

[a]Before 1963 includes some shipments under authorization other than PL 480.
Source: USDA (1977c).

tries. These goods were mostly raw materials, but the programme was never large and was phased out by 1967, having been insignificant since the early 1960s (Table 64). The term 'Title III' has recently been reactivated for a very different purpose which will be discussed below.

The first major change in the legislation came in 1966 with the Food for Peace Act (PL 808, Eighty-ninth Congress) which altered the emphasis of PL 480 in three important ways. The poor Indian grain harvest of 1966 coincided with a period when stocks of grain in the United States were relatively low and surplus disposal was no longer an important criterion for food aid programmes. As a result, the revised wording of the Act concentrated on 'combatting hunger and malnutrition using the abundant agricultural resources of the United States'. 'Surplus' was now changed to 'abundant' and there was now explicit reference to the use of food aid in cases of hunger and malnutrition (Mettrick, 1969; USDA, 1977c). Secondly, as emphasis had shifted from surplus disposal, the new legislation could also emphasize general economic development in the recipient countries to build up the potential for increased commercial trade with the United States. The legislation stressed self-help and that recipient countries should devote energies and resources to increasing the production of food crops rather than increasing the land planted to cash crops at the expense of food production. When the PL 480 Title I shipments arrived in a country they were to be sold by the recipient governments. The funds accumulated from these sales were to be used for development projects established by the recipient government and approved by the United States. Annual reports on the expenditure of this locally generated currency were required. The third change brought about by the revised legislation consolidated the shift from local currency sales to dollar credit. Loan terms varied depending on the economic state of the recipient countries and, if possible, 5 per cent of the total value was required as a deposit on the signing of the PL 480 agreement. The wording of the law may have changed, but the original intention of the legislation obviously remained in the minds of those close to its administration. For example, it was possible for Paarlberg (1973) to report to a Congressional hearing on the world food situation in October 1973 that 'It is my understanding that the USDA considers PL 480 to be what it was legislated to be namely a trade development and surplus disposal operation.' The hearing established that the USDA did not include food aid shipments in its annual estimates of demand as the United States in 1972–73 had no surpluses and PL 480 would not apply without surplus.

The next change occurred with the International Development and Food Assistance Act of 1975 (PL 94–161). This followed the world oil crisis and the balance of payments problems which this presented to most developing countries, coinciding with the world food shortages of 1973–74. Again there were three significant changes. Firstly, the chronic need for relief food was recognized. Reinforcing agreements reached at the World Food Conference in 1974, a minimum of 1.3 million tons of cereals was allocated annually to Title II aid. This was the first time that a floor quantity had been established and this minimum amount was to be delivered irrespective of the existence of agricultural surplus in the United States.

Many recipient countries had been worried by the halving of United States' food aid in 1973 and this minimum allocation was a form of guaranteed free availability regardless of the state of world supply. Secondly, Congress insisted that at least 75 per cent of available food under Title I went to countries with a GNP of $300 per head or less. This was a reaction to the overemphasis on foreign policy motives for food aid and a recognition of the desperate plight of the poorest nations, many of which then, and now, receive no food aid. Finally, Title III was reactivated to reinforce the self-help development aspects of the 1966 Act. Local funds available from the sale of Title I food, invested by the recipient government in development projects approved by the United States, would be taken as payment for a proportion of the Title I shipments. This was to start at 5 per cent of the Title I shipments in 1979 and rise to 15 per cent in 1981. Few new Title III agreements have been signed, partly because of the difficulty of monitoring the developmental expenditure and partly because such agreements are taken by many recipients as undue interference in their internal affairs. The Act also reconfirmed the importance of self-help by stating that food aid is to be related to the efforts by the receiving countries to increase their own agricultural production with emphasis on the development of small, family farm agriculture and to improve their facilities for transportation, storage and distribution of food commodities. This is the first reference to the income distribution problems of agricultural development in the developing countries, although the 1966 Act had tried to discourage the development of cash crop farming. From November 1975 to March 1976 PL 480 shipments to Bangladesh were delayed until the Bangladesh government raised the ration price at which Title I food was to be sold within the country. By raising the ration price it was hoped that the food aid would be less of a disincentive for domestic producers (McHenry and Bird, 1977).

It has been suggested that the State Department artificially inflated the worldwide food aid need in 1976 in order to be able to ship more to the Philippines and South Korea under the 75 per cent rule established by the 1975 Act. Possibly this is an explanation for the shipment of too much food aid to Bangladesh in 1976, coinciding with a good local harvest and overwhelming local storage facilities (McHenry and Bird, 1977). At the same time it appeared likely that Egypt would fall out of the major food aid category as GNP rose, just at a time when Egyptian/United States relations were reaching *rapprochement*. It is certainly true that the 75 per cent rule led to a high degree of inflexibility and the limiting figure was raised to $550 per capita GNP in 1976 dollars, a figure which can now vary depending on the World Bank's criterion for the allocation of 'soft' loans. Also the 75 per cent rule as a whole can now be waived if it can be demonstrated that the full 75 per cent cannot be efficiently utilized for humanitarian and development purposes (USDA, 1977c).

The latest addition to the criteria for the allocation of food aid has been the matter of human rights. Countries which are considered consistently to deny basic human rights to their citizens, determined by such measures as the number of political prisoners, are not to receive food aid from the United States. This limitation has proved difficult to enforce and in some cases it clearly conflicts with other objectives of the PL 480 programmme, particularly the furtherance of US foreign policy, as in the Philippines and Indonesia, for example.

The responsibility for the management of PL 480 is jointly in the hands of USAID (a division of the Department of State) and the Department of Agriculture. The Secretary for Agriculture is empowered to decide on the amount of agricultural produce available for PL 480 shipments each year, even though the strict surplus requirements of these shipments have been lifted since 1966. His department also decides on the commodities available and the terms of sale for these commodities and arranges the shipping. USAID decides on the needs of the recipient countries, based on requests from potential recipients and information from its field officers located in the relevant US embassies. Within Congressional budget restraints laid down each year, the Department of Agriculture and USAID jointly decide on the allocation recommendations. The amount to be allocated depends on the state of the Commodity Credit Corporation stocks since, if the food has to be purchased directly from the Congressional aid budget, the amount available is smaller. In addition to the Congressional allocation there is also available the income to the CCC from earlier PL 480 sales, the credits for which are maturing all the time. The joint recommendations for the allocations and the terms of sale are then passed to the Interagency Staff Group (ISG) which is chaired by the USDA and has representatives from USAID, the Office of Management and Budget (OMB), the State Department, Department of the Treasury, Department of Commerce, and the Department of Defense.

The multiple objectives of the US food aid programme are well illustrated by the diversity of membership of this group. The important members are the OMB, Treasury, and State (here the State Department represents different views from USAID, particularly those relating to foreign policy). The OMB is particularly powerful as the watchdog of Congressional spending. The OMB has resisted shipments of commodities for which there are no price-support policies in the United States, regardless of the needs of potential recipients. Three shipments of beans were resisted by the OMB in 1976 and two requests from recipients were not forwarded to the ISG in the face of known OMB objections. The ISG is generally not liked as a mechanism by either the USDA or USAID because of the conflicting interests expressed by its membership and because there is effectively no appeal against its decisions. USAID and USDA can be outvoted on the group and neither are represented at the only appeal, which is to the National Advisory Council. This does not imply that USDA and USAID see eye to eye on all issues of food aid in the face of opposition from other members of the ISG. The present division of responsibility is unhappy, with need being defined by USAID and allocation strongly influenced by USDA. In particular, the Congressional insistence on the use of local funds generated from the sale of PL 480 Title I for agricultural development, presents difficulty. The State Department and USAID have the field officers in the recipient countries to attempt to monitor development progress, but the agricultural expertise rests largely with the USDA, which lacks the field strength in the developing countries. The conflict has come to a head over the new Title III which both agencies would like to control.

Recent proposals reaching the Senate, first put forward by the late Senator Hubert Humphrey, would co-ordinate all United States' aid activity, both food aid and other aid, and take it all out of the direct realm of foreign policy and the influence of both the Department of Agriculture and the State Department by the creation of a new aid and development agency directly responsible to the President's Office. If this proposal fails it seems likely that USDA will achieve a more important role in PL 480 programmes, partly because of its greater political muscle at home and partly because of its distance from foreign policy issues, Congressional attitudes to which have shifted considerably since the end of the Vietnam War. The linking of agricultural interests in the United States with the distribution of food aid has certainly been in the interest of the recipient countries because of the political favour in which US domestic agricultural programmes are held and the incidental spin-off that these created in food aid flows.

Despite all changes in the wording of the legislation, surplus disposal, foreign policy and encouraging United States' trade, remain important criteria for the allocation of US food aid. For example Title II shipments, which are the only ones which are not direct government-to-government transactions, were no higher a proportion of total PL 480 shipments in 1976 than they had been in 1969. In addition, food aid has fallen dramatically in importance in relation to total agricultural exports, falling from nearly 30 per cent in the early 1960s, the years of the big surpluses, to less than 4 per cent in 1976 (Table 62). Such a shift has been quite unrelated to any change in the needs of recipient countries.

The European Economic Community Food Aid

In 1967 a Food Convention was called which resulted in the International Wheat and Food Aid Treaty of the same year. The Convention was held on the initiative of the United States, faced by increased calls upon its food aid potential, largely from India, at a time when food stocks were low. The United States considered that it was time for 'burden sharing' with the rest of the developed world (Mettrick, 1969). However, many of the developed countries, including the EEC at that time and the United Kingdom, were food importers and the extent to which food aid could be considered in isolation from all other sorts of aid, and the burden of food aid alone shared, was questionable. There was little enthusiasm for food aid within the United Kingdom or in many of the member countries of the EEC. It was seen as aid to wheat producers masquerading as aid to the developing countries. Certainly, tying aid to another country's goods is not an attractive proposition for any donor. At least with untied aid (cash) a small porportion comes back in orders (Mettrick, 1969). None the less, the grain-importing developed countries agreed to the Food Aid Convention and were signatories to an agreement for a minimum food aid level and for contributions from all participating countries (Table 65). These shipments were to continue until July 1971. The grain-importing countries agreed to this as a part of horse-trading over trade liberalization as the International Grains Agreement of 1967 was a part of the General Agreement on Tariffs and Trade (GATT), Kennedy Round. The EEC agreed to shipments of 1.035 million tons of grain but, in 1973, with the enlargement of the Community to nine members, its contribution rose to 1.287 million tons under the Second Food Aid Treaty (ISMOG, 1977). Dairy products are separate, milk powder aid shipments starting in 1973 and butter-fat shipments in 1974. The annual shipments of these products rose rapidly, based on the state of the internal dairy market in the EEC and not in any way related to the needs of the recipient countries or to the shipments of grains by the EEC or by other donors.

Table 65. Agreed minimum annual shipments under the Food Aid Convention, 1967[a]

Country	Minimum shipment ('000 tons)	Percentage
United States	1890	44.4
EEC	1035	24.3
Canada	495	11.6
Australia	225	5.3
Japan	225	5.3
United Kingdom	225	5.3
Sweden	54	1.3
Switzerland	32	0.8
Denmark	27	0.6
Argentina	23	0.5
Finland	14	0.3
Norway	14	0.3
Total	4259	100.0

[a]Contribution in cash was calculated at the rate of $1.73 per bushel.
Source: Mettrick (1969).

Criteria for the shipment of EEC aid are as follows:

1. A demonstrated food need *outside commercial channels*. To this end the great majority of EEC aid agreements contain the following clause: 'The contracting parties to implement the agreement in such a way as to avoid any interference with the normal pattern of production and international trade. To this end they will take any necessary steps to ensure that supplies as aid will supplement, not replace, commercial transactions which might reasonably be expected in the absence of such supplies. Recipient countries to prevent (a) re-export of product received as aid as well as products derived from it, (b) the commercial and non-commercial export, within six months of last delivery, of similar locally obtained commodity or products derived from it.' The United States has similar agreements and both the United States and the EEC specify a 'usual marketing requirement', the volume of a commodity which is expected to flow through the normal marketing channels if that commodity is received as aid.

2. That the country's average per capita income does not exceed $300 per annum. In 1976 this income requirement was altered to indicate two groups of countries with different priorities, those with per capita incomes of less than $100 and those with less than $600.

3. That the recipient country has a balance of payments problem, taking into account the price of imports and aid already received.

If these criteria are met the country concerned will not be excluded from the possibility of EEC food aid, but all such countries are not included. The amount of aid delivered is not related to the overall need of the country concerned, allocation within eligible countries is determined more or less arbitrarily (ISMOG, 1977).

Food aid from the EEC is normally distributed in the recipient countries through open-market sales designed to increase the market supply of basic foodstuffs and depress prices. This is not necessarily a particularly effective way of reaching the poor and malnourished in the recipient countries as the price effects of the generally small quantities of EEC aid are small (Jones, 1976).

The EEC has three food aid programmes, each of which has different administrative procedures:

1. Normal aid. The annual programmes for cereals, milk powder and butter-fat are drafted separately by the EEC Commission and sent to the Council and its committees. Once the Council has finally approved the overall programmes for these three groups of commodities the Food Aid Department draws up provisional agreements with recipient countries. These agreements usually make specific reference to the use of the local funds generated by the government sales of this food aid, requiring that these be used for developmental purposes. When the agreements are signed (the Council does not have to approve each agreement separately)

the Directorate General (Agriculture) is responsible for deliveries. The quantities concerned are obtained, either from the EEC intervention stocks, or if necessary, by public tender and resulting commercial purchase. Shipping costs are normally paid by the recipient country.

2. Temporary aid. This is intended to tide a recipient country over a bad harvest period when it is expected that the following harvest will remove the food shortage. Applications for temporary aid are processed individually and not considered as a part of the division of any annual allocation. The supplies, either as goods or as money to buy goods in the market, are met from Community reserves. The Council approves individual applications which then form the basis of agreements between the EEC and the countries concerned and delivery is arranged as for normal aid.

3. Disaster aid. This is emergency assistance and can be rendered by the Community at short notice. Limitations are 250 tons of wheat and 50 tons of dairy produce for each action taken without specific Council approval. This plus the transport costs, limits the effectiveness of this type of aid. In addition to the three types of Community aid, all the member countries operate their own food aid schemes independent of EEC control.

With the exception of Japan and Finland all other food aid donors distribute food aid in the form of grants. Some donors, notably Australia (96.5%) and France (99.1%, except EEC contribution), and to a lesser extent New Zealand (81.7%) and Japan (83.7%) ship the bulk of their food aid through bilateral agreements. The remaining donors, especially the smaller countries, prefer to make food available to various international agencies for multilateral distribution. Austria, Ireland, Norway, and the German Federal Republic used only such agencies while the United Kingdom (85.8%), the Netherlands (85%), and Denmark (67%) favoured this method of distribution.

Food Aid Recipients

An examination of the major recipients of food aid over the last twenty-five years exposes all the contrasting and conflicting reasons for food aid. In the early years of the PL 480 programmes, European countries suffered from chronic shortage of foreign exchange and, under the last years of United States' support for the post-war European countries, PL 480 food was shipped in considerable quantities. This was paid for in local, non-convertible, currencies which the United States spent in the recipient country by joint agreement. Alternatively, some food was bartered for goods required in the United States, especially from the United Kingdom and West Germany, explaining why these countries were apparently recipients of food aid. Some 15 per cent of PL 480 shipments between 1955 and 1964 went to countries of Western Europe, most of it under Title I agreements (Table 66). In later periods, the picture is dominated by shipments to the developing countries, especially to India, South Korea and South Vietnam. It is noticeable that in those countries where the political objectives of food aid were paramount, for example South Korea, South Vietnam, Egypt and Cambodia, the bulk of the food aid shipments were under Title I, allowing the recipient government to sell the produce and strengthen their budget. This type of aid was also bilateral and was clearly seen as originating in the United States rather than going through a neutral third party such as the United Nations. Although the emphasis is clearly shown as shifting to the developing countries, the presentation of information in Table 66 has a number of disadvantages, particularly as it does not indicate the relationship between food aid and food need. Several developing countries, notably Sri Lanka, do not appear at all and the absence of African countries south of the Sahara is equally strking. The

Table 66. Major recipients of PL 480, 1955–76

Country	1955–64	1965–74	1975–76	1955–76		Total[a]
		('000 tons)		Title I	Title II	
India	2,084	2,933	301	4,406	836	5,318
Pakistan	736	906	175	1,688	129	1,817
South Korea	493	1,034	128	1,399	310	1,655
South Vietnam	130	1,307	27	1,308	156	1,464
Egypt	690	222	220	976	143	1,132
Indonesia	212	757	56	940	83	1,025
Brazil	501	385	7	607	224	893
Israel	289	375	24	621	21	688
Turkey	452	218	4	550	106	674
Bangladesh	—	66	364	378	52	430
Taiwan	237	158	—	293	86	395
Morocco	97	264	24	155	226	385
Chile	128	112	110	238	107	350
Tunisia	96	200	12	166	141	308
Khmer Republic	—	207	91	295	3	298
Philippines	89	167	25	134	132	281
Colombia	118	131	18	110	142	267
Yugoslavia	783	238	—	848	153	1,021
Spain	604	18	—	474	117	622
Poland	535	33	—	498	60	568
Italy	403	3	—	140	232	406
United Kingdom	342	11	—	48	—	353
Greece	202	43	—	144	88	245
West Germany	212	3	—	1	66	215
World total	11,692	11,463	1,932	17,853	5,502	25,087

[a]Includes Title III barter arrangements.
Source: USDA (1977c).

248

reasons are twofold. Firstly, many countries did not, or do not, receive food aid from the United States, even if they have, or had, a severe food gap. Secondly, some of those developing countries excluded from this list have small populations so that the total aid shipments were small, even if of considerable significance to the recipients.

To correct for this problem of data specification Figure 49 shows total food aid from all sources plotted against the food energy ratio in each of the recipient countries receiving significant amounts of food aid per capita. The food energy ratio is the energy value of food available to the country as a proportion of the energy required by the population, based on FAO calorific standards. The ranking of countries in this way may be misleading because the food energy ratio results from dividing one large number by another,

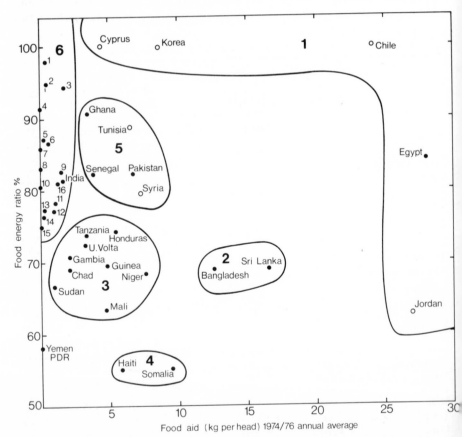

Figure 49. Food aid and food need. 1 = Malagasy, 2 = Burma, 3 = Mozambique, 4 = Ivory Coast, 5 = Cameroon, 6 = Burundi, 7 = Nepal, 8 = Uganda, 9 = Benin, 10 = Sierra Leone, 11 = Ethiopia, 12 = Ruanda, 13 = Afghanistan, 14 = Kenya, 15 = El Salvador, ● = most seriously effected countries, ○ = other countries with food aid over 4 kg per head. Source, based on data from Mellor and Huddleston (1978)

both of which are subject to considerable errors. Also, a national average figure for consumption gives no indication of food consumption by individuals, being an average of often very unequal consumption by different sectors of the population (Hay, 1978). For example, although Cyprus and Chile have similar food energy ratios, Chile is more likely to have a larger proportion of its population malnourished and to have more unequal food distribution. For this reason this ratio should be interpreted with caution.

The countries can be grouped into several cateogries. In Group 1 we have three countries whose food energy ratios are in excess of 100 per cent and yet they are in receipt of substantial amounts of food aid per capita. There are also two countries which are receiving substantial amounts of food aid per capita but which have food energy gaps and therefore need the food aid. In all five countries a major proportion of the food aid was from United States' sources and the political importance of each country during the period 1974–76 is obvious. The second group of only two countries have both high levels of food aid and high levels of need for extra supplies. Of course, as is the case in Bangladesh, high levels of food aid do not necessarily do much to reduce food need as the aid is not targeted at those most in need. It is noticeable that India does not fall into this group. This is partly because of her immense population which means that food aid shipments, although large, remain small measured on a per capita basis, and partly because the improved harvests of recent years have reduced the need for aid shipments. Group 3 contains a large number of countries with food aid needs about as high as in Bangladesh and Sri Lanka, but with lower, often much lower, food aid receipts. The majority of these countries are in or near the Sahel and the gap between need and aid seems to have been particularly acute in the Sudan, Chad, and The Gambia. The worldwide strategic importance of these countries is minimal and provides no additional justification for special consideration. Group 4, to which could be added the Yemen PDR, includes countries in which the food shortage is acute but food aid levels vary greatly depending on political circumstances. It is not surprising to find that the Yemen should not be in receipt of food aid from Western countries. Haiti now finds itself in conflict with the basic human rights criteria applied by the United States and its food energy ratio has probably worsened since 1976. In Group 5 food aid levels appear reasonably related to need, continuing the trend for Bangladesh and Sri Lanka. Group 6 contains seventeen countries of very diverse size and food need, but which have low food aid levels in common. In some cases a small population means that food aid levels are small or non-existent, in others, particularly India, food aid levels have been high, though lower than in previous years. To this picture should be added a further group of countries including Western Samoa, Laos PDR, Lesotho, Mauritania, Cape Verde, Guinea-Bissau, and the Central African Empire in which food gaps occur and to which food aid flows, but for which data problems do not allow their

K

inclusion in the analysis (Mellor and Huddleston, 1978). There are also a number of countries in receipt of food aid amounting to less than 4 kg per head per year which do not fall into the FAO category of most seriously affected, including Indonesia, Zaïre, Zambia, Bolivia, Nigeria, Uruguay, and the Lebanon.

Such an analysis is not entirely fair to food aid because, in addition to political circumstances, there are other reasons why food aid may not be well related to food energy needs. In particular there is the ability of the country to absorb large levels of aid. India, Bangladesh, and Sri Lanka have well-established mechanisms for distributing food aid shipments and the agricultural sectors of their economies are sufficiently large to be little affected by large food aid shipments. The same is certainly not true for most African countries. If food aid could be supplied according to the level of need measured by the energy gap in countries like Chad, the Sudan, and Upper Volta, the management of such shipments would be beyond the capabilities of the recipient countries and international organizations, and the effects on a small commercial agricultural sector would be severe. None the less, as is illustrated by Figure 49, it clearly pays to live in a food-deficit country which has some international political significance rather than in one that has not.

Comparison of total development aid with food aid yields no correlation for the most seriously affected countries (Table 67). In addition there are countries not specified as MSA which receive development aid, just as some receive food aid. In particular, Israel received $76.35 per head per year development aid with an average national income of $3235 per head per year. Tunisia, Panama, Nicaragua, Jordan, and Zambia are also significant recipients of food aid.

Value of Food Aid

It is difficult to calculate the actual value of food though there are several methods of doing this. One would be to take the world market value of the foods at the time of shipment as this is the price which a recipient would have had to pay for a similar shipment, bought in the world market. There are two problems here; the recipient country almost certainly would not have purchased an equal amount in the commercial market, indeed one of the main objectives of, and main arguments for, food aid is that it provides extra food to the recipient countries. Also, if the food delivered as aid had been placed on the world market, the price on that market would have fallen, in the case of some commodities which are shipped as aid in large quantities it would have fallen very sharply. Between 1955 and 1965 two-thirds of all shipments of wheat from the United States were delivered as aid. Clearly, this quantity of wheat on the free market would have significantly lowered world prices and therefore the price which the recipient country would have paid in a commercial transaction. The cost of

Table 67. Comparison of food aid, total development assistance, and income

Country (MSA countries only[a])	Food aid[b] kg per capita 1974–76 average	Food energy[b] ratio	Total development[c] aid per capita ($US)	Income per[c] capita ($US)
Ivory Coast	—	91.7	16.98	600
Guatamala	1.4	81.2	5.19	470
El Salvador	—	75.0	7.37	382
Guyana	—	83.3	12.82	360
Honduras	5.4	74.1	10.24	306
Senegal	3.8	82.2	24.41	248
Egypt	27.9	84.2	5.16	245
Ghana	3.2	90.8	6.94	236[d]
Sri Lanka	16.4	69.3	6.72	223
Mozambique	1.6	94.2	0.47	216
Sierra Leone	—	80.7	4.78	200
Kenya	0.2	76.2	8.70	197
Haiti	5.9	55.6	5.66	158
Pakistan	6.6	82.1	5.17	149
Tanzania	3.2	74.0	na	147
Sudan	0.9	66.7	4.49	143
India	1.5	81.5	1.87	136
Uganda	—	83.3	1.27	127
Malaysia	0.4	98.1	8.65	127[d]
Gambia	2.0	70.8	13.22	101[d]
Cameroon	0.2	87.0	74.45	97[d]
Yemen PDR	—	58.4	8.50	92[d]
Somalia	9.4	55.5	14.80	87[d]
Nepal	—	86.0	2.97	84
Afghanistan	0.2	77.3	2.41	83[d]
Niger	7.4	68.7	22.19	81[d]
Guinea	4.8	69.9	2.21	79[d]
Burma	0.3	95.7	2.51	73[d]
Upper Volta	3.1	71.7	13.15	72
Chad	2.0	69.0	13.93	70[d]
Ethiopia	1.0	78.3	3.80	68[d]
Burundi	0.5	86.6	9.55	60[d]
Bangladesh	12.5	69.2	8.14	59[d]
Rwanda	0.9	77.3	13.32	54[d]
Mali	4.7	63.8	16.81	53[d]

[a]Ecludes Western Samoa, Laos PDR, Yemen PDR, Lesotho, Mauritania, Cape Verde, Guinea-Bissau, Central African Empire—for which data are inadequate.
[b]Source: Mellor and Huddleston (1978).
[c]Source: United Nations Statistical Yearbook (1977)—data available for early 1970s.
[d]1970 data.

aid to the donor appears easier because so much of the aid has come from stocks already acquired as a result of government price-support programmes. In the United States during the first ten years of the PL 480 programmes, almost all the food and other goods shipped came from the stockpiles of the Commodity Credit Corporation. The acquisition may have taken place the previous year, or even earlier, under different price conditions, but the costs to the donor were the CCC procurement price at the time plus the storage charges incurred after procurement. Such a calculation would certainly overvalue food aid because of the market effects discussed above; indeed, Schultz (1960) used only 33 per cent of the CCC price in evaluating food aid from the United States.

Calculations of value using this basis also overvalue food aid in another way.

A cynical but probably reasonably accurate explanation is that for a number of major food producers, food aid has, in the past, gone a long way to legitimise financial losses arising from the production of surpluses under protective agricultural policies. Consequently policy makers in donor countries have tended to behave as if the real costs of providing food aid was considerably less than its market value (Jones, 1976).

With the decline in stockpiles of many commodities the value problem is somewhat easier in the mid 1970s as the commodities had to be bought specifically for aid. Such purchases must, however, be considered as at least partly support buying if, at the same time, the aid donors are to argue that food aid is additional to normal commercial trade.[1]

Title II and III shipments are more costly forms of food aid to the United States as more of the foodstuffs shipped are processed and fortified foods and all freight charges are included in the aid, except for distribution costs in the recipient countries. The charging of freight costs to the recipients of Title I aid may be a disincentive for the participation of very poor countries in the programme.

Food Aid Assessment

There are few other issues which have so divided agricultural and development economists as the effects of food aid on recipient countries. The arguments have spread far beyond these disciplines for they include wide-ranging debates on foreign policy and on problems of world hunger. The controversy started soon after the passing of PL 480, rapidly increased during the 1960s with the large aid shipments from the United States, and continues today, especially in the context of the long-term effects of food aid

---

[1] In the foregoing tables where value has been used in order to compare the shipments of unlike commodities, world market value has been used. This is an exaggeration of the true worth of the food aid but useful for comparative purposes.

on the poorest in the recipient developing countries. The extreme view is that 'food aid is received with cynicism by its recipients and with scepticism by American development experts' (McHenry and Bird, 1977), but an early general condemnation of food aid by academic economists has been replaced by a feeling that food aid, if properly conducted, can at least be a necessary evil and at best play a useful part in economic development (Bard, 1972).

The main criticisms of food aid hinge on the extent to which the additional supplies of food in the recipient countries either replace normal imports or replace normal domestic production. In theory the former should rarely happen because of the constraints on shipment placed by the donor countries. However, displacement of normal imports seems to be fairly general (Stevens, 1977). The extent to which food aid displaces normal domestic production depends on the extent to which the food is supplied to people who would not have access to that amount of food under normal market conditions. The early criticisms concentrated on the production effects of food aid, with depressed prices reducing domestic production, while more recent criticisms have dwelt upon the extent to which food aid actually reaches those in need of additional food (Merrill, 1977). The evidence is conflicting, not least because domestic production depends on so many other variables besides the level of food aid. Conclusions reached in one set of circumstances do not apply elsewhere. 'It does not follow that conclusions on, for example, India, where food grain imports represent a small proportion of total grain supplies but where food aid forms a large proportion of grain imports, are directly applicable to, say, Lesotho, where the opposite is true' (Stevens, 1977). The bulk of food aid goes to countries where such aid makes up only a small fraction of domestic production and supply. For example, even at the height of food aid shipments to India, PL 480 made up only between 4 and 6 per cent of the total wheat supply on the Indian domestic market (Shenoy, 1974).

Production and Price Effects

The basic case for the effects of food aid on domestic production and price has already been made (Chapter 4), but the size of the 'income effect' in moving the demand curve to the right remains unclear. A relatively early attempt to model the disincentive effects brought about by lowered domestic prices was by Seevers (1968). He estimated that there would be a 6.7 per cent depression in domestic market prices for the food aid product, assuming that shipments were fully additional to normal commercial imports, the domestic demand curve remained unchanged, the aid made up 5 per cent of the domestic supply and was sold at or near market prices. Some of these assumptions are unreasonably far from the real world and the price effects are normally considered to be less than this (Merrill, 1977). The most telling argument against food aid's negative effects on domestic production is provided by the fact that it was precisely in those countries which were the major recipients of food aid that the dramatic production increases took place in the 1960s (OECD, 1971). Over the fourteen years of PL 480 shipments to India, Sen (1971) argues that India's own wheat production had risen from 7 to 22 million tons per annum, at least part of which increase was in advance of the arrival of the high-yielding seeds. Most studies of the effects of food aid have been conducted on the Indian food-grain market, partly as that country has been a recipient of very large amounts of aid, and partly because data for that country are reasonably available and reliable. A bibliography on the effects of food aid covering the period from the mid 1960s to the mid 1970s produced by Schneider (1975) lists twenty-two Indian case studies, with the next most popular country being Colombia with only seven studies, followed by Israel and Pakistan with five each. Even in India the results are confused by the base year for the studies and the effects of the poor crop years in the mid 1960s and early 1970s. In many years domestic production can appear to be depressed as a result of large food aid shipments, but often an equally plausible explanation is that crop yields declined for essentially climatic reasons and food aid shipments were increased to fill this shortfall in domestic production.

If food aid is additional to commercial imports then its effects on domestic prices depend on the creation of additional domestic demand, and this in turn depends on the method chosen for the distribution of the food aid. (For a useful summary of the distribution methods used in Turkey, Colombia, Greece, Spain, Israel, and India see Barlow and Libbin, 1969.) The Indian ration shop distribution has been estimated to have increased consumption so that 93 per cent of the PL 480 shipments went towards increasing demand, and thus had no effect on producer prices. The remaining 7 per cent is assessed as having depressed producer prices by a mere 0.02 per cent during the 1960s (Srivastava et al., 1975). Different figures are given in different studies but all agree that extensive additional demand was created by the PL 480 shipments. A more recent, detailed, study by Isenman and Singer (1975) found that relative Indian food prices (compared with all other consumer items) were depressed only in the 1960 to 1962 period during the total food aid period of 1956 to 1971. Not only did the ration shops create an additional demand, but the government revenue created through the sale of the food aid, invested in development projects of all sorts, increased employment generally. This additional employment in turn increased the demand for food as a high proportion of wages is spent on food. Rogers et al. (1972) found that the net loss to Indian domestic food-grain production was about 3 per cent of the food aid provided, but Isenman and Singer point out that this study did not consider the long-term effects on employment and hence on the future increased demand for food grains.

If the food provided as aid is distributed through a government agency there can be a temptation for that agency to maximize government revenue by deliberately undercutting domestically produced food-grain prices and thereby maximizing sales (Stevens, 1977). There is some evidence that this took place in Colombia. Imports, both commercial and as aid, of wheat to Colombia rose from 50 to 90 per cent of domestic consumption between 1953 and 1971, and home production of wheat was reduced to about a third of the level of the 1950s (Dudley and Sandilands, 1975). The domestic wheat price fell from 467 to 345 pesos per ton (Merrill, 1977). Aid only made up about 25 per cent of total shipments, however, and the commercial imports were subsidized by an overvalued exchange rate (Isenman and Singer, 1975). It is, therefore, hardly fair to blame all the ills of the Colombian wheat producers on to the food aid. Indeed, food aid, in so far as it may be sold at below the market price, creating additional demand, has less effect on the domestic prices than an equivalent amount of commercial imports (Mann, 1967).

Colombia continues to be quoted as the classic example of production and price disincentive effects of food aid, but equally impressive examples can be quoted to support the role of food aid. The importation of cheap corn to Israel under PL 480 stimulated the livestock sector of the economy of that country which in turn stimulated the local production of corn. Here the PL 480 shipments had the pump-priming function that many hoped, and hope for, elsewhere in the world (Merrill, 1977). Also, the security of supply provided by food aid shipments may, in certain circumstances, allow producer prices to rise. This was the case in Indonesia between 1967 and 1971 when the guaranteed supply provided by PL 480 Title I aid meant that the government procurement agencies did not have to be so keen to push producer prices as low as possible to ensure that they acquired sufficient supplies for the urban consumers. The evidence from Africa is that food aid has been generally neutral to producers, it has mostly been used to create additional demand and to replace commercial imports (Stevens, 1977).

The intense criticisms of food aid in the 1960s certainly had their effects (Schultz, 1960). The changed wording of the PL 480 legislation is an example. Throughout the life of the PL 480 programme there has been an increasing emphasis on the use of the funds generated by food aid sales for developing domestic agriculture. British attitudes to food aid were also influenced, although in this case the fact that the United Kingdom was, and remains, a food importer meant that the criticism was easier as food aid had no domestic benefits. 'We ought to recognise that food aid can only be a palliative and may be a dangerous one. The aim should be to replace food aid as quickly as possible with more constructive aid to development' (Prentice, 1967). The current view of food aid in the development community is that it can be harmful to domestic production but it need not be. The evidence remains divided (Tolley and Gwyer, 1967) but tends to show little price or production effects on the recipient country.

However, these studies of the effects of aid can never be positive. They all leave the unanswerable question, what if? If food aid had *not* been available would domestic prices have risen fast and would this have stimulated more dramatic food production increases in countries which have been major food aid recipients?

Part of this dilemma is that we know little about the price elasticity of supply of food in the developing countries. Generally this is low, probably between 0.1 and 0.2 (Mellor, 1966) and so the response by producers to changes brought about by food aid shipments is likely to be small, even if the food aid takes from the existing demand rather than creating new demand. On the other hand, the marketed surplus may have a higher elasticity than production as, with a fall in prices, producers may retain a higher proportion of the production on the farm and consume more themselves (Mettrick, 1969). Also, most of the marketed surplus of food grains which finally reaches the major urban centres comes from the larger farmers, who are better placed to respond to price increases and may shift to other cash crops when the price of food grains falls. The response of the large farmer to price increases is limited by his access to inputs, particularly fertilizers, since declining unit costs are more important in increasing production than are price rises (Mellor, 1969). This was obviously the case for wheat production in India during the green revolution. Declining unit costs can be encouraged by a proper investment of the government funds accumulated from the sale of the food aid commodities. If the price of one grain falls significantly then many farmers may shift to another food crop; in Colombia the shift was from wheat to barley, and overall agricultural incomes were little affected (Merrill, 1977). Finally, the price elasiticity of supply will be influenced by the year-on-year price stability, as the elasticity is clearly related to risk. Food aid can contribute to long-term price stability to the benefit of food producers and consumers. Production effects of food aid are complex and probably neutral in most circumstances.

Policy Effects

The second major argument concerning the effects of food aid is that it allows, or even encourages, the governments of recipient countries to follow policies which ignore the problems of agriculture and food production because a safe level of food supply is available from the food aid shipments. The lack of attention to the agricultural sector can either be deliberate or can result from the fact that the food aid obscures the real nature of the rural problems, by providing a secure source of food, and governments do not notice the need for agricultural investment and development (Stevens, 1977). Many developing countries have followed, and many continue to follow, policies which ignore or pay little attention to national agricultural sectors. The best publicized case was the concentration on industrial development contained within the Indian second and third five-year plans. In the early 1960s there was heavy political concentration on industrial development but it is doubtful that food aid *caused* that emphasis, rather allowing policies to be carried through more effectively (Isenman and Singer, 1975). Food aid was used to ensure that prices of cereals did not rise too fast following any shortage of supply. If such a rise had occurred there would have been general inflation, effects of which would have hindered Indian industrialization. Whatever we might think of policies which discouraged agricultural development in favour of industrialization, they reflected a widely held view of the nature of, and the requirements for, economic development at the time and were certainly not the result of food aid shipments (Papanek, 1972).

Again we are left with a 'what if' question. Without the food aid would the Indian government have been forced to give a higher priority to agriculture, and if so, what would have been the effects on the demand, supply and price of food? Such questions cannot be answered realistically. The obvious anxiety of the United States to be rid of surpluses in the early 1960s coincided with India's obvious anxiety for industrial development. Industry and mining received by far the largest share of government investments resulting from Title I sales and agriculture benefited little (Wightman, 1968). Agriculture still receives only about 20 per cent of the development budget of the government of Bangladesh, despite the obvious need for increased domestic food production. Food aid shipments make a contribution to the prevention of widespread food shortages in that country and could be said to be contributing to the continuance of these policies. It remains very doubtful, however, that major policy shifts would be made if the food aid were not available. Again, as with price and production effects of food aid, the evidence is equivocal. Food aid is certainly not all good in its effects on policy, but it should not be the scapegoat for all that is bad about the development policies of the developing nations. The criticisms have had their impact. The increasing emphasis on self-help programmes for increased food production within the United States' food aid policy is evidence. Specifically, the new Title III food aid is a real attempt to shift recipient countries towards policies of agricultural development.

Budgetary and Employment Effects

The generation of government income from the sale of food recieved as aid can be of the greatest importance to the major recipients of food aid. For most recipient countries, with a very poorly developed tax structure and inadequate tax income, the sales of food may make a substantial contribution to the total budget, a proportion of which will be used for development purposes. Between 14 and 18 per cent of the budgetary income to the government of Bangladesh presently comes from the sale of food aid, although at certain crisis times it has been as high as 40 per cent. Although this income is supposed to be used for developmental purposes, additional to that which the government would otherwise spend, poor budgetary accounting makes this hard to monitor or control A proportion of such funds may *replace* government expenditure on development and a proportion may be used for straight budgetary support, that is, on expenditure not related to economic development. Part of the objectives of the PL 480 programme is to impart political stability in countries which are friendly to the United States and which are strategically important. The use of food aid-generated funds to this end in Egypt, for example, is central to the objectives of the American food aid programme. A similar argument over the role of food aid can develop about budgetary support as developed over government policy for agricultural development. To what extent is the food aid encouraging, or allowing, the government to avoid the politically difficult issue of tax reform? The collection of property taxes in Bangladesh, even from the largest of landowners, is rudimentary. Only 0.7 per cent of government revenue is raised from land tax.

Apart from general budgetary support, food aid can make a major contribution towards keeping down domestic inflation, especially in the developing countries where a major proportion of personal income is spent on food. Although a shortage of food would raise prices and encourage domestic production, it would also lead to increased wage rates and rising costs of agricultural inputs by fuelling a general level of inflation. The availability of ration foods in Bangladesh allows government wages to be kept low (Chapter 4). The holding down of wage rates reduces the relative advantage of capital-intensive, labour-scarce investments and therefore encourages a higher level of employment (Merrill, 1977). This is a point developed by Isenman and Singer (1975). When two-thirds or more of the income of the poor is spent on food, then available food supplies become a constraint on employment-creating investment. The authors ask us to imagine the effects on government programmes to increase employment if two thirds of the wages in a developed country were spent on purchases of oil-related products, at a time of national shortage of oil and high prices. Food aid allows some investment in employment-creating activities, without fear of a resulting shortage of food. This employment increases the demand for food so that domestic production may remain relatively unaffected by the food aid shipments. Hopefully, the economic development which follows from this investment will result in an increase in purchasing power, increased domestic demand and increased domestic production, coupled with a phasing out of food aid. This is very close to the sequence of events followed in India until the food crisis and poor harvests of the early 1970s.

Another constraint on investment in employment-generating projects, is foreign exchange. Where food aid substitutes for imports, foreign exchange is saved. This substitution is far more widespread than the food aid rules of the EEC and the United States would imply (Stevens, 1977). The foreign exchange thus saved can be used for the development of any, or all, sectors of the economy, and if there is a concentration on the industrial sector the 'blame' for this can hardly be put at the door of the food aid. We are in danger of judging food aid by different standards than those used to judge other aid. Any aid which saves foreign exchange—and most forms of aid do this either directly or indirectly—can have the same criticism applied to it. The fault, if any, lies with the development policy followed by the recipient country, not with the food aid itself.

There are circumstances where, if aid substitutes for commercial imports, it can damage the economic position of other developing countries. Food aid to South Asia is mostly in wheat which encourages a shift in taste from rice to wheat. Some aid also arrives as rice from the United States. Although the effect may not be large there has been some reduction in the demand for rice from Burma and Thailand as a result of aid shipments to India, Pakistan, Sri Lanka, Bangladesh, and Indonesia (OECD, 1963).

Debts and Dependency

The majority of food aid is available under the terms of Title I from the United States and has to be paid for. The aid element lies in the terms of repayment. Although many recipients will obtain 'soft' loans, considerable long-term debts are accumulating in the recipient countries. At June 1977 outstanding debts for PL 480 food in Indonesia alone amounted to $760 million. Indonesia has oil export income with which to repay the debts, but other countries are not so fortunate. India has accumulated debts of $607 million and Bangladesh $394 million, from food shipments over a period of only five years. The grace period (at only 2 per cent interest), is ending for many existing loans and future annual payments will be at 3 per cent interest and will include the repayment of capital. The poorest countries, unable to meet these repayments, even at the nominal rate of interest, will sink further into debt. The position is even more serious if the government revenues have not been invested in development projects but have been used solely for a largely middle-class consumer subsidy and for other government expenditure. Then there will be no extra national resources resulting from the aid which could provide the additional revenues with which to repay the debts. This is the purpose of the low-interest grace period. Bangladesh, for example, is faced with a continuing need for food aid and very little extra resources to repay the outstanding, and rapidly accumulating, international debts. These debts have accumulated not only for food aid, but food makes up a substantial part of the total. Of course it is possible that these debts will ultimately be forgiven, in which case the Title I shipments will become grants. Hopefully, the example of the United Kingdom in writing off debts to the poorest of developing countries will be followed by other more important lenders. Bangaldesh's debt forgiven by the United Kingdom in 1978, was only a minute fraction of that country's international debts.

The debt question is part of the larger issue of dependency. This issue reached a head, as far as food dependency is concerned, in 1973–74 when the shortage of wheat supplies led to drastic reductions in aid shipments from the United States, although commercial trade remained relatively unaffected. It is supposed that the dependence on United States wheat, created during times of surplus food production in the Unites States, left the developing countries particularly vulnerable to reduction in aid flows. Without the PL 480 shipments perhaps the recipient countries would have developed alternative domestic supplies. There is, however, no evidence that domestic demand would have been made effective and thereby simulated domestic production in the absence of food aid, remembering that the poor cannot afford to buy food at low prices, let alone at incentive prices for producers. Furthermore, domestic production is constrained by many things apart from demand and price, notably by shortage of fertilizer and irrigation. Also, domestic supply is just as liable to short-term fluctuation as is the food aid (Mellor and Huddleston, 1978). The domestic production of rice in Bangladesh varies from about 9 million tons to 11.5 million, depending on the nature of the harvest.

Perhaps the most insidious danger of all is that aid of all sorts encourages a beggar mentality. Requests for aid are couched in humanitarian terms, but are really motivated by budgetary and financial considerations (McHenry and Bird, 1977). High aid levels are requested even when good harvests exist. The autumn of 1975 and the spring of 1976 was a period of good Bangladesh harvests but it coincided with the arrival of 250,000 tons of food grains under PL 480. The need for food was not there and the storage facilities could not cope. Losses of between 100,000 and 200,000 tons of grain occurred as a result (Merrill, 1977). 'There is no question of the extreme importance, to the Bangladesh leaders, of a continued flow of imported food grains to fuel the ration system and above all to keep potentially active Dacca dwellers supplied with low priced food grains' (State Department, Bangladesh Mission Cable, January 1976). The political need encouraged aid requests regardless of the need for food or the country's capabilities for dealing with it. The people of Bangladesh remained malnourished, not because of a shortage of aid, nor a shortage of food, but because of an inability to pay for the available food and a distribution system biased in favour of the urban population. The cycle of constant requests for aid and, at least a political, dependency on that aid, is well advanced and the expressed need for aid from Bangladesh seems unabated. The political slogan of food self-sufficiency is of doubtful reality when that country would lose a major source of income should food self-sufficiency be reached.

Programme Versus Project Food Aid

Most of the previous discussion has concentrated on government-to-government food aid, typified by the PL 480 Title I programme. The amin alternative, so-called project aid, is where food is made available, usually through international organizations such as UNESCO or charitable groups like OXFAM and CARE, for specific projects in the recipient countries rather than for government distribution and sale. There are three main groups of such projects:

1. Supplemental feeding programmes for nutritionally vulnerable groups, particularly mothers and young children.
2. School meals programmes—provided at all levels of education, but concentrated in primary schools.
3. Food for work schemes, where public works are financed in part by the payment of workers in food.

Although there has been considerable debate, the consensus is that project aid is preferable to other food aid programmes because:

1. it is clearly targeted to the poor and to those whose need for extra nutrition is greatest
2. for this reason it is more obviously additional to existing food consumption, and will therefore have less effect on domestic production and on domestic prices.
3. it is managed by internationally respected agencies, project aid is less obviously political than are government-to-government transactions. Such aid can be acceptable, perhaps even where countries are known to be violating basic human rights, or even where they are politically unfriendly to the food donors. The basis of this type of aid is that the poor of such countries cannot be held responsible for the political perspectives of their governments.

There are also disadvantages. Project aid is considerably more expensive to the donor countries because additional processing and transport costs are involved. The foods are often enriched and the transport costs are borne by the donor country or agency. This raises an issue which is not usually a real argument with programme aid, especially in times of surplus production, namely would it be better to spend the same amount of money on other forms of aid rather than food? We will return to this issue in a later section (p.269), but it can be argued that food delivered as aid is better sold by the recipient government and the cash raised used to buy local foods for supplementary feeding programmes (Stevens, 1977). This has a dual advantage of providing locally acceptable foods and aiding domestic producers by adding to the overall demand for their production. The local administration costs of such a programme would be considerable.

The World Food Programme

The World Food Programme (WFP), a joint United Nations and FAO organization based in Rome, is the largest organizer of project aid and has been in operation since 1963. At that time the United Nations First Development Decade had been launched with a good deal of enthusiasm and the WFP was established to make food aid available without any political strings. Many countries were to contribute to the programme, making available a range of foodstuffs and allowing countries with small or intermittent surpluses of food to participate in food aid programmes. Countries without surplus foods could contribute cash to help pay for the organization and the shipping of the food aid. Many of the country contributions are small and largely symbolic, but it is significant that of the thirty-six countries which make pledges of food or cash aid in all five of the pledging periods between 1963 and 1972, eighteen were developing countries. However, the major participants are Canada ($34 million worth between 1963 and 1972), Denmark ($24 million), EEC ($19 million), Germany ($12 million), Netherlands ($19 million), Sweden ($15 million), and the United States ($110 million). The contributions of the United States were made under the Title II programme of PL 480.

The WFP is directed almost entirely at project aid and if projects are to be supported they have to have specified developmental aims to promote social as well as economic welfare (WFP, 1973). Although food sales have been organized, these are rare and the programme works generally by paying special attention to meeting otherwise unsatisfied nutritional requirements. The programme covers specifically pre-school and school feeding, projects to increase agricultural productivity, labour-intensive projects, and rural welfare, as well as emergency relief. Help is also given where the food shortage is chronic on a multiyear basis, and such help might include the establishment of food security stocks. Contributions to the programme come from United Nations member countries in the form of pledges, plus contributions from the World Aid Convention where the member-country contribution come under the International Wheat Agreements. Development projects absorb about 65 per cent of total revenue, emergency assistance about 15 per cent, and the remainder is used for administration and shipping costs. As most of the WFP aid goes to supplemental feeding and food for work schemes, each of these will be examined below.

Supplemental Feeding

The WFP devotes about 40 per cent of its resources to what is called the development of human resources and the greatest proportion of this is used for supplemental feeding programmes, particularly provision of school meals. By 1976 projects were reaching 6,793,800 primary school children (Ronchi and Lopez, 1976). Other international agencies, particularly UNICEF, contribute to similar programmes for the distribution of food aid. The objectives of providing free school meals are threefold:

1. The meal is planned to act as a nutritional supplement to the existing diet of the child, thereby improving the quality and quantity of the diet and hopefully reducing levels of malnutrition.
2. The meals themselves can be used as vehicles for the teaching of food preparation, food hygiene, and basic nutrition. In a few cases such programmes have been combined with the development of a school garden to help provide the necessary food, and take the education function one stage further.
3. Improved nutrition of school children improves the effectiveness of education by providing an incentive to come to school and improving the attention and learning of the pupils, both of which suffer when nutrition is inadequate.

The particular advantage of school feeding programmes at all levels is that there is an existing institutional framework which can be used for the distribution of the food. There are also considerable disadvantages:

1. The most serious deficiency of school meals programmes stems from taking advantage of the administrative structure, because this type of programme reaches the children after the most critical years of early growth and weaning. Even though most of the effort is expended on primary school feeding programmes to reach the children at as young an age as possible, it is still past the most critical nutritional period. Not only will a large number, perhaps as high as one in four children, never reach school age because of malnutrition-induced infant mortality, but many of those who do may have already incurred nutritional damage. The incurable damage, especially to mental development, often comes before school age (Jones, 1976).
2. Related to this issue is the fact that many of those children most in need of the supplemented diets never go to school to benefit from the school feeding programmes. In poor households the young children will be required to search for employment, no matter how financially unrewarding, and a proportion of the children may be too weak from disease, parasites and malnutrition to attend school.
3. The supplied mid-day meal may be used as a substitute for a domestic meal, probably in the evening, so that the child is nutritionally little better off. Other children in the household may be better off as the available food can be redistributed. In this case the intervention may improve the overall nutritional standard of the community by small amounts, rather than helping the specified target group as much as expected. This type of 'leakage' of school meals acts as an income supplement to poor families by lowering family expenditure on food. Perhaps half the food distributed to Indian school children may leak as family income supplements (Maxwell, 1978a).

4. Finally, although the school structure provides a convenient medium for the distribution of food, the administrative network is most sketchy where the intervention feeding is most needed, in the isolated rural areas. Also, the general administration expenses of school feeding are great, and the possibilites of many recipient countries taking over responsibility for such programmes in the immediate future are remote. School feeding, once embarked upon, will probably become a long-term commitment for the aid agencies.

The second major supplemental feeding programme concerns mother and child feeding. These schemes attempt to boost the diet of pregnant and lactating mothers and their young, pre-school, children. By 1976 these programmes were reaching over 2 million mothers and 7.8 million pre-school children. Recognizing that this is the critical period for nutrition intervention is one thing, but carrying out any extensive programme is another. Reaching the mothers in need is difficult. Such programmes can be usefully coupled with rural health care, vaccination programmes and family planning services, helping to encourage attendance at rural health centres, but the administration and distribution costs remain very high. If food is available only at selected centres, the energy expended in the collection has to be set against the nutritional benefit. Alternatively, food distribution for home use, either through school children, or by weekly pick-ups from the supply centres, will not necessarily be used by the targeted groups (Ronchi and Lopez, 1976). Berg (1973) discusses the feeding order in households as one reason for continued malnutrition in this group of mothers and children, and a report of the efficacy of Title II food aid concluded that ' . . . it is highly questionable that food which is distributed for home use . . . has a measurable impact on newborn infants, especially those who are severly malnourished' (Checci and Co., 1972). Such supplemental feeding programmes can have a valuable nutritional impact but they require considerable expenditure on administration, a long-term commitment for food aid, and recipient countries will have a limited capacity to absorb aid of this sort. Useful though it may be, it can never hope to reach more than a small fraction of the population in need.

Very few objective assessments have been made concerning the effectiveness of supplemental feeding programmes. Many of the assessments which have been made have methodological problems (Maxwell, 1978a). It is important to remember that the food supplied is not really free to the recipient country, it could be sold and the income used by government to purchase local food for distribution both on supplemental feeding programmes and as food for work, which generally has been assessed as of more direct benefit (Maxwell, 1978b). The use of such local food would provide some incentive to local producers, not develop tastes for expensive 'foreign' foods, provide the basis for appropriate nutrition training and involve foods which were more acceptable to the poor. Although the motivation for such targeted food aid programmes is admirable, the practice seems to have very little positive impact on the nutritional problems of the most vulnerable.

Food for Work Programmes

About half of the WFP's resources are spent on projects linked to agricultural development, and most of this is spent on land development of one sort or another. This usually involves labour-intensive projects where food is provided as part payment, complete payment or in what the WFP calls 'incentives for voluntary work'. Major public works are often undertaken under food for work programmes. These involve land drainage, flood control and irrigation, and rural roads. Although such projects can help agricultural development there are a few points worth making about them. The projects themselves are sometimes little researched and the effects can be short-lived. Rural roads constructed with plenty of labour but few materials are unlikely to survive the following rainy season in a country like Bangladesh. River channels deepened in the dry season silt up again the following year. At best, these sorts of project are little more than 'make-work', utilized to help give the local community a sense of identity and provide supplemental feeding. Although these may be admirable objectives, agricultural development may be minimal. Secondly, the work itself increases the calorific requirements of the participants and it is possible that the net nutritional results will be low. Thirdly, it is mistaken to assume that food is the only requirement of the rural poor. Some other basic purchases are necessary, fuel for example to cook the food, and Berg (1973) has shown how food needs can be made secondary to the demands for other consumer goods.

In such circumstances a proportion of the food received under the food for work programmes will be sold to raise cash for other purchases. If the food issued is not the locally preferred food, for example, wheat in a predominantly rice-eating country, almost all the food received may be sold. This greatly depresses the local market price, perhaps affecting some producers, and certainly reducing the amount of cash raised by the workers and also the amount of alternative food which can purchased. The overall nutritional impact will be considerably smaller than the nutritional value of the total food distributed (ISMOG, 1977). Finally, there are climatic limitations to the food for work programmes. The physical conditions mean that rural works can only be carried out successfully in the dry season. In Bangladesh and India, for example, this is the food 'fat' season following the main rice harvests. In the wet season the nutritional needs of the population will be higher, opportunities for alternative employment are lower, and the food for work programmes are not operating. The rural poor are picked up and dropped by such programmes at exactly the wrong times. It is also important to consider who are the recipients of the benefits accruing from the rural works projects. Mostly such land development and rural infrastructure building will be of greater benefit to the larger farmers and to the landowners and of little benefit to the rural poor. In fact the end product of the improvements brought about by the rural works programmes may be to raise the number of the rural poor such programmes are designed to help (Chapter 5).

The combined effects of administrative costs, absorption limitations and other difficulties with project aid, mean that its total value remains limited and it should be seen as complementing, rather than as an alternative to, programme aid. It is doubtful that the international agencies could manage a much larger flow of food aid than they at present handle and bilateral food aid, providing money for the recipient countries to invest in rural development, can be a more efficient and effective way of improving both the nutritional status of the population and the rate of rural development.

Emergency Aid

Food to meet emergency conditions created by natural disaster, war, or extreme food shortage, creates little opposition within the donor or the recipient countries. The speed with which the international media relays information and pictures from disaster areas ensures that the charitable and international agencies are aware of the problems and that the general public are awakened to the situation, can respond to the calls for help from the agencies, and are unlikely to be opposed to the shipment of relief food. Bilateral and multilateral food aid may be provided in such circumstances. Unfortunately, the organization in the recipient country, perhaps weak to start with, may be unable to cope with the strains of the emergency and with the distribution of the relief commodities. Considerable delays often occur and a proportion of the relief goods are spoiled or pilfered. Also, such shipments do lead to great opportunities for corruption. The post-cyclone relief operations in Bangladesh in 1970 suffered greatly from corruption within the Bangladesh Red Cross and at one time aid was stopped for this reason. Another important point is that food is not necessarily the most important commodity needed, for example after an earthquake. Shelter and health care are far more important in the short term. Existing country stores of food may not have been adversly affected by the disaster, but large quantities of food aid, coupled with the distribution problems of such aid in addition to normal supplies, may considerably disrupt local markets and prices with long-term effects on producers. Clearly, where, for example, a massive flood has destroyed food stocks, some food aid will be needed, but it will be extremely difficult to ensure that this food is distributed and used within the disaster area in accordance with the quantities of food lost.

On the whole, emergency aid presents the least controversy because it can be seen to be obviously directed for humanitarian reasons, is normally small in quantity and, with the disruptions already existing, probably has the least effect on normal production and marketing within the recipient country. However, the administration and distributional problems should not be overlooked nor should absolute priority be given to *food* aid. Others have gone further and suggest that food aid for emergencies should be replaced by financial aid (Jones and Tullock, 1974).

Speed and Dependability of Food Aid

One thing which is essential if the emergency aid is to be effective is speed. Delays in shipments of food aid can be disruptive, but delays in the relief of famine conditions can be catastrophic. Rivers *et al.* (1976) conclude chillingly that 'in total, in Ethiopia there were, between 1972 and 1975 an excess of at least 100,000 deaths due to starvation and associated diseases. They occurred in spite of massive injections of aid from overseas. The aid failed to prevent these deaths simply because it was, with a few exceptions, too late.' The great majority of the food aid shipments to the Ethiopian districts of Wollo and Tigrai arrived after most of their problems were over. The reasons for the delay are put down to two basic causes. The international relief agencies are not able or willing to devote many resources to long-term predictive studies. They react to the event of starvation. The roots of the Ethiopian famine went back through many years of unreliable rainfall, but the starvation was a *sudden* and late event. When the national government and the agencies reacted it was too late for aid of all sorts to save the great majority of the suffering. A contributory cause is that the Ethiopian famine became of interest to the international media long after the worst was over and so aid continued to flow, but too late. To have prevented the bulk of the starvation deaths, action should have been taken many months earlier.

The similarities between famine and other natural disasters are worth exploring. Cyclones in the Bay of Bengal are regularly recurring features. They give rise to flooding, loss of foodstuffs and widespread death wherever they strike on the east coast of India, Bangladesh, or the west coast of Burma. The 1970 cyclone and floods in Bangladesh are estimated to have killed at least 350,000 people. Many more died as a result of the food shortage and health problems which followed the cyclone. The event is sudden and catastrophic. Famine is also sudden. Although malnutrition can build up over several years, sudden rises in death rates characterize the onset of famine. The famine may be almost as sudden as an earthquake or cyclone. Earthquake zones and coasts vulnerable to cyclones are known with reasonable accuracy. Although the date of the arrival of such disasters cannot be predicted, everyone knows that one will eventually occur. Thus, considerable sums of money can be allocated and spent in advance, providing cyclone early warning systems based on satellite pictures, flood embankments, and a number of solid, two-storey houses to provide at least some protection for the population. Similarly, the onset of famines are not totally unpredictable. Bihar suffers regularly, as does Ethiopia. The successful type of food and other aid is that which attempts to offset the effects of a future disaster and does not wait until it arrives. National nutrition surveys and food balance studies can help provide the data similar to the climatological and geophysical data for cyclone and earthquake zones. The establishment of buffer stocks and early warnings for intervention are the only ways in which aid can hope to be in time really to alleviate the effects of famine by preventing it. Action which awaits the event will be too late.

Speed for other types of aid is less problematic, but delays are often so great that food aid deliveries arrive at totally inappropriate times. Food shortages will be the result of poor previous harvests. The food aid designed to supplement this poor harvest must arrive as soon as possible after that harvest, and at the very least, well before the next harvest. The majority of United States Title I and Title II aid is planned and dispatched within the fiscal year and therefore the delays between recipient countries' requests, consideration by the United States, and food delivery are not long. There may be occasions when it arrives just after a good harvest, but USAID does try to arrange deliveries to coincide with the 'lean' season in the recipient country. Other considerations, especially port access and transport to landlocked states such as Nepal and Afghanistan present additional constraints.

Delays for EEC normal aid are often ludicrously long (ISMOG, 1977). The time from the submission of the application for aid by Bangladesh (one or two months before the beginning of October) and the time at which the food was delivered at the European port ready for onward shipment to Bangladesh, has varied from 198 days to 856 days with an average period of 479 days. At least another 50 days should be added for shipment, unloading, warehousing, and distribution in Bangladesh. Similar, though shorter, delays occurred for shipments to Sri Lanka and to Egypt. In all cases there seemed little doubt that the deliveries would be approved, but the bureaucratic process ensured delays. Such delays between the calculation of need and the arrival of the aid provide great difficulties in the recipient countries, quite apart from the fact that the delays themselves make the assessment of the request by the EEC irrelevant. The arrival of the aid is not linked to the level of need at that time and, therefore, the effects of food aid in levelling out price fluctuations are not as great as they could be, indeed in some circumstances the food aid can increase these fluctuations. The probability of depressing effects on domestic production is increased, as the aid may arrive in coincidence with good domestic harvests. The general assessment of the advantages and disadvantages of food aid is weighted in favour of the disadvantages because of the effects of food aid delays.

Closely related to the question of delays in food aid, is the regularity of supply. Congressional agreements to ship a minimum quantity of Title II food aid, and pledges to the World Food Programme, provide some measure of continuity. The WFP, in particular, is able to embark on multiyear programmes because of the reliable supply of food. The bulk of food aid is not delivered under such programmes, however, and just as the food for work programmes can pick up and drop needy people at inappropriate times, so also can the various bilateral food aid flows. The total aid available each year for United States Title I aid is assessed by the Department of Agriculture, and then the division is made between the various recipient countries. Such a process provides no security for the recipients to allow for the initiation of genuine development programmes based on the sale of the food aid commodities. Most such development programmes should be multiyear. Such annual consideration of needs encourages overbidding for aid and there is no doubt that, if food aid is to be used successfully for development purposes, the donor countries must find a better way of allocating the aid according to need and provide a more regular supply (Mellor and Huddleston, 1978).

Conclusions

In making a final assessment of the values and disadvantages of food aid one important issue is the extent to which the food aid can be considered to be additional to other types of aid. There is generally little doubt among development economists that aid in cash is preferable to aid in food as it is more flexible and can be used for food by the recipient country if the conditions warrant. There seems equally to be little doubt that most aid is additional to other forms of aid, and that potential food-surplus countries would not replace food aid with an equivalent amount of cash aid (Isenman and Singer, 1975). It seems highly unlikely that the United States Congress, for example, would agree to the substitution of cash aid for present levels of food aid. The food aid costs are not fully accounted as so much of the cost is hidden within a programme of support to agriculture. The effects of a change to cash aid would be simultaneously to appear to increase the development budget at the same time as to increase the agricultural budget, as alternatives to the aid channels would have to be found for the disposal of surplus production. Agricultural policies have a much broader support base in Congress than does overseas aid, which has lost one of its main champions with the death of Senator Humphrey. Where non-food surplus countries are involved in food aid programmes, the aid is less likely to be additional. For example, the United Kingdom meets its contributions to the EEC food budget from its general development assistance budget (Jones, 1976). As most food aid comes from surplus countries, we can conclude that it is largely additional and that a recipient country deciding to forgo food aid would not expect to increase its share of cash or any other sort of aid.

The second point in a general assessment of food aid is that we tend to judge the value and difficulties of food aid by different standards from those used for other aid (Isenman and Singer, 1975; Stevens, 1977). Although cash aid is generally preferred because of its flexibility, this very flexibility will allow the aid to be used for projects which are equally or even potentially more harmful to domestic agriculture. The available cash can be used for projects of industrialization, mechanization of agriculture, or even military purposes. Food aid should be judged, not only by its effects on the agricultural sector of the recipient economy, but also by its effects on the nutritional status of the population. Nutritional status in Taiwan and South Korea has improved very greatly since the onset of the PL 480 shipments. Other things have, of course, happened in both those countries, but food aid has made a major contribution to this nutritional improvement. What would have been the nutritional status of the population of India in the mid 1960s without the PL 480 shipments? As we have seen, the evidence for long-term harmful effects on domestic agriculture is mixed and the evidence for short-term improvements in nutrition are considerable.

> ... It is surprising how many studies and policy discussions either dismiss or miss entirely the direct purpose of food aid as if food aid were to be judged solely on the basis of its contribution to food production. ... Food aid provides food for the hungry both by direct subsidised distribution often to nutritionally vulnerable groups such as children, and by helping contain price increases, which tend to hit the nutritionally vulnerable groups the hardest ... it provides financing for specific government development projects ... it can be used to build up food stocks ... and it eases a major constraint on growth and employment (Isenman and Singer, 1975).

A third point is that other forms of aid are needed along with the food, to help in the absorption of the food aid. Distribution costs are considerable. The educational value of school feeding programmes needs to be supported by other forms of aid to education. The use of local funds from the sale of food to help in agricultural development needs other forms of aid, both of experience and skill and of capital investment. Even the food for work programmes cannot exist entirely on large amounts of unskilled labour. Health, education and development budgets in the recipient countries will need to be assisted in parallel with food aid if the latter is to be successful in its objectives. One of the serious limitations of the WFP is that it only has *food* to offer as aid (Mettrick, 1969). The programme would be more successful if it received not only pledges of food from participating nations, but also if it received, and was able to manage, other forms of development assistance. The amalgamation of all forms of aid agencies within the United States, if it should come to pass, should allow a greatly improved co-ordination of food aid with other forms of aid.

The final consideration in the overall assessment of food aid is that food is not a single commodity but that supply and food tastes vary throughout the world. The food provided as aid may be unknown, unsuitable or even 'luxury' foods quite inappropriate for staple cereal eaters. An extreme, and rather trivial, example of this was the shipment of quantities of tomato sauce to Bangladesh in 1970 from an Eastern European country. The starving people of Bangladesh had no use for such food. In fact it was sold in the markets. The money gained was used for the purchase of more suitable foods, and eventually the tomato sauce started to appear in hotels catering to Western visitors. Very little harm was done in this case, although the people who profited from the sale of the sauce were certainly not those most in need of food. Other possibilities exist with potentially more severe consequences.

Several times comments have been made about the fact that the largest recipients of food aid are rice-eating people, while most of the aid is in the form of wheat and wheat products. Sri Lanka grows no wheat, but most of its food aid is of this commodity. A taste is being developed for bread which can only be met in the future by further food aid or by commercial imports (Jones, 1976). Part, at least, of the greater availability of rice in the Philippines in the late 1960s and early 1970s is not the result of greatly increased production but because rice has been foregone in favour of wheat by the poorest sections of the population, the wheat being derived from PL 480 shipments. The types of food available to the World Food Programme are relatively limited and it is not always possible to provide foods which are known, or easily available at low cost, in the recipient countries. This situation creates problems in nutrition education, which should be carried out on the basis of locally produced foods. It also makes the take-over of the feeding projects by the recipient government more difficult at the planned end of the involvement of the World Food Programme (Ronchi and Lopez, 1976).

A potentially more serious, and certainly more controversial, problem of inappropriate foods is the increasing shipment of dried skimmed milk (DSM) especially from the EEC, to developing countries. There are three reasons for the criticism of such shipments, the first of which we have already discussed in Chapter 5, stems from unhygienic and improper use of the DSM by mothers and the consequent decline in breast feeding. The second criticism is potentially even more serious, though it now appears to be not as great a problem as was at first thought. Milk contains a carbohydrate, lactose, the milk sugar. A proportion of the world's population has an enzyme, lactase, in the small intestine which helps to digest this milk sugar and enables the milk protein to be utilized by the body. The process of DSM manufacture concentrates the lactose by the removal of the milk fats. The problem arises because a substantial proportion of the world's population does not have the enzyme, lactase, and, therefore, is unable to digest the milk. Not only is digestion not possible, but the lactose can create severe diarrhoea; given, for example, to a child suffering from kwashiokor DSM could potentially add to the problems of nutrient and water loss from the body and hasten death. A band of Africa from South West Africa through Tanzania is characterized by agricultural peoples with no cattle. This lack of cattle is the result of the presence of the tsetse fly. Almost all of South-East Asia contains non-milk drinkers. These people have very low lactase levels and low digestive tolerance to milk. It appears that DSM is not only an inappropriate food for aid because it is not locally produced, but that it may be positively harmful as a result of the digestive problems added to the hygiene and nutrition questions raised earlier. Recent experiments (Kretchmer, 1971), however, conclude that lactose tolerance can be built up quickly despite low lactase levels and that an intake of a small daily quantity of milk will not produce the expected drastic digestive effects and may be beneficial. The overall value of DSM, especially as an aid to non-milk-drinking populations, must, however, remain doubtful.

Milk products are used as food aid because they are in surplus production, especially in the EEC. It has even been suggested that the EEC should produce more in order to have more for use as aid. Animals are not good converters of the food value of their fodder and a third argument against DSM as food aid is that '. . . if a donor country wishes to give away food it should not waste three-quarters of it by first passing it though a cow. It would, in most cases, be preferable to provide as aid the cereals and high protein feeds that go into dairy production, rather than the milk which comes out' (Jones, 1976).

The balance of advantage and disadvantage of food aid will have to be assessed by each developing country and donor. Schneider (1975) outlines four requirements for food aid to be valuable:

1. The amount of aid should be closely linked to the size of the deficit in the recipient country.
2. As far as possible, domestic producers should be isolated from price effects by the use of food aid in differentiated marketing channels creating additional demand.
3. The recipient countries should ensure that they have development policies which continue to encourage domestic food production.
4. Donors should ensure that the recipients are not developing a 'beggar mentality', especially through long-term feeding in refugee camps, and that they are adopting genuine self-help schemes.

To these I would add:

5. The development policies of the recipient countries should be more closely monitored by the donors, despite the resulting accusations of paternalism and neo-colonialism. Brown (1975) goes so far as to suggest that food aid should be denied to those countries which do not implement effective population and development policies. Food tied to such performance criteria mitigates against the poorest of the

developing countries as they are the least able to implement such effective policies. Encouragement and some control are needed but not a strict adherence to performance criteria.

6. Food aid should be additional to other aid and generally, the larger the food aid shipments the larger should be the complementary other aid flows.

7. There must be increased security in the amounts of food aid available over a period of years. This could be achieved by the donor countries agreeing to meet some proportion of the overall food deficit, an issue which will be returned to when considering world food security stocks in Chapter 9.

One thing remains clear—food deficits will continue and will grow in most developing countries (IFPRI, 1977) and food aid will be the only available short-term alternative to large-scale starvation. It is inescapable that food aid is needed, though as a complement, not as a substitute, for the development of domestic agricultural production (Sanderson, 1975). At best, food aid can be little more than a nutritional palliative to a problem, the basic cause of which is poverty. 'Given that there is a world food problem not only is food aid not the only solution, it is not even the best solution. It might, however, be the only practical one' (Mettrick, 1969).

Neo-Malthusia, Triage and Lifeboat Ethics

A discussion of food aid should not end without a mention of some of the more extreme views. The three considered here are related and equally unsound. The first borrows from the writing of Malthus in suggesting that birth rates are largely biologically controlled, and that to reduce malnutrition and starvation in the developing countries today is merely to encourage the poor in those countries to have more children, and for the improved health of such children to lead to further mouths to feed. Healthy mothers are assumed to be capable of having, and to want to have, more children. This gloomy view assesses the situation as hopeless and food aid as self-defeating, leading to a hastening of the ultimate Malthusian catastrophe. It is demographically unsound. We have already considered how children can be regarded as economic and social insurance and that *decreased* well-being will *increase* the incentives for higher birth rates and faster population growth (Rich, 1974). Decisions to have children are much more complex than the result of simple biological controls.

The evidence appears somewhat contradictory. Hull and Hull (1977) are able to cite several examples where the expected negative relationship between fertility and economic status is not found. Indonesian evidence, using the education level attained by women as a surrogate for economic development, shows that fertility climbed steeply with increasing education level, then flattened out and declined at the highest levels of education.

Suggested reasons are that there is greater disruption of marriage because of divorce and widowhood among the poor; the poor also practice longer periods of abstinence from sexual relations after the birth of a child during breast feeding, and finally that the poor have shorter reproductive lives. The latter point has been strongly supported by Frisch (1974) who shows that fecundity is strongly related to nutritional status. As nutrition improves, a woman's *ability* to have children and her reproductive life increases. On the other hand in most of the developing countries, birth rates are falling (Kirk, 1972). True fertility rates (which is fertility related to the number of women in each child-bearing age group) are falling in the great majority of the developing countries, although not particularly fast in most of those with very large populations (Tsui and Bogue, 1978).

The true picture is probably a combination of both views. A reduction in malnutrition will increase the *capability* of the population to increase itself at a faster rate. Improvement in the conditions of life will reduce the *desire* to have more children. Changes in fertility might be expected to follow an inverted U shape with a relatively short-lived increase in fertility and birth rate followed by a longer, and more significant, decline (Simon, 1977). The fact that the relationship is non-linear helps to explain the several examples of the weak, usually not statistically significant, positive relationships, found between birth rates and economic growth (Yotopoulos, 1977). That author finds, however, that these positive relationships are also the result of using birth rates rather than the true fertility rate and using growth in the gross national product as a measure of economic development. Using the true fertility and the GNP per capita plus a measure of the income distribution (the income share of the worst-off 40 per cent of the population), Yotopoulos finds a statistically significant negative relationship for a number of different samples of countries throughout the world. If, as seems to be established, fertility can be negatively related to the quality of life of the population, and food aid can be shown to improve the quality of life, then this neo-Malthusian argument against food aid turns, on closer examination, into a potent argument in favour of it.

Two similar attempts have been made to provide moral arguments against food aid. The first is the so-called 'triage' or sorting analogy first put forward in 1967 (Paddock and Paddock) from the operation of field hospitals during wartime. A limited medical facility is faced with a large influx of wounded. The medical staff must decide who to treat first. The wounded are placed into three categories: those who will live without immediate treatment; those who will die regardless of treatment; and those who can probably be saved by immediate treatment. The last group is treated first. The parallel with food aid would have us divide up the potential recipients into the same categories and not waste our resources on those countries which are thought to be beyond hope regardless of the extent of outside help. In particular, a country should be denied food aid if the population growth rate has already surpassed its agricultural potential.

Such an analogy rests on a number of false assumptions. Firstly, it assumes that such a division can be made in the case of countries. Undoubtedly, through shortage of time, tiredness, and shortage of diagnostic aids, mistakes were made at the field hospitals and people died unnecessarily, but the range of the variation of the injuries was generally not large and the personnel skilled and experienced. On what basis could a choice reasonably be made for the developing countries? Our data base is weak and often virtually non-existent, and our 'surgeons' certainly lack experience of such choices. Secondly, and more telling, is the whole basis of the medical analogy. The manpower of the field hospital is clearly limited and is much less than would be required to treat all patients at once. Equally, we can be reasonably certain of the recovery rate from the various courses of treatment. We can by no means be certain that the resources, food aid and otherwise, of the developed nations are less than is required to treat all the developing nations, and we know virtually nothing about the recovery rates following treatment. What is required is the will to treat the patients; symptoms certainly, but primarily the cause of these symptoms. The resources of the rich nations are almost certain to be sufficient if the will is there.

The same critical assumption that resources are not adequate to save all, appears again in the so-called lifeboat ethic (Hardin, 1977). Here the analogy goes as follows. The world is a lifeboat with limited resources. It is already full but a number of people are swimming around the boat attempting to get in. The choice facing the lifeboat occupants is to let the others aboard, thus swamping the boat and drowning everyone, or to fight them off thereby saving themselves. The countries of the developed world are seen as the occupants of the lifeboat, the resources of which will run out if the weakest of the developing nations are helped aboard. The crux of the error in this analogy is that the developed world is not a lifeboat at the limits of its resources. There is ample evidence of potential for increased food production in the world. Admittedly, the possibilities are certainly finite, but the world is not yet at the point of limiting resources. Secondly, to continue the analogy perhaps beyond reasonable limits, the developed world in the lifeboat has considerable excess weight, which if jettisoned could make room for more. We have seen (Chapter 5) that eating less in the West will not automatically improve the lot of the poor, but the assumptions of equality between all occupants of the lifeboat and among all the occupants of the water is nonsense in the context of world food production and consumption. The analogy of triage predicts impending disaster to all those helped unless a choice is made, and the lifeboat ethic predicts disaster to all, both the helper and the helped. Both are based on a view of the world at the edge of its supplies of useful resources. In the case of food, crises have occurred but they were in no way the result of, or premonitions of, a world running out of food. The food potential is there if we have the will to use it and if we act in time.

The lifeboat analogy could be turned around. It is close to the shore, the healthy can be left to swim to the shore while the weak are helped by the lifeboat. Perhaps that is overly optimistic, but it is closer to reality than the original use of the analogy.

CHAPTER 8

Food Crises

Introduction

'Food crisis' is a term which came into popular usage most recently in the two years following August 1972. The events of these two years, popularized through the news media scenes of chaos on the Chicago grain exchange, and stories of malnutrition and hunger throughout the world, drew attention to a series of events which appeared unique and to signal a dramatic and potentially explosive political change in world relations. The earth seemed to have suddenly reached a point of being unable to supply enough food for its rapidly growing population.

There have been many such food crises during man's occupation of the earth and they have all been characterized by shortfalls in supply relative to the growing food demand of the population. Primitive hunters and gatherers had and, where such societies still remain, still have, periods of severe food shortage. Adverse weather conditions and other circumstances led to food shortages in the United Kingdom in the seventeenth century. Early settlers in North America suffered times of acute food shortage until they were able to adapt to the local conditions and raise agricultural production. Johnson (1975a) identifies four main periods during the last eighty years when a part or all of the world appeared to be in a food crisis. The first of these was at the end of the nineteenth century when Britain's wheat supply seemed limited in the face of ever rising demand. At this time there appeared to be little possibility of increasing world wheat supply and that imported supplies available to the United Kingdom must decline as North America needed more and more grain to meet domestic demand. The prospects of increasing yields to meet this increased demand looked bleak. The second period of impending crisis which Johnson identifies was in the early 1920s in the United States. Again it was a threat of supplies not increasing fast enough to meet demand. Potential increases in yields were considered unlikely to be fast enough to raise food production in sufficient time. After a further brief food scare in the late 1940s following unpredicted increases in the population and fertility in the United States, the next major crisis occurred in the mid 1960s. Significantly, this food crisis had two characteristics which it was to share with the most recent crisis ten or so years later; it was felt worldwide and it involved important changes in the policies of the centrally planned economies of China and Russia. In 1961 China became a net importer of wheat and in 1963 Russia also began to import large quantities of food. World wheat stocks fell in all the major wheat-exporting countries and India had poor grain harvests in 1965 and 1966. Overall world wheat production dropped slightly in 1961–62 and again in 1963–64 and in 1965–66. Although these falls were not marked, demand was rising all the time and stocks were drawn down. The coincidence of increased world wheat demand from China and Russia, combined with poor Indian harvests, is a pattern which was to be repeated in 1972. This crisis was quickly over as grain crops in the Indian subcontinent increased and 1966–67 was a record year for world wheat production. By the late 1960s world stocks of wheat had begun to climb again.

Between these crises of supply not matching demand were crises of another kind. To major food-producing countries a surplus of production over demand is a crisis. Prices fall necessitating government action to support prices or to mitigate the effects of the fall. This leads to considerable expenditure and the creation of food stockpiles. All this is necessary to avoid hardship among producers. Press headlines change as the crisis now becomes one of oversupply, and photographs of starvation in India are replaced by those of overflowing grain silos in the United States. Starvation in India may continue more or less unabated throughout this time but the outward face of the crisis has changed. Well-known commentators changed sides with great rapidity. Johnson (1975a) notes contrasting statements made by Lester Brown in 1964 and 1968. In the latter he predicts a new era of production of food and conditions of food plenty. By 1973 he, and many others, had again swung the other way, suggesting that the events of 1972–73 were ushering in a new era of food shortage. In hearings before a Senate subcommittee on the world food situation Brown commented: 'One of the most basic questions concerning the current food situation is to what extent it is temporarily just a departure from a trend and to what extent we are witnessing a fairly basic transformation in the nature and dimensions of the world food problem . . . I lean towards the latter' (US Senate, 1973). At the same hearings Paarlberg, representing the views of the United States Department of Agriculture, drew attention to the similarities between the early 1970s and the mid 1960s when 'with two successive droughts in South Asia we saw a rash of books and articles on the bleak outlook for the world food situation'. One such book had the predictive title of *Famine 1975* (Paddock and Paddock, 1967). As in the past, the 'new era' of shortage and high food prices turned out to be remarkably short-lived. There certainly are problems in world food production and demand but they are not of the sort postulated by these writings.

The world has swung, often with great rapidity, from situations of surplus to situations of shortage of food (McGovern, 1975). The essence of the present world food situation is not an overall shortage of food but the inability of producer and consumer countries to predict supply and demand and to manage supplies to allow for basic instabilities in production. One of the important aspects of future world food supply is that the climatic instability is probably increasing. Although experts disagree about whether the earth is entering a cooling or a warming period they appear agreed that the future climate is likely to be more unstable than the recent past. In many ways it matters little whether the climate gets warmer or cooler on a world scale. Warmer conditions will probably mean drier conditions and this will reduce cereal production on the important, but already marginal, frontiers of cultivation in the American West and the Russian East. If the climate gets significantly cooler and wetter this will reduce yields as a result of lack of sunshine and shorter growing seasons. In this case the effects are likely to be most severely felt in the cool temperate production areas. Even if there is no overall climatic change, a change in the stability of conditions will increase food production instabilities and, without remedial measures, will create food crises of mismatched supply and demand. As countries have become increasingly interdependent so local food shortages begin to have repercussions elsewhere. Increased demand from one sector reduces supplies for another. As the world increasingly relies on supplies from just one country, the United States, to meet any shortfall in domestic production, so any local food crisis soon becomes a world food crisis.

The world food problem consists of two very different dimensions, supply and demand. All the recognized food crises have been the result of essentially short-term inelasticities of supply. For short periods the supply of food has been limited or reduced in the face of rising demand. Most analyses of such crises have emphasized supply questions, for example, the problems of limitations on world food production provided by limited resources of arable land. 'We ought not to delude ourselves that there are vast acreages of good land waiting to be brought into production' (Brown before the Senate hearings, US Senate, 1973). The World Food Conference, in 1974, concentrated almost exclusively on the supply side of the crisis; food production potential, world food stock management and the distribution of food and food aid. These supply problems turned out to be as short-lived in 1974 as they had been in 1965, meanwhile the other dimension of the world food problem continued more or less unchanged. Malnutrition and starvation existed in the world before, during and after the 1960s food crisis and before, during and after the similar crisis of the 1970s. The World Food Conference paid little heed to the lack of effective demand as a major world food problem. Supply inelasticities and the resulting price response were not new or long-lived phenomena, but malnutrition continued. In fact the effects of the 1970s crisis on the people of most developing countries was probably less than on the people in the developed countries. Price changes in basic foodstuffs were small in many developing countries as a result of government food price policies and a high degree of rural family self-sufficiency in food. Changes in the world market price for cereals had little effect on the majority of the population. Although a higher price had to be paid for imported grain and the shortage of world supplies limited food aid shipments, in general, levels of malnutrition remained high in the Third World because of an inability of much of the population to purchase food whatever its price, not because of the world food shortage or world food price rises (Taylor, 1975). The 'crisis' was a failure in the management of the world food supply, while the real food problem continued more or less unaffected.

The remainder of this chapter will examine the events of 1972–74, tracing as far as possible the causes of the supply problems and the instabilities in food supply which will continue to lead to further world food crises. Just as 1972 was not the first crisis, without drastic policy changes it certainly will not be the last.

The Events of 1972–75

Between 1971–72 and 1975–76 world wheat production remained more or less static with 1973–74 showing a slight improvement. Between 1966–1967 and 1970–71 world wheat prices had fallen steadily in absolute and, more dramatically, in real terms. World and United States' stockpiles of unsaleable wheat accumulated. Stock levels, production and price seemed to give little cause for concern, except among producing countries, until August 1972 when obviously something happened which had not occurred in the past, even in the crisis of the mid 1960s. Prices increased almost fourfold, stocks fell to record low levels, more or less disappearing in the United States. It was not until 1976–77, when production increased greatly, that stocks and prices started to regain their previous levels (Figure 50). Both production and stock levels have fallen before, but without the dramatic price rise of the early 1970s. There were several interrelated causes of these events.

Climatic Conditions

The onset of the crisis was a very poor production year in 1972. These poor conditions were worldwide. The Asian monsoon was very poor, seriously affecting the size of harvests in India, Bangladesh, and Pakistan; there was drought in the USSR, especially in European Russia, following a very cold dry winter over the whole of the country. Bad harvests were recorded in China and in Mexico and the cereal harvests in Argentina and

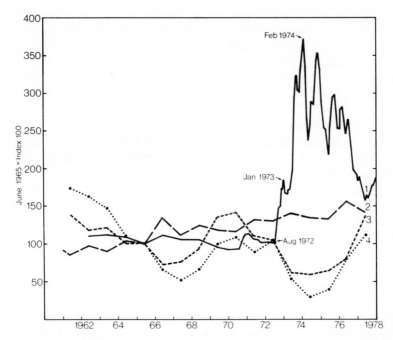

Figure 50. World production, stocks and price of wheat, 1961–78. 1 = Wheat (US export) price, 2 = world wheat production, 3 = world wheat stocks, 4 = US wheat stocks, Source: FAO, *Production Yearbooks* and unpublished data; *World Wheat Statistics*, International Wheat Council, and USDA *Foreign Agricultural Trade of the United States* (June, 1978)

Australia were below trend in 1971–72. This bad season was not a one-year event. The Asian monsoons were again poor in 1974 and a severe drought struck much of the United States' corn belt at the same time. In 1972 the world cereal harvest was down by about 40 million tons, or some 3 per cent of world production. Production of major cereal crops fell, not a larger fall than had been experienced previously, but this time the production of wheat, corn, rice, and barley all fell together (Figure 3) showing the worldwide nature of the poor growing conditions. A similar combined fall occurred again in 1974, led by the sharpest drop in corn production, but in 1975, although wheat and barley production continued downwards, rice and corn production moved sharply upwards. In 1976 wheat production reached record levels, partly as a result of policies for increased production in the United States and other major wheat-producing countries, and partly as a result of better growing conditions. Barley and corn production were also up, although less dramatically, and although rice production registered a slight fall from the previous year's record peak, the food crisis was over and prices were falling rapidly, the fall continuing into 1977.

As an explanation of the food crisis the coincidence of poor climate, and therefore poor cereal production, on a global scale is an oversimplification. Climate had a greater impact as the poor conditions of 1972 came at the end of what, with hindsight, was a long run of favourable cereal-growing conditions. Viewed over a longer time period the climate of 1972 was probably more or less normal, as was cereal production, but 1972 followed an exceptional period, and it was on these conditions that food production planning was based. The effects of the 1972 climate were more severe than they need have been if planning had been based on more reasonable average conditions (Thompson, 1975). Although wheat and corn production were down in 1972, this followed exceptional rises in production the previous year and the 1972 harvest remained the second highest ever for corn and barley and the third highest for wheat. About half of the drop of 16 million tons of coarse grains production was the result of the United States' production controls, maintained because of the previous years' good production and the intense political desire not to increase stock levels. Only in the case of rice was the drop of 14 million tons, or 5 per cent, added to a fall the previous year. Agricultural planners in the FAO, USDA and in the USSR all assumed that climatic factors in agricultural production would vary, but around a more or less constant trend (Allen, 1976) and production, withdrawn acreage and livestock plans were based on this assumption. The effects of the weather in 1972 were aggrevated by the planners' assumptions that the good years would continue. Cereal crop production was again at a record level in 1973, but falls for most cereals the following year, and for wheat in 1975, were significant as the world cereal market had not had time to recover from the bad year of 1972.

Population and Demand

Although cereal production declined in 1972 and again in 1974, world population continued to increase and the decline in cereal production per capita was greater. This was particularly marked in the rice-eating, developing countries. At the same time increasing affluence, especially in the developed countries, but also significantly in the centrally planned economies of Asia and Europe and in the oil-rich countries of the Middle East, meant that per capita demand for meat and processed cereals rose fast. Plans for production, and for stock levels, of grains for human and for animal consumption were made without sufficient attention to such changes in world demand (Biggs, 1976). The rapid world economic recovery from the slump of 1969–71 meant that per capita demand for food rose rapidly. Johnson (1975a) estimates that it grew by an average of 0.7 per cent annually in the 1960s, by 0.55 per cent in 1971, by 0.8 per cent in 1972 and by 1.0 per cent in 1973. Such an increase in demand per capita would explain about 20 per cent of the world food price rise of 1972, assuming that the supply of food was reasonably elastic.

High-Protein Animal Feeds

In 1972, for reasons little understood, the cold El Nimo ocean current off the west coast of South America altered and the anchovy harvest of Peru failed almost totally. The anchovies feed on the plankton brought to the surface by the cold current as it meets warmer tropical waters from the north. In 1970 the Peruvian fish catch, most of which was anchovies, made up nearly 19 per cent of the total world fish catch. By 1973 this proportion has fallen to 3.5 per cent of a slightly reduced world fish catch (Figure 51). Recovery since that date has been slow with Peruvian fish catches now at about 60 per cent of the level of 1963 and making up about 6 percent of the world fish catch. The anchovies were used to produce fishmeal, a high-protein animal feed used in North America and in Europe. The best alternative animal food was soybeans, and the price of soybeans rose sharply as fishmeal became scarce. Soybeans compete with corn for land in the American Mid-west and so the rise in soybean prices stimulated a rise in corn prices. As the same crops compete elsewhere in the world the imposition of the temporary soybean export ban by the United States to protect the home cattle industry, resulted in the price of animal feed of all sorts, including coarse grains, rising even more sharply elsewhere in the world.

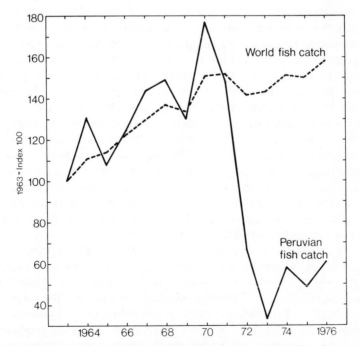

Figure 51. World and Peruvian fish catch, 1963–77. Source: FAO, *Fishery Statistics* (1971; 1977)

Oil and Fertilizer Shortages

This provides one reason why the technology of the green revolution was not able to compensate for the less favourable climatic conditions. World supplies of nitrogen fertilizers were down by 2.3 per cent in 1973–74 and in 1974–75. Demand was rising fast in the developing countries with the fertilizer requirements of the HYV seeds. Supply constraints led to sharply increased prices, to black market trading in fertilizers and to smuggling. Even though most developing countries subsidized fertilizer (Timmer, 1976a), acute supply shortages meant that government organizations were unable to control the real farm-gate prices. Fertilizer application rates fell. The early HYV seeds probably grew less well without fertilizer than did the traditional varieties.

Fertilizer production is characterized by cycles of investment, overproduction and falling prices, followed by a lack of new plant investment and subsequent shortage. During the mid 1960s the world demand for fertilizers was high and high prices encouraged an over-expansion of production capability. Prices fell and investment in fertilizer plant came to a halt between 1968 and 1971. This was followed by a shortage and high prices, but by 1977 with new investment world fertilizer prices had fallen again. This production cycle was aggravated by some locally important production plant failures (i.e. in Bangladesh) and more importantly by the oil crisis. Oil and natural gas are the basic feedstocks for nitrogen fertilizer manufacture. Price rises and the oil embargo limited production capability and contributed to the raising of the fertilizer price. Although it may be politically and economically expedient to blame the oil crisis for the fertilizer shortage, the impact was not as great as that resulting from the investment problems of the industry. Whatever the reason, the world shortage and the high price meant that fertilizer was obtained by those able to afford it and not by those whose production would have benefited most. Fertilizer trade was reduced and aid shipments of fertilizer to the developing countries more or less stopped. Fertilizer usage in the United States, on golf courses as well as on farm land (George, 1976), remained little affected. It was greatly reduced in those countries in the developing world, whose position at the bottom of the fertilizer response curve would have ensured a much greater grain production per unit of fertilizer used (Table 6).

The effects of the oil crisis went beyond fertilizer production. Although the agriculture sector of the United States was able to avoid fuel rationing, shortage and high prices in the developing countries had considerable effects. The Third World countries were not the target of the Arab oil boycott but, because world oil distribution is controlled by the multinational oil companies and not directly by the Arab producers, oil deliveries were severely cut to all places which were marginal markets. Deliveries of the available supplies were concentrated on to the developed countries, the major markets. Oil and petrol rationing was much more severely felt in the small developing countries of the Pacific, for example, than in either the United States or the United Kingdom. Fuel shortages affected the distribution of fertilizers, the marketing of surplus food grains and the operation of mechanized farm equipment and pumps for irrigation. This contributed to the apparent failure of the green revolution technology to compensate for the poor climatic conditions.

Cattle Cycles

Cattle production is subject to the same cycles as other forms of agricultural production (Chapter 3). During times of rapidly rising beef prices cattle herds increase, but because of the production lag between the decision to increase herd sizes and the ultimate slaughter, the resulting falls in price are delayed. The beef price falls, coinciding with the slaughter of the increased herds and the resulting low prices do not encourage full herd replenishment. This is an oversimplification as herds are constantly being culled and replenished, but in 1972 the cattle production cycles of Argentina, North America, Australia, and Europe were in phase, with large herd sizes in all regions, probably for the first time (Johnson, 1975a). Despite the substantial proportion of the world cattle herd raised on range lands large herd sizes require large amounts of cattle feed. This increased demand for cattle feed came just at the time when it was in short supply and highly priced.

Conjunctional Accidents

The above are the major economic and physical reasons for the events of 1972. No one of these factors alone would have been responsible for the dramatic rises in food prices. Individually most had happened before. The coincidence of 1972 was that a number of apparently unrelated events affected agricultural production and demand in the same direction and at the same time. We have already seen that 1972 was the first time in recent years when the production of all major cereals turned down at once. The coincidence of factors in 1972 was far more widespread, with climatic, fertilizer, food demand, cattle production, animal feed, and oil factors, all operating together to lead to a downturn in food production and a sharper upturn in price.

Though wide-ranging and severe this conjunctional accident was not the only, or perhaps the major, factor in the food price rises of 1972. The politics of food production and consumption, and the political reactions to the food situation in 1972, greatly amplified these events.

The Politics of the 1972 Food Crisis

The United States

Within the United States there was again a coincidence of different factors which worked together to stimulate the events of 1972. The first of these was the desire of a Republican President (Nixon) and his Secretary for Agriculture (Butz) to remove as much as possible of government interference from agriculture and return it to free market conditions. The two main instruments of government policy were support buying by the CCC and the idling of productive land to reduce production and hold up prices. The first of these policies had led to the steady build-up of world wheat stocks, most of which were in the United States, from the low point of 1967 (Figure 50) to in excess of 40 million tons in 1970. Stocks were held at about that level and remained embarrassingly high and expensive to maintain. The other form of food stocks was the potential of the land withdrawn from production under government programmes. Although this had been reduced from the levels of the 1960s, it remained considerable (Table 68) until the rise in food prices led the USDA to encourage farmers to plant 'fence row to fence row'. Idled land was less of a political embarrassment than were stockpiles, as the latter had a purchase price as well as a storage cost. Payments for acreage withdrawn, although costly, did not produce the same accumulation of costs over successive years. In 1972 there was a political eagerness to dispose of stockpiled food which probably overrode all or any consideration of the food security value of such reserves. The overall costs of government intervention had risen nearly fourfold between 1955 and 1970 (Figure 35) so the political stage was set to take advantage of any opportunity to reduce these costs, and overseas sales were a most attractive way to do this.

At the same time the overall balance of payments of the United States was in deficit. In the fiscal year 1971–72 the trade deficit was $8.4 billion, three times greater than the previous year. Any increase in exports was vital, especially at a time of rapidly rising oil import bills. The stockpiles of American food were available if a market could be found. Thirdly, President Nixon was anxious to continue to develop the political *détente*

Table 68. United States cereal acreage planted and withdrawn

	1956–60	1961–65	1966–70	1971–72
		(million acres)		
Cereal acreage withdrawn (1)	23.9	57.5	53.7	50.0
Cereal acreage planted (2)	303.7	304.4	304.8	317.2
(1) as percentage of (2)	7.2%	18.9%	17.6%	15.8%

Source: Biggs (1976).

between the United States and the Soviet Union, which had been started by President Johnson's removal of trade embargoes.

In summary, by 1972, grain sales from the United States, especially to the USSR, looked attractive to the President because:

(a) they would hold up agricultural prices and help with the farm vote during the Congressional elections year;
(b) agricultural prices could be supported without expansion of CCC intervention and resulting high costs, a matter of concern to all taxpayers in the United States. The prospects of large export sales appeared as the long-sought-after panacea of rising domestic agricultural prices without government expenditure;
(c) such exports would help the balance of payments and, at the same time the President's favoured area of international relations.

It is hardly surprising that the prospect of grain sales to the USSR was welcomed. Trade negotiations with the USSR started early in 1972 on a broad front with the negotiating team led by USDA, their position strengthened by the available stocks of food in the United States.

The USSR

Meanwhile the physical circumstances in the USSR, and the political reaction to the reduced harvests, encouraged the possibility of food purchases from the United States. The five-year plan for agriculture for the period 1971–75 was based on production, and production conditions, of 1968. The growing conditions in that year, especially in the new cereal lands of Kazakhstan and Siberia, appear to have been exceptionally good. In the 1971–72 growing season, the second of the five-year plan period, conditions were very different. The winter was very cold but exceptionally dry. The lack of snow cover meant that about one-third of the winter cereals (sown the previous autumn) had germinated but were then killed by frost, lacking the insulating snow cover. Winter-sown crops make up about one-third of the total USSR cereal production. Additional spring sowing of cereals took place to compensate for this loss, but a spring drought in much of European Russia delayed germination and reduced yields. Also, most of the additional area was sown to feed grains not to wheat. This was in accordance with the five-year plan's emphasis on livestock production. The drought in European Russia also reduced the potato crop, which is particularly susceptible to drought but which is usually a convenient substitute for cereals. The spring cereal yields in Kazakhstan and Siberia were good, but wet weather delayed the harvest and a shortage of local drying facilities together with transport congestion led to crop wastage. The 1972 Russian production of cereals was 134 million tons, only about 90 per cent of the previous year's production and 8 per cent down on the target production indicated for that year in the five-year plan. Cereals for direct human consumption were even further below target. Potato production was 15 per cent down on the previous year while production of milk, meat, and eggs were all above the previous year's levels.

The five-year plan placed heavy emphasis on livestock production. Economic growth rates had been slowing down in Russia since the 1950s and consumption was to be increased to stimulate growth. Consumer goods of all sorts became more freely available, demand being met, largely but not exclusively, by domestic production. Meat production was planned to increase fast to match consumer demand, aid increased consumer spending and increase the GNP. Unfortunately, the five-year plan for agriculture was based on a year of favourable weather and adequate production potential for feed grains. Previous USSR policy had always made the livestock sector particularly volatile. Animals would be slaughtered, often in huge numbers, to ensure adequate cereal production for direct human consumption. Bread always had a higher priority than beef. Domestic cereal supply for human consumption was rendered fairly constant by a flexible livestock programme. Thus, for example, livestock numbers declined in 1969, a year of poor harvests, but in 1972 to 1974 continued a sharply rising curve despite poor cereal harvests (Figure 52). It was only after a second poor harvest in 1974 and again, after an even worse harvest in 1975, that the trend of increasing livestock production was reversed. Such a situation of increased livestock production and reduced cereal yields could be met either by drastic reductions in domestic cereal consumption

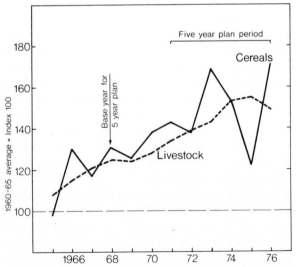

Figure 52. Cereal and livestock production in the USSR, 1965–77. Source: FAO, *Production Yearbooks*

(not a feasible solution because of the importance of cereals in the staple diet in Russia) or by the import of cereals on a large scale.

The Russians also had political reasons for encouraging *détente* with the West, particularly with the United States. Relationships with China were deteriorating and the desire not to have enemies in both East and West provided a favourable climate for bilateral trade negotiations. The stage was set for what was to be recognized as one of the largest commercial coups ever. The Russians were prepared for the necessity of grain imports, and the Americans, as the dominant world grain supplier, had the available surpluses and a government committed to increased agricultural trade, especially with the USSR.

The reasons that the resulting USSR/US grain deals had such an impact on the international grain markets are a combination of miscalculation, secrecy of negotiations, astute bargaining by the Russian buyers and over-enthusiasm on the part of the American sellers, or at least by their government.

The Grain Deals

In early 1972 USDA grossly underestimated the likely size of the USSR cereal needs. USDA estimates of grain sales to the USSR were set at 5 million tons in 1972 with a 10 per cent increase over the succeeding years of the five-year plan. Such estimates were based on the livestock numbers in the five-year plan but assuming the same grain production conditions as 1968. Despite the weather and winter crop reports available to USDA, these estimates of grain imports were apparently not revised upwards. Negotiations started in May 1972. Interestingly, in the light of later developments, the Russians wished to deal government-to-government, but the United States insisted that the sales be made through private companies even though the CCC had to sell surpluses to these companies first. The resulting negotiations were split between the government-to-government discussions and the private company dealings, increasing the general confusion. Throughout May and June intense diplomatic activity continued over the overall size of the deal and the credit terms to be available to the Russians. USDA public announcements still made no reference to wheat deals even as late as May, referring only to sales of coarse grains (*Foreign Agriculture,* May 1972). On 9 July 1972 an official deal was signed between the two countries. The Russians agreed to buy at least $750 million worth of grain over the next three years and the Secretary of Agriculture assured all that no more than this amount of grain would be purchased in any one year. He also assured the American people that the credit terms and the sale price would involve no subsidy to the Russians by the American taxpayer. Several days before that, on 30 June, the Continental Grain Company had agreed to sell $480 million worth of grain *that year*, about half of which was to be wheat. It is significant that this deal had been declared to USDA before being finalized, as clearance over the position of the export subsidy was necessary before the price could be negotiated. This will be discussed below. Between 1 July and 21 July the Russian buyers negotiated for an additional 5 million tons of cereals, including 1 million tons from Canada. In three *weeks* the buying team had purchased $705 million worth of cereals, nearly as much as the official deal allowed for a three-*year* period! The negotiations had been carried out with each grain company separately, with Continental Grain doing most of the business. The only organization in a position to know the true size of the total deal was USDA, which cleared the subsidy position with each company before the deals were signed. Subsequent charges levelled at the Russians for secrecy and underhand dealing are hardly fair. They negotiated with the private companies at the specific request of the American government and then proceeded to operate in the way in which any commercial company buying in the market place would operate. Full information was available to the American government at all times, although not at the request of the Russians. In early August the buying team returned and purchased another $450 million worth of cereals, about half of which was wheat.

The export subsidy is an important aspect of the grain deals. To encourage the depletion of cereal stocks before these deals began, an export subsidy was paid to United States' grain exporters to make up the difference between the high, government-supported, domestic price and the lower, world market price. All the deals with the Russians were for such enormous quantities of grain that even the largest companies did not have sufficient stocks on hand so had to purchase some of this grain on the open market. Such purchasing activity raised the domestic grain price during the time the companies were accumulating sufficient grain to meet their contractual obligations to the Russians. The companies needed to be assured that the export subsidy would remain in effect, regardless of any changes in the domestic price. This assurance they obtained from USDA. The export subsidy rose from a few cents a bushel in May 1972 to 24 cents by 3 August and to 38 cents by 24 August. This rise in subsidy reflected a rise in the domestic price of grain, which in turn reflected the purchasing activities of the large grain companies. Previous regulation of the subsidy had allowed a delay between the negotiations of a sale and the registration of that sale for subsidy purposes. At the time of the drafting of these regulations no one anticipated a very rapid rise in the domestic price of grain. It had been very stable for the previous ten years. The domestic price which pertained to the sale for subsidy purposes was the price at the time of registration, not the price at the time of actual sale. Most of the sales to Russia were not registered until some time later as the dealers allowed the subsidy to rise with the domestic price. The negotiated price which the grain companies reached with the Russian buyers was actually below the likely break-even price. The companies speculated, correctly, that the rise in domestic prices would occur and would raise the subsidy. Having first cleared the continuance of the regulations with USDA, the late registration of the sales enabled the companies to make a profit. In fact, as the deals were proceeding concurrently with a number of companies in secret, the companies underestimated the rise in the domestic price of grain. The purchase price to the companies, and the subsidy, went up more than they expected. However, as the domestic price and the subsidy rose together the only people who made really profitable deals were the Russians.

On 25th August 1972 USDA acted on the subsidy which was rapidly getting out of hand. A week's grace was allowed during which all sales made before 23 August could be registered for a subsidy of 47 cents a bushel. After that week the subsidy would be successively lowered until 22 September, when it would be eliminated entirely. About 30 per cent of the total sales were registered during that week at a cost of $480 million to the United States taxpayers. So much for the unsubsidized sales to the Russians.

The Instability of World Grain Markets

The size of the Russian grain deals were staggering and the use made of the capitalist system and company secrecy was equally impressive, but the deals do not explain all the instability of the world market which followed. A major part of the cereal price change during this period was the result of the limited nature of the world cereal market and the role of stocks in stabilizing this market. All the feed grains bought by the Russians and 80 per cent of the wheat, was purchased from the United States. Other countries, notably the EEC and Japan, protected their consumers from high domestic grain prices by limiting exports. The world market effects were amplified in the reduced market (Johnson, 1975a). Josling (1978b) estimates that such domestic price stability schemes in the developed countries reduced the amount of wheat available to the world market by over 19 million tons in 1971–74. This is close to the size of the Russian purchases. In the period 1971–74 consumer wheat prices more than tripled in the United States, while they increased only 35 per cent in the EEC, 52 per cent in Japan and 60 per cent in Australia (Hathaway, 1978). The same thing happened in reverse during the depression in the 1930s when price falls were much less in the protected markets of Europe than in the United States. The rice market, smaller than the wheat market showed even more spectacular price rises. The world trade in rice was made smaller by raising the rice premium in Thailand, one of the world's major rice exporters, to protect domestic consumers from high rice prices.

In 1972–73 the United States exported 32.1 million tons of wheat and 39 million tons of feed grains, representing 44 per cent and 58 per cent of all world wide sales respectively. This concentration of sales and price effects in the American domestic and export markets, and therefore on her Third World customers, was further amplified by the suddenly imposed transport demands, both internal and for export, of all the grain company deals at one time. Huge transport bottlenecks occurred, increasing the degree of panic and speculation over prices. Prices of other goods on the American market also rose as they had to compete with the grain companies for limited transport rolling stock and were also affected by the transport delays.

At the same time food imports from the United States appeared more attractive to other food-short countries. The dollar was devalued in relation to most currencies in 1971 and again in 1973. With the effects of inflation in the importing countries, United States' food appeared cheaper. The relative price of United States' food to Japanese importers fob gulf ports declined from an index value of 120 in 1964 to 72 in 1972 because of these factors. The Russians paid for most of their purchases in gold, which rose in value on world markets with the decline of the dollar. The nature of the world markets, and the United States' domestic economy, concentrated the world food sales in the United States, and protectionist policies elsewhere amplified the price effects on the United States and on the world markets.

The general nervousness of the world food market was accentuated by rapidly depleted stocks of cereals. As the stock levels declined so the market became more nervous about the requirements to meet the Russian deals. Wheat prices had remained more or less stable at stock levels from in excess of 60 million tons to about 35 million tons. As stocks declined below this level so prices rose rapidly (Figure 53). According to Biggs (1976), in the United States the critical stock level lies about one and a half times domestic consumption. Increased instability in the world wheat market following the events of 1972–75 has perhaps meant that the critical stock level is now more like 40 million tons. Without the Russian sales in 1972 the year-end stocks would have been about 40 million tons. This is less than the level of the previous year as production had fallen and all other traditional purchasers stayed at their same level of demand, but above the apparently critical level of stockholding.

Speculation and panic by dealers probably contributed a relatively small amount to the general price rise. It has been suggested that the slide in the value of the dollar led some speculators and dealers to get out of dollars and into commodities (Paarlberg, before United States Senate, 1973). Also dealer margins increased as one would expect with increased prices, transport difficulties and uncertainties in the future markets. Biggs (1976) quotes wheat price to the Kansas farmer as $1.57 a bushel, the United States' terminal price as $1.82 a bushel and the Rotterdam cif price as $1.94 a bushel during the first quarter of 1972. In the first quarter of 1973 these prices were $3.73, $4.19 and $5.04. The rises in margins were largely effects of, rather than causes of, the world price instability at the time.

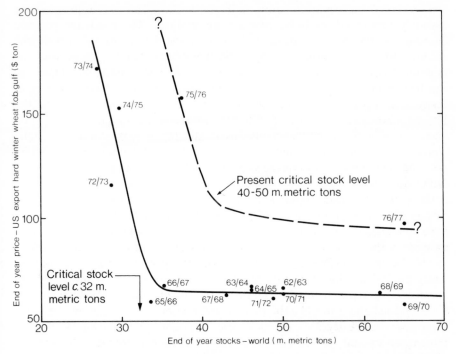

Figure 53. Wheat export price and world wheat stocks, 1962–77. Source: FAO, *Production Yearbooks*; International Wheat Council

Summary

Physical and political factors are inextricably linked in the events of the food crisis of 1972. It is convenient to blame the weather for which no one has responsibility. It is equally tempting to blame the Russians for disrupting the world's cereal markets. Neither explanation is sufficient. The weather was certainly bad throughout much of the world, and agricultural production was reduced as a result, but this was not sufficient in itself to create such market instability. The Russians certainly chose to react in a surprising way to domestic food shortages, but most commentators suggest that they did not deliberately set out to disrupt the grain markets (Biggs, 1976). The most significant factors were the political ones. In the United States there was a fixation with surpluses and their disposal which blinded officials to the need for security stocks. There was a lack of available information from USDA about the overall size of probable Russian purchases so farmers sold early, unable to take advantage of later price rises, a fact which left much of the farming community bitter towards the way in which USDA handled the matter. This was tempered somewhat as prices remained high the following year. The secrecy of the deals, and the lack of clear information from USDA as the deals were progressing, certainly stimulated the nervousness of the markets. There was the political decision on the part of the government of the USSR to go outside the country to reduce domestic food shortages and, finally, there was the reaction of other developed countries, especially in the EEC and Japan, to insulate their domestic markets from world price events by export taxes, thus thrusting the full market effect of the grain sales on to the United States market and its purchasers. Much of the human suffering that occurred as a consequence of all this in the low-income countries of the world (Chowdhury and Chen, 1977) was the result of human action and not the inevitable consequence of the adversities imposed by nature (Johnson, 1978).

One of the most significant outcomes of the crisis has been the recognition of the importance of grain stocks. Attitudes to food stockpiles have undergone an abrupt reversal. 'Grain and soybean reserves that existed in the past were more often considered surpluses than reserves' (S. H. Sabin, Vice-President, Continental Grain, at United States Senate hearings, 1973). The previous storage policy of the United States had been accidental, derived from the necessity of making purchases through the CCC and lacking a market channel for their disposal. The size of the stock level was a reflection of domestic production and world market circumstances and not based on any consideration of security or stability of the world grain supply. Present attempts to construct a system of security stocks will be discussed in the next chapter.

The complexity of the factors influencing food production has been well illustrated by the events of 1972–75 and in some cases lessons have been learnt. There is a need for management not only of domestic agriculture but more particularly of the international aspects, particularly trade. Since 1972 the Russian need for grain has been recognized and the advantages of a more orderly method of purchasing on the world market have persuaded the Russians and the Americans to reach bilateral agreements concerning grain trade. The Russians had wanted such an orderly trade through government-to-government transactions in the first place. The dramatic shortening of world grain supply and the effect that this had on the disbursement of food aid to the needy nations have led to greater efforts to stabilize food aid regardless of the state of the world markets. Such agreements have a long way to go before the world grain market and trade can be stabilized. It is to be hoped that the memory of the events of 1972 does not fade faster than the remedial action progresses.

This is the lasting problem of such food supply crises, they are temporary. Despite the comments from Lester Brown to the United States Senate hearings (1973), there is no evidence that 1972 ushered in a new period of world food shortage any more than the similar predictions made in the 1960s proved to be correct. Both supply crises were followed by supply crises of another sort. Overflowing grain stocks in the developing as well as the developed world presently concentrate the mind on the problems of oversupply. One difference on this latest occasion is that a longer-term view would allow the creation of security stockpiles to be undertaken when world prices are down, rather than as the World Food Conference recommended, when they were very high as in 1974. The creation of stocks at that time would have added to the demand for grain and would have pushed prices even higher. It would also have been an unacceptable expense at a time of high prices. Stockpiling at times of oversupply is cheaper and politically more acceptable as it supports the price of grain to the producers. If the organization can be created and adequate stocks properly managed we are perhaps close to a solution to the problems created by wild swings in supply (Walters, 1978).

One should not forget that the food crises of the 1960s and 1970s were not expressions of the real world food problem and therefore their solutions will not be appropriate to it either. These crises were sudden events brought on by a combination of circumstances, a combination that, like the crisis itself was short-lived. The *real* problem that remains is the long-term inability of the world to feed its continuously growing population *at a price that this population can afford to pay*. There is considerable potential to raise food production in the world, but it will be expensive food. Much of the world's population is too poor to purchase food at its current prices. The problem is not so much the technical fix of increased food production, although this will get progressively more difficult, but the social and economic development in the Third World which will enable the population to purchase food at all. Raised food prices encourages more production, but by doing so places more people in the category of being too poor to afford sufficient food. The world as a whole faces the same dilemma as many developing countries with the potential to increase food production.

The next chapter will assess the future world food needs and prospects of meeting these, and the present efforts at the management of the world food supply. Unless these efforts are successful—and little real progress has been made since 1974—the probability is very high that there will be a food crisis of the 1980s to add to those of the 1960s and the 1970s.

CHAPTER 9

The Future

Looking into the future of food supply, demand and policies involves two types of projection. The first of these is to see where trends in production and consumption are likely to lead. The almost universal conclusion of such projections is that the gap between food demand and supply in most developing countries will increase very substantially over the next ten to fifteen years. If the predictions of increasing instability of climate are correct then not only will the demand/supply gap increase but it will also fluctuate in a more extreme fashion than in the past. The events of 1972–76 seem very likely to be repeated, but also some years will show overflowing grain storage. There are certainly no physical conditions which can lead to optimism that the cycles of under and overproduction will not continue and that the world will become even more dependent on food supplies from a limited number of major grain producers, particularly the United States.

The second area of prediction follows naturally, namely the probable changes in the reactions of national governments and international agencies to future world shortages. For the food gap to be reduced, food production would have to be greatly increased in the developing countries, at a much faster rate than has been evident over the last fifteen years. An increase of the necessary magnitude does not seem to be impossible, but its economic and political feasibility is more questionable. Production increases will not be sufficient but will have to be supported by commodity and trade agreements. The political dilemma is that it is only in times of apparent crisis that there is the momentum for action on national and international food stocks and other food security measures. But, as in 1973–74, food stocks are extremely expensive to acquire at such times. When they are cheap, and when no food crisis exists, the drive for the creation of the security stocks is lost in the face of more immediately pressing short-term political demands.

About the only thing all predictions have in common is that they will be wrong. With the best techniques in the world it is not possible to anticipate future events except in so far as they may be outcomes of continuation of trends evident at the present, and established over a sufficiently long time to provide an adequate base for extrapolation. Predictions of the future level of population in many Third World countries, for example, depend on the anticipated rate of the demographic transition. By how much, how soon and determined by what factors will birth rates begin to fall? Projections simply on the basis of present birth rates soon produce horrifying population figures for countries like Bangladesh with a 3 per cent population growth rate. That Banglandesh's population will more or less double by the end of the century is fairly certain, but the rate of growth must begin to slow down at some point.

Projections of future food demand are even more difficult than population projections. Population is only one parameter in the food equation. Others, such as the reasons for shifts in production and per capita food demand make food gap analysis even more of a gaze into a crystal ball. Prediction of policy reactions to future food scenarios is equally difficult as few recognizable trends are evident to provide a basis for projection. This chapter will examine various attempts to assess the future size of the food gap in developing countries and the prospects for filling it.

The Food Gap

Assessments of the food gap of any country or group of countries will be the product of projections of food production and food consumption. The gap, if it exists, will have to be filled by imports, either commercial or aid, or will have to be reduced by changes in policy not assumed in the projections. Demand may have to be curtailed or shifted to different foods and faster growth in production encouraged. A projected food gap is no indication of the actual size of a country's food import demand in any one year, but gives only an indication of how the future might look if all present trends continue.

It is clear from Chapter 2 that predicting future trends in food production in developing countries will be present special problems. Very different results can be expected by 1990 if we project developing country food production growing as in 1966 to 1970 at the height of the green revolution, compared to projections based on the trend of 1970 to 1975. Since then food production has shown a more encouraging rate of growth. The length, and the start and end year, of the period used for projections of the future are obviously critical to the projection results. Different base periods will also influence decisions on the nature of the growth rates, whether they can be considered to be linear or have some curvilinear function. The pattern of growth in food production for many developing countries is actually a step function, where rapid spurts in food production have been followed by periods with slower growth rates. One such step was triggered by the adoption of the green revolution technology, and for reasons discussed in Chapter 5, the improvements brought about by this technology grew less dramatic a few years after its adoption. If the stepped nature of growth in food production is accepted it helps little for the future projection of food supply as the timing, and even the existence, of future technological innovations is unknown. Future technological developments in food production will probably be slower and less dramatic than in the recent past, but nothing is more difficult to see than the effects of tomorrow's technology. In the mid 1950s the upward step in the production of food brought about by the green revolution would have seemed like fantasy to most people.

The International Food Policy Research Institute (1977b) has made projections of future food production based on trends established over the period 1960 to 1975, while the World Bank (1976) uses the period 1960 to 1974. The IFPRI study projects the rate of growth in food production established over this period while the Bank Report notes that the rate of growth appears to be slowing over the latter years of the period and modifies the future rates of growth to take account of this and other specific conditions. The Bank study assumes that the production spurt in wheat in South Asia is over and that future growth rates will be lower. There is still assumed to be potential for rapid growth in wheat production in Latin America and for rice in South and South-East Asia. The growth rates, once set, are assumed to remain the same throughout the projection period. As different crops have shown very different rates of growth in the recent past, for example a comparison of wheat and pulses in South Asia (Figure 33), some studies of future food production and consumption disaggregate the analysis by major crop type (IFPRI, 1977b), but most include only cereal crops providing the major component of most diets (IFPRI, 1976; OECD, 1976a; World Bank, 1976). Food production in the developing countries is critically dependent on the use of various agricultural inputs, particularly fertilizer and irrigation. The use of these inputs is in turn dependent on the relationship between input and output prices in agriculture and on the diffusion of the technology itself. Some USDA studies (Rojko, 1975; World Bank, 1976) assume different rates of production increase depending on different utilization levels of agricultural inputs. Annual production growth rates in the various projections vary between a high of 3.7 per cent per annum used for the most optimistic of USDA forecasts to 2.4 per cent used in the first IFPRI study (IFPRI, 1976). The future food supply and demand situation depends critically on what happens to production. Although lower growth rates are more likely than higher ones, the alternatives allow a type of sensitivity analysis of future food production.

Projection of future consumptions is at least as difficult as that of production. The major influence on food consumption is obviously population (Chapter 6). All projections of the future food gap use the

United Nations medium variant for population growth. There is little significant possibility of altering world population growth rates by 1985 or 1990 (World Bank, 1976). If and when the population growth rates of the developing countries begins to slow then the increasing food demand per head which comes from the ageing of the population will start to become a significant factor, especially in the developing countries with very large populations. As this slowing is unlikely to start before the end of this prediction period this factor has not been included in any of the food gap analyses.

The other major variable affecting food demand is income. Food consumption per capita will rise as per capita incomes rise, and this rise in demand will be complicated by a shift towards more expensive food and away from basic cereals. The World Bank Study projects the rate of growth in cereal consumption as the rate of growth of the population plus the growth rate in per capita income times the income elasticity of demand for grain. The income elasticity of demand is assumed to remain the same throughout the projection period although the report recognizes that it should fall as incomes rise. On the other hand, as incomes rise so also does the demand for animal products of all sorts and, if we include this indirect use of grain, the income elasticity for all grains may rise with income. Again a range of growth rates of income per capita are included in the various attempts to estimate the food gap. The most disaggregated approach is adopted by the IFPRI study using three developing country groups, with high and low income growth rates allowed for each group. OPEC countries have allocated a high income growth of 10 per cent per annum and a low estimate which is the same as for the 1965 to 1973 period. Developing countries with incomes per head of less than $200 have actual income growth between 1965 and 1973 as the high estimate and 1.8 per cent per year as the low estimate. Poorer developing countries have the actual growth as the high estimate and 0.5 per cent as the low estimate.

The IFPRI estimates of consumption growth rates are rather lower than in other studies which have adopted more optimistic income growth assumptions. The IFPRI estimates of food consumption increases vary from 2.65 per cent per year, assuming existing per capita consumption, to 3.0 per cent and 3.2 per cent for the low- and high-income assumptions respectively. In contrast the World Bank Study estimates consumption growth at 3.5 per cent per annum, the FAO (1974c) 3.3 per cent and USDA between 3.0 and 3.7 per cent.

All the studies ignore the effects of income distribution implicitly or explicitly assuming that it will remain unchanged as incomes per capita rise (World Bank, 1976). This seems an unlikely assumption in the light of Third World experience to date. Income per capita for the majority of the population of the Third World can be expected to grow less fast than projected national figures would suggest as the wealth tends to be

Table 69. Projection of future food gaps

	1 IFPRI 1990 All Low-income food-deficit LDCs	2 IFPRI 1990 All All food- deficit LDCs	3 IFPRI 1990 All All LCDs	4 OECD 1990 cereals poorest LDCs	5 WB 1985 cereals All LDCs	6 FAO 1985 cereals All LDCs	7 USDA 1985 cereals All LDCs
Source Date Food Countries							

Deficit
Food balance (million tons)

Food balance	1	2	3	4	5	6	7
150							
140		– A					
130		– B					
120			– A				
110							
100				– D		– J	
90			– B				
80	– A				– I		
70	– B					– K	– L
60		– C					

50

40

30

20

10

Surplus

10

20

30

40

50

60

70

−M
−N
−O
−4

−E

−3

−F
−2
−G

−4

−I

−1
−C

−H

−C

−1

Key to table: A = High income growth assumptions (1.5 per cent per annum). B = Low income growth assumptions (0.5 per cent per annum). C = At 1975 per capita consumption; D = Assuming 1 per cent growth in production. E = Assuming 2 per cent growth in production. F = Assuming production growth continues at 1964–73 average rate.. G = Assuming 3 per cent growth in production. H = Assuming 4 per cent growth in production. I = Using World Bank predictions for increased production. J = Unadjusted—using paddy production. K = Paddy production adjusted to rice equivalent. L, M, N = Alternatives modifying existing trends in the use of agricultural inputs, in production, and in agricultural policies. O = Assumes expansion of agricultural investment and improvement of the internal terms of trade for agriculture and the use of greater volumes of agricultural inputs. 1 = Actual gap in 1975. 2 = Actual gap in 1972. 3 = Actual gap in 1974. 4 = Gap for base years 1969–71 average.
Source: FAO (1974c); IFPRI (1976; 1977b); OECD (1976a); Rojko (1975); World Bank (1976).

accumulated in the hands of relatively few. The effects on overall consumption will be the same as if there was a lower growth in aggregate income.

Direct comparison of the different food gap studies is difficult because of the different end year of the projection, the different countries included and the different foods included. Table 69 summarizes the various projections. The effects of different income assumptions are particularly marked for the IFPRI projections for all food-deficit developing countries (column 2).

The size of the food gap nearly trebles if we move from today's per capita income to high income growth. The projected gaps are lower for all developing countries (column 3) as this means adding in food-exporting developing countries. The OECD projections (column 4) are of smaller food gaps, but the study includes only cereals and only the poorest of the developing countries and the inclusion of the high-income-growth OPEC countries would increase the cereal deficit considerably. Sustained food production increases close to 4 per cent per annum (projection H) seems highly unlikely in the poorest of the developing countries. The World Bank's 1985 projection for all developing countries, based as it is on higher income growth rates, projects larger food gaps. The FAO study, once adjusted to include rice rather than paddy (IFPRI, 1977b), falls very close to that of the World Bank and is generally more pessimistic than the projections of USDA.

Despite the differences in technique and assumptions there is a good level of agreement between the various projections. In all probability the food gap by 1985 or 1990 will be much larger than it is today, just how much larger depends on which of the various assumptions turns out to be closest to the truth. The more optimistic production records of many developing countries in recent years have led to decreases in the size of the estimated food gap (IFPRI, 1976; 1977b). An annual rate of growth in food production in excess of 2.0 per cent seems unlikely, which from the OECD projections would give a deficit of 45 million tons of cereals in the poorest developing countries by 1990. This is some four times the present gap. The poorest developing countries will see little real income growth per capita for the bulk of the population, giving a total food gap between B and C in the IFPRI projections or about 45 million tons of food for the poorest of the food-deficit countries alone. Including all developing countries, the opportunity for higher income growth may exist, giving a possible deficit in 1990 of close to B in column 3, say 90–100 million tons of food.

On the basis of these studies a food gap of about four times that in 1975 would seem to be a distinct possibility for 1990. The developing countries would need to import about 100 million tons of food to meet effective demand over and above domestic production. The size of this projected food gap will be no indication of the state of malnutrition and starvation in the developing world. Actual food demand will continue to be very much higher than effective demands as the latter will be depressed by continuing poverty—a point frequently made elsewhere in this book.

The world food situation by 1990 will not be the outcome of the continuation of present trends of supply and demand. No authors of projections based on such trends would claim this to be the case. Interacting with these trends will be changes in weather and technology to which we can perhaps attach probabilities, and responses by societies and governments to the constantly changing situation. At least one sophisticated projection combining all three elements has been tried (Enzer et al., 1978). In this projection the trends were established using a world simulation model of supply and demand. Probabilities were attached to various technological and environmental changes and developments by a panel of experts. Alternative scenarios were presented to a Delphi panel for each year of the projection. The panel members took the role of the decision-makers presented with the various scenarios. The panel's decisions of political action in the light of the developments in the forecast period were then incorporated in the projections for the future years. Such an analysis attempts to include changes which may result, or which may be forced upon governments and decision-makers by changing events. It seems probable that the governments of many developing countries will be forced by circumstances to act to increase investment in domestic agricultural production before the food gaps predicted by IFPRI (1977b) materialize. Such forecasting methods indicate areas where changes are particularly necessary in the near future, for example, the provision of food stocks and increasing food self-reliance brought about by changes in domestic agricultural policy. No matter what these changes are the food gaps of the developing countries will increase.

The Implications of Future Food Gaps

The demand for close to 100 million tons of food in the developing countries in little more than ten years raises three questions:

1. Can the developed countries produce this extra amount additional to their own needs?
2. Is the trading of this quantity of food physically possible?
3. Can the developing countries afford to pay for this extra food?

The answers to these questions at present would seem to be respectively yes, possible, and definitely not, given a continuation of present trading circumstances. The extra food requirements amount to some 20 per cent more than the developed countries produce at present. This is a realistic target for 1990 provided that the increased market is reflected in higher prices to producers in the developed countries with food export potentials. Projections based on probable demand and production situations show that not only does the developed world increase its total volume of exports to the developing countries but the trend of a concentration of these exports originating in the United States will continue. Projections show that by 1985 the share of the world wheat trade held by the United States will be 57.5 per cent (47.8 in 1975–76), will be 67.5 for all feed grains and remain unchanged at about 75 per cent of soybean trade (Crosson and Frederick, 1977). The shipping of an additional 100 million tons of food would require major investments, not only in shipping tonnage, but also in port docking and handling facilities in exporting and importing countries. Such difficulties are very real but there is no reason to feel that such movements are impossible because they have not been done before (Josling, 1978b). Other commodities such as oil are moved in much larger tonnages.

The financial implications of such food movements are much more difficult. The long term brings in the terms of trade of the developing countries and encompasses the issues discussed in the North/South dialogue and in the New International Economic Order. The short-term problems of coping with future world food shortages, perhaps on a greater scale than 1972, raise issues of food aid, food security schemes and food stocks.

Terms of Trade

Action is needed both to make investment in agriculture in the developing countries more attractive, and thereby stimulate domestic production, and to make exports of the developing countries' agricultural and industrial goods show a higher and more stable rate of return, allowing these exports to pay for necessary food imports. Domestic agricultural policies have manipulated the terms of trade for agriculture to such an extent that, in most developed and in many developing countries, the world market prices for food commodities have little significance. In the developed countries prices have become related to costs of production or parity, and have tended to creep upwards towards the maximum governments appear willing to pay (Josling, 1978b), while in the developing world prices are depressed both as a result of subsidized imports from the developed world and by the subsidized consumer prices these imports allow. There continues to be a net transfer from the developing country producers and the developed country consumers to the producers of the developed countries and the consumers of the developing countries. In such circumstances agricultural investment in the developing countries appears unattractive. Alternative investments in industrial and urban sectors, also finding political support, have little effective opposition when subsidized imports of grain and other foodstuffs are available and domestic prices are depressed.

The best way to tackle the future food gap is to continue to strive to reduce it by raising investment in food production in the developing countries. Although this will be true for the majority of the developing countries there are two caveats. It seems most improbable that such a redirection and increase in investment will be sufficient in practice significantly to raise food production above trend, reducing the size of the food gap by 1990. The political motivation for such a redirection does not seem to be present in many developing countries. On the other hand the donor community is increasingly, and rightly, concerned with the distributional aspects of such agricultural investment. Unfortunately, rural investment projects which do not increase income differentials between the rich and the poor are hard to devise and slow to implement.

There are also developing countries whose comparative advantage does not lie in food production. Although many analysts have concluded that the purchase of the necessary additional cereals by the developing world would be commercially impossible (100 million tons would cost in excess of $10,000 million at world prices), they have tended to ignore the role of international trade in financing food imports (Sanderson, 1978). The cost of the increased import requirements is only a small percentage of the anticipated export receipts of the developing countries. Even in 1974, when imported cereals were at their highest prices, the developing countries as a whole were in trade surplus for agricultural commodities. The problem will remain one of distribution. The food gap will grow fastest in the poorest developing countries, with continued rapid population increase, and these countries have the least export earning potential. None the less, probably the greatest contribution which the developed world can make to lessening the food gap in the developing countries would be to ease trade restrictions on agricultural and labour-intensive manufactured goods from the developing world. Unfortunately, this is neither easy to accomplish nor probable in the near future (Johnson, 1978).

The concept of trade preferences for the goods of the developing countries on a worldwide basis has its origins in the 1964 meeting of the United Nations Committee on Trade and Development (UNCTAD), which placed great emphasis on the importance of developing countries in the pattern of world trade. In 1971 the signatories of the General Agreement of Tariffs and Trade (GATT) adopted a waiver to allow tariff preferences to the developing countries for ten years. This was the Generalized System of Preferences (GSP). It was not until 1975, eleven years after the original UNCTAD agreement, that the GSP was adopted by the United States. Between 1975 and 1977 2.6 per cent of the total United States imports, worth $3.9 billion, entered the United States duty free under GSP. Agricultural imports under the scheme amounted to 4.1 per cent of all agricultural imports (Good, 1978).

Despite the GSP, which covers processed as well as primary products, the more processed the exports from the developing countries generally the more duty is payable in the developed countries and the higher the trade protection is in other ways. The EEC most-favoured-nation rate for import taxes on roasted coffee beans is 15 per cent, but is only 7 per cent on unroasted beans (Nagle, 1976). Cotton and jute fibres are generally traded free of duty, but cotton and jute fabrics are subject both to high duties and to controls on the quantity traded. Such import quotas set by the developed countries are the most important of the non-tariff barriers (NTB) to trade and are at least as important in restricting trade as are tariffs. Such restrictions and tariffs are permissible under the GATT safeguards clause where duties can be regarded as necessary to protect the domestic industry of the importing countries. The superior bargaining power of the developed countries persuades the exporting developing country to impose 'voluntary' quantity restrictions on exports (UNCTAD, 1978). The cheap labour available in the developing countries is regarded as 'unfair' competition for the declining industrial sectors of the economies of the developed countries, an issue especially important for textiles. Thus the developing countries have a comparative cost advantage which they are unable fully to exploit (Nagle, 1976). This form of protection has been growing since the early 1970s and most developing countries regard freer entry into the markets of the developed world for their manufactured goods as of vital importance. It would help to free the dependence of the developing countries on trade in primary commodities with very unstable prices, and would assist in the financing of future food imports.

There is a contrary view. Production of trade in manufactured goods by the developed countries can be regarded as of little significance as it affects only a small number of the developing countries and certainly not the poorest or those with the largest present or future food gaps. Exports of manufactured goods from developing countries are generally small in relation to the total world manufactured production and a large part of the benefits of such trade goes to transnational corporations which account for up to 50 per cent of these exports (UNCTAD, 1976). This minority view suggests that the development of industrialization in the developing countries is the worst possible strategy as it leads to economic and technological dependency, to the creation of a dual economy and to increased indebtedness for the developing countries. Certainly, at least in the short term, the economic future of the developing countries has much more to do with commodities than it does with manufactured goods. Also trade between the developing countries has been increasing. Although only 10 per cent of the manufactured goods imported to developing countries come from other developing countries this trade is growing rapidly (10.6 per cent per year between 1960 and 1975) (World Bank, 1978b).

The supply management of commodities and their prices relative to manufactured goods have occupied most of the limelight in international negotiations between the developed and the developing countries. Even when they have the resources the poor countries remain poor because of their inability to influence world prices and because of the rising prices of imported manufactured goods and the gyrating prices of primary production which the developing countries export to the industrialized countries (spokesman for the 'Group of 77' at UNCTAD, fourth session, Nairobi, 1976; UNCTAD, 1977). In 1974, out of 87 developing countries sampled, 43 showed deteriorating terms of trade, 23 of these (representing 40 per cent of the population of the developing countries) showed terms of trade deteriorated by by more than 10 per cent in one year (UNCTAD, 1976). The terms of trade problems of that time were especially severe in the developing countries of South Asia because their export commodities did not share in the commodity price boom. While this general deterioration in 1973–74 was partly the result of a combination of high food and oil import prices, a small improvement in 1975–76 was followed the next year by a further decline of 0.7 per cent for all developing countries. The balance of payments deficit forecast for all developing countries for 1978 is $30 billion while, in the poorest developing countries, import volume is growing faster than export purchasing power (UNCTAD, 1978).

It is this increasing disparity between export earnings of the developing countries, and their import costs, which gives rise to the discussions of the New International Economic Order, the main plank of which is a scheme to index prices of commodities, exported from the developing countries, to the prices of imported manufactured goods. Such proposals were discussed in the General Assembly of the United Nations at its Sixth Special Session in 1976 (General Assembly resolutions 3201 and 3202S–vi), and at the UNCTAD Fourth Session in Nairobi in 1976. A number of objections have been raised to such an indexation scheme, principally by Germany, the United States and Japan. Although these objections must reflect self-interest there are genuine difficulties with such a scheme. The first and most obvious is that, although raw commodity costs are a relatively small part of finished product costs, such a scheme would tend to be inflationary. As the costs of manufactured goods rise, so they would drive up the cost of raw materials, which in turn drives up the price of manufactured goods and so on. Also, if the price of commodities are to be maintained above the level determined by the market supply and demand equilibrium, the supply will have to be firmly controlled. Without such controls more would be produced than could be sold; the same position which results from the maintained high prices for agricultural commodities in the EEC and in the United States. In the case of most commodities, where the market is not dominated by a single country, a supply agreement would have to be international. Previous commodity agreements have succeeded only in times of surplus not shortage, or failed because they did not include all countries. Participating countries had a reduced share of the market in competition with non-participants (Huddleston, 1977). The international coffee agreement (1968) contributed to price stability for some years, but it broke down in 1972–3 in times of shortage and high prices encouraging producer countries to 'go it alone' (Nagle, 1976). Other difficulties occur over specification of the baskets of commodities, both imports and exports, which would be used to create the index. Whichever commodities are chosen, such regulation would tend to stabilize the present supply and to hinder diversification. Finally, payments and benefits of such a scheme would accrue to those developing countries with a large resource base and would not be distributed according either to deteriorating terms of trade or import requirements (Huddleston, 1977).

With most developing countries supporting indexation and most developed countries opposing it, intense debates took place between 1975 and 1978 on the necessity for a new economic order or at least some way of improving the economic terms of trade of the developing countries or compensating them for this deterioration. They took place at the Commonwealth Conference at Kingston, Jamaica in May 1975; at the 'Group of 77' meeting in Manila in January and February 1976, and at the Fourth Session of UNCTAD at Nairobi in 1976. The outcome of these discussions was an agreement by UNCTAD to an integrated programme for commodities supported by a common fund. The integrated programme makes specific reference to bananas, bauxite, cocoa, coffee, cotton and cotton yarn, hard fibres and products, iron ore, jute and products, manganese, meat, phosphates, rubber, sugar, tropical timber, tin, vegetable oils, including olive oil, and oil seeds. Facilities exist to add other commodities to this list. Although the list includes many agricultural commodities, all grains are excluded, awaiting the outcome of renegotiations of the International Wheat Agreement. Future negotiating sessions were agreed to harmonize national stock policies and to establish a system of international stocks. Despite opposition to indexation of prices, the agreement included a clause that future price arrangements should take account of prices of manufactured goods, exchange rates and inflation. A common fund was to be established from which developing countries, as producers of commodities, can be compensated if the price of the commodity(s) they export fall relative to imported manufactured goods. A number of countries pledged financial contributions to this common fund at the conference. The common fund would be administered by the International Monetary Fund, which already had a scheme to tide countries over balance of payments problems created by falling commodity prices (Huddleston, 1977). Although the proposed size of the common fund has recently been scaled down, no agreement has been possible over the size of government contributions to the fund nor the ratio of cash payments to borrowing rights for each commodity. The UNCTAD proposals were that cash payments should be no less than 25 per cent of drawing rights for countries interested in a commodity, the countries borrowing the remaining 75 per cent as and when needed. The lowest that the negotiators for the rich countries would go in November 1978 was a ratio of 40/60. Negotiations continue in early 1979 (*Economist*, 1978c).

Such a proposal is not new. On its formation the EEC had to absorb the special trading arrangements between member countries and their colonial and dependent territories around the world. The most important such connections were between France and a number of countries in Africa, the Caribbean, and the Pacific (ACP). For these, the Yaoundé Convention allowed special trading privileges with the EEC. The group of privileged countries was expanded when the United Kingdom became a full member of the EEC, but many Commonwealth countries, particularly in South Asia, were not included. The Lomé Convention, which replaced the Yaoundé, has fifty-three signatory countries, primarily still in Africa. Virtually all ACP exports to the EEC enter duty free, although about 75 per cent would have done so without the Convention as they include goods not in competition with EEC production (*Economist*, 1978a). The Convention includes a scheme (Stabex) for stabilizing the export earnings of the ACP countries. If export earnings fall below 7.5 per cent (or 2.5 per cent for the least developed countries in ACP) of a rolling average of the previous four years on twelve products, there is a compensation scheme financed from the EEC aid budget. Only for the twenty-four poorest countries, where exports to the EEC are the least significant, is Stabex in the form of outright aid, other countries have to repay the compensation. The scheme, by concentrating on exports which are not in competition with EEC production (sugar and beef exports are subject to special arrangements designed to protect the EEC farmers), and by limiting the countries which it covers, is of restricted benefit. The poor countries of South and South-East Asia are considered to be too poor, and therefore to be potentially too much of a drain on Stabex's limited budget (Nagle, 1976), or to have too many exports, primarily textiles, in close competition with EEC industry (*Economist*, 1978), to be included in the Lomé club. Also the stabilization of export prices may do little to stabilize the developing country's capacity to import manufactured goods or food, as this capacity is more effected by rising import prices than by falling export prices.

The obvious thrust of the earlier UNCTAD negotiations had been directed at trade liberalization on the basic assumption that free trade, in commodities especially, is in the best interests of the developing countries. Some countries have expressed doubts about this assumption. Because the trade between the developing and the developed countries represents primary commodities moving in one direction and manufactured goods in the other, the exchange is inherently unequal and it can be argued that the developing countries would suffer from the liberalization of this trade. The move towards price indexation, although not formally adopted by UNCTAD, is a move towards trade management and away from free market trade. The example of the operation of market control by OPEC afforded an incentive to other commodity producers to consider the possibilities of commodity cartels. Some producers regard the end of negotiations with the developed world as the only real hope for the future, replacing them with tight supply control to put the bargaining power in the hands of the developing country commodity producers (UNCTAD, 1978). Such policies have shown few signs of success so far. Commodity cartels assume that the overall political and economic interest of *all* producers are the same. The actions of Saudi Arabia within OPEC shows what happens when this is not the case. Also, such cartels encourage the adoption of substitute commodities and/or a reduction in demand, market glut conditions and ultimately perhaps a breakdown of the cartel in the face of conflicting national self-interest. Producer/consumer commodity agreements tend to break down under conditions of shortage and high price while producer cartels have difficulties surviving market glut and low prices.

Free trade in agricultural commodities, especially food, is made impossible by the multitude of national price-support policies. Although a world model constructed to show the effects of free trade in agricultural commodities (FAO, 1971) showed a net gain of the GDP of almost all countries if free trade replaced all forms of agricultural protection, progress in this direction has been non-existent and seems likely to be so for many years. The $80 million improvement in aggregate GDP shown by this model was shared more or less equally by the developing and the developed countries, but the distribution of losses and benefits within countries provides the main stumbling block to adoption. Present agricultural policies provide transfers from consumers to producers in the developed countries and from producers to consumers in the developing countries. The costs and benefits of dismantling such policies would end these net transfers, changing the *status quo* in ways which are likely to be politically unacceptable for all the reasons outline in Chapter 3. Moves in the reverse direction have been encouraged by the events of 1972–76 with increased efforts at food self-sufficiency having been the result of a short-term world supply shortage. Completely free trade, and no government intervention in agriculture, would be bound to result in wide fluctuations in supply so that national and /or international stocks would be needed to control supply and prevent acute food shortages. Such stocks imply a large measure of management in the world's food trade, and therefore trade is no longer free and controlled only by market forces. Finally, with a substantial portion of the world under centralized socialist economic management with state trading corporations, and such countries as the USSR taking increasingly active roles in world food trade, the free operation of the world food market becomes impossible (Nagle, 1976).

Abortive attempts have been made, notably at the Kennedy Round of GATT, to prevent the present state protection of agricultural production and trade from increasing. Proposals were put forward for the freezing of national self-sufficiency ratios so that countries would not increase their self-sufficiency at the expense of the comparative advantage of others. The events of 1972–76 and the nervousness which these years imparted to the world's major food importers, ended all hopes of such a stablization of self-sufficiency policies, at least for the time being. Further proposals were made to freeze the present levels of government support to agriculture. Again political self-interest means that this is unlikely and there are also considerable operational difficulties in any such agreement. Government support to agriculture includes such a diverse range of activities from direct price support to grants for education and training (Chapter 4) that agreed definitions of what constitutes agricultural support would be difficult to come by. Enforcement would also be impossible. Within the EEC, member countries are constantly breaking EEC rules concerning domestic as against Community support to farmers. A worldwide agreement, covering a much wider range of production, would not be feasible. Domestic agricultural policies will continue for the foreseeable future and so international agreements are necessary to govern trade, prices and stocks.

The current debate over international agreements for food commodities is driven partly by the recognition of the need to act over the future food gaps of the developing countries, and partly by the desire to include the management of food commodities within UNCTAD and GATT. The emphasis is on international food stocks and their role in international price stability, and on food security schemes for the major food-deficit countries. Without any change in world food management it is certain that countries found exposed during 1972–76 will be equally, if not more, exposed by future food shortages. The developing countries were the main casualties of these events and the world needs to ensure that future sudden food shortages do not occur, or if they do, that the costs shall be borne more evenly by all countries. Without change, those who rely on world food markets will be as exposed as in 1972, and those countries which go for increased food self-sufficiency, ignoring the economic advantages which could and should stem from international trade, will risk a far from optimal investment of limited resources and a general slowing down of economic development (Johnson, 1978).

Grain Stocks and Food Security

The one common agreement to come out of the food crisis was recognition of the need for international stocks of grain. Unfortunately, little progress has been made beyond this recognition and there is no agreement as to who should hold such stocks, how they should be accumulated and paid for, the purposes to which they should be put and the trigger mechanisms which would result in their use.

The stockpiling of cereals is a good example of externalities in the overall assessment of the costs and benefits of investment. Storage costs can be considerable ($10,000 per 1000 tons of grain per year Konandreas and Huddleston, 1979) but so also can be the costs of a world cereal shortage. Unfortunately, the costs of storage presently falls on different governments to those who have the costs of a shortage and high prices. Cereals could be stockpiled by the producing countries, which means predominately the

United States, or by the importing countries, especially in the Third World. Storage is physically easier in the surplus countries, but the producer countries who benefit least from stable international prices do not find it acceptable that they should bear the full costs of storage of security stocks. Also many Third World countries are suspicious of a world grain reserve under the control of a small group of producer countries, a group which must be dominated by the United States (ODI, 1977). A compromise would be to have the cereal stocks under the control of an international agency, perhaps the World Food Council, operating management rules agreed by the international community.

More intractable difficulties are evident in the management of an international grain stock. The stock could be used to avoid rapid price rises, with grain released from stock triggered by either a shortfall in production or by a rise in world price. Price is obviously related to production and so, in practice, the trigger would work in similar ways. The United States prefers a stock release policy based on price changes while the EEC prefers the trigger to be the result of production changes. This difference of opinion is based on the fact that, in the EEC, price is artificially fixed for agricultural commodities, while the United States, as a major exporter, is more directly concerned with the world price. To use stocks completely to stabilize the price of grains would be self-defeating unless it operated with sympathetic changes in domestic production policies. Suppose the stock release trigger price is set at $100 a ton. If world production is good and price falls, grain must be diverted to stock, thereby maintaining the world market price. Conversely, if the price rises above $100 a ton, stocks are used to supply the market and depress prices. Changed production circumstances without price adjustment means that two or more years of low or high production will either totally deplete stocks or lead to the accumulation of excessively large amounts of grain at great cost. Even if the trigger price is replaced by a band, with upper and lower limits to control acquisition and release, the band will have to be wide and coupled with domestic policies to alter consumption and to encourage or discourage domestic production. A stabilization policy using only world stocks will not work without initial stock levels of a least 60 million tons (Walters, 1978), and even then the lack of sufficient price adjustment to production circumstances may soon make the stock system unworkable (Josling, 1978b). Additional problems are posed by the choice of currency for the price bands and by changing exchange rates. Such a scheme would soon find itself in the complications of the EEC, with green exchange rates and monetary compensation amounts (Chapter 4).

To these operational difficulties of using stocks to control world cereal prices must be added the obvious difficulties of ensuring that all supplying and importing countries agree to it. If some remain outside the scheme then a trade war will result. It is far from clear that agreement can even be reached by the importing and exporting interest groups. In times of good harvests and low prices the importing countries have no motivation to join such a scheme, and in times of shortage and high prices the suppliers have no such motivation. Limited political time horizons make the necessary long-term planning unlikely. Additionally, there are problems in sharing the considerable costs of such a scheme which requires huge world stocks.

All these difficulties have not prevented agreement on the role of world food stocks to supply a guaranteed minimum level of food aid. In this case the stocks can be held by donor countries against pledges of food aid made through the World Food Council. The figure for this guaranteed food aid agreed at the World Food Conference in 1974 was 10 million tons, and this or some slightly smaller figure seems to have been fairly widely accepted (Walters, 1978). Additionally, perhaps 500,000 tons is needed for emergency relief aid in the event of major natural disasters.

In the face of the difficulties of devising a scheme for the more general use of food stocks to stabilize prices for food commodities, a number of crop insurance proposals have been put forward (IFPRI, 1978; Konandreas and Huddleston, 1979). The objectives are to provide a reserve of either cash or grain which can be drawn upon by an individual country if the need arises in that country. The scheme would be designed to compensate for major production shortfalls in a single country and not to work by modifying the world market price directly. One scheme (Johnson, 1978) allows a country to have drawing rights from a centrally held grain reserve only when and if that country's production of grain falls more than 6 per cent below trend. The drawing rights would be sufficient to raise domestic grain availability to the level of 6 per cent below the trend production level for that year. The trigger is set this far below trend to provide for domestic price incentives to producers, to encourage a reduction in consumption in times of low production and high prices and to encourage some national storage of food grains. Such a security scheme removes only the effects of the most severe upward movements in price following a shortfall in domestic production. As such a scheme would work country by country and allow a substantial margin for domestic adjustment, international grain stocks to service it need not be large. Johnson estimates that such a scheme would have required an average of 4 million tons of grain per year between 1954 and 1973 with high points of 14.8 million in 1966 and 13.4 million in 1973. An insurance reserve of 20 to 30 million tons should be sufficient for this scheme (Walters, 1978).

This proposal would cater for domestic production shortfalls, but there remains the problem of world price rises, with resulting increases in the size of the import bill for a country, even if that country's domestic food production remained much as before. Such a rise in food import costs would reduce food availability in that country in just the same way as reduced domestic production. A solution to this would be to make the

M

drawing rights dependent on the expected size of the food import bill over and above the normal trend for such import costs (Reutlinger, 1977). This should allow some margin to encourage domestic adjustment in both production and consumption. Suppose production falls to 90 per cent of trend. The consumption trend is calculated and target consumption is set at 95 per cent to allow for some consumption adjustment. On the basis of these production and consumption levels, the import bill is calculated. If this is above a trigger level, say 108 per cent of trend, then compensation is allowed, either as cash or as grain.

As these are grain *insurance* schemes, the purchase costs of the grain stocks necessary could be met by premium payments. The size of a country's premium would determine the size of their allowable drawing rights and could be assessed by each country on the basis of the perceived risk and on that country's desire to maintain independent domestic grain security stocks. For the poorest countries the international donor community might pay the premiums as a part of a normal aid programme. The grain reserves would probably be held in the grain-exporting countries, and in some cases, notably the United States, the carrying costs might be borne as a part of the domestic price-support policies of the surplus countries.

Unfortunately, a good statistical base would be needed for such a food security scheme, especially in major food-deficit countries where data collection is presently weak or lacking. There needs to be sufficient data to establish trends in consumption and to assess production levels early enough in the year to allow the drawing from the insurance fund to prevent major domestic shortages. Satellite monitoring of crop production holds out some hope for such data gathering in the future.

Without suitable external monitoring, akin to the assessment of damage by an insurance company, there is a temptation for countries to under-represent production in any one year, especially if production falls to just above the trigger level in relation to trend. This would ultimately lead to a reduction in the production trend itself and therefore would be self-defeating in the long term, but the short-term horizons of many developing country governments means that this remains as a potential problem (Johnson, 1978). There is also the very important question of countries where grain does not form a major part of the staple diet. To be comprehensive such a food insurance scheme would have to consider the production of all food crops, although the insurance payments would have to be in cash or in grain rather than in other traditional food crops.

Unfortunately, all such schemes remain only designs. It is characteristic of all international negotiations on food that there has been plenty of talk, especially in times of food crisis, but very little action. The challenge is to devise a scheme which is not only practical but which can be seen as of benefit to food-surplus and food-deficit countries in times of food shortage and food surplus. The food insurance schemes come closest to this ideal.

Conclusion

The world has not yet entered a new era of increasing food shortages. Although the situation cannot help but become increasingly critical in the chronic food-short countries such as Indonesia and Bangladesh, on a world scale the next ten years seem likely to be characterized by increasing variability of production, but not by overall world shortage of food. Even if the food gap for the next ten years can be filled there is less certainty about the longer-term future. The Malthusian dilemma is still very much with us although for the past 200 years technological change has allowed us to push it into the future. At some point the world's population will stabilize, and also at some future time the limited resources of the world will prevent further increases in food production, at least of the conventional foods we eat today. The question remains now as always, which of these will come first? Will population growth stabilize before food shortages play a more direct part in population limitation? Because we have so far been able to avoid the Malthusian prophecy does not mean that the prophecy was wrong. Recently, the predicted world population of 7 billion people by the year 2000 has been reduced as there have been falls in the population growth of many countries, especially the middle-income developing countries (Table 70). None the less, changed life styles reflecting changed birth rates have to continue for seventy years or so to grow through a human population to stabilize it. Estimates of the ultimate stable world population are widely varying, as they depend on so many assumptions about changed rates of economic development and social change. They range between 12 and 25 billion, at least three times the present population and probably very much larger.

Food production more than kept pace while the world's population last

Table 70. Falling birth rates in middle-income developing countries

Country	Crude birth rate per 1000	Percentage change 1960–75
Singapore	18	−52.6
Hong Kong	18	−48.6
Taiwan	23	−42.5
South Korea	24	−41.5
Trinidad and Tobago	23	−39.5
Costa Rica	29	−38.3
Chile	23	−37.8
Tunisia	34	−27.7
Colombia	33	−26.7
Thailand	34	−26.1
All middle-income countries	40	− 9.2
All industrial countries	18	−13.6

Source: *Economist* (1978b).

doubled, hopefully it will be able to do so for the next doubling, perhaps by the end of this century. Beyond that it is increasingly hard to be certain but more difficult to be optimistic.

Increased food production will depend mainly on yield increases and, in the developed countries, these have been attributed more or less equally to genetic improvements and to technological development (Jensen, 1978). The genetic improvements have resulted in shorter cereal plants; for example, wheat varieties issued in the United States have decreased in height from 116 cm in 1920 to 85 cm in 1973. A further reduction of about 15 cm is believed to be possible and there are other genetic possibilities which have considerable potential, but there are obvious limits. Technological developments will also be less freely available, particularly those which use large amounts of energy. Environmental factors will become increasingly important, with a banning of certain toxic pesticides and herbicides because of their undesirable side effects already having a significant effect on the agriculture of many developed countries. Agriculture has so far escaped many of the constraints placed on economic growth by energy shortages and environmental controls, but this position is unlikely to continue for very much longer. In the Third World, where technological and energy developments are necessary to raise yields closer to those obtained in the developed world, the impact of the increasing costs of the technology will be felt most severely. Food production will certainly continue to increase for many years to come, but absolute yield limits are possible in the not too distant future (Jensen, 1978).

In speculating about conditions up to and beyond the year 2000 one is an optimist or pessimist almost by instinct. Because of the importance of population growth on demand the issue must be widened to consider the whole question of the economic development of the developing countries over which some recent reports have been relatively optimistic (World Bank, 1978b), while other attempts to project population, natural resource use, and economic development together, taking account of the interactions between each aspect, have been more pessimistic than attempts to project each aspect separately (Hughes and Mesarovis, 1978). Whatever one's instincts it is necessary to have faith in man's technological ability to constantly produce more food to meet increasing demand. While this technology may not be limited to conventional food sources, and has to be appropriate to the available limited energy supplies and to the economic and social systems within which it is applied, it seems certain that no worldwide solution to the world food problem beyond the year 2000 lies in images of domestic self-sustaining self-sufficient agriculture in the developed world (Merrill, 1976). Such Utopian dreams ignore the vast food needs of the developing countries which have no prospect of food self-sufficiency in the foreseeable future. These dreams are as self-centered as the agribusiness corporations which the designers are so ready to criticize.

The one thing that is certain is that the increasing instability in world food markets, and future food shortages, will increase rather than decrease the role of government in national and international food policy. Today's level of intervention may soon appear to be trifling as the political pressures for self-sufficiency and protectionism increase with food shortage. Food supplies have been domestic and international political weapons in the past and they will be increasingly so in the future.

Bibliography

Abercrombie, K. C. (1975). Agricultural mechanisation and employment in developing countries, *FAO Monthly Bull. Agr. Econ. and Stat.*, **24** (5), 1–9.

Ahmed, R. (1977). Food grain production in Bangladesh. An analysis of its growth; its sources and related policies. *Bangladesh Agricultural Research Council, Agricultural and Rural Social Science Papers*, 2. Dacca.

Akino, M. and Hayami, Y. (1975). Efficiency and equity in public research: rice breeding in Japan's economic development. *Am. J. Agr. Econ.* **57** (1), 1–10.

Allen, G. (1972). An appraisal of contract farming. *J. Agr. Econ.* **23** (2), 89–98.

Allen, G. (1976). Some aspects of planning world food supplies. *J. Agr. Econ.*, **27** (1), 97–120.

Arteaga, L. A. (1976). The nutritional status of Latin American adults. In N. S. Scrimshaw and M. Béhar (eds.), *Nutrition and Agricultural Development*. Plenum Press, New York, 66–76.

Bailey, K. J. (1975). Malnutrition in the African region. *WHO Chronicle*, **29**, 354.

Baldwin, W. L. (1974). The Thai rice trade as a vertical market network: structure, performance and policy implications. *Econ. Dev. and Cult. Change*, **22** (2), 179–197.

Bard, R. L. (1972). *Food Aid and International Agricultural Trade*. Heath, Lexington, Mass.

Barlow, F. D., and Libbin, S. A. (1969). Food aid and agricultural development. *Foreign Agr. Report*, 51, USDA.

Belden, J., and Forte, G. (1977). *Towards a National Food Policy*. Explanatory report for Economic Alternatives, Washington, DC.

Berg. A. (1973). *The Nutrition Factor: Its Role in National Development*. The Brookings Institution, Washington, DC.

Bergmann, D. (1977). Agriculture in the EEC—taking stock—another view. *Food Policy*, **2** (1), 85–88.

Biggs, T. S. (1976). *Political Economy of East–West Trade: The Case of the US–Russian Wheat Deal*. Unpublished PhD Thesis, University of California, Berkeley.

Billings, M. H., and Singh, A. (1969). Labour and the green revolution. *Econ. and Pol. Weekly*, **4** (52), 27 Dec., A221–A224.

Blakeslee, L. L., Heady, E. O., and Framingham, C. F. (1973). *World Food Production*. Iowa State University Press, Ames, Iowa.

Bogert, L. J., Briggs, G. M., and Calloway, D. H. (1973). *Nutrition and Physical Fitness*. 9th edn. Saunders, Philadelphia.

Borlaug, N. E. (1968). Wheat breeding and its impact on world food supply. *Proc. 3rd International Wheat Genetics Symposium*. Canberra.

318

Brandow, G. E. (1969). On bargaining in agriculture. *World Agriculture*, **18** (3), 8–11.

Breimyer, H. F. (1977). A new farm and food law. *Challenge*, Nov.–Dec., pp. 56–59.

Breimyer, H. F. (1978). Agriculture's three economies in a changing resource environment. *Am. J. Agr. Econ.*, **30** (1), 37–47.

Briscoe, J. (1976). *Infection and Nutrition: The Use of Public Health Programs as Nutrition Interventions*. Harvard University Center for Population Studies, Cambridge, Mass.

Britton, D. K., and Hill, B. (1975). *Size and Efficiency in Agriculture*. Saxon House, Farnborough.

Brown, L. (1975). The politics and responsibility of the North American bread basket. *World Watch Paper*, 2, Oct.

Brown, L. (1976) World population trends: Signs of hope, signs of stress. *World Watch Paper*, 8, Oct.

Buringh, P., van Heemst, H. D. J., and Staring, G. J. (1975). *Computation of the Absolute Maximum Food Production of the World*. Dept. of Tropical Soil Science, Agricultural University, Wageningen, the Netherlands.

Byres, T. J. (1972). The dialectic of India's green revolution. *South Asian Review*, **5** (2), 99–116.

Campbell, A., Converse, P., Miller, W., and Stokes, D. (1964). *The American Voter*. Wiley, New York.

Checci and Company (1972). *Food for Peace: An Evaluation of PL 480, Title II*. Washington, DC.

Chowdhury, A. K. M. A., and Chen, L. C. (1977). Interaction of nutrition, infection and mortality during recent food crises in Bangladesh. *Food Research Institute Studies*, **16** (2), 47–62.

Clarke, C, and Turner, J. B. (1977). Family consumption and marketable surplus. *Oxford Agrarian Studies*, **6**, 1–25.

Clarkson, K. W. (1975). Food stamps and nutrition. *Evaluative Studies*, **18**. American Enterprise Institute for Public Policy Research, Washington, DC.

Cochrane, W. W. (1958). *Farm Prices, Myth and Reality*. University of Minnesota Press, Minneapolis.

Cochrane, W. W., and Ryan, M. E. (1975). *American Farm Policy 1948–1973*. University of Minnesota Press, Minneapolis.

Colmenares, J. H. (1975). *Adoption of Hybrid Seeds and Fertilisers among Columbian Corn Growers*. Centre Internacional de Mejaramiento de Maiz y Trigo (CIMMYT) Mexico.

Congressional Record (1973). *Senate 93rd Congress 1st Session*, **119**, 10, 12 April, S7205–S7214.

Corden, W. M., and Richter, H. V. (1967). Trade and the balance of payments. Chapter 6 in T. H. Silcock (ed.), *Thailand: Social and Economic Studies in Development*. ANU Press, Canberra.

Cravioto, J., and De Licardie, E. R. (1976). Microenvironmental factors in severe protein–calorie malnutrition. In N. S. Scrimshaw and M. Béhar (eds.), *Nutrition and Agricultural Development*. Plenum Press, New York.

Crosson, P. R., Frederick, K. D. (1977). The world food situation: Resource and environmental issues in developing countries and the United States. *Resources for the Future Research Paper*, R-6, Washington, DC.

Cutié, J. T. (1975). *Diffusion of Hybrid Corn Technology, The Case of El Salvador*. (CIMMYT) Mexico.

Dalrymple, D. G. (1971). *Survey of Multiple Cropping in Less Developed Nations*. Foreign Economic Development Service, USDA, Washington, DC, Oct.

Deaton, R. (1978). Agricultural trade act paves the way for gain in US farm exports. *Foreign Agriculture*, 30 Oct., 2–4.

De Hoogh, J., Keyzer, M. A., Linneman, M. A., and van Heemst, H. D. J. (1977). Food for a growing world population. *Technological Forecasting and Social Change*, **10**, 27–51.

Demeny, P. (1974). The populations of the under-developed countries. *Scientific American*, **231**, 148–159.

Dexter, K. (1978). Farm size in relation to technology and competition. *Bledisloe Memorial Lecture*, Royal Agr. Coll. Cirencester.

Doorenbos, J. (1975). The role of irrigation in food production. *Agriculture and Environment*, **2**, 23–54.

Dudley, L., and Sandilands, R. J. (1975). The side effects of foreign aid: the case of the Public Law 480 wheat in Colombia. *Econ. Dev. and Cult. Change*, **23** (2), 325–336.

Eckholm, E. (1975). The other energy crisis: firewood. *World Watch Paper*, 1.

Eckholm, E., and Record, F. (1976). The two faces of malnutrition. *World Watch Paper*, 9.

Economist (1977). Germany and the CAP, 5 Nov., 54–56.

Economist (1978a). Rewriting Lomé, 23 Sept., 93.

Economist (1978b). The not impossible dream, 19 Aug., 63–66.

Economist (1978c). Stalemate on the Common Fund, 2 Dec., 81.

Economist Intelligence Unit (1977). *Bangladesh Fertiliser Marketing and Distribution Study*. Economist Intelligence Unit, London.

Edwards, C. E., Biggs, S., and Griffith, J. (1978). Irrigation in Bangladesh: on contradictions and under-utilised potential. *Development Studies Discussion Paper*, 22. University of East Anglia, Norwich.

Enzer, S., Drobnick, R., and Alter, S. (1978). Neither feast nor famine: world food 20 years on. *Food Policy*, **3** (1), 3–17.

Falcon, W. P. (1970). The green revolution: generations of problems. *Am. J. Agr. Econ.*, **52** (5), 698–710.

Falcon, W. P. (1978). Food self-sufficiency; lessons from Asia. In USDA (1978b) *International Food Policy Issues: A Proceedings*, pp. 13–20.

FAO (1948). Rice and rice diets. *Nutritional Studies* 1, Washington, DC.

FAO (1970a). *Indicative World Plan*, Rome.

FAO (1970b). Amino acid content of foods and biological data on proteins. *Nutritional Studies*, 24. Rome.

FAO (1971). *World Price Equilibrium Model*, Nov. Rome.

FAO (1973). Energy and protein requirements, report of a joint FAO/WHO ad hoc Committee, 22 March–2 April 1971. *FAO Nutrition Meetings Report Series,* 52, and *WHO Technical Report Series*, 522. Rome.

FAO (1974a). Handbook on human nutritional requirements. *Nutritional Studies*, 28. Rome.

FAO (1974b). *Annual Fertiliser Review*. Rome.

FAO (1974c). *Assessment of the World Food Situation; Present and Future*, Nov. Rome.

FAO (1974d). Rice Parboiling, *Agricultural Development Paper*, 97. Rome.

FAO (1975). Agricultural protection and stabilisation policies: a framework of measurement in the context of agricultural adjustment. *FAO Conference, Eighteenth Session*, 8–27, Nov. Rome.

FAO (1976). *Production Yearbook*. Rome.

FAO (1977a). *Annual Fertiliser Review 1976*. Rome.

FAO (1977b). *Selected Policy Issues in Agriculture*. FAO/UNDP Mission, Bangladesh.

Field, J. O., and Levinson, F. J. (1975). Nutrition and development: the dynamics of commitment. *Food Policy*, **1** (1), 53–61.

Freeman, H. E. (1977). Relationship between nutrition and cognition in rural Guatemala. *Am. J. Public Health*, **67** (3), 233–239.

Frisch, R. E. (1974). Demographic implications of the biological determinants of female fecundity. *Social Biology*, **22** (1), 17–22.

Gaffney, M. (1965). The benefits of farm programs: incidence shifting and dissipation. *J. Farm Econ.*, **47**, 1252–1263.

Gavan, J. (1977). *The Calorie Energy Gap in Bangladesh and Strategies for Reducing It*. Paper read at the Conference on Nutrition Oriented Food Policies and Programs at Villa Serbelloni, Bellagio, Italy, Aug.

George, S. (1976). *How the Other Half Dies*. Penguin, London.

Gifford, R. M. (1976). Energy in agriculture. *Search*, **7** (10), 411–417.

Government of Bangladesh (1974). *Integrated Rural Development Programme—An Evaluation*. Planning Commission, June.

Government of Bangladesh (1978a). *Bangladesh Rural Transport Survey*. Planning Commission, Dacca.

Government of Bangladesh (1978b). *Development Statistics for Bangladesh Agriculture*. Ministry of Agriculture and Forests, Planning and Evaluation Section, Dacca.

Government of Bangladesh (1978c). *Performance of the Agriculture Sector during 1977–78 and Annual Plan for 1978–79*. Ministry of Agriculture and Forests, Planning and Evaluation Section, Dacca, June.

Government of Bangladesh (1978d). *Report of the Task Force for Rice Processing and Byproduct Utilisation in Bangladesh*. Ministry of Agriculture, Dacca, March.

Good, D. L. (1978). US generalized system of preferences: the first two years. *Foreign Agriculture*, Supplement, July, USDA.

Greeley, M. (1978). Appropriate rural technology recent Indian experience with farm level food grain storage research, *Food Policy*, **3** (1), 39–49.

Green, D. (1975). *The Politics of Food*. Gordon Cremonesi, London.

Grigg, D. G. (1974). *The Agricultural Systems of the World: an Evolutionary Approach*. Cambridge University Press, UK.

Griliches, Z. (1960a). Hybrid corn and the economics of innovation. *Science*, **132**, 275–280.

Griliches, Z. (1960b). Measuring inputs in agriculture: a critical survey. *J. Farm Econ.*, **42**, 1411–1427.

Grossmann, G. (1977). The 'Second Economy' of the USSR. *Problems of Communism*, **26** (5), 25–40.

Hakim, P., and Solimana, G. (1975). Supplemental feeding as a nutritional intervention: the Chilean experience in the distribution of milk. *International Nutritional Planning Program Discussion Paper*, 2, MIT, Cambridge, Mass.

Halcrow, H. G. (1977). *Food Policy for America*. McGraw-Hill, New York.

Hardin, G. (1977). Living in a lifeboat. In G. Hardin and J. Baden (eds.), *Managing the Commons*, Freeman, San Francisco, pp. 261–279.

Harpstead, D. D. (1971). High-lysine corn. *Scientific American*. Aug. Reprinted as Chapter 27 in *Food: Readings from Scientific American*. Freeman, San Francisco, 1973.

Harrison, A., Tranter, R. B., and Gibbs, R. S. (1977). Landownership by public and semipublic institutions in the UK. *Centre for Agricultural Strategy Research Paper*, 3. Reading University.

Hathaway, D. E. (1959). Agriculture in an unstable economy revisited. *J. Farm Econ.*, **41** (3), 487–489.

Hathaway, D. E. (1963). *Government and Agriculture: Public Policy in a Democratic Society*. Macmillan, New York.

Hathaway, D. E. (1978). The relationship between trade and world food security. *Foreign Agr. Econ. Report*, 143, USDA, pp. 55–58.

Hay, R. W. (1978). The statistics of hunger. *Food Policy*, **3** (4), 243–255.

Heady, E. O. (1967) (ed.). *Alternatives for Balancing World Food Production and Needs*. Iowa State University Press, Ames, Iowa.

Heidhues, T. (1976). Price and market policy for agriculture. *Food Policy*, **1** (2), 116–129.

HMSO (1975). *Food From Our Own Resources*. HMSO, Cmnd 6020.

Hopkins, R. F. (1977). How to make food work. *Foreign Policy*, **27**, 89–108.

House of Representatives (1977). *Conference Report—Food and Agriculture Act 1977*, Report 95–599.

Huddleston, B. (1977). Commodity trade issues in international negotiations. *International Food Policy Research Institute Occasional Paper*, 1, Jan.

Hughes, B. B., and Mesarovic, M. D. (1978). Population, wealth and resources up to the year 2000. *Futures*, **10** (4), 267–282.

Hull, T. E., and Hull, V. J. (1977). The relation of economic class and fertility: an analysis of some Indonesian data. *Population Studies*, **31** (1), 43–57.

Ingram, J. C. (1971). *Economic Change in Thailand 1850–70*. Stanford University Press, Stanford, California, 1971 edn.

International Food Policy Research Institute (1976). *Meeting Food Needs in the Developing Countries: the Location and Magnitude of the Task in the Next Decade*. IFPRI, Washington, DC.

International Food Policy Research Institute (1977a). Recent and prospective developments in food consumption: some policy issues. *Research Report*, 2.

International Food Policy Research Institute (1977b). Food needs of developing countries: projections of production and consumption to 1990. *Research Report*, 3.

International Food Policy Research Institute (1978). Food security; an insurance approach. *Research Report*, 4.

Isard, W. (1962). *Location and Space Economy*. MIT, Cambridge, Mass.

Isenman, P. J., and Singer, H. W. (1975). *Food Aid: Disincentive Effects and Their Policy Implications*. Institute of Development Studies, University of Sussex.

Islam, M. A. (1977). The importance of deep water rice. *Proceedings of the Workshop on Deep Water Rice*. International Rice Research Institute, Philippines.

Islam, N. (1978). *Development Strategy of Bangladesh*. Pergamon Press, Oxford.

ISMOG (1977). (Instituut voor sociaal-economische studie van minder ontwikkelde gebieden). *Study of EEC Food Aid* (in Dutch). Universiteit van Amsterdam.

Jennings, P. R. (1974). Rice breeding and world food production. *Science*, **185** (Dec.), 1085–1088.

Jensen, N. F. (1978). Limits to growth in world food production. *Science*, **201** (July), 317–320.

Johnson, B. L. C. (1975b). *Bangladesh*. Heinemann, London.

Johnson, D. G. (1975a). *World Food Problems and Prospects*. American Institute for Public Policy Research, Washington, DC.

Johnson, D. G. (1978). International food security: issues and alternatives. *Foreign Agr. Econ. Report*, 143, USDA, pp. 81–90.

Johnson, G. L. (1957). Sources for expanded agricultural production. *Policy for Commercial Agriculture*. Joint Economic Committee, 85th Congress, 1st Session, pp. 127–144.

Johnson, G. L., and Quance, C. L. (1972) (eds.). *The Over-Production Trap in US Agriculture: A Study of Research Allocation from World War II to the Late 1960's*. Johns Hopkins University Press, Baltimore.

Johnston, B. F. (1978). *Nutrition in Developing Countries: Issues and Perspectives*. Report prepared for FAO, March.

Johnston, B. F., and Meyer, A. J. (1977). Nutrition, health and population in strategies for rural development. *Econ. Dev. and Cult. Change*, **26** (1), 1–23.

Jones, B. D., and Tullock, P. (1974). Is food aid good aid? *ODI Review*, **2**, 1–6.

Jones, D. (1976). *Food and Interdependence: The Effect of Food and Agricultural*

Policies of the Developed Countries on the Food Problems of the Developing Countries. Overseas Development Institute, London.

Jones, W. O. (1970). Measuring the effectiveness of agricultural marketing in contributing to economic development: some African examples. *Studies of Agr. Econ., Trade and Dev.,* **9** (3), Food Research Institute, Stanford, 175–196.

Jones, W. O. (1972). *Marketing Staple Foodstuffs in Tropical Africa.* Cornell University Press, Ithaca, New York.

Josling, T. (1978a). Review of H. G. Halcrow 'Food policy for America', and J. Belden 'Towards a national food policy'. *Food Policy,* **3** (1), 72–73.

Josling, T. (1978b). Agricultural trade policies: issues and alternatives. *Foreign Agr. Econ. Report,* 143, USDA, pp. 59–68.

Joy, L. (1973). Food and nutrition planning. *J. Agr. Econ.,* **24** (1), 165–197.

King, J. W., Hurst, E., Slater, A. J., Smith, P. A., and Tamkin, B. (1974). Agriculture and sunspots. *Nature,* **252** (Nov.), 2–3.

Kirk, D. (1972). Prospects for reducing birth rates in developing countries: the interplay of population and agricultural policies. *Food Research Institute Studies,* 11 (1), 3–10.

Klein, R. E., Habicht, J-P., and Yarborough, C. (1971). Effects of protein/calorie malnutrition on mental development. *Advances in Pediatrics,* **18,** 75–91.

Kon, S. K. (1972). Milk and milk products in human nutrition. *Nutritional Studies,* 27. FAO, Rome.

Konandreas, P., and Huddleston, B. (1979). Cost analysis of a food insurance scheme for developing countries. *Food Policy,* **4** (1), 3–14.

Kovda, V. A. (1971). The problem of biological and economic productivity of the Earth's land areas. *Soviet Geography,* **12** (1), 6–23.

Kretchmer, N. (1971). Lactose and lactase; an historical perspective. *Gastroenterology,* **61** (6), 805–813.

Ladejinski, W. (1969). The green revolution in the Punjab. *Econ. and Pol. Weekly,* **4** (26), A73–A83.

Lamb, H. H. (1976). Understanding climatic change and its relevance to the world food problem. *Climatic Research Unit Research Paper,* 5. University of East Anglia, UK.

Lane, S. (1978). Food distribution and food stamp program effects on food consumption and nutritional 'achievement' of low income persons in Kein Country, California. *Am. J. Agr. Econ.,* **60** (1), 108–116.

Latham, M. C. (1976). Nutritional problems in the labor force and their relation to economic development. In N. S. Scrimshaw and M. Béhar (eds.), *Nutrition and Agricultural Development.* Plenum Press, New York.

Latham, M. C., and Brooks, M. (1977). The relationship of nutrition and health to worker productivity in Kenya. *Technical Memorandum,* 26, World Bank, Washington, DC.

Leach, G. (1975). The energy costs of food production. In F. Steel and A. Bourne (eds.), *Man Food Equation,* Academic Press, London.

Lele, U. J. (1971). *Food Grain Marketing in India: Private Performance and Public Policy.* Cornell University Press, Ithaca, New York.

Lele, U. J. (1975). *The Design of Rural Development: Lessons from Africa.* Johns Hopkins University Press, Baltimore.

Lele, U. J. (1976). *Considerations relating to optimum pricing and marketing strategies in rural development.* Paper presented at the 16th International Conference of Agricultural Economists, Nairobi, Kenya, July/Aug.

Leveille, G. A., Rosmos, D. R. (1974). Meal eating and obesity, *Nutrition Today,* **6** (9), 4–9.

Lewis-Beck, M. S. (1977). Agrarian political behavior in the US. *Am. J. Pol. Science,* **21** (3), 543–565.

324

Lockwood, B., Mukerjee, P. E., and Shand, R. T. (1971). *The HYVP in India.* Research School of Pacific Studies, Dept. of Economics, ANU, Canberra.

MacCorquodale, D. W., and De Nova, H. R. (1977). Family size and malnutrition in Santo Domingo. *Public Health Reports.* **92** (5), 453–457.

McGovern, G. (1975) (ed.). *Food and Population: The World in Crisis.* Arno Press, New York.

McGregor, I. (1976). Comments on food and nutrition problems. In N. S. Scrimshaw and M. Béhar (eds.), *Nutrition and Agricultural Development.* Plenum Press, New York, pp. 63–66.

McHenry, D. F., and Bird, K. (1977). Food bungle in Bangladesh. *Foreign Policy*, **27**, 72–88.

MacKerron, G., and Rush, H. J. (1976). Agriculture in the EEC: taking stock. *Food Policy*, **1** (4), 286–300.

McQuigg, J. D. (1974). Meteorological variability and economic modelling. In *World Food in Changing Climate*, proc. of the Sterling Forest Conference, 2–5 Dec., Sterling Forest, New York, pp. 40–46.

Maddock, R. T. (1978). The economic and political characteristics of food as a diplomatic weapon. *J. Agr. Econ.*, **29** (1), 31–41.

Mann, J. S. (1967). The impact of PL 480 imports on prices and domestic supply of cereals in India. *J. Farm Econ.*, **49** (1), 131–146.

Marsh, J. S. (1975). The CAP and the British interest. *J. Agr. Econ.*, **26** (2), 183–196.

Mata, L. (1972). Influence of recurrent infections on nutrition and growth of children in Guatemala. *Am. J. Clinical Nutrition*, **25** (11), 1267–1275.

Mayer, J. (1975). Management of famine relief. In P. H. Abelson (ed.), *Food: Politics, Economics, Nutrition and Research.* Am. Ass. Adv. Science, Washington, DC, pp. 79–83.

Maxwell, S. (1978a). Food aid for supplementary feeding. *Food Policy*, **3** (4), 289–298.

Maxwell, S. (1978b). Food aid, food for work and public works. *Discussion Paper*, 127. Institute for Development Studies, University of Sussex.

Meadows, D. H., Meadows, D. L., Randers, J., and Behrens, W. W. (1972). *The Limits to Growth.* Earth Island, London.

Mears, L. (1974). *Rice Economy of the Philippines.* Quezon City.

Mellanby, K. (1975). *Can Britain Feed Itself?* Merlin Press, London.

Mellor, J. W. (1966). *The Economics of Agricultural Development.* Cornell University Press, Ithaca, New York.

Mellor, J. W. (1969). Agricultural price policy in the context of economic development. *Am. J. Agr. Econ.*, **51** (5), 1413–1420.

Mellor, J. W. (1976). *The New Economics of Growth: A Strategy for India and the Developing World*, Cornell University Press, Ithaca, New York.

Mellor, J. W., and Huddleston, B. (1978). *Programming US Food Aid to Meet Humanitarian and Developmental Objectives.* IFPRI, Washington, DC.

Merrill, A. K. (1977). *PL 480 and Economic Development in Recipient Countries*, (draft report). National Security and International Affairs Division, Congressional Budget Office, Washington, DC.

Merrill, R. (1976). Towards a self-sustaining agriculture. Chapter 16 in R. Merrill (ed.), *Radical Agriculture.* Harper & Row, New York.

Mettrick, H. (1969). *Food Aid and Britain*, ODI, London.

Missiaen, E. (1978). Government incentives spur increased Brazilian soybean products exports. *Foreign Agriculture*, 16 Oct., 7–9.

Mönckeberg, F. (1976). Definition of the nutrition problem—poverty and malnutrition in mother and child. In N. S. Scrimshaw and M. Béhar (eds.), *Nutrition and Agricultural Development.* Plenum Press, New York, pp. 13–24.

Nagle, F. C. (1976). *Agricultural Trade Policies*. Saxon House, Farnborough.
National Defense University (1978). *Climate Change to the Year 2000*. Washington, DC.
National Research Council (1973). *The Relationship of Nutrition to Brain Development and Behaviour*. National Academy of Sciences, Washington, DC.
National Research Council (1976). *Climate and Food: Climatic Fluctuations and US Agricultural Production*. National Academy of Sciences, Washington, DC.
National Research Council (1977). *World Food and Nutrition Study*. National Academy of Sciences, Washington, DC.
Nelson, F. (1975). *An economic analysis of the impact of past farm programs on livestock and crop prices, production and resource adjustments*. Unpublished PhD thesis, University of Minnesota, Minneapolis.
ODI (1977). The world food grain situation and the 1977 World Food Council Conference. *Overseas Development Institute Briefing Paper*. London, Oct.
OECD (1963). *Food Aid: Its Role in Economic Development*. Paris.
OECD (1971). *Development Assistance*. Paris.
OECD (1973). *Agricultural Policy Reports*. Paris.
OECD (1974). *Agricultural Policy Reports*. Paris.
OECD (1975). *Agricultural Policy Reports*. Paris.
OECD (1976a) *Study of Trends in World Supply and Demand of Major Agricultural Commodities*. Report by the Secretary-General, Paris.
OECD (1976b). *Final Report on Rural Road Planning in Development Countries*. Paris.
O'Hagan, J. P. (1976). National self-sufficiency in food. *Food Policy*, **1** (5), 355–366.
Paarlberg, D. (1973). Evidence before the Hearing on the United States and the World Food Situation. *Senate 93rd Congress 1st Session*. October.
Paddock, W., and Paddock, P. (1967). *Famine, 1975*. Weidenfeld, London.
Papenek, G. F. (1972). The effects of aid and other resource transfers on savings and growth in less developed countries. *Econ. J.*, **83**, 934–950.
Parthasarthy, G. (1976). Dilemmas of marketable surplus: the Indian case. Paper presented at seminar on agricultural price policy, Cornell University, Ithaca, New York, Feb.
Payne, P. R. (1977). Review of Reutlinger and Selowsky (1976). *Food Policy*, **2** (2), 164–165.
Perelman, M. (1976). The green revolution: American agriculture in the Third World. Chapter 8 in R. Merrill (ed.), *Radical Agriculture*. Harper & Row, New York.
Perrin, R., and Winkelmann, D. (1976). Impediments to technical progress on small versus large farms. Paper prepared for the Am. Agr. Econ. Ass. CIMMYT, Mexico.
Pimentel, D., Hurd, L. E., Bellotti, A. C., Forster, M. J., Oka, I. N., Sholes, O. D., and Whitman, R. J. (1973). Food production and the energy crisis. *Science*, **182**, 443–449.
Pinthong, C. (1978). *A Price Analysis of the Thai Rice Marketing System*. Unpublished PhD thesis, Stanford University.
Planning Commission (PEO) (1968). *Evaluation Study of the HYVP Report for the Rabi 1967–68 Wheat*. Government of India, New Delhi.
Poleman, T. T. (1975). World food, a perspective. *Science*, **188**, 510–518.
Prentice, R. Rt. Hon. (1967). *Speech to the 14th FAO Conference*, 7 Nov. Rome.
Price, D. W., West, D. A., Scheier, G. E., and Price, D. Z. (1978). Food delivery programs and other factors affecting nutrient intake of children. *Am. J. Agr. Econ.*, **60** (1), 609–618.
Ray, D. E., and Heady, E. O. (1974). Simulated effects of alternative policy and

326

economic environments on US agriculture. *Centre for Agricultural and Rural Development Report*, 46T, Iowa State University, Ames, Iowa.

Reidinger, R. B. (1974). Institutional rationing of canal water in northern India: conflict between traditional patterns and modern needs. *Econ. Dev. and Cult. Change*, **23**, 79–104.

Renaud, B., and Suphaphiphat, P. (1971). The effect of the rice export tax on domestic price level in Thailand. *The Malayan Econ. Review*, April.

Reutlinger, S. (1977). *Food Insecurity: Magnitude and Remedies*. World Bank, Washington, DC, June.

Reutlinger, S., and Selowsky, M. (1976). Malnutrition and poverty. *World Bank Staff Occasional Paper* 23, Washington, DC.

Revelle, R. (1974). Food and population. *Scientific American*, **231**, 160–171.

Rich, W. (1974). Smaller families through social and economic development. *Monograph* 7, Overseas Development Council, Washington, DC.

Rivers, J. P. W., Holt, J. F. S., Seaman, J. A., and Bowden, M. R. (1976). Lessons for epidemiology from the Ethiopian famines. *Ann. Soc. Belge Méd. Trop.*, **56** (4–5), 345–357.

Robinson, K. L. (1960). Possible effects of eliminating direct price supports and acreage control programs. *Farm Econ. J.*, 5813–5820.

Rogers, E. M. (1958). Categorising the adopters of agricultural practices. *Rural Sociology*, **23**, 136–145.

Rogers, K. D., Srivastava, U. K., and Heady, E. O. (1972). Modified price, production and income impacts of food aid under market differentiated distribution. *Am. J. Farm Econ.*, **54** (2), 201–208.

Rojko, A. S. (1975). Alternative futures for food in world grain–oilseed–livestock economics: commodity projections to 1985. Unpublished manuscript, ERS, USDA.

Ronchi, F. F., and Lopez, J. G. (1976). Evaluation of supplementary feeding programmes assisted by the World Health Programme. *Food and Nutrition*, **2** (4), 19–25.

Roy, S., and Blase, M. G. (1978). Farm tractorisation; productivity and labour employment: a case study of the Indian Punjab. *J. Dev. Econs.*, **14** (2), 193–209.

Ruch, H., Marstrand, P., Gribbin, J., and MacKerron, G. (1976). 'When enough is not enough'. *Nature*, **261**, 181–182.

Rudra, A. (1971). The green and greedy revolution. *South Asian Review*, **4**, 291–305.

Rural Health Research Center (1975). *The Narangwal Population Study—Integrated Health and Family Services*. Punjab, India.

Ruthenburg, H. (1971). *Farming Systems in the Tropics*. Clarendon Press, Oxford.

Sanderson, F. H. (1975). The great food fumble. *Science*, 9 May, 503–509.

Sanderson, F. H. (1978). The role of international trade in solving the food problem of the developing countries. *Foreign Agr. Econ. Report* 143, USDA, pp. 69–74.

Schneider, H. (1975). *The Effects of Food Aid on Agricultural Production in Recipient Countries: An Annotated Selective Bibliography*. OECD, Paris.

Schneider, S. H. (1974). Climate variability and food production. In *World Food Supply in Changing Climate*, proc. of the Sterling Forest Conference, Sterling Forest, New York, 2–5 Dec., pp. 32–39.

Schuftan, C. (1978). Nutrition planning—what relevance to planning? *Food Policy*, **3** (1), 59–65.

Schulter, M. (1971). Differential rates of adoption of the new seed varieties in India: the problem of the small farm. *Occasional Paper* 47, Dept. of Agricultural Economics, Cornell University, New York.

Schultz, T. S. (1961). Investment in human capital. *Am. Econ. Review*, **51** (1), 1–17.

Schultz, T. W. (1960). Value of US farm surplus to underdeveloped countries, *J. Farm Econ.*, **42** (5), 1019–1030.

Schultze, C. L. (1971). The distribution of farm subsidies: who gets the benefits? Staff paper, Brookings Institution, Washington, DC.

Scobie, G. M., and Posada, T. R. (1978). The impact of technical change on income distribution: the case of rice on Colombia. *Am. J. Agr. Econ.*, **60** (1), 85–92.

Scrimshaw, N. S. (1976). An analysis of past and present recommended dietary allowances for protein in health and disease. *New England J. of Med.*, 15 and 27 Jan.

Scrimshaw, N. S. (1978). Nutrition considerations in food aid. *Foreign Agr. Econ. Report* 143, USDA, 37–44.

Scrimshaw, N. S., and Béhar, M. (1976) (eds.). *Nutrition and Agricultural Development*. Plenum Press, New York.

Scrimshaw, N. S., Taylor, C. E., and Gordon, J. E. (1968). Interactions of nutrition and infection. *WHO Monograph Series* 57, Geneva.

Scrimshaw, N. S., and Young, U. R. (1976). The requirements of human nutrition. Chapter 3 in *Food and Agriculture: Readings from Scientific American*. Freeman, San Francisco.

Seevers, G. L. (1968). An evaluation of the disincentive effect caused by PL 480 shipments. *Am. J. Agr. Econ.*, **50** (3), 630–642.

Sen, S. R. (1971). Whither aid. *Am. J. Agr. Econ.*, **53** (5), 768–776.

Setthawong, P. (1977). *The Structure of the World Rice Market and a Model of Thai Rice Exports*. ESCAP Consultants Report, Bangkok.

Shapley, D. (1977). Soviet grain harvests: CIA study pessimistic on effects of weather. *Science*, **195**, 377–378.

Sharp, R. (1972). Desertification—holes in the bucket. *Food Policy*, **2** (1), 69–71.

Shenoy, B. R. (1974). *PL 480 Aid and India's Food Problem*. East West Press, New Delhi.

Siamwalla, A. (1975). A history of rice policies in Thailand. *Food Research Institute Studies*, **14** (3), 233–249.

Silcock, T. H. (1970). *The Economic Development of Thai Agriculture*. ANU Press, Canberra.

Simon, J. (1977). *The Economics of Population Growth*. Princeton University Press, Princeton, NJ.

Simontov, A. (1976). World food consumption: can we achieve a balance? *Food Policy*, **1** (3), 232–238.

Singh, S. (1976). *Modernisation of Agriculture: A Case Study in Eastern Uttar Pradesh*. New Delhi.

Slesser, M. (1975). Energy requirements in agriculture. Chapter 1 in J. Lenihan and W. W. Fletcher (eds.), *Environment and Man*, Vol. 2: *Food, Agriculture and Environment*. Blackie, Glasgow.

Souter, G. N. (1977). Export instability and concentration in the less developed countries. *J. Dev. Econ.*, **4** (3), 279–297.

Srivastava, U. K., Heady, E. O., Rogers, K. D., and Myer, L. V. (1975). *Food Aid and International Economic Growth*. Iowa State University Press, Ames, Iowa.

Stevens, C. (1977). Food aid: more sinned against than sinning? *ODI Review*, **2**, 71–85.

Symons, L. (1972). *Russian Agriculture: A Geographic Approach*. Bell, London.

Talbot, R. (1977). The three US food policies. *Food Policy*, **2** (1), 3–16.

Tarrant, J. R. (1974). *Agricultural Geography*, David & Charles, London.

Tarrant, J. R. (1979). Rural transport and development in Bangladesh. *Bangladesh Institute of Development Studies Journal*, in press.

Taylor, L. (1975). The misconstructed crisis: Lester Brown and world food. *World Development*, **3** (11/12), 827–837.

Thompson, L. M. (1974). The world food situation as related to weather variability and grain production. In *World Food Supply in Changing Climate*, proc. of the Sterling Forest Conference, 2–5 Dec., Sterling Forest, New York, 12–31.

Thompson, L. M. (1975). Weather variability, climatic change and grain production. *Science*, **188**, 535–541.

Timmer, C. P. (1974). The demand for fertilisers in developing countries. *Food Research Institute Studies*, **13** (3), 197–224.

Timmer, C. P. (1976a). Fertiliser and food policy in LDC. *Food Policy*, **1** (2), 143–154.

Timmer, C. P. (1976b). Interaction of energy and food prices in developing countries. *Development Digest*, **14** (3), 54–58.

Timmer, C. P., and Falcon, W. P. (1973). The impact of price on rice trade in Asia. In G. S. Tolley and P. A. Zadrozny (eds.), *Trade Agriculture and Development*. Ballinger, Cambridge, Mass., 57–89.

Tolley, G. S., and Gwyer, G. D. (1967). International trade and agricultural products in relation to economic development. In H. M. Southworth and B. F. Johnson (eds.), *Agricultural Development and Economic Growth*. Cornell University Press, Ithaca, New York, 403–407.

Tongpan, S. (1974). Agricultural exports and economic development: a case study of Thailand. Chapter 10 in N. Islam (ed.), *Agricultural Policy in Developing Countries*. Macmillan, London, 240–253.

Tracy, M. A. (1976). Fifty years of agricultural policy. *J. Agr. Econ.*, **27** (3), 331–348.

Tropical Products Institute (1976). *Report on the Production, Handling and Marketing of Pineapple and Other Fresh Horticultural Produce in the Chittagong Hill Tracts*, London.

Trowell, H. C. (1973). Kwashiorkor. Chapter 7 in *Food: Readings from Scientific American*. Freeman, San Francisco.

Tsui, A. O., and Bogue, D. J. (1978). Declining world fertility: trends, causes and implications. *Population Bull.*, **33** (4).

Tyner, F. H., and Tweeten, L. G. (1964). Excess capacity in US agriculture. *Agricultural Economics Research*, **16**, ERS, USDA, 23–31.

UK Select Committee on Overseas Development (1976). *World Food Crisis and Third World Development*. HMSO, London.

UNCTAD (1976). *New Directions in International Trade and Development Policies*. Report by Secretary-General of UNCTAD, United Nations, New York.

UNCTAD (1977). *Proc. of the UNCTAD 4th Session, Nairobi*, 1. United Nations, New York.

UNCTAD (1978). The main issues for UNCTAD in the 1980s. *UNCTAD Seminar Programme Report Series*, 4, United Nations, New York.

UN Dept. of Economics and Social Affairs (1975). *Poverty, Unemployment and Development Policy: A Case Study of Selected Issues with Reference to Kerala*. United Nations, New York.

US Depts. of Commerce and Agriculture (1976). Farm population of the United States. *Current Population Reports*, 49.

USDA (1956). The effects of acreage allotment program 1954 and 1955: a summary report. *Production Research Report*, 3. Washington, DC.

USDA (1963). Composition of foods. *Agriculture Handbook*, 8. Washington, DC.

USDA (1974). US agricultural exports under PL 480. *ERS*, 395, Washington, DC.

USDA (1975). The food and fiber system—how it works. *Agr. Inf. Bull.*, 383. Washington, DC.

USDA (1976). Fact book of US agriculture, *Misc. Publication*, 1063, Washington, DC.

USDA (1977a). Farm income statistics. *Stat. Bull.*, 576, Washington, DC.

USDA (1977b). Balance sheet of the farming sector 1977. *Agr. Inf. Bull.*, 411, Washington, DC.

USDA (1977c). PL 480 concessional sales. *Foreign Agr. Econ. Report*, 142, Washington, DC.

USDA (1978a). US Department of Interior's proposed rules for enforcement of the Reclamation Act of 1902: an economic impact analysis. *Economics Statistics and Co-operative Service Staff Report*. Washington, DC, Jan.

USDA (1978b). International Food Policy Issues, a proceedings. *Foreign Agr. Econ. Report*, 143. Washington, DC.

US Government (1976). Appropriations and budget estimates: statements. *93rd Congress, 2nd Session*, 76-8796. Washington, DC.

US Senate (1973). Hearings on US and world food situation. *93rd Congress, 1st Session*, Oct. 74-5161. Washington, DC.

Van Liere, W. J. (1974). Weather and crop production in S.E. Asia. In *World Food Supply and Changing Climate*, proc. of the Sterling Forest Conference, 2–5 Dec., Sterling Forest, New York, 103–116.

Veeman, T. S. (1977). Indian food grain performance. *Food Policy*, **2** (2), 168–171.

Vieira, C. (1976). Comment. In N. S. Scrimshaw and M. Béhar (eds.), *Nutrition and Agricultural Development*. Plenum Press, New York, 317–323.

Vyas, V. S. (1975). *India's High Yielding Varieties Programme in Wheat 1966–7 to 1971–2*. CIMMYT Mexico.

Wade, N. (1974). Green revolution: a just technology, often unjust in use. *Science*, **186**, 1093–1096, 1186–1192.

Walters, H. E. (1978). International food security: the issues and the alternatives. *Foreign Agr. Econ. Report*, 143, USDA, pp. 91–98.

Ward, G. M., Know, P. L., and Hobson, B. W. (1977). Beef production options and requirements for fossil fuel. *Science*, **198**, 265–271.

Watts, H. D. (1971). The location of the sugar beet industry in England and Wales, 1912–36. *Transactions of the Inst. of British Geographers*, **53**, 95–116.

Waugh, F. J. (1967). Reserve stocks of farm products. *Agricultural Policy: A Review of Programs and Needs*, 5. Govt. Printing Office, Washington, DC.

Whittlesea, D. (1936). Major agricultural regions of the earth. *Annals of Ass. Am. Geographers*, **26** (4), 199–240.

WHO (1972). A survey of nutritional–immunological interactions. *WHO Bull.*, **46**, 537–546.

Widdowson, E. M. (1976). Changes in the body and its organs during lactation: nutritional implications in breast feeding and the mother. *CIBA Foundation Symposium 45*, Elsevier, Amsterdam, 103–118.

Wightman, D. R. (1968). Food aid and economic development. *International Conciliation*, 567.

Wilson, G. K. (1977). *Special Interests and Policy Making: Agricultural Policies and Politics in Britain and the USA, 1956–70*. Wiley, London.

Winkelmann, D. (1976). *The Adoption of New Maize Technology in Plan Puebla, Mexico*. CIMMYT, Mexico.

Wong, C. M. (1978). A model for evaluating the effects of Thai government taxation of rice exports on trade and welfare. *Am. J. Agr. Econ.*, **60** (1), 65–73.

World Bank (1976). Developing country food grain projections for 1985. *World Bank Working Paper*, 247, Washington, DC.

World Bank (1978a). *Bangladesh Food Policy Review*. Washington, DC.

World Bank (1978b). *World Development Report, 1978*. Washington, DC.

World Food Programme (WFP) (1973). *Ten Years of World Food Programme Development Aid 1963–72*. FAO, Rome.

Wortman, S., and Cummings, R. W. (1978). *To Feed This World*. Johns Hopkins University Press, Baltimore.

Yotopoulos, P. (1977). The population problem and the development evolution. *Food Research Institute Studies*, **16** (1).

Index

336